UNITED NATIONS CONFERENCE ON TRADE AND DEVELOPMENT

UNCTAD

WORLD INVESTMENT REPORT 2022

INTERNATIONAL TAX REFORMS AND SUSTAINABLE INVESTMENT

UNITED NATIONS
Geneva, 2022

United Nations Publications
405 East 42nd Street
New York, New York 10017
United States of America

Email: publications@un.org
Website: https://shop.un.org

This publication has been edited externally.

United Nations publication issued by the United Nations Conference on Trade and Development.

UNCTAD/WIR/2022

ISBN 978-92-1-113049-2
eISBN 978-92-1-001543-1
Print ISSN 1020-2218
Online ISSN 2225-1677
Sales No. E.22.II.D.20

PREFACE

Global flows of foreign direct investment recovered to pre-pandemic levels last year, reaching $1.6 trillion. Cross-border deals and international project finance were particularly strong, encouraged by loose financing conditions and infrastructure stimulus. However, the recovery of greenfield investment in industry remains fragile, especially in developing countries.

This fragile growth of real productive investment is likely to persist in 2022. The fallout of the war in Ukraine with the triple food, fuel and finance crises, along with the ongoing COVID-19 pandemic and climate disruption, are adding stresses, particularly in developing countries. Global growth estimates for the year are already down by a full percentage point. There is significant risk that the momentum for recovery in international investment will stall prematurely, hampering efforts to boost finance for sustainable development.

The *World Investment Report* supports policymakers by monitoring global and regional investment trends and national and international investment policy developments. The report reviews investment in the Sustainable Development Goals and in climate change mitigation and adaptation. It also looks at sustainable finance trends in capital markets and among institutional investors.

The coming years will see the implementation of fundamental reforms in international taxation. These reforms are expected to have major implications for investment policy, especially in countries that make use of fiscal incentives and special economic zones. The report of this year provides a guide for policymakers to navigate the complex new tax rules and to adjust their investment strategies.

I commend this report to all engaged in promoting investment in sustainable development.

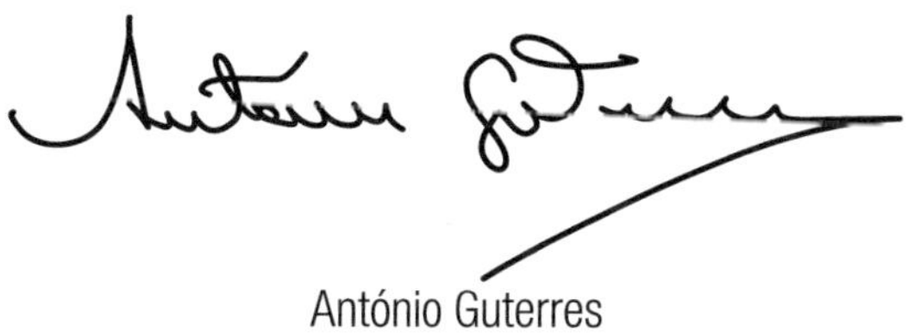

António Guterres
Secretary-General of the United Nations

FOREWORD

The global environment for international investment changed dramatically with the onset of the war in Ukraine, which occurred while the world was still reeling from the impact of the pandemic. The war is having effects well beyond its immediate vicinity, causing a cost-of-living crisis affecting billions of people around the world, with rising prices for energy and food reducing real incomes and aggravating debt stress. Investor uncertainty and risk aversity could put significant downward pressure on global FDI this year.

The effects on investment flows to developing countries in 2022 and beyond are difficult to anticipate. Apart from direct effects on countries in Central Asia with close investment ties in the region, the impact on others will be mostly indirect and depend on the extent of their exposure to the triple crisis – in food, fuel and finance – caused by the conflict and their consequent economic and political instability – key determinants of international private investment. If the past is an indication, the last time food prices were this high – during the 2007–2008 food crisis – there were riots in more than 60 countries.

The outcome will be of enormous significance for development prospects. The need for investment in productive capacity, in the Sustainable Development Goals (SDGs) and in climate change mitigation and adaptation is enormous. Current investment trends in these areas are not unanimously positive. Although global FDI flows rebounded strongly in 2021, industrial investment remains weak and well below pre-pandemic levels, especially in the poorest countries; SDG investment – project finance in infrastructure, food security, water and sanitation, and health – is growing but not enough to reach the goals by 2030; and investment in climate change mitigation, especially renewables, is booming but most of it remains in developed countries and adaptation investment continues to lag well behind.

Worryingly, some emerging indicators suggest that the war in Ukraine could become a setback in the energy transition, with increased fossil fuel production in countries previously committed to reducing emissions. In the first quarter of 2022, most of the 5,000 largest multinational enterprises revised downward their earnings forecasts for 2022. Alarmingly, while extractive industries revised upwards their expected earnings, with oil and gas at +22 per cent and coal at +32 per cent of expected earnings, renewable energy companies released downward revisions of an average of -22 per cent of expected earnings, lending credence to the intuition that current conditions risk reversing years of progress towards investing in sustainable energy. This is especially worrying as global CO2 emissions from energy combustion and industrial processes rebounded in 2021 to reach their highest ever annual level.

To achieve the SDGs it is imperative that more funds are channeled to where they are most needed, on the ground, in developing countries. But also an important effort will have to come from domestic resource mobilization. From that perspective, the ongoing international tax reforms led by the G20 and the OECD, which we study extensively in this report, are a major step forward. They aim to ensure that multinationals pay their fair share of taxes where they operate, and they have the potential to give a significant boost to tax revenues in developing countries.

However, the war in Ukraine has further complicated domestic resource mobilization in developing countries, already worsened by the COVID-19 pandemic and the increased frequency of natural disasters in the context of climate change. In the midst of rising and unsustainable debt levels, without adequate multilateral mechanisms for restructuring, countries are being forced to reduce their fiscal space at a time when they should be increasing it.

The International Labour Organization suggests that the social protection financing gap stands at $1.2 trillion per year in developing countries, part of the $4.3 trillion we at UNCTAD estimate as the yearly gap in SDG financing. And even with food and energy import bills, and worsening costs of borrowing due to higher interest rates, developing countries' primary fiscal balance has shrunk by $315 billion since the start of the war.

That is why international investment plays a critical complementary role to domestic public investment. And the new tax rules will affect how countries have traditionally promoted – and often competed – for international investment, through low tax rates, fiscal incentives and special economic zones.

The tax reforms are an opportunity for developing countries, not only from a revenue perspective, but also from an investment attraction perspective. Strategically, tax competition will decrease. Practically, the need to review the investment promotion toolkit is a chance to make costly incentives more sustainable.

There will be challenges. Developing countries face constraints in their responses to the reforms, because of a lack of technical capacity to deal with the complexity of the tax changes, and because of investment treaty commitments that could hinder effective fiscal policy action. The international community has the obligation to help. It can do so through technical assistance, by agreeing a solution to problems caused by international investment agreements, and by putting in place safeguards that protect the tax revenues of the poorest countries. These efforts should be part of a broader multilateral endeavor towards reining in illicit financial flows, especially in the developing world. This report points the way.

It is important that we act now. Even though countries face very alarming immediate problems stemming from the cost-of-living crisis, it is important we are able to invest in the long term. Because the short term and long term start at the same time. And the time is now.

Rebeca Grynspan

Rebeca Grynspan
Secretary-General of UNCTAD

ACKNOWLEDGEMENTS

The *World Investment Report 2022* was prepared by a team led by James X. Zhan. The team members included Richard Bolwijn, Bruno Casella, Joseph Clements, Berna Dogan, Hamed El Kady, Kumi Endo, Anastasia Leskova, Massimo Meloni, Anthony Miller, Abraham Negash, Yongfu Ouyang, Diana Rosert, Amelia U. Santos-Paulino, Changbum Son, Astrit Sulstarova, Claudia Trentini, Joerg Weber and Kee Hwee Wee.

Research support and inputs were provided by Gregory Auclair, Hamidreza Bakhtiarizadeh, Magdalena Bulit Goñi, João de Camargo Mainente, Malou Celander, Antoine Cornevin, Juliette Gailly, Tiffany Grabski, Vicente Guazzini, Maxime Ladrière, Corli Le Roux, Iana Miachenkova, Josef Ostřanský, Hayley Marie Pallan, Sang Hyun Park, Lisa Remke, Samuel Ringier, Rita Schmutz, Baptiste Souillard, Irina Stanyukova, Ilan Strauss, Yihua Teng and Anqi Wang.

Comments and contributions were provided by Yoseph Asmelash, Chantal Dupasquier, Isabel Garza Rodriguez and Paul Wessendorp, as well as the Office of the Secretary General.

Statistical assistance was provided by Mohamed Chiraz Baly and Bradley Boicourt. IT assistance was provided by Chrysanthi Kourti.

The manuscript was copy-edited by Lise Lingo. The design of the charts and infographics, and the typesetting of the report were done by Thierry Alran, assisted by Alexandra Sonia Garcês. Production of the report was supported by Elisabeth Anodeau-Mareschal and Katia Vieu. Additional support was provided by Nathalie Eulaerts and Sivanla Sikounnavong.

Michael Keen acted as principal advisor on the theme chapter of the report. The theme chapter also benefited from the collaboration with the team at the WU Global Tax Policy Centre of Vienna University of Economics and Business led by Jeffrey Owens, including Ivan Lazarov, Belissa Ferreira Liotti, Ruth Wamuyu Maina and Joy Waruguru Ndubai.

At various stages of the preparation of the theme chapter, in particular during the kick-off event at the World Investment Forum and various expert meetings organized to discuss drafts, the team benefited from comments and inputs received from external experts: Flurim Aliu, David Bradbury, Julien Chaisse, Alex Cobham, Michael Devereux, Lorraine Eden, Javier Garcia-Bernardo, Ana Cinta Gonzalez Cabral, Tibor Hanappi, Liselott Kana, Anita Kapur, Petr Janský, Michael Lennard, Pierce O'Reilly, Zahira Quattrocchi, Augustin Redonda, Tove Maria Ryding and Logan Wort.

The team is grateful for advice, input and comments at all stages from colleagues in international organizations and other experts, including Vincent Beyer, Martin Dietrich Brauch, Abdul Muheet Chowdhary, Sabrine Marsit, Suzy H. Nikièma, Marcelo Olarreaga, Joshua Paine, María Florencia Sarmiento, Alessandro Turina, Christian Volpe Martincus and Sebastian Wuschka.

Numerous officials in central banks, national government agencies, international organizations and non-governmental organizations also contributed to the report.

TABLE OF CONTENTS

ABBREVIATIONS

AETR	average effective tax rate
AfCFTA	African Continent Free Trade Area
ASEAN	Association of South-East Asian Nations
AUM	assets under management
BEA	Bureau of Economic Analysis
BEPS	Base Erosion and Profit Shifting
BIT	bilateral investment treaty
CbCR	country-by-country reporting
CDP	Carbon Disclosure Project
CIS	Commonwealth of Independent States
CIT	corporate income tax
COVID-19	coronavirus disease 2019
CPTPP	Comprehensive and Progressive Agreement for Trans-Pacific Partnership
CSR	corporate social responsibility
DTT	double taxation treaty
ECT	Energy Charter Treaty
EIA	Economic Impact Assessment
ESG	environmental, social and governance
ETR	effective tax rate
EU	European Union
FET	fair and equitable treatment
FTA	free trade agreement
GATS	General Agreement on Trade in Services
GATT	General Agreement on Trade and Tariffs
GCI	Guidance on Core Indicators
GDP	gross domestic product
GHG	greenhouse gas
GILTI	global intangible low-taxed income
GloBE	Global Anti-Base Erosion
GSSB	GRI Standard Setting Board
GTED	Government Tax Expenditure Database
GVC	global value chain
ICCC	Independent Consumer and Competition Commission
ICT	information and communication technology
ICMA	International Capital Market Association
ICSID	International Centre for Settlement of Investment Disputes
IFC	International Finance Corporation
IFRS	International Financial Reporting Standards
IIA	international investment agreement
IIR	Income Inclusion Rule
IMF	International Monetary Fund
IOSCO	International Organization of Securities Commissions
IP	intellectual property
IPA	investment promotion agency
IPFSD	Investment Policy Framework for Sustainable Development
ISDS	investor–State dispute settlement
ISSB	International Sustainability Standards Board
LDC	least developed country
LLDC	landlocked developing country
M&A	merger and acquisition
METR	marginal effective tax rate
MFN	most favoured nation
MNE	multinational enterprise
NAFTA	North American Free Trade Agreement
NT	national treatment
OFC	offshore financial centre
OIC	Organisation of Islamic Cooperation
PPP	public-private partnership
QDMTT	qualified domestic minimum top-up tax
R&D	research and development
RCEP	Regional Comprehensive Economic Partnership
SDGs	Sustainable Development Goals
SEZ	special economic zone
SIDS	small island developing States
SMEs	small and medium-sized enterprises
SSE	Sustainable Stock Exchanges
STR	statutory tax rate
STTR	Subject to Tax Rule
TIP	treaty with investment provision
TRIPS	Trade-Related Aspects of Intellectual Property Rights
UNCITRAL	United Nations Commission on International Trade Law
UNEP	United Nations Environment Programme
UNODC	United Nations Office on Drugs and Crime
USMCA	United States–Mexico–Canada Agreement
WAEMU	West African Economic and Monetary Union
WFE	World Federation of Exchanges
WHT	withholding tax
WIR	World Investment Report
WTO	World Trade Organization

KEY MESSAGES

INVESTMENT TRENDS AND PROSPECTS

Global foreign direct investment (FDI) flows in 2021 were $1.58 trillion, up 64 per cent from the exceptionally low level in 2020. The recovery showed significant rebound momentum, with booming merger and acquisition (M&A) markets and rapid growth in international project finance because of loose financing conditions and major infrastructure stimulus packages.

However, the global environment for international business and cross-border investment changed dramatically in 2022. The war in Ukraine – on top of the lingering effects of the pandemic – is causing a triple food, fuel and finance crisis in many countries around the world. Investor uncertainty could put significant downward pressure on global FDI in 2022.

The 2021 growth momentum is unlikely to be sustained. Global FDI flows in 2022 will likely move on a downward trajectory, at best remaining flat. New project activity is already showing signs of increased risk aversion among investors: preliminary data for Q1 2022 show greenfield project numbers down 21 per cent and international project finance deals down 4 per cent.

The 2021 FDI recovery brought growth in all regions. However, almost three quarters of the global increase was due to the upswing in developed countries, where FDI reached $746 billion – more than double the 2020 level. The increase was mostly caused by M&A transactions and high levels of retained earnings of multinational enterprises (MNEs). Those, in turn, led to sizeable intrafirm financial flows and major FDI fluctuations in large investment hubs.

The high levels of retained earnings in 2021 were the result of record MNE profits. The profitability of the largest 5,000 MNEs doubled to more than 8 per cent of sales. Profits were high especially in developed countries, because of the release of pent-up demand, low financing costs and significant government support.

Despite high profits, the appetite of MNEs for investing in new productive assets overseas remained weak. While infrastructure-oriented international project finance was up 68 per cent and cross-border M&As were up 43 per cent, greenfield investment numbers increased by only 11 per cent, still one fifth below pre-pandemic levels. The value of greenfield announcements overall rose by 15 per cent, to $659 billion, but remained flat in developing countries at $259 billion – stagnating at the lowest level ever recorded. This is a concern, as new investments in industry are crucial for economic growth and development prospects.

FDI flows to developing economies grew more slowly than those to developed regions but still increased by 30 per cent, to $837 billion. The increase was mainly the result of strong growth performance in Asia, a partial recovery in Latin America and the Caribbean, and an upswing in Africa. The share of developing countries in global flows remained just above 50 per cent.

- FDI flows to Africa reached $83 billion, from $39 billion in 2020. Most recipients saw a moderate rise in FDI. The total for the continent was inflated by a single large intrafirm financial transaction. Greenfield announcements remained depressed, but international project finance deals were up 26 per cent, with strong growth in extractive industries.

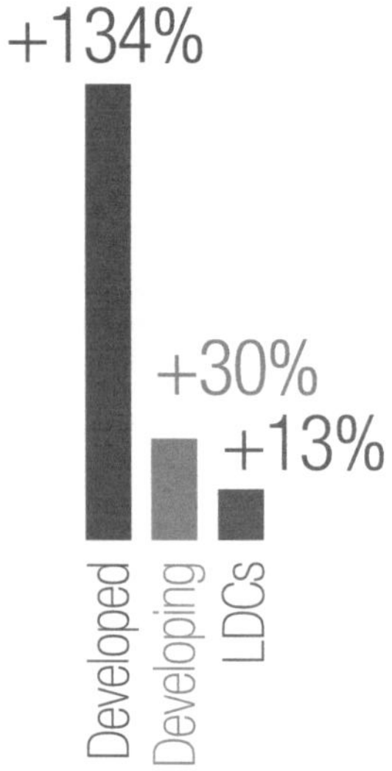

- In *developing Asia*, despite successive waves of COVID-19, FDI rose to an all-time high for the third consecutive year, reaching $619 billion. Asia is the largest recipient region, accounting for 40 per cent of global FDI. However, inflows remain highly concentrated; six economies account for more than 80 per cent of FDI to the region.
- FDI in *Latin America and the Caribbean* rose by 56 per cent to $134 billion. Most economies saw inflows rebound, with only a few experiencing further declines, caused by pandemic-induced economic crises. Total inflows remained about 15 per cent below the pre-pandemic level.
- FDI flows to the structurally weak, *vulnerable and small economies* rose by 15 per cent to $39 billion. Inflows to the least developed countries (LDCs), landlocked developing countries (LLDCs) and small island developing States (SIDS) combined accounted for only 2.5 per cent of the world total in 2021, down from 3.5 per cent in 2020.

International investment in sectors relevant for the Sustainable Development Goals (SDGs) in developing countries increased substantially in 2021, by 70 per cent. The combined value of greenfield announcements and international project finance deals in SDG sectors exceeded the pre-pandemic level by almost 20 per cent. Most of the growth went to renewable energy. Investment activity in other SDG-related sectors – including infrastructure, food and agriculture, health, and WASH – saw only a partial recovery.

Renewable energy and energy-efficiency projects represent the bulk of climate change investments. International private investment in climate change sectors is directed almost exclusively to mitigation; only 5 per cent goes to adaptation projects. More than 60 per cent is invested in developed countries, where 85 per cent of projects are purely privately financed. In contrast, almost half of the projects in developing countries require some form of public sector participation.

International project finance is increasingly important for SDG and climate change investment. The strong growth performance of international project finance can be explained by favourable financing conditions, infrastructure stimulus and significant interest on the part of financial market investors to participate in large-scale projects that require multiple financiers. The instrument also enables governments to leverage public investment through private finance participation.

Finally, comparing the largest, the smallest and the digital MNEs shows starkly contrasting investment trends. Sales of UNCTAD's top 100 digital MNEs grew five times faster than those of the traditional top 100 over the past five years, with the pandemic providing a huge boost. The largest MNEs engage more in greenfield investment, and digital MNEs more in M&As. Digital MNEs are FDI light, needing relatively little investment in physical assets to reach overseas markets. International production by both digital and large MNEs has grown continuously, albeit at different speeds. In contrast, FDI by SMEs is in decline. Over the past five years, the share of SMEs in greenfield investment projects declined from 5.7 to 1.3 per cent.

INVESTMENT POLICY DEVELOPMENTS

In 2021, the pace of investment policymaking returned to pre-pandemic levels, with 109 new measures, 28 per cent fewer than in 2020. That signalled an end to the emergency investment policymaking that characterized the first year of the pandemic; however, the crisis still affected the nature of the measures.

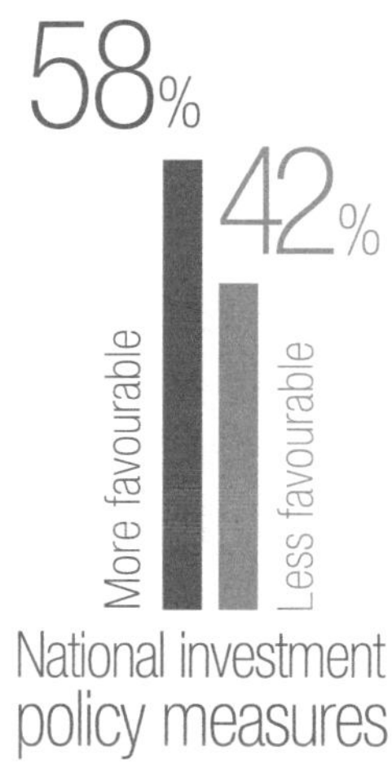

Developed countries expanded the protection of strategic companies from foreign takeovers, bringing the share of measures less favourable to investment to an all-time high (42 per cent). Four new countries adopted FDI screening mechanisms (including one developing country), and at least twice as many tightened existing mechanisms. Together, countries that conduct FDI screening account for 63 per cent of global FDI inflows and 70 per cent of stock (up from 52 and 67 per cent, respectively, in 2020).

Conversely, developing countries continued to adopt primarily measures to liberalize, promote or facilitate investment, confirming the important role that FDI plays in their economic recovery strategies. Investment facilitation measures constituted almost 40 per cent of all measures more favourable to investment, followed by the opening of new activities to FDI (30 per cent) and by new investment incentives (20 per cent).

The first quarter of 2022 registered a record number of new investment policy measures (75), mainly in response to the war in Ukraine. Sanctions and countersanctions affecting FDI to and from the Russian Federation, Belarus and the non-government-controlled areas of eastern Ukraine constituted 70 per cent of all measures adopted in Q1 2022.

Several notable developments accelerated the reform of the international investment agreement (IIA) regime in 2021. They included the conclusion of new-generation megaregional economic agreements and large-scale terminations of old-generation bilateral investment treaties (BITs). Greater policy attention to investment facilitation, climate change and human rights will also affect international investment governance.

For the second consecutive year, the number of terminations exceeded the number of newly concluded IIAs. In 2021, countries concluded 13 IIAs and effectively terminated at least 86 IIAs, bringing the size of the IIA universe to 3,288. In line with UNCTAD's IIA policy recommendations, IIAs signed in 2021 continue to feature many reform-oriented provisions aimed at preserving regulatory space while promoting investment for development.

The total count of investor–State dispute settlement (ISDS) cases reached 1,190 at the end of 2021, with at least 68 new arbitrations initiated during the year. Most of the cases initiated were brought under old-generation IIAs. In 2022, the war in Ukraine brought into the spotlight past and potential future ISDS claims related to armed conflict.

Trends in the taxation of investment

Tax policy is used around the world as an instrument to promote international investment. Countries rely on a variety of fiscal incentives to attract investors to priority sectors or regions. An analysis of tax-related investment policy measures adopted worldwide over the last decade shows that profit-based incentives, such as tax holidays and reduced corporate income tax (CIT), are among the most frequent and widespread.

Incentives are typically not time-bound, nor allocated on the basis of transparent criteria. Although the governance of incentives varies greatly across countries, on average, 70 per cent of incentives are allocated on the basis of discretion, criteria not available to the public or negotiation with individual investors. In addition, only about half of all tax incentives introduced worldwide over the last decade were time-bound, with lower shares in Africa (35 per cent) and Asia (40 per cent).

IIAs impose obligations on States that can create friction with tax measures undertaken at the national level. Most IIAs do not exclude taxation from their scope, which means that they cover a wide range of tax-related measures, whether of general or specific application. UNCTAD data suggest that investors have challenged tax-related measures in 165 ISDS cases based on IIAs. UNCTAD's guide for tax policymakers on IIAs, published in 2021, contains IIA reform options to minimize the risk of friction with tax policy.

THE IMPACT OF A GLOBAL MINIMUM TAX ON FDI

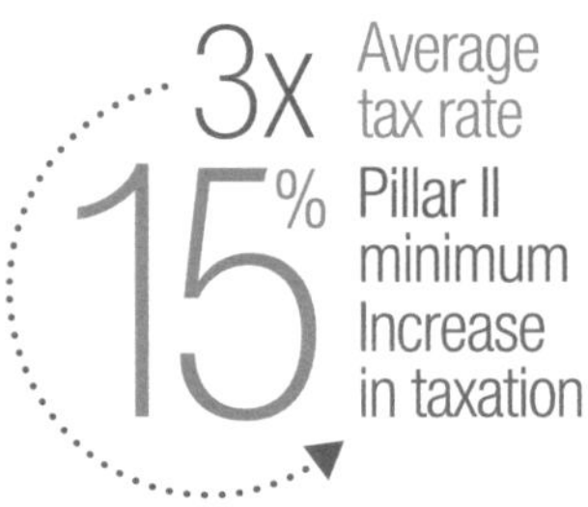

The introduction of a minimum tax of 15 per cent on the foreign profits of the largest MNEs proposed in the context of the G20/OECD Base Erosion and Profit Shifting (BEPS) project has important implications for international investment and investment policies. BEPS Pillar II is expected to discourage MNEs from shifting profits to low-tax countries and to reduce tax competition between countries. Further objectives are to stabilize international tax rules and reduce tax uncertainty, to create a more level playing field for companies and to prevent the proliferation of unilateral measures that would lead to a deterioration of the investment climate. In addition, increased tax revenues will support domestic resource mobilization for the SDGs.

Statutory rates of corporate income tax (CIT) have declined over the last three decades in a race to the bottom to attract international investment. They now hover at about 25 per cent in both developed and developing countries. Effective tax rates (ETRs) on the reported profits of foreign affiliates tend to be lower, less than 20 per cent on average, mainly because of fiscal incentives offered by host countries.

MNEs often pay significantly less tax on their foreign income because they can shift part of their profits to low-tax jurisdictions. As a result, the actual tax rates faced by MNEs on their foreign income are about 15 per cent, significantly lower than the headline rate. This is captured by a new metric introduced in this report, the FDI-level ETR, reflecting the average taxes paid by MNEs on their entire FDI income, including shifted profits.

Pillar II will increase the corporate income tax faced by MNEs on their foreign profits. First, MNEs will reduce profit shifting, as they will have less to gain from it, and will pay host-country tax rates. Second, foreign affiliates that pay an ETR below the minimum on profits reported in host countries will be subject to a top-up tax. The expected rise in the (FDI-level) ETR faced by MNEs is conservatively estimated at 2 percentage points. This corresponds to an increase in tax revenues paid by MNEs to host countries of about 15 per cent – more for large MNEs that are directly affected by the reform.

Both developed economies and developing economies are expected to benefit substantially from increased revenue collection. Offshore financial centres stand to lose a substantial part of CIT revenues collected from MNEs' foreign affiliates. For smaller developing countries – which generally have lower ETRs – the application of the top-up tax could make a major difference in revenue collection.

The flipside of increased tax revenues is the potential downward pressure on the volume of investment that the increase in CIT on FDI activities will exert. The baseline scenario places the potential downward effect on global FDI at about -2 per cent.

At the same time, the reduction in tax rate differentials will result in the diversion of investment from low- to higher-tax jurisdictions, with developing countries benefiting relatively more because of their higher corporate tax rates.

The diversion effect could counterbalance investment losses caused by the volume effect. However, this will not occur automatically. In a world of smaller tax rate differentials, countries stand to gain more from improvements in other investment determinants – including those related to infrastructure and the regulatory and institutional environment.

No country can afford to ignore Pillar II. The mechanism that has been devised for implementation is such that it is sufficient for a relatively limited number of investor home countries (e.g. G20 and OECD members) to apply the top-up tax for the effects to become almost universal. Host countries, including many developing economies, then have the option to apply the top-up tax first – before home countries can do so – to protect tax revenues. But the effectiveness of competitive tax rates or traditional tax incentives to attract FDI will be diminished.

The Pillar II reforms will thus have major implications for national investment policymakers and investment promotion institutions, and for their standard toolkits. Fiscal incentives are widely used for investment promotion, including as part of the value proposition of most special economic zones. Looking specifically at the incentives most used to attract FDI:

- Accelerated depreciation and loss carry-forward provisions will remain effective.
- Tax holidays and exemptions will lose all or most of their attraction for investors.
- A range of other incentives will be affected to various degrees depending on their design.

Investment policymakers urgently need to review their incentives packages, for both existing and new investors. Some fiscal policy options to promote investment remain, including amplifying the benefit to investors of the so-called substance-based carve-out; shifting to incentives that are less affected by Pillar II; or reducing taxes that are not covered by Pillar II, to the extent that they have a bearing on investment decisions.

International investment policymakers and negotiators of IIAs need to consider the potential constraints that IIA commitments may place on the implementation of key provisions of Pillar II. If host countries are prevented by IIAs and their ISDS provisions from applying top-up taxes or removing incentives, the tax increase to the global minimum will accrue to home countries. Host countries would lose out on tax revenues without the compensating investment-attraction benefit. Existing old-generation IIAs, of the type predominantly in force in many developing countries, are likely to be particularly problematic.

The strategic implications of the reforms for investment policy are also important. Reduced competition from low-tax locations could benefit developing economies. Nevertheless, as competition shifts from tax levers to alternative investment determinants, and from fiscal incentives to financial incentives, many could still find themselves at a disadvantage because they are unable to afford the substantial upfront financial commitments associated with infrastructure provision or subsidies.

Looking ahead, many important details of Pillar II still need to be defined. *Therefore, it will be key for developing countries to strengthen cooperation and technical capabilities to ensure effective participation in the process of negotiating the final shape of the reforms.*

Finally, the implementation of BEPS Pillar II by tax authorities will be highly complex, and so will the translation of the reforms into investment policies, incentives regimes, and the value propositions of investment promotion agencies and special economic zones. Moreover, the tax revenue implications for developing countries of constraints posed by IIAs are a major cause for concern. *The international community, in parallel with or as part of the Inclusive Framework discussions, should alleviate the constraints that are placing developing countries, and especially LDCs, at a disadvantage:*

- Vastly scale up technical assistance to developing countries to support BEPS implementation and investment policy adjustment.
- Adopt a multilateral solution to remove implementation constraints posed by IIAs and mitigate ISDS risks.
- As a stopgap measure, establish a mechanism to return any top-up revenues raised by developed home countries that should have accrued to developing host countries, but that they were unable to raise because of capacity or treaty constraints.

CAPITAL MARKETS AND SUSTAINABILITY

sustainable finance

$5.2 trillion in 2021 up 63%

UNCTAD estimates that the value of sustainability-themed investment products in global financial markets amounted to $5.2 trillion in 2021, up 63 per cent from 2020. These products include sustainable funds ($2.7 trillion), green bonds (over $1.5 trillion outstanding), social bonds ($418 billion), mixed-sustainability bonds ($408 billion) and sustainability-linked bonds ($105 billion). Most are domiciled in developed countries and targeted at assets in developed markets.

The global market for sustainable funds experienced another year of exceptional growth in 2021. Net investment reached $557 billion, up 58 per cent from 2020 and more than three times the 2019 level. European funds attracted net inflows of $472 billion, or 85 per cent of the world's total. Sustainable funds now account for 18 per cent of the assets of the European fund market. Globally, however, sustainable funds still only account for about 4 per cent of total open-ended funds.

New global sustainable bond issuance surpassed $1 trillion in 2021, including green, social and mixed-sustainability bonds, as well as sustainability-linked bonds. The increase in sustainable bond issuance was especially visible in emerging markets. The European Union and the corporate sector continue to push social and mixed-sustainability bond issuance to new heights.

Concerns remain about greenwashing and the real impact of sustainability-themed investment products. That is because most of these products are self-labelled and there is a lack of consistent standards and high-quality data to assess sustainability credentials. Also, developing economies are largely bypassed by the sustainable fund market.

In 2021, public pension funds held more than $22 trillion in assets, or almost 40 per cent of global pension fund assets. The assets of sovereign wealth funds grew to $11 trillion. *Institutional investors can exert a significant influence over their investees and the sustainable investment market through asset allocation and active ownership.*

Currently, more than half of the 100 largest public pension and sovereign wealth funds do not disclose or report on sustainability issues. Making progress on ESG reporting by these funds will require strengthening national regulations.

Exchanges continue to play an important role in promoting sustainable finance, especially ESG disclosure. The number of exchanges with written guidance on ESG disclosure for issuers grew to 63 at the end of 2021. Mandatory ESG disclosure, supported by both exchanges and security market regulators, now exists in 30 markets.

Mandatory ESG disclosure in 30 markets

Exchanges also have an important role in promoting gender equality. The number of exchanges engaged in annual "Ring the Bell for Gender Equality" events has grown from just 7 in 2015 to over 110 in 2022. Beyond raising awareness, exchanges support mobilizing finance for gender-equality-themed investment products, improving women's access to financial markets and promoting greater levels of female participation in corporate board rooms.

The climate emissions of publicly listed companies vary significantly from one market to another and can present systemic risks in some markets in a transition to net-zero emission economies. Exchanges, regulators and policymakers should monitor the emissions of companies listed on public markets to ensure an orderly transition.

Stock exchanges are playing an important role in helping listed companies take action on climate change, including through intensive training of their issuers on climate disclosure reporting.

With the rise of sustainability-themed financial products, governments around the world are stepping up their efforts to develop regulatory frameworks for sustainable finance. By the end of 2021, 35 countries and economic groupings – both developed and developing – had 316 sustainable finance-dedicated policy measures and regulations in force, more than 40 per cent of which were introduced in the last five years. Almost half of these policies are dedicated to sustainability disclosure. Sector-specific regulations with respect to asset management, sustainable banking and sustainable insurance are the second biggest policy area, representing about 20 per cent of all measures. Policy and regulatory gaps are more visible in three relatively new policy areas: taxonomies, product standards and carbon pricing.

In 2021, efforts to coordinate and consolidate sustainable finance regulations and standards at the international level gathered momentum. The International Organization of Securities Commissions (IOSCO) and the International Financial Reporting Standards (IFRS) Foundation are now leading a global effort in consolidating the major ESG reporting standards, effectively reducing the fragmentation that has persisted over the past decade.

CHAPTER I

GLOBAL INVESTMENT TRENDS AND PROSPECTS

A. INVESTMENT TRENDS

1. Global trends

Global foreign direct investment (FDI) flows in 2021 were $1.58 trillion, up 64 per cent from the level during the first year of the COVID-19 pandemic of less than $1 trillion (figure I.1). FDI flows appeared to have significant momentum mainly because of booming merger and acquisition (M&A) markets and rapid growth in international project finance as a result of loose financing conditions and major infrastructure stimulus packages.

However, the global environment for international business and cross-border investment changed dramatically in 2022 with the onset of the war in Ukraine, which occurred while the world was still reeling from the impact of the pandemic. The war is having effects well beyond its immediate vicinity, causing a triple food, fuel and finance crisis, with rising prices for energy and basic commodities driving inflation and worsening debt spirals (box I.1). Investor uncertainty and risk aversity could put significant downward pressure on global FDI in 2022.

The war, with its direct implications for investment in and from the Russian Federation and Ukraine, and its ripple effects through sanctions, supply shortages in energy and basic commodities, and broader macroeconomic impact, is not the only factor cooling FDI prospects for 2022. The flare-up of COVID-19 in China, which is resulting in renewed lockdowns in some areas that play a major role in global value chains (GVCs), could further depress new greenfield investment in GVC-intensive industries.

Figure I.1. FDI inflows, global and by economic grouping, 2008–2021 (Billions of dollars and per cent)

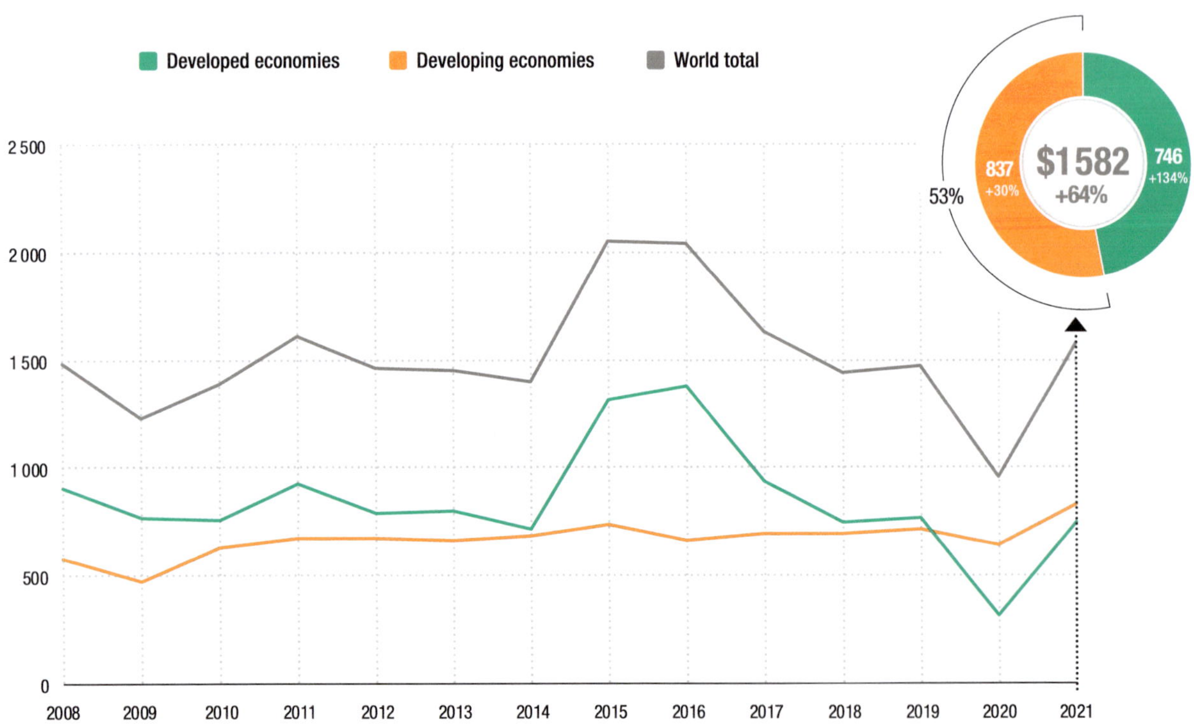

Source: UNCTAD, FDI/MNE database (https://unctad.org/fdistatistics).

Box I.1. The impact of the war in Ukraine on global FDI flows

The war in Ukraine will have far-reaching consequences for international investment in economic development and the Sustainable Development Goals (SDGs) in all countries. It comes as a fragile world economy was just beginning an uneven recovery from the effects of the pandemic. Global FDI in 2022 and beyond will be affected by the security and humanitarian crises, by macroeconomic shocks set off by the conflict, by energy and food price hikes, and by increased investor uncertainty.

The direct effects of the war on investment flows to and from the Russian Federation and Ukraine include the halting of existing investment projects and the cancellation of announced projects, an exodus of MNEs from the Russian Federation, widespread loss of asset values and sanctions virtually precluding outflows.

The value at risk is significant. MNEs from developed economies that support the sanctions account for more than two thirds of FDI stock in the Russian Federation (with a significant part of the rest accounted for by offshore financial centres (OFCs)). In contrast, to date, MNEs from China and India account for a negligible share of FDI stock in the Russian Federation (less than 1 per cent), although their share in ongoing projects is larger. Box table I.1.1 shows the top 10 non-financial MNEs ranked by assets held in the Russian Federation. Energy sector MNEs hold the largest share. In Ukraine, similarly, a number of MNEs hold significant assets, mostly in steel, information and communication technology (ICT), pharmaceuticals and agricultural commodities. Arcelor Mittal (Luxembourg) is the largest investor, with assets of $6.5 billion.

Box table I.1.1. **Top 10 non-financial MNEs by assets held in the Russian Federation, 2021**
(Billions of dollars)

Company	Home country	Industry	Estimated assets[a]
Fortum	Finland	Utilities	32.6
Renault	France	Automotives	15.9
BP	United Kingdom	Oil and gas	14.4
TotalEnergies	France	Oil and gas	13.7
Exxon Mobil	United States	Oil and gas	7.5
Shell	United Kingdom	Oil and gas	5.7
PepsiCo	United States	Food and Beverages	5.6
Carlsberg	Denmark	Food and Beverages	3.7
Japan Tobacco	Japan	Tobacco	3.9
Siemens	Germany	Machinery	2.6

Source: UNCTAD, based on data from Refinitiv SA.
[a] Because companies rarely report country-by-country segment figures, assets are estimated in many cases using subsidiary data.

The wider effects on global investment flows are mostly indirect and difficult to anticipate. Apart from its importance as a natural resource exporter, the Russian Federation plays a relatively minor role in international investment and global value chains (GVCs). Moreover, both its inward and outward investments had already declined significantly after the international sanctions imposed in 2014. Inward FDI fell by more than three quarters immediately following those sanctions and remained 43 per cent lower than the pre-sanctions average in the subsequent years (box figure I.1.1). It can be expected that only a few economies – mainly in Eastern Europe and Central Asia – will be significantly affected now as a result of Russian links with their FDI profile.

Box figure I.1.1. **FDI inflows to the Russian Federation, 2008–2021**
(Billions of dollars)

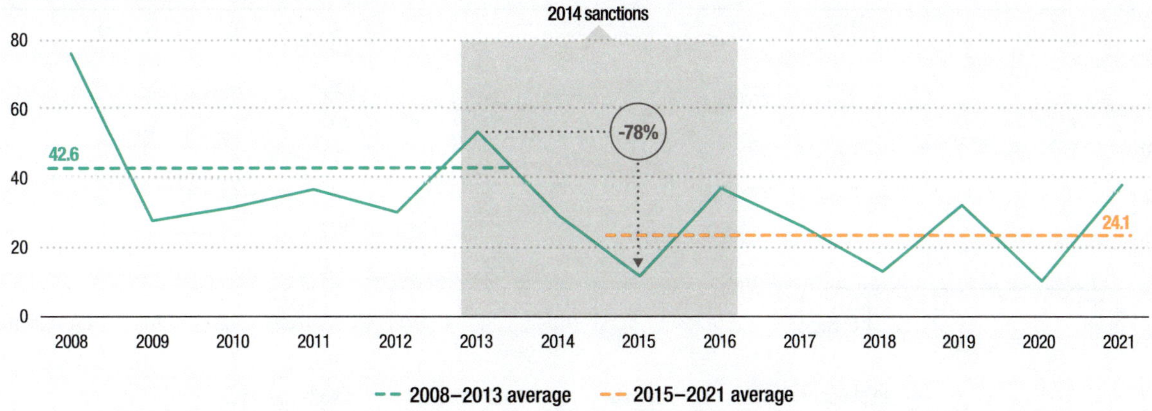

Source: UNCTAD, FDI/MNE database (https://unctad.org/fdistatistics).

/...

Box I.1. The impact of the war in Ukraine on global FDI flows (Concluded)

The indirect effects on investment flows to developing countries will mostly depend on the extent of their exposure to the triple "food, fuel and finance" crises caused by the conflict and their consequent economic and political instability – key determinants of international private investment.

An early indication of investment prospects for individual sectors and industries can be found in the profit expectations of MNEs. Since the start of the war, the majority of the top 5,000 MNEs have revised earnings forecasts for 2022. Due to high commodity prices, extractive industries (mining, oil and gas) have revised their forecasts upward. Industries that require commodities as production inputs (such as manufacturing and construction) or that depend on fuel (such as airlines) have revised their earnings forecasts downwards. Geographically, companies in Eastern Europe and North Africa appear to face relatively more downward pressure on earnings.

Source: UNCTAD.

Furthermore, the expected interest rate rises in the United States, Europe and other major economies that are seeing significant rises in inflation could slow down M&A markets later in the year and dampen the growth of international project finance. Negative financial market sentiment and signs of a looming recession could accelerate an FDI downturn.

There are also factors that point towards making FDI relatively resilient to drastic decline at times of global economic downturn. The part of FDI that is most closely correlated with financial markets has not yet lost its strength. Cross-border M&As and international project finance in infrastructure sectors may provide a floor to global FDI in 2022. Greenfield investment in industry, which saw only a partial recovery in 2021 and remains weak in many sectors, is likely to suffer more.

Early indicators reveal a worrisome FDI outlook: FDI project activity in the first months of 2022 shows investors' uncertainty and risk aversity. According to preliminary data, the number of greenfield project announcements in the first quarter of 2022 was 21 per cent below the quarterly average in 2021. Cross-border M&A activity was 13 per cent below the 2021 average and international project finance deals were down 4 per cent (figure I.2). However, in terms of value, cross-border M&As were up 59 per cent from last year. The value of announced international project finance deals was 37 per cent below the record levels of 2021 but remains at a very high level compared with the pre-pandemic period.

Figure I.2. **Announced greenfield projects, cross-border M&As and international project finance deals, Q1 2020–Q1 2022** (Number and per cent)

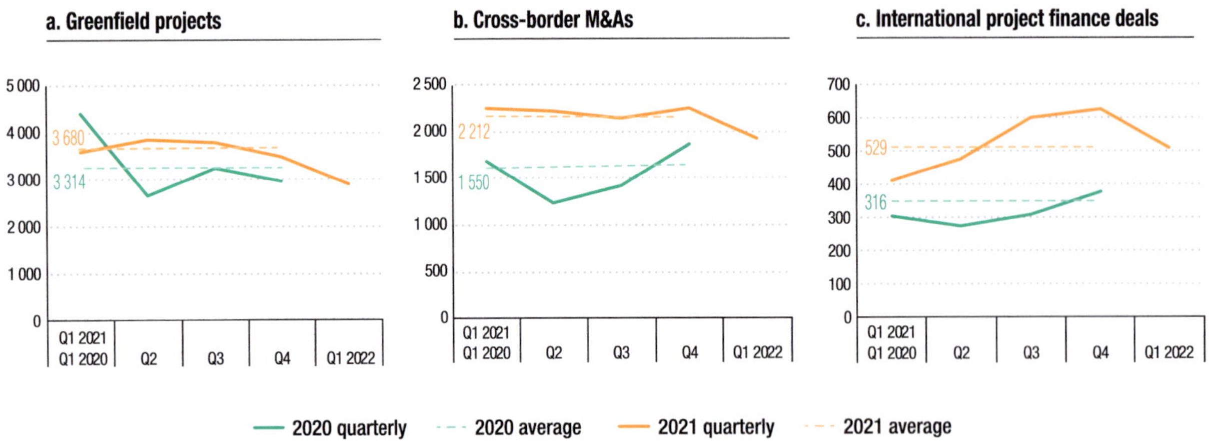

Source: UNCTAD, cross-border M&A database (https://unctad.org/fdistatistics) for M&As, information from the Financial Times Ltd, fDi Markets (www.fDimarkets.com) for announced greenfield FDI projects and Refinitiv SA for international project finance deals.

Overall, UNCTAD foresees that the growth momentum of 2021 cannot be sustained and that global FDI flows in 2022 will likely move on a downward trajectory, at best remaining flat. This projection takes into account the various downward pressures and potential stabilizing factors and considers the composition of the 2021 value of $1.6 trillion, which for some recipient regions (especially Europe) does not represent historically high levels and could therefore cushion the decline. However, even if flows should remain relatively stable in value terms, new project activity is likely to suffer more from investor uncertainty.

Looking at the global FDI trend over the course of the pandemic to date, a clear contrast emerges with other economic variables (table I.1). In 2020, FDI was much more severely affected than global trade and GDP, which had already started their recovery in the second half of the year. In 2021, FDI accelerated faster than other variables.

The large swings in FDI observed between the first and second year of the pandemic, especially in developed countries, were mainly caused by the substantial financial flow component of FDI and by transactions that are closely linked to the performance of financial markets. The booming M&A market and retained earnings of MNEs explain much of the rapid rebound of growth in 2021. The corollary is visible in much weaker growth of greenfield investments in industry and in the low share of new equity in FDI flows.

The reinvested earnings component of FDI – profits retained in foreign affiliates by multinational enterprises (MNEs) – accounted for the bulk of FDI growth in 2021. In the United States, reinvested earnings reached $200 billion – the highest level ever recorded. Other developed countries, including Switzerland, the Netherlands, Canada, Australia and Belgium, in that order, also saw large jumps in their reinvested earnings. Global equity investment grew more moderately, reflecting the more limited growth of new project investments and the shift towards international project finance, which often includes a much smaller equity component and greater reliance on debt financing. Intracompany loans remained negative in many countries (figure I.3).

The importance of retained earnings in 2021 FDI flows reflects the record rise in profit levels of MNEs, especially in developed economies, with

Figure I.3. **Global FDI inflows, by components, 2020 and 2021** (Billions of dollars and per cent)

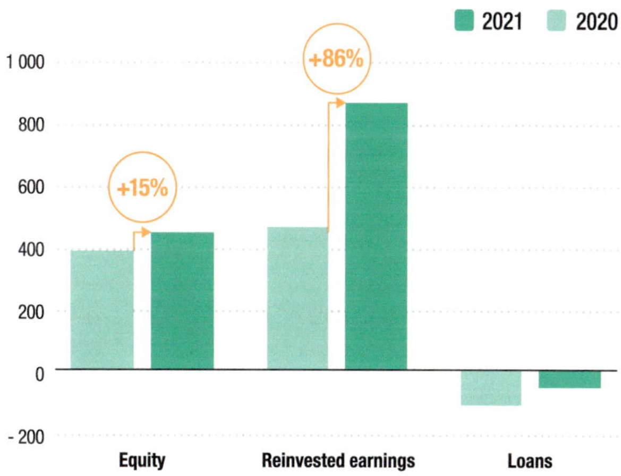

Source: UNCTAD, FDI/MNE database (https://unctad.org/fdistatistics).

Table I.1. **Growth rates of global GDP, GFCF, trade and FDI, 2015–2022** (Per cent)

Variable	2015	2016	2017	2018	2019	2020	2021	2022[a]
GDP	3.4	3.3	3.7	3.6	2.9	-3.1	6.1	3.6
Trade	3.0	2.3	5.6	4.0	0.9	-7.9	10.1	5.0
GFCF	-4.7	0.9	4.1	5.0	0.5	-2.9	8.0	3.2
FDI	47	-1	-20	-11	2	-35	64	-
Memorandum								
FDI value (Trillions of dollars)	2.1	2.0	1.6	1.4	1.5	1.0	1.6	1.6

Source: UNCTAD, FDI/MNE database for FDI; IMF (2022b) for GDP, GFCF and trade.
Note: GFCF = gross fixed capital formation.
[a] Forecasted.

the release of pent-up demand, low financing costs and significant government support. The profitability of the largest MNEs doubled to 8.2 per cent (figure I.4).

As a result of these growth factors, developed economies saw the biggest rise by far, with FDI reaching $746 billion in 2021 – more than double the exceptionally low level in 2020. In Europe, FDI rose in most countries, although half of the increase was caused by large fluctuations in major conduit economies. Inflows in the United States more than doubled, with much of the increase accounted for by a surge in cross-border M&As. Although much of the growth in FDI in developed countries was driven by financial flows and M&As, there were indications of investment strength in actual new projects. Investor confidence was high in infrastructure sectors, supported by favourable long-term financing conditions and recovery stimulus packages. International project finance deals in developed economies were up 70 per cent in number and 149 per cent in value (table I.2).

FDI flows to developing economies increased by 30 per cent, to $837 billion, with 19 per cent growth in developing Asia (to a record $619 billion), a partial recovery in Latin America and the Caribbean (to $134 billion) and an uptick in Africa (to $83 billion). International project finance deals rose by 64 per cent in number (142 per cent in value). Investor confidence in industry remained weak, although the low points seen in GVC-intensive industries in 2020 were not repeated and several industries registered a partial recovery. Greenfield project announcements in developing countries were flat in value terms, although activity (project numbers) increased by 16 per cent.

Figure I.4. **Profitability and profit levels of MNEs, 2010–2021** (Billions of dollars and per cent)

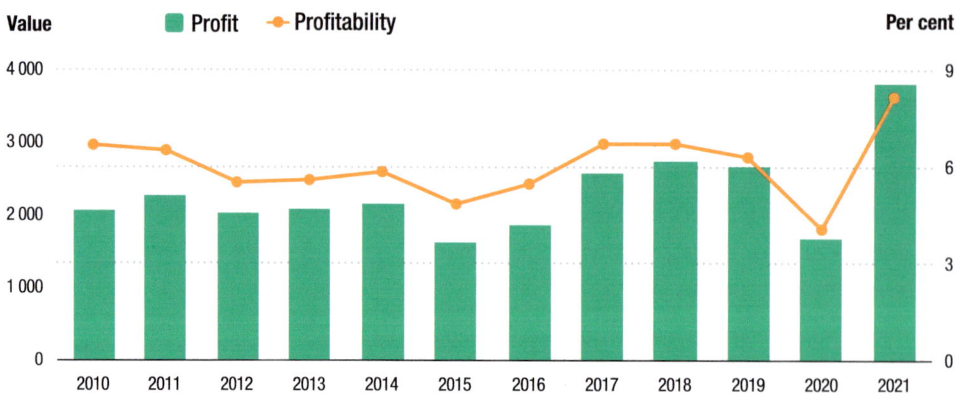

Source: UNCTAD, based on data from Refinitiv SA.

Table I.2. **Announced FDI greenfield projects, cross-border M&As and international project finance deals, by economic grouping, 2020–2021**

Group of economies	Type of FDI	Value (Billions of dollars) 2020	Value (Billions of dollars) 2021	Growth rate (%)	Number 2020	Number 2021	Growth rate (%)
Developed economies	Cross-border M&As	389	615	58	5 333	7 838	47
	Greenfield projects	316	401	27	8 993	9 790	9
	International project finance	264	656	149	742	1 262	70
Developing economies	Cross-border M&As	86	113	31	868	1 008	16
	Greenfield projects	259	259	-	4 255	4 920	16
	International project finance	220	532	142	520	853	64

Source: UNCTAD, cross-border M&A database (https://unctad.org/fdistatistics) for M&As, information from the Financial Times Ltd, fDi Markets (www.fDimarkets.com) for announced greenfield FDI projects and Refinitiv SA for international project finance deals.

2. Trends by geography

a. FDI inflows

FDI flows recovered strongly in 2021 in all regions (figure I.5; box I.2). The increase in FDI flows to developed economies (+134 per cent) – from the exceptionally low values in 2020 – accounted for most of the global growth. The jump in developed economies showed the effect of stimulus packages, resulting in record earnings for MNEs, and reflects the more volatile nature of FDI flows in developed markets because of the larger financial component. However, FDI flows to developing regions also increased significantly. FDI inflows to developing Asia increased by 19 per cent to reach a new high of $619 billion, driven mostly by East and South-East Asia (table I.3). Flows to Latin America and the Caribbean increased by 56 per cent, recovering part of the ground lost in 2020. Flows to Africa more than doubled, but most of the increase was due to a single corporate transaction, without which they would have increased moderately.

The share of global flows accounted for by developed countries returned to pre-pandemic levels, at about half of the total, from just one third in 2020. Structurally weak economies continued to attract only a small share of global FDI, at 2.5 per cent of the total.

Figure I.5. **FDI inflows by region, 2020–2021**
(Billions of dollars and per cent)

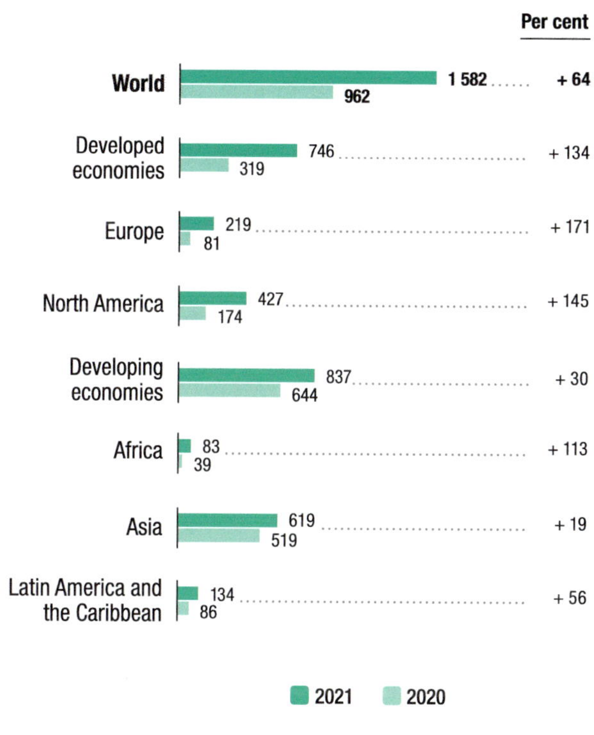

Source: UNCTAD, FDI/MNE database (https://unctad.org/fdistatistics).

Box I.2. Changes in geographical classifications in *WIR22*

Several changes in the definition – for statistical purposes – of regions and economic groups have been introduced in this year's *World Investment Report*, following the reclassification of some countries by the United Nations Statistical Division (UNSD).

Transition economies have been discontinued as an economic group. The economies in it have been distributed across other groups and regions. Europe now includes five countries of the western Balkans, namely Albania, Bosnia and Herzegovina, Montenegro, North Macedonia and Serbia, and four countries from the Commonwealth of Independent States (CIS) namely Belarus, the Republic of Moldova, the Russian Federation and Ukraine. These nine countries are now included among developed countries under "other Europe". Armenia, Azerbaijan and Georgia are included in West Asia and Kazakhstan, Kyrgyzstan, Tajikistan, Turkmenistan and Uzbekistan are included in Central Asia. They are all part of developing Asia. In addition, at its 1215th plenary meeting, the Trade and Development Board approved the application of the Republic of Korea, endorse by Group B, and with the agreement of the Asia-Pacific Group, to be moved from the States in list A to the list B States annexed to General Assembly resolution 1995 (XIX). Therefore, the Republic of Korea is now included in the group of developed countries throughout the WIR. Thus, invarious data presentations, it no longer features under developing Asia, but under other developed countries.

All references to developed economies, developing economies, Europe and developing Asia in *WIR22* refer to the new classification; growth rates have been calculated on the basis of adjusted series, unless stated otherwise

Source: UNCTAD.

Table I.3. FDI flows, by region, 2019–2021 (Billions of dollars and per cent)

Other Europe	FDI inflows			FDI outflows		
Region	**2019**	**2020**	**2021**	**2019**	**2020**	**2021**
World	**1 481**	**963**	**1582**	**1 124**	**780**	**1 708**
Developed economies	764	319	746	737	408	1 269
Europe	405	81	219	343	-21	552
EU	402	210	138	368	66	398
Other Europe	3	-129	81	-26	-87	154
North America	275	174	427	108	281	493
Other developed countries	84	64	100	286	147	225
Developing economies	716	645	837	387	372	438
Africa	46	39	83	5	-1	3
Asia	512	519	619	336	378	394
Central Asia	8	6	7	-3	-2	2
East Asia	232	285	329	203	268	244
South Asia	59	71	52	13	11	16
South-East Asia	175	122	175	80	62	76
West Asia	37	35	55	43	39	56
Latin America and the Caribbean	159	86	134	47	-5	42
Oceania	0.1	-0.1	0.1	-0.8	-0.8	-0.2
Structurally weak, vulnerable and small economies[a]	**41**	**34**	**39**	**-0.2**	**0.4**	**2.4**
LDCs	23	23	26	-1.0	1.5	-0.1
LLDCs	22	14	18	0.8	-1.3	1.7
SIDS	4	3	3	0.8	1.0	0.5
Memorandum: percentage share in world FDI flows						
Developed economies	51.6	33.1	47.1	65.6	52.3	74.3
Europe	27.3	8.4	13.8	30.5	-2.6	32.3
EU	27.1	21.7	8.7	32.8	8.5	23.3
Other Europe	0.2	-13.4	5.2	-2.3	-11.1	9.0
North America	18.6	18.1	27.0	9.6	36.1	28.9
Other developed countries	5.7	6.6	6.3	25.5	18.9	13.2
Developing economies	48.4	66.9	52.9	34.4	47.7	25.7
Africa	3.1	4.1	5.2	0.4	-0.1	0.2
Asia	34.6	53.9	39.1	29.9	48.5	23.1
Central Asia	0.6	0.7	0.4	-0.2	-0.3	0.1
East Asia	15.7	29.6	20.8	18.0	34.3	14.3
South Asia	4.0	7.4	3.3	1.2	1.4	0.9
South-East Asia	11.8	12.7	11.1	7.1	8.0	4.4
West Asia	2.5	3.6	3.5	3.8	5.0	3.3
Latin America and the Caribbean	10.7	8.9	8.5	4.2	-0.6	2.5
Oceania	0.0	-0.0	0.0	-0.1	-0.1	-0.0
Structurally weak, vulnerable and small economies[a]	2.8	3.5	2.5	-0.0	0.1	0.14
LDCs	1.5	2.4	1.6	-0.1	0.2	-0.01
LLDCs	1.5	1.5	1.2	0.1	-0.2	0.1
SIDS	0.3	0.3	0.2	0.07	0.12	0.0

Source: UNCTAD, FDI/MNE database (https://unctad.org/fdistatistics).
Note: LDCs = least developed countries, LLDCs = landlocked developing countries, SIDS = small island developing States.
[a] Without double counting countries that are part of multiple groups.

(i) Developed economies

In 2021, most developed countries – 34 out of 48 – saw an increase in FDI. The overall rise was characterized by strong fluctuations in conduit FDI, financial flows resulting from corporate restructurings, and M&As. Among subregions, flows rose in North America, other Europe and other developed countries while they fell in the EU (figure I.6).

In North America, flows to the United States more than doubled to $367 billion, the third highest level ever recorded, after those of 2015 and 2016. The United States remained the largest recipient of FDI (figure I.7). The increase in corporate profits had a direct impact on reinvested earnings, which rose to a record $200 billion. In addition, equity investments were up by 54 per cent, reflecting a steep increase in cross-border M&As. New greenfield project announcements also increased, by 28 per cent to $86 billion.

Cross-border M&A sales of United States assets to foreign investors in the services sector reached $200 billion. They were spread across many services industries, including information and communication ($43 billion), trade ($40 billion), transport and storage ($37 billion), finance and insurance ($30 billion) and professional services ($21 billion). Among the 18 cross-border M&As sales of more than $10 billion in 2021, nine took place in the United States. They included the acquisition of Alexion by AstraZeneca (United Kingdom) for $39 billion, the purchase of GE Capital Aviation Services by AerCap Holdings (Ireland) for $31 billion, the purchase of Kansas City Southern by Canadian Pacific Railway (Canada) for $31 billion and the acquisition of Speedway by Seven & I Holdings (Japan) for $21 billion. The boom in cross-border M&A deals explained much of the increase in FDI in the United States.

Figure I.6. FDI inflows in developed economies, 2020–2021 (Billions of dollars)

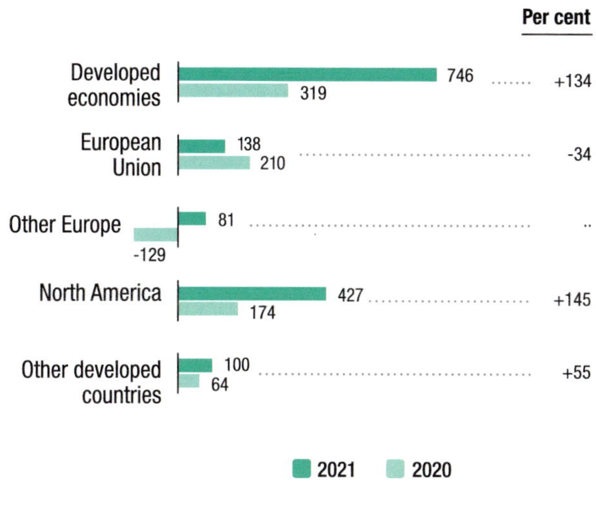

Source: UNCTAD, FDI/MNE database (https://unctad.org/fdistatistics).

Figure I.7. FDI inflows, top 20 host economies, 2020 and 2021 (Billions of dollars)

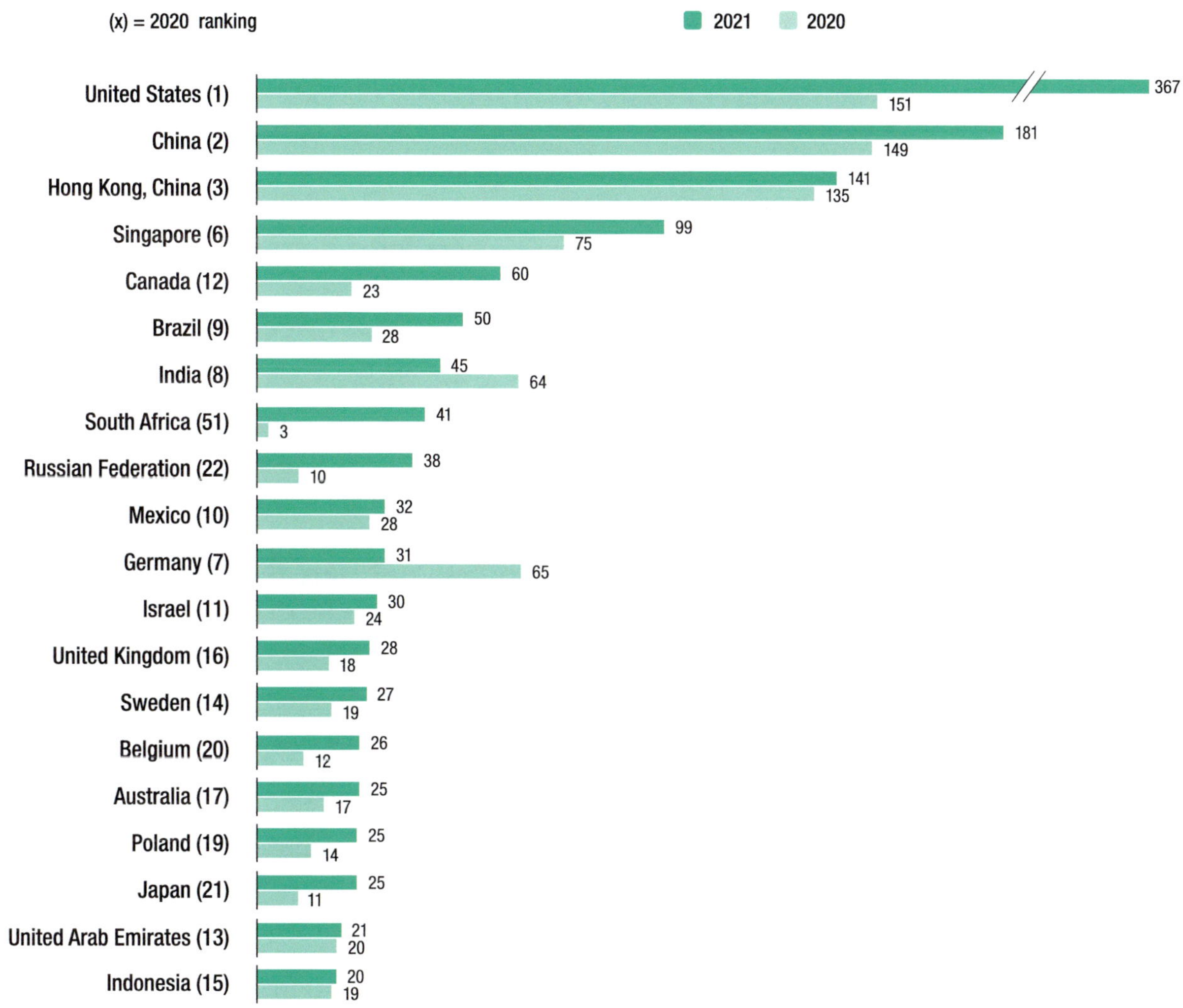

Source: UNCTAD, FDI/MNE database (https://unctad.org/fdistatistics).

FDI in Canada increased by 157 per cent to $60 billion, 30 per cent above the 10-year average before the pandemic. Reinvested earnings reached a record $29 billion, from only $3 billion in 2020. Equity flows rose also, by 50 per cent to $25 billion, driven by a doubling of cross-border M&A sales to $29 billion. Sales – predominantly to MNEs from the United States – increased in extractive industries ($7 billion) and services ($14.5 billion), mainly in information and communication ($7 billion) and finance and insurance ($4 billion).

FDI flows to the European Union (EU) reached $138 billion – the lowest level since 1997– mostly due to continued large swings in conduit flows, including negative values in the Netherlands (-$81 billion in 2021 from -$105 billion in 2020) and an enormous drop of flows to Luxembourg (from $102 billion in 2020 to -$9 billion in 2021). Equity flows in EU countries fell sharply from $220 to -$4.2 billion. Cross-border M&A sales dropped also by 26 per cent to $139 billion. While intra-EU sales doubled, mainly because of acquisitions by French and German MNEs, sales to MNEs from outside the EU declined. The fall was due in part to several sizeable divestments of foreign affiliates to domestic firms, which led to negative values in net cross-border M&As. For example, the sale in France of Aviva France (United Kingdom) to Aema Groupe (France) for $3.9 billion.

The fall in EU inflows occurred despite record reinvested earnings of foreign affiliates in the group, at $252 billion. The decline was not limited to conduit locations: FDI flows also decreased in large EU host countries. Flows to Germany fell by 52 per cent, to $31 billion, from $65 billion in 2020.

The overall positive growth in Europe was driven by FDI flows registered in Switzerland which, after three consecutive years of negative flows, turned positive to $1 billion. In addition to intrafirm financial flows, M&A activity drove part of the increase. Among the larger deals were the acquisition of Sunrise by Liberty Global (United Kingdom) for $5.4 billion. FDI flows to the United Kingdom also rose, by 51 per cent to $28 billion, still one of the lowest levels ever recorded. Equity investment there more than doubled, together with cross-border M&A values. Large deals in the United Kingdom included the merger of Fiat Chrysler Automobiles with Peugeot (France) for $22 billion and the purchase of GW Pharmaceuticals by Jazz Pharmaceuticals (United States) for $6.8 billion. Two large divestments included the sale by PPL (United States) of its Bristol-based electric power distributor to National Grid for $20 billion and the sale by Telefonica (Spain) of its O2 Holdings to Virgin Media for $13 billion. Most other developed economies also saw FDI inflows rise in 2021. In Israel, FDI continued its upward trend, to $30 billion – a record. Cross-border M&A sales there reached $22 billion, more than half of which was in information and communication. For example, Thoma Bravo (United States) merged with Ironsource, for $10 billion. Flows to Australia rose by 50 per cent to $25 billion, driven in part by M&A sales in food and beverages; Coca-Cola European Partners (United Kingdom) acquired a 69 per cent in Coca-Cola Amatil for $5.2 billion. Despite some large divestments, FDI flows to Japan more than doubled, to $25 billion, and flows to the Republic of Korea doubled to $17 billion.

Although developed economies are more prone to large fluctuations in FDI caused by financial flows and M&A transactions – clearly the case in the 2021 rebound from the 2020 lows – there were upswings in new productive project announcements as well. The value of new greenfield projects announced in developed economies rose by 27 per cent to $401 billion. Projects in the primary sector remained minimal (at $7 billion), while the value of projects in the services sector rose slightly, by 9 per cent, to $215 billion. Manufacturing industries experienced a return to pre-pandemic values, at $179 billion. Greenfield projects announced in electronics and electrical equipment, strongly affected during the first year of the pandemic by supply chain concerns, more than doubled to $73 billion. The value of announced projects in information and communication kept rising in 2021 to $68 billion.

The two largest deals announced were in semiconductors: Intel (United States) intends to build a semiconductor plant in Germany for $19 billion, and Samsung (Republic of Korea) plans to build a semiconductor factory in the United States for $17 billion.

In 2021, the number of announced international project finance deals continued its upward trend, reaching 1,262 projects – a record. The total value of deals more than doubled, to $656 billion. Renewable energy remained the most important industry with two thirds of the deals (805), a 52 per cent increase from 2020. Deals in residential and commercial real estate quintupled to 78 from 16. Many international project finance deals target sustainability or climate change objectives; in 2021 projects included, for example, the construction of a zero-carbon retail and residential precinct in Australia for $1 billion.

For 2022, FDI trends in developed economies are highly uncertain, as the war in Ukraine could have far-reaching consequences for investment – especially in Europe where, apart from the direct impact on investment in the Russian Federation and Ukraine, the main channel through which the war and the sanctions will affect investment is the rise in energy prices and energy insecurity. Supply chain disruptions will also hurt some industries – including automotive – as the war and sanctions hinder production of key inputs. Nonetheless, cross-border M&As – the most important type of FDI in developed economies – rose by 39 per cent, to $285 billion, in the first four months of 2022, compared with the $205 billion four months average in 2021. One third of M&A sales ($87 billion) took place in the extractive industries, reflecting the higher commodity prices.

(ii) Developing economies

FDI flows to developing economies in 2021 increased by 30 per cent to $837 billion, the highest level ever recorded. The increase was mainly the result of strong growth performance in Asia, a partial recovery in Latin America and the Caribbean, and an upswing in Africa. The share of developing countries in global flows remained just above 50 per cent. FDI flows continue to be an important source of external finance for developing economies, together with other cross-border capital flows, which also saw a rise in 2021 (figure I.8).

Figure I.8. **Developing economies: sources of external finance, 2011–2021**
(Billions of dollars)

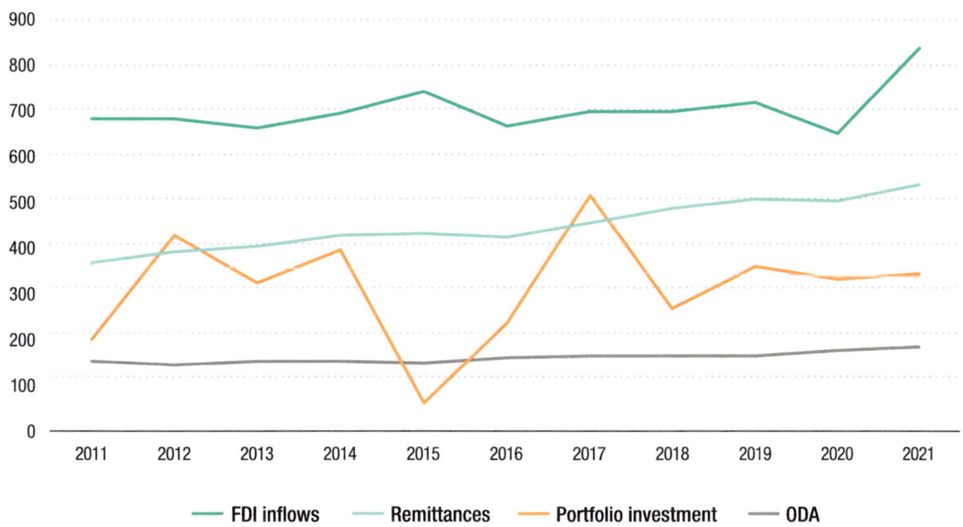

Source: UNCTAD, FDI/MNE database (https://unctad.org/fdistatistics) (for FDI inflows), OECD (for ODA flows) and World Bank (for remittances).

In 2022, FDI flows to developing economies are expected to be strongly affected by the war in Ukraine and its wider ramifications, and by macroeconomic factors including rising interest rates. The main drivers of a possible contraction of FDI are the impact of higher energy prices on domestic demand; high food prices, which can lead to political instability; and tighter financial conditions. Fiscal space in many countries will be significantly reduced, especially in oil- and food-importing developing economies. Rising investor uncertainty and downgrades of country risk ratings will be important factors for FDI. Higher commodity prices may provide some offsetting investment increases for resource-based economies in Africa and in Latin America. As in developed economies, cross-border M&A sales in developing economies also rose – by 13 per cent, to $42 billion in the first months of 2022, 40 per cent of which targeted extractive industries.

Africa

FDI flows to Africa reached $83 billion – a record level – from $39 billion in 2020, accounting for 5.2 per cent of global FDI. Most recipients saw a moderate rise in FDI after the fall in 2020 caused by the pandemic. The total for the continent was inflated by a single intrafirm financial transaction in South Africa in the second half of 2021. Excluding that transaction, the increase in Africa is moderate, more in line with other developing regions. Southern Africa, East Africa and West Africa saw their flows rise; Central Africa remained flat and North Africa declined (figure I.9).

Flows to North Africa fell by 5 per cent to $9.3 billion. Egypt saw its FDI drop by 12 per cent as large investments in exploration and production agreements in extractive industries were not repeated. Despite the decline, the country was the second largest host of FDI on the continent. Pledges from Gulf States to invest some $22 billion in various sectors may boost FDI going forward. Announced greenfield projects in Egypt more than tripled, to $5.6 billion; for example, Reportage Properties (United Arab Emirates) announced a real estate project for $1.5 billion. Flows to Morocco rose by 52 per cent to $2.2 billion. A large international project finance deal was announced there: the $20 billion construction of a 3,800 km transmission line to the United Kingdom with 3.6 GW of capacity, sponsored by Xlinks (United Kingdom).

Figure I.9. **FDI inflows in Africa, by subregion 2020–2021** (Billions of dollars)

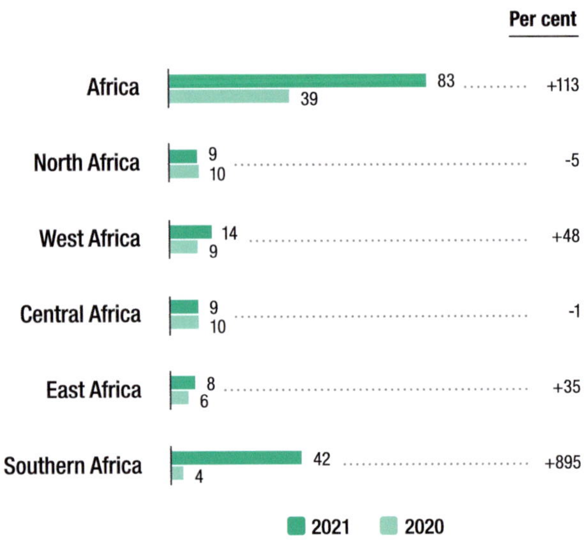

Source: UNCTAD, FDI/MNE database (https://unctad.org/fdistatistics).

FDI in West Africa increased by 48 per cent to $14 billion. Nigeria saw its flows double to $4.8 billion, mainly because of the resurgence in oil investment and expansion in gas. International project finance deals in the country jumped to $7 billion, with some large projects in residential and commercial real estate. These included, for example, the $2.9 billion Escravos Seaport project, involving construction of an industrial complex with a refinery, international airport, industrial estate and free trade zone. FDI flows to Ghana rose by 39 per cent to $2.6 billion, again mainly owing to projects in extractive industries; for example, the construction of an $850 million gold mining facility by Newmont Corp (United States) and the construction of a cement factory by Ciment d'Afrique (CIMAF) (Morocco) for $436 million.

FDI to East Africa grew by 35 per cent to $8.2 billion. Flows to Ethiopia reached $4.3 billion. Chinese investments tripled in 2021 (Ethiopia is a central hub for China's Belt and Road Initiative).

Four (out of five) international project finance announcements in the country were in renewables; for example, the Masdar solar project involves construction of a 500 MW solar power plant for $135 million, with Abu Dhabi Future Energy as a sponsor. Uganda saw its FDI rise by 31 per cent to $1.1 billion. FDI to the United Republic of Tanzania rose by 35 per cent to $922 million, and new greenfield project announcements tripled in value. The two largest projects announced in 2021 were the development of nickel project from Kabanga Nickel (United Kingdom) for $318 million, and an investment in food and beverages by Associated British Foods (United Kingdom) for $238 million.

Flows to Central Africa remained flat at $9.4 billion. FDI to the Democratic Republic of the Congo rose by 14 per cent $1.9 billion, with investment remaining buoyant because of flows in offshore oil fields and mining. Other projects include a facility for treatment of municipal organic waste by Biocrude Technologies (Canada) for $136 million. Flows to Congo fell by 8 per cent to $3.7 billion, but two international project finance deals were announced; the largest involves the construction of an oil facility for $166 million, sponsored by China National Chemical and Beijing Fortune Dingheng Investment (China).

FDI to Southern Africa jumped to $42 billion due to a large corporate reconfiguration in South Africa – a share exchange between Naspers and Prosus in the third quarter of 2021. New project announcements included a $4.6 billion clean energy project finance deal sponsored by Hive Energy (United Kingdom) and a $1 billion greenfield project by Vantage Data Centers (United States), with its first African campus.

Despite the overall positive FDI trend on the continent, total greenfield announcements remained depressed, at $39 billion, showing only a modest recovery from the low of $32 billion in 2020 (down from $77 billion in 2019).

In contrast, international project finance deals targeting Africa showed a rise of 26 per cent in number (to 116) and a resurgence in value to $121 billion (after $36 billion in 2020). The rise was supported by strong investment by multilateral finance and capital market investors targeting power ($56 billion) and renewables ($26 billion). The largest project was the announcement in Mauritania of a power-to-x hydrogen project for $40 billion by CWP Renewables (Australia).

European investors remain by far the largest holders of foreign assets in Africa, led by the United Kingdom ($65 billion) and France ($60 billion).

Developing Asia

Despite successive waves of COVID-19, FDI in developing Asia rose for the third consecutive year to an all-time high of $619 billion, underscoring the resilience of the region. It is the largest recipient region of FDI in the world, accounting for 40 per cent of global inflows.

The 2021 upward trend was widely shared in the region, with South Asia the only exception (figure I.10). However, inflows remain highly concentrated. Six economies (China, Hong Kong (China), Singapore, India, the United Arab Emirates and Indonesia, in that order) accounted for more than 80 per cent of FDI to the region.

FDI in East Asia increased 16 per cent to $329 billion in 2021. FDI growth in China picked up pace, growing by 21 per cent to $181 billion, after

Figure I.10. FDI Inflows in developing Asia by subregion, 2020–2021 (Billions of dollars)

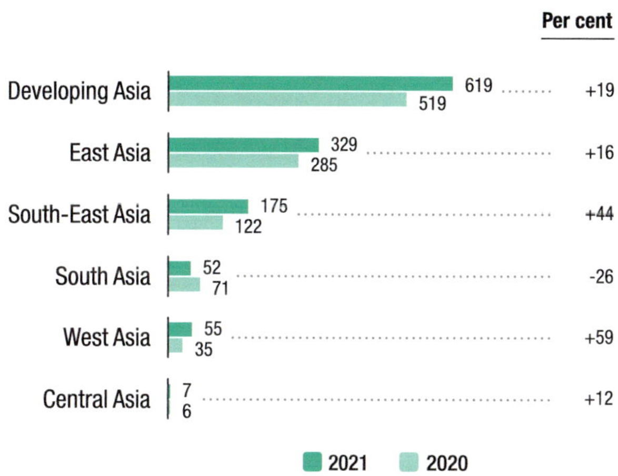

Source: UNCTAD, FDI/MNE database (https://unctad.org/fdistatistics).

only a 6 per cent increase in 2020. China's robust FDI growth was powered by strong investment in services and high-tech sectors, where the outlook also remains robust; for example, TSMC (Taiwan Province of China) plans to invest $2.8 billion in China to ramp up the production of semiconductors used in automobiles. The number of foreign-invested enterprises in China registered in 2021 reached 48,000, up 24 percent year on year. International project finance deals reached 25 – a record number, with the most projects announced in renewables and industrial real estate. One of the largest projects was the construction of a data centre in Shanghai for $1 billion, sponsored by Princeton Digital Group (Singapore). Flows to Hong Kong, China, reached $141 billion – 4 per cent higher than 2020, mostly accounted for by reinvested earnings ($108 billion). FDI trends in China in 2022 will be affected by renewed lockdowns in parts of the country, with significant implications for industrial production and global supply chains.

South-East Asia resumed its role as an engine of growth for FDI in developing Asia and globally, with inflows up 44 per cent to $175 billion and increases across most countries. The rise was underpinned by strong investment in manufacturing, the digital economy and infrastructure. Singapore, the largest recipient, saw inflows up 31 per cent to $99 billion, driven by a jump in cross-border M&As. The largest deal was the merger of Altimeter Growth Corp (United States) with Grab, a Singapore-based software publisher, for $34 billion. Announced greenfield projects also rose to $13 billion with a $4 billion project of GlobalFoundries (United Arab Emirates) to build a chipmaking plant in Singapore. Malaysia also attracted chipmakers; its largest greenfield project announcements were all in semiconductors – Risen Solar Technology (China) for $10 billion, Intel (United States) for $7 billion and AT&S (Austria) for $2.1 billion.

FDI in West Asia increased by 59 per cent to $55 billion in 2021 from $35 billion in 2020, mainly driven by a significant rise in cross-border M&As. While the United Arab Emirates remained the largest recipient with stable flows at $20 billion, inflows more than tripled in Saudi Arabia and rose by 60 per cent in Turkey. In the United Arab Emirates, DHL Global Forwarding (Germany) and Total (France) announced the building of a solar energy project in Dubai for $633 million. FDI inflows to Saudi Arabia rose to $19 billion from $5.3 billion in 2020 thanks to two large deals. In Turkey, after two consecutive years of decline, inflows reached $13 billion, with a rise in new equity investments. Deals included the refinancing of project debt across several oil and gas assets in Turkey by Socar (Azerbaijan), for $1.3 billion.

FDI in South Asia fell by 26 per cent, to $52 billion, as the large M&As registered in 2020 were not repeated. Flows to India declined to $45 billion. However, a flurry of new international project finance deals were announced in the country: 108 projects, compared with 20 projects on average for the last 10 years. The largest number of projects (23) was in renewables. Large projects include the construction in India of a steel and cement plant for $13.5 billion by Arcelormittal Nippon Steel (Japan) and the construction of a new car manufacturing facility by Suzuki Motor (Japan) for $2.4 billion.

Flows to Central Asia rose by 12 per cent to $7 billion. Flows to Kazakhstan – the largest host in the subregion – fell by 14 per cent to $3.2 billion, with declines in extractive industries and transportation. Flows rose by 18 per cent to $2 billion in Uzbekistan and by 24 per cent to $1.5 billion in Turkmenistan.

Across developing Asia, investment in sectors relevant for the SDGs rose significantly. International project finance values in these sectors increased by 74 per cent to $121 billion, primarily because of strong interest in renewable energy. Project values in this industry rose 123 per cent, to $77 billion, from $34 billion in 2020.

Latin America and the Caribbean

In 2021, FDI in Latin America and the Caribbean rose by 56 per cent to $134 billion, sustained by strong inflows in traditional target industries such as automotive manufacturing, financial and insurance services, and electricity provision, and pushed up by record high investments in information and communication services across the region. Most economies saw inflows rebound, with only a few experiencing further declines caused by the pandemic-induced economic crisis, in some cases combined with political instability. Flows rose in all three subregions in Latin America and the Caribbean (excluding financial centres) (figure I.11).

Figure I.11. **FDI inflows in Latin America and the Caribbean, by subregion,** (Billions of dollars)

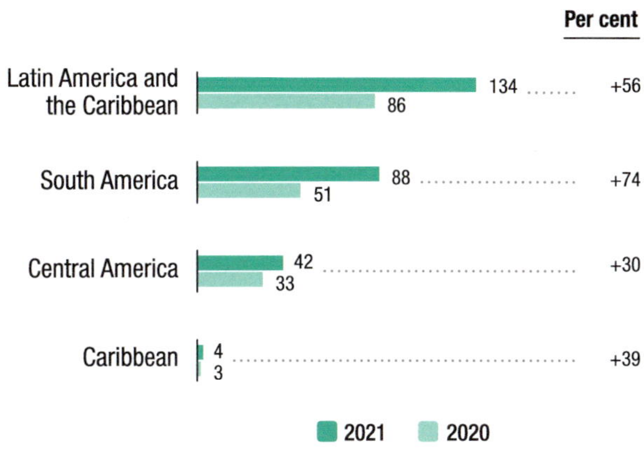

Source: UNCTAD, FDI/MNE database (https://unctad.org/fdistatistics).

In South America, FDI grew by 74 per cent to $88 billion, sustained by higher demand for commodities and green minerals. All major recipients, which include Brazil, Chile and Colombia, saw their FDI flows rise, driven by the resumption of flows into mining and hydrocarbons. In Brazil investments in agribusiness, automotive and electronics manufacturing, information technology and financial services led to an increase of total FDI by 78 per cent, to $50 billion. The value of announced greenfield projects and number of international project finance deals in the country rose by 35 per cent and 32 per cent, respectively. One of the largest greenfield projects was the kick-off by Bravo Motor (United States) of a $4.4 billion project to produce electric vehicles as well as batteries and components in Brazil. Among international project finance deals, the largest was the construction of a 2 GW offshore wind farm for $5.9 billion, sponsored by Ocean Winds (Spain). Flows to Chile rose by 32 per cent to $13 billion, sustained by several large acquisitions and renewed interest in mining projects. The number of international project finance deals there rose 80 per cent to 88 projects. One of the largest is the construction of a $3 billion ammonia plant with onshore wind farm, electrolysers, and port facility. Flows to Colombia grew by 26 per cent to $9 billion, led by inflows in the manufacturing sector and in transport, logistics and communication services. Flows to Argentina and Peru recovered to pre-pandemic levels. In Argentina, inflows grew to $6.5 billion, largely in mining projects.

In Central America, FDI reached $42 billion. Flows to Mexico, the second largest recipient in the subregion, increased by only 13 per cent to $32 billion, with new equity investments in the mining and extractive industries as well as in automotive. Greenfield investment announcements, an indicator of future investment plans, were up 43 per cent from 2020, with the biggest jump in information and communication; for example, Huawei (China) announced that it will open a cloud data centre in Mexico for $4.5 billion. Flows to Costa Rica returned to pre-pandemic levels, almost doubling to $3.2 billion with new investments in special economic zones. In Guatemala flows reached a record level of $3.5 billion.

In the Caribbean, FDI increased by 39 per cent to $3.8 billion, mainly driven by growth in inflows to the Dominican Republic, to $3.1 billion. Flows increased in mining, financial services and special economic zones.

Overall, in Latin America and the Caribbean, cross-border M&A activity increased, with a higher number of deals, although the total value of net sales was virtually unchanged from 2020 at $8 billion. The services sector recorded the highest increase of net sales, especially in the financial and energy supply industries. Announced greenfield investment increased by 16 per cent, with most commitments going to the automotive, information and communication, and extractive industries. The value of announced international project finance deals doubled, exceeding pre-pandemic levels, pushed by large projects in transportation infrastructure (especially in Brazil), mining (across the region) and renewable energy.

Structurally weak, vulnerable and small economies

FDI flows to 82 structurally weak, vulnerable and small economies rose by 15 per cent to $39 billion (figure I.12). Inflows to the least developed countries (LDCs), landlocked developing countries (LLDCs) and small island developing States (SIDS) combined[1] accounted for only 2.5 per cent of the world total in 2021, down from 3.5 per cent in 2020. The impact of the pandemic continued to intensify the fragility of the structurally weak economies. Investment in various sectors relevant for achieving the SDGs, especially in food, agriculture, health and education, continued to fall in 2021.

FDI in LDCs increased by 13 per cent to $26 billion, despite the acceleration of funds repatriation by oil companies, which resulted in negative inflows to Angola of -$4.1 billion (from -$1.9 billion in 2020). Flows remained concentrated, with the top five recipients (Mozambique, Ethiopia, Cambodia, Bangladesh and Senegal, in that order) accounting for 69 per cent of total FDI in the group.

FDI inflows to the 33 African LDCs increased by 17 per cent to $16 billion, accounting for almost two thirds of all LDC inflows. Inflows exceeded $1 billion in five African LDCs. In Mozambique, inflows grew by 68 per cent to $5.1 billion, and the country saw a jump in greenfield projects; for example, Globeleq Generation (United Kingdom) plans to build power plants for $2 billion. Flows to Ethiopia rose by 79 per cent to $4.3 billion as FDI from China tripled in 2021. FDI in Senegal rose by 21 per cent to $2.2 billion, and the country registered a 27 per cent rise in announced greenfield projects. Flows to Zambia remained negative at -$457 million, due to a $1.5 billion copper mine divestment by Glencore (Switzerland) to State-owned ZCCM Investments Holdings.

In the nine Asian LDCs, FDI inflows rose by 6 per cent to $9.8 billion, or one third of the LDC total. In Cambodia, the largest LDC recipient, FDI was down by 4 per cent, at $3.5 billion. While greenfield projects fell to only $124 million (from $1.6 billion in 2020), there were eight international project finance deals (compared with only two in 2020). For example, a 50-hectare car tire manufacturing facility is under construction for $350 million, sponsored by Sailun Group (China). In Bangladesh, inflows rose by 13 per cent to $2.9 billion – around the pre-pandemic level. The number of international project finance deals tripled to 14, reaching $4.7 billion. The largest project was the construction of a container terminal in Ananda Bazar for $2 billion.

The number and value of greenfield project announcements in LDCs continued their downward trend in 2021. The number of projects fell to the lowest level since 2008. Their value fell to the lowest ever recorded, $12 billion. This is a major concern as these investment types are crucial for building productive capacity and thus for prospects of sustainable recovery. By value, the largest projects were announced in energy and gas supply and in information and communication.

Figure I.12. FDI inflows in structurally weak, vulnerable and small economies, 2020–2021
(Billions of dollars)

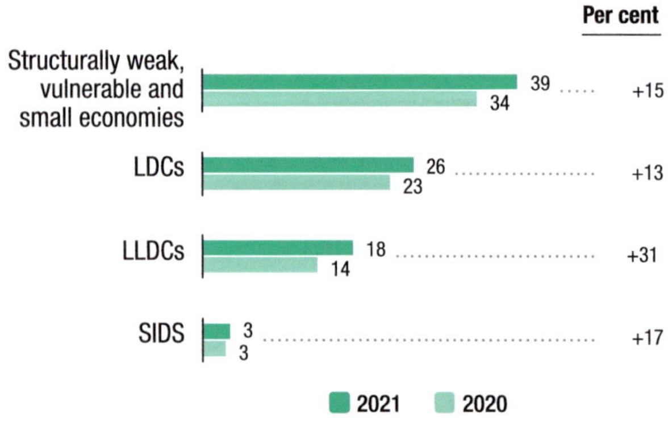

Source: UNCTAD, FDI/MNE database (https://unctad.org/fdistatistics).

International project finance deals targeting LDCs decreased by 6 per cent in number (to 73) but rose by 69 per cent in value. Renewable energy projects accounted for the largest number (34), while power was the largest in terms of value ($41 billion).

Investment in SDG sectors in LDCs remains weak. The number of foreign investment projects (both greenfield and international project finance deals) fell in important SDG sectors, including renewables, power, food and agriculture, and health. They rose in transport, WASH (water, sanitation and hygiene) and education.

MNEs from developing countries play an increasingly important role in LDCs. China continues to be the largest source of FDI, with its FDI stock in the group reaching $46 billion – a 38 per cent rise from 2016.

Since 2011, FDI flows to LDCs as a group have increased only marginally. The pandemic has further undermined the attainment of the goals of the Istanbul Programme of Action for LDCs, as well as the SDGs. FDI remains an important external source of finance for LDCs, but the growth of FDI lags other sources; ODA and remittances are by far the largest external financial flows to LDCs (figure I.13).

Although international project finance is an increasingly important source of investment in most countries and in a diverse set of industries, including SDG-relevant sectors, in LDCs extractive industries continue to be the main target of project finance. This points to the continued dependence of LDCs on resource-driven FDI.

A few LDCs have seen some sectoral diversification. Looking at the types of investment that are most important for the development of productive capacities in LDCs, only investment in energy generation and distribution grew significantly during the decade, while investment in other infrastructure sectors and projects important for private sector development and structural change barely increased. During the pandemic, investment in several priority sectors for developing productive capacity almost completely dried up, making the next programme of action for LDCs – recently adopted – particularly challenging (table I.4).

Figure I.13. | **LDCs: FDI inflows, ODA and remittances, 2011–2021** (Billions of dollars)

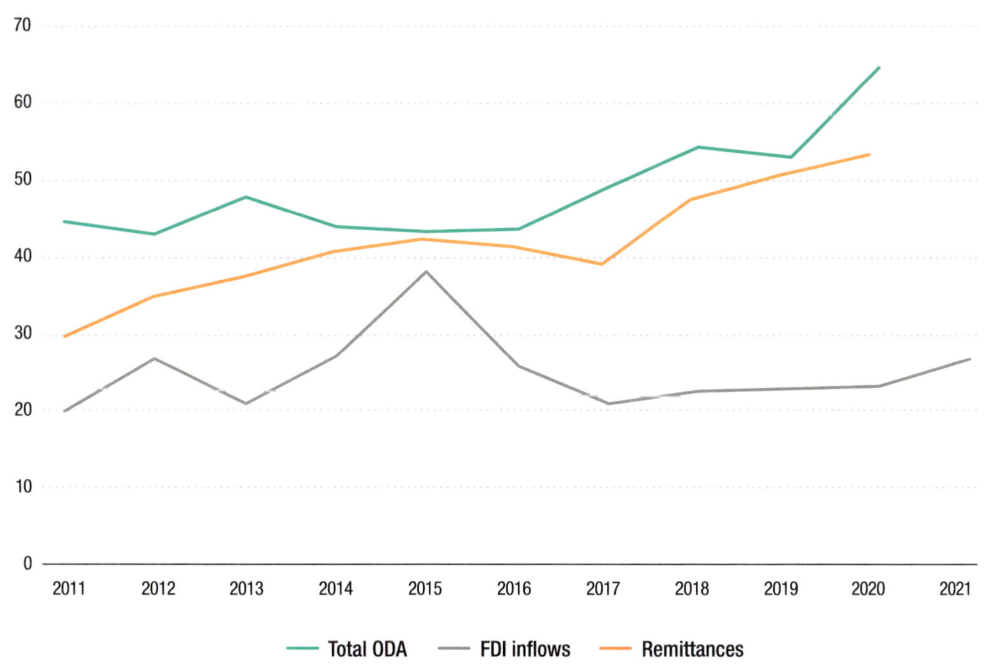

Source: UNCTAD, FDI/MNE database (https://unctad.org/fdistatistics) (for FDI inflows), OECD (for ODA flows) and World Bank (for remittances).

Table I.4. LDCs: announced investment in productive capacity, 2011–2012 and 2019–2021
(Millions of dollars and per cent)

Productive capacity-relevant sector	Greenfield projects						International project finance deals					
	2011	2012	2019	2020	2021	2020–2021 growth rate (%)	2011	2012	2019	2020	2021	2020–2021 growth rate (%)
Total												
Value	**28 741**	**24 765**	**33 779**	**17 314**	**11 368**	**-34**	**96 765**	**115 265**	**67 376**	**32 401**	**60 474**	**87**
Number of projects	**492**	**556**	**421**	**207**	**160**	**-23**	**24**	**27**	**83**	**60**	**63**	**5**
Energy												
Value	4 398	4 265	3 483	7 047	3 260	-54	93 370	54 821	59 267	18 208	55 855	207
Number of projects	3	9	17	24	7	-71	14	19	67	49	47	-4
Human capital												
Value	177	438	201	43	244	467	387	100	130	351	216	-38
Number of projects	10	8	10	5	7	40	2	1	1	2	3	50
ICT												
Value	1 120	771	337	2 248	1 898	-16			320		410	..
Number of projects	27	41	19	31	31	0			2		2	..
Natural capital												
Value	12 159	6 374	11 214	3 059	1 568	-49			181			..
Number of projects	44	22	19	10	7	-30			1			..
Private sector development												
Value	2 322	3 128	1 377	838	524	-37						..
Number of projects	147	178	108	45	31	-31						..
Structural change												
Value	8 488	9 110	14 754	4 078	3 364	-18	1 844	1 112	314	992	858	-14
Number of projects	256	287	232	92	72	-22	5	2	3	5	5	0
Transportion												
Value	77	678	2 413		509	..	1 164	59 231	7 164	12 849	3 135	-76
Number of projects	5	11	16		5	..	3	5	9	4	6	50

Source: UNCTAD, information from the Financial Times Ltd, fDi Markets (www.fDimarkets.com) for announced greenfield FDI projects and Refinitiv SA for international project finance deals. For the methodology on investment in productive capacities, see *WIR21*, chapter IV, and UNCTAD's Productive Capacities Index.

FDI inflows to the 32 LLDCs rose by 31 per cent to $18 billion. Flows to these countries in Africa, Latin America and the Caribbean, and Europe rose. Only flows to LLDCs in Central Asia fell. Flows remained concentrated in a few economies, with the top five recipients (Ethiopia, Kazakhstan, Mongolia, Turkmenistan and Uzbekistan, in that order) accounting for more than 71 per cent of total FDI to the group.

In Africa, flows to the group increased by 53 per cent to $7.8 billion, accounting for 42 per cent of total FDI in LLDCs. Ethiopia became the largest LLDC recipient. Flows to Mali rose by 23 per cent to $660 million; Ciment d'Afrique (CIMAF) (Morocco) intends to construct a factory for $436 million. Uganda saw its FDI rise by 31 per cent, to $1.1 billion.

In the two Latin American LLDCs, FDI inflows turned positive in 2021, to $716 million, after large divestments in 2020 in the Plurinational State of Bolivia. In Paraguay, flows remained flat, rising by 1 per cent to $594 million. The country's lockdown, nationwide for two months and in selected areas afterwards, proved effective and the economy reopened relatively quickly.

Inflows to the LLDCs in developing Asia contracted by 6 per cent to $9.1 billion. After the increase in 2020, flows to Kazakhstan fell by 14 per cent to $3.2 billion. Investment in extractive industries and in transportation and storage declined, but they rose in manufacturing and in finance and insurance. Top investors in the country included MNEs from the United States ($1.6 billion, up 11 per cent), the Russian Federation ($865 million, doubling from 2020) and China ($491 million from -$851 million in 2020). Flows to Mongolia rose by 24 per cent, to $2.1 billion. There were three international project finance deals; for example, the South Gobi green hydrogen pilot plant project for $262 million. Flows rose in Turkmenistan, Uzbekistan and the Lao People's Democratic Republic. In Azerbaijan, flows turned negative to -$1.7 billion because of the repatriation of funds by oil companies.

Looking at the LLDCs group as a whole, the value of greenfield project announcements decreased to $9.9 billion in 2021, although the number of projects rose by 26 per cent, to 173. The decrease in value was particularly pronounced in in manufacturing and services. There was a jump in value in extractive industries, mainly because Zimplats (South Africa) plans to expand investment in the production of platinum in Zimbabwe by $1.2 billion.

The number of international project finance deals in LLDCs was 46 per cent higher than in 2020, at 76 projects. The majority (41) targeted renewables, but projects were also announced in other sectors, including mining, power generation and infrastructure. Examples include the construction of a gas-fired power plant in Kazakhstan for $1.2 billion, sponsored by Siemens Energy (Germany), the expansion of Almaty International Airport in Kazakhstan for $780 million, sponsored by TAV Havalimanlari Holding (Turkey) and the construction of a wind farm and 69 wind turbines in North Macedonia for $610 million, sponsored by WPD (Germany).

FDI to LLDCs originates mostly from a few key investor countries. With $20 billion, China was by far the largest investor in LLDCs (with $6 billion in Kazakhstan alone), followed by Thailand, the Netherlands and Canada.

FDI inflows to the SIDS in 2021 rose by 17 per cent to $3.3 billion, continuing to hover around 0.2 per cent of global FDI. Reflecting differences in levels of development and factor endowments, a handful of SIDS continued to attract the bulk of inflows. The top five recipients (Maldives, Fiji, the Bahamas, Trinidad and Tobago, and Mauritius, in that order) accounted for 56 per cent of FDI flows to the group. The 2021 increase represented only a partial recovery, as pre-pandemic levels were about 25 per cent higher than current levels. This reflects the multiple problems that several of these countries face resulting from the pandemic, including stagnant international tourism.

Inflows to the 10 Caribbean SIDS rose by 4 per cent to $1.7 billion, after dropping 27 per cent in 2020. In the Bahamas, inflows decreased by 60 per cent to $360 million. However, there was a rise in announced greenfield projects and international project finance deals. CGrowth Capital (United States) sponsored the construction of a refinery in the Bahamas for $262 million. Flows to Trinidad and Tobago turned positive (to $342 million from -$103 in 2020); Digicel (Jamaica) plans to invest $137 million in telecommunication.

FDI rose in the two Asian SIDS. In Maldives, FDI inflows rose by 27 per cent, to $443 million, still about half of the 2019 level. In Timor-Leste, a large project was announced in 2021—the construction of a carbon capture and storage scheme in the Timor Sea for $1.6 billion sponsored by a group of investors from Italy, Australia, the Republic of Korea and Japan.

In the five African SIDS, FDI rose by 25 per cent to $592 million. Mauritius saw its FDI flows rise by 13 per cent to $253 million. Decathlon (France) opened its fourth global warehouse in that country – an investment with a value of $17 million. In Seychelles, FDI flows rose by 28 per cent (to $157 million), more than recovering the loss during the pandemic. Cross-border M&As rose in information and technology as ICOA (United States) acquired iBG, a provider of custom computer programming services, for $185 million.

In the 11 SIDS in Oceania, inflows also recovered to pre-pandemic levels, with a 64 per cent rise to $517 million. In Fiji, the largest host country by far, FDI was up by 67 per cent to $401 million, as Sevens Pacific (Singapore) acquired a 44 per cent stake in the state-owned Energy Fiji for $210 million.

b. FDI outflows

In 2021, MNEs from *developed economies* more than doubled their investment abroad to $1.3 trillion, from $408 billion. Their share in global outward FDI rose to three quarters of global outflows. The strong volatility of conduit countries continued in 2021.

Aggregate outward investment by European MNEs rebounded from the anomalously low level in 2020 of -$21 billion to $552 billion.

Outflows from the Netherlands reversed direction, jumping back to $29 billion from -$191 billion in 2020, with the difference accounting for two thirds of the rise in investment by EU MNEs. A sharp increase in outflows from Germany to $152 billion (from $61 billion in 2020) made it the second largest investor home country in the world (figure I.14). Among the components, reinvested earnings of German MNEs abroad jumped to $66 billion – the highest level ever recorded. Large acquisitions by German MNEs included the purchase of Varian Medical Systems (United States) by Siemens Healthineers for $16 billion and the purchase of the petrochemicals business of BP (United Kingdom) in the United States by INEOS Styrolution Group for $5 billion. Outflows from Ireland increased also, to $62 billion from -$45 billion in 2020, mainly owing to several large acquisitions, such as the purchase of GE Capital Aviation Services (United States) by AerCap Holdings for $31 billion.

Outward investments by MNEs from other European countries turned positive to $154 billion from -$87 billion in 2020. MNEs from the United Kingdom increased their investment abroad to $108 billion from -$65 billion in 2020, mainly in the form of reinvested earnings. Outward FDI flows from the Russian Federation increased to $64 billion from $7 billion, mostly directed to Cyprus.

Outflows from North America reached a record $493 billion. MNEs from the United States increased their investment abroad by 72 per cent, to $403 billion. Flows to the EU and the United Kingdom doubled to $154 billion and $79 billion, respectively. Outflows from the United States to Mexico almost tripled (to $11 billion), and to Singapore they increased significantly ($25 billion). By industry, the biggest rises were in wholesale trade (to $38 billion from -$1 billion) and finance (to $39 billion from -$30 billion).

Outward FDI from other developed countries rose by 52 per cent to $225 billion, mainly because of increases from Japanese and Korean MNEs. Outflows from Japan rose by 53 per cent to $147 billion, making it the third largest investor country. Cross-border M&As from Japan rose to $60 billion from $18 billion, mainly in information and communication and in chemicals. For example, Renesas Electronics (Japan) acquired Dialog Semiconductor (United Kingdom) for $6 billion. Outflows from Korean MNEs doubled to $61 billion, with announced greenfield projects overseas jumping from $9.4 billion to $33 billion.

The value of investment activity abroad by MNEs from *developing economies* rose by 18 per cent, to $438 billion. Developing Asia remained a major source of investment even during the pandemic. Outward FDI from the region rose 4 per cent to $394 billion, contributing to almost a quarter of global outflows in 2021. The rise included robust outflows from Saudi Arabia (with a five-fold increase to $24 billion), Singapore (up 49 per cent to $47 billion) and the United Arab Emirates (up 19 per cent to $23 billion). Investment from China and Hong Kong (China), the region's two largest investors, fell by 6 per cent to $145 billion and

Figure I.14. **FDI outflows, top 20 home economies, 2020 and 2021**
(Billions of dollars)

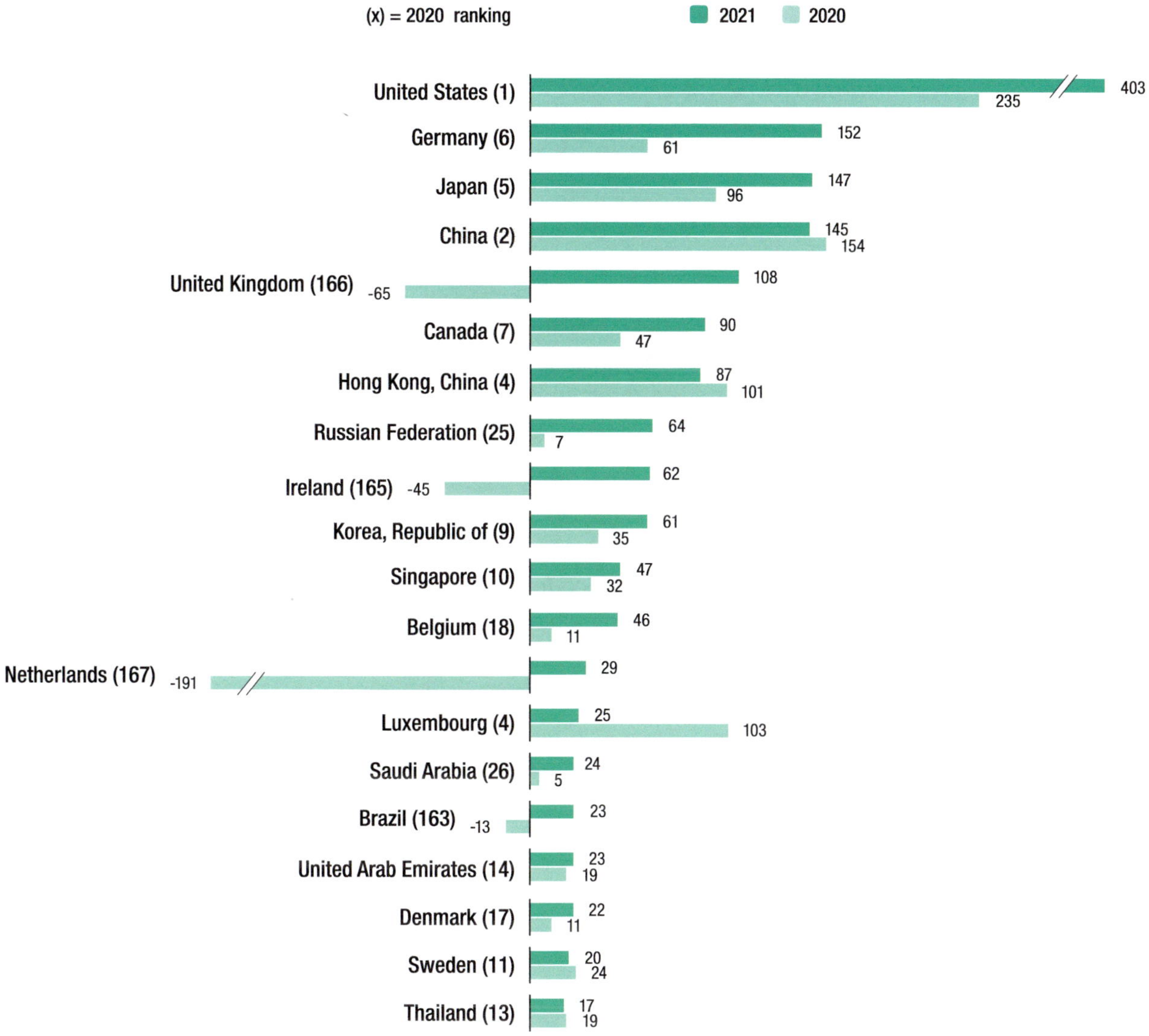

Source: UNCTAD, FDI/MNE database (https://unctad.org/fdistatistics).

13 per cent to $87 billion, respectively. Outward FDI from South Asia, mainly from India, rose by 43 per cent to $16 billion. In South-East Asia, only outflows from Singapore and Malaysia increased.

Although overall outward investment from developing Asia increased, companies headquartered in the region made fewer acquisitions in 2021. Cross-border M&A purchases fell by 35 per cent to $45 billion. Acquisitions by MNEs headquartered in East Asia (mainly China) plummeted, from $44 billion in 2020 to just $6.3 billion. South-East Asia, however, saw cross-border M&A purchases rise by 19 per cent to $29 billion and West Asia saw a rise from -$1.3 billion to $7.7 billion.

Outward FDI from Latin America and the Caribbean jumped back to 2019 levels at $42 billion. The increase is mostly explained by the investment behaviour of Brazilian MNEs, as $13 billion of negative outflows turned to a positive $23 billion. Chilean MNEs also increased their foreign investments to $12 billion.

3. Trends by type and sector

In 2021, cross-border M&As, greenfield project announcements and international project finance deals all increased, both in value and in number (figure I.15). Strong financial markets and loose financing conditions led to robust growth in international project finance numbers, up by 68 per cent, and a boom in M&A activity, with a corresponding increase in cross-border M&As of 43 per cent. The recovery of greenfield project announcements after the steep drop in 2020 was more moderate, with project numbers up 11 per cent.

a. Greenfield investment trends

The value of announced greenfield investment projects rose by 15 per cent to $659 billion (table I.5). It remained flat in developing countries at $259 billion – stagnant at the lowest level ever recorded as MNEs' appetite for investing overseas in real productive assets remained weak. This is a major concern, as these investments in industry are crucial for economic growth and development prospects.

Greenfield projects targeting the primary sector – mainly in extractive industries – remained small. At $13 billion, the aggregate value of announced greenfield projects represented less than 2 per cent of the total, compared with 24 per cent in 2003, 13 per cent in 2009 and 7 per cent in 2016. The long-term decline in primary sector projects is the result of continued low international investment in agriculture, and – in extractives – a shift from greenfield projects by individual investors to international project finance investments that allow risk sharing among multiple investors.

The number of projects in manufacturing rose by 8 per cent. The increase represents only a hesitant initial recovery after the 2020 drop in investment activity by more than a third, and it leaves manufacturing project numbers about a quarter below the average of the last 10 years.

Figure I.15. **Value and number of cross-border M&As and announced greenfield projects, 2012–2021** (Billions of dollars, number and per cent)

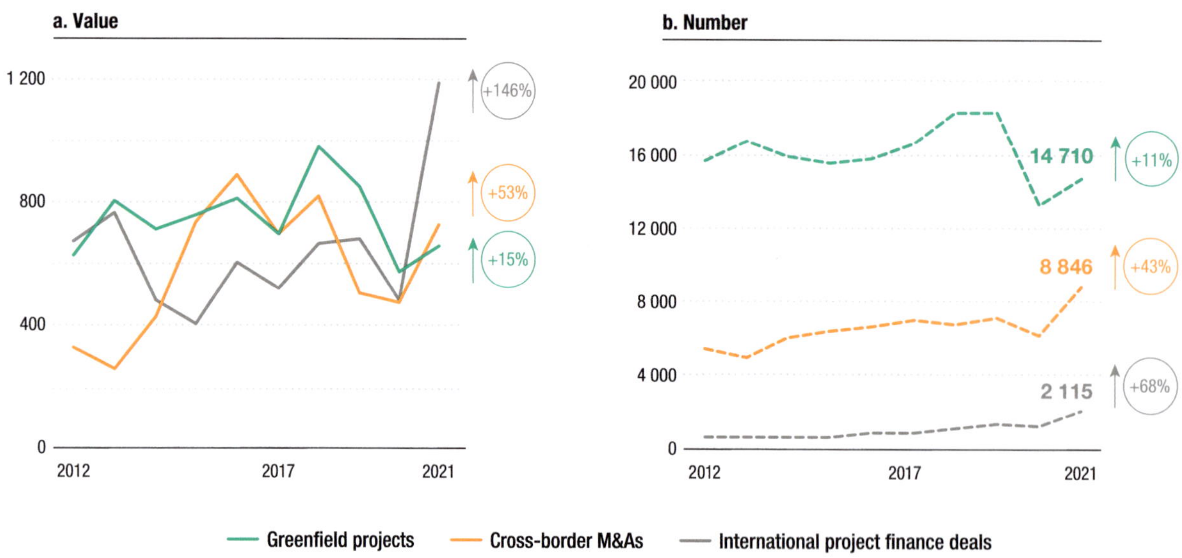

Source: UNCTAD, cross-border M&A database (https://unctad.org/fdistatistics) for M&As, information from the Financial Times Ltd, fDi Markets (www.fDimarkets.com) for announced greenfield FDI projects and Refinitiv SA for international project finance deals.

Table I.5.	Announced greenfield projects, by sector and selected industries, 2020–2021					
	Value (Billions of dollars)			**Number**		
Sector/industry	**2020**	**2021**	**Growth rate** (%)	**2020**	**2021**	**Growth rate** (%)
Total	**575**	**659**	**15**	**13 248**	**14 710**	**11**
Primary	11	13	15	100	98	-2
Manufacturing	240	297	23	5 258	5 688	8
Services	323	350	8	7 890	8 924	13
Top 10 industries in value terms						
Electronics and electrical equipment	47	120	156	882	1 028	17
Information and communication	85	104	23	2 962	3 743	26
Electricity and gas supply	103	90	-13	546	484	-11
Construction	33	49	49	320	329	3
Automotives	33	34	3	571	692	21
Transportation and storage	27	33	25	639	737	15
Chemicals	40	28	-30	452	445	-2
Trade	23	24	4	580	638	10
Food, beverages and tobacco	18	19	9	432	431	0
Pharmaceuticals	15	19	26	360	378	5

Source: UNCTAD, based on information from the Financial Times Ltd, fDi Markets (www.fDimarkets.com).

Among the stronger performers in 2021 were a few typical GVC-intensive industries such as electronics and automotive, which were hit hard during the first year of the pandemic. Announced greenfield values in electronics and electrical equipment more than doubled to $120 billion. Booming demand for microchips prompted producers to start several mega investment projects. The two largest deals announced in 2021 were in semiconductors: Intel (United States) intends to build a semiconductor plant in Germany for $19 billion and Samsung (Republic of Korea) plans to build a $17 billion semiconductor factory in the United States. Several other large projects were announced in electronic components; for example, Risen Energy (China) will invest $10 billion in a new production facility in Malaysia to manufacture high-efficiency photovoltaic modules.

The moderate recovery in the number of greenfield project announcements was mostly driven by services, which now account for 61 per cent of total projects – the highest on record. The fast-growing global demand for digital infrastructure and services led to a significant rise in greenfield FDI project activity in the ICT industry, with values up by 23 per cent to $104 billion and numbers up by 26 per cent to a record 3,743 projects. Amazon (United States) stood out as the most active foreign investor in 2021, with $20 billion worth of investments.

b. International project finance trends

International project finance activity in 2021 was frenetic. The number of projects reached 2,115, a 68 per cent increase over 2020 and almost three times the average of the last 10 years. The value of international project finance deals was above $1 trillion for the first time ever.

The rise of projects led by domestic sponsors was even higher (90 per cent) than internationally sponsored deals (as reported in table I.6), reaching 3,924 projects. While conducive long-term financing conditions favoured both types, recovery stimulus packages benefitted domestic markets more than international ones.

Table I.6. Announced international project finance deals, selected industries, 2020–2021

Industry	Value (Billions of dollars) 2020	Value (Billions of dollars) 2021	Growth rate (%)	Number 2020	Number 2021	Growth rate (%)
Total	**484**	**1 188**	**146**	**1 262**	**2 115**	**68**
Top 10 industries by number						
Renewable energy	198	502	154	802	1 193	49
Industrial real estate	52	135	160	52	152	192
Residential/commercial real estate	13	30	137	45	143	218
Mining	21	39	88	65	109	68
Power	30	116	293	55	109	98
Oil and gas	60	139	131	71	102	44
Telecommunication	42	61	45	52	92	77
Transport infrastructure	41	49	20	52	90	73
Petrochemicals	19	90	370	25	59	136
Water and sewerage	3	9	176	21	18	-14

Source: UNCTAD, based on data from Refinitiv SA.

Investment in renewable energy has been the main engine of growth in international project finance for several years running. It now makes up more than half the annual number of projects. In 2021, activity growth in the sector was exceptionally high (up 49 per cent). Values increased even more because of some megaprojects. Six projects were worth more than $10 billion, including the largest, the $74 billion construction in Australia of a 50 GW green energy hub over 15,000 square km that could convert wind and solar power into green fuels, sponsored by Intercontinental Energy Corp (United States), CWP Europe SARL (Luxembourg) and Mirning Green Energy (Australia).

International project finance announcements in industrial real estate have also grown continuously for several years, with no let-up during the pandemic. In 2021, deal numbers tripled to 152 projects with a value of $135 billion. Large projects include the construction of a steel and cement manufacturing plant in India for $14 billion and the construction of a 960 -hectare pharmaceutical park in Viet Nam for $10 billion. The number of deals targeting residential and commercial real estate also tripled, to 143. The biggest increase took place in developed countries, where the number of such projects rose from 16 to 78.

Investment in the oil and gas industry in 2021 rose by 131 per cent in value and 44 per cent in number. The most significant rise across developing regions was reported in Asia, where the value of announced investment rose to $62 billion from $19 billion. The largest project involved the construction of a 1,700-km oil pipeline in Iraq for $18 billion.

Telecommunication investment continued its rise, reaching $61 billion and 92 projects following the pandemic-induced acceleration of the digital economy. While most projects targeted Europe (46), the number of projects in developing Asia more than doubled, from 7 to 18. The largest projects include the acquisition by Telxius Telecommunication Towers (United States) of telecommunication towers in Argentina, Brazil, Chile, Germany, Peru and Spain, from Telefonica (Spain) for $9.4 billion and the construction by Dito Telecommunity (China) of 10,000 towers in the Philippines for $5.4 billion.

In petrochemicals, the value of projects also rose strongly to a record $90 billion, driven mainly by a few very large projects; for example, in Oman, the $30 billion construction of a plant to produce over 1.8 million tonnes per year of green hydrogen.

c. Cross-border M&As

Cross-border M&A sales reached $728 billion in 2021 – up 53 per cent compared with 2020 (table I.7). In the services sector, cross-border M&As doubled to $461 billion – one of the highest levels ever recorded. Deals targeting manufacturing firms rose slightly, by 5 per cent, to $239 billion. In the primary sector, M&A values remained at a low level ($28 billion), continuing the decade long downward trend, reflecting reduced investment in the upstream activities of the oil and gas industry.

Information and communication and pharmaceuticals remained in the top ranking as the pandemic pushed up activity in the digital and health sectors. Sales of assets in digital industries rose by 69 per cent to $136 billion – a record level. In deal numbers information and communication has been the most active sector since 2000; in 2021 it was also the largest in value terms. An important deal was the $34 billion merger of Altimeter Growth (United States) with Grab (Singapore), a leading Asian "superapp" for food delivery, mobility and digital payments.

After the fall in value in 2020, the value of M&A sales in pharmaceuticals rose by 31 per cent, to $73 billion, and the number of deals by 6 per cent, reaching 223 deals – the highest number ever recorded. The largest deal of the year was recorded in the pharmaceutical industry: the acquisition of Alexion (United States) by AstraZeneca (United Kingdom) for $39 billion.

In developed countries, where cross-border M&As are a significant part of total FDI, the value of deals rose by 58 per cent to $615 billion, mostly from tripling in North America, while in Europe the value remained flat at $258 billion.

In other sectors, M&A sales in transportation and storage rose more than seven-fold to a record $53 billion, mainly because of a single large deal in which Canadian Pacific Railway acquired Kansas City Southern (United States) for $31 billion. Some large divestments were recorded in the electric and electrical equipment sector. For example, PPL (United States) sold its Bristol-based electric power distributor to National Grid (United Kingdom) for $20 billion.

Table I.7. Net cross-border M&As, by sector and selected industries, 2020–2021

Sector/industry	Value (Billions of dollars)		Growth rate (%)	Number		Growth rate (%)
	2020	2021		2020	2021	
Total	**475**	**728**	**53**	**6 201**	**8 846**	**43**
Primary	25	28	11	658	639	-3
Manufacturing	228	239	5	1 136	1 674	47
Services	221	461	108	4 407	6 533	48
Top 10 industries in value terms						
Information and communication	80	136	69	1 248	2 114	69
Pharmaceuticals	56	73	31	211	223	6
Finance and insurance	28	72	157	562	733	30
Trade	18	63	255	495	663	34
Transportation and storage	7	53	651	224	324	45
Automotives	17	42	144	41	81	98
Professional services	11	41	268	447	689	54
Electronics and electrical equipment	40	38	-4	165	311	88
Real estate	22	35	57	327	420	28
Administrative and support services	6	28	413	206	303	47

Source: UNCTAD, cross-border M&A database (https://unctad.org/fdistatistics).

B. SDG AND CLIMATE CHANGE INVESTMENT TRENDS

1. SDG investment trends

Cross-border investment in SDG sectors in developing economies was growing before the COVID-19 pandemic, although not at a sufficient rate to fill the SDG investment gap. International SDG investment was significantly hit in the first year of the pandemic, with double-digit declines across all sectors except renewable energy (*WIR21*). In 2021, with the overall investment recovery, SDG investment increased substantially, by 70 per cent, compared with 2020. The combined value of greenfield investment and international project finance in SDG sectors, which had dropped to $218 billion in the first year of the pandemic (from $312 billion in 2019) rebounded to $371 billion in 2021, thus surpassing the pre-pandemic level. However, most of the recovery growth was due to international project finance activity in the renewable energy sector, where project values reached more than three times the pre-pandemic level.

While the 2021 recovery in value terms is positive, investment activity in most SDG-related sectors in developing economies, as measured by project numbers, remained below pre-pandemic levels (table I.8). Apart from renewables, only investment activity in education fully recovered to prior levels. Other sectors, including food and agriculture, health, physical infrastructure and WASH, partially recovered.

Greenfield investment in SDG sectors – mostly by individual firms – has started its recovery from the fall of 2020 but remains well below pre-pandemic levels (table I.9). In contrast, international project finance – large projects, often with the involvement of multiple investors, including financial institutions – is now well above pre-pandemic levels (table I.10).

Table I.8. International private investment in the SDGs: 2021 project numbers compared to pre-pandemic levels (Per cent)

Sector	SDGs	Change
Infrastructure Transport infrastructure, power generation and distribution (except renewables), telecommunication	7 Affordable and clean energy; 9 Industry, innovation and infrastructure; 11 Sustainable cities and communities	-11
Renewable energy Installations for renewable energy generation, all sources	13 Climate action	+2
WASH Provision of water and sanitation to industry and households	6 Clean water and sanitation	-9
Food and agriculture Investment in agriculture, research, rural development	2 Zero hunger	-35
Health Investment in health infrastructure, e.g. new hospitals	3 Good health and well-being	-25
Education Infrastructural investment, e.g. new schools	4 Quality education	+17

Source: UNCTAD.

Table I.9. Announced greenfield projects in SDG sectors in developing economies
(Millions of dollars and per cent)

SDG-relevant sector	Developing economies 2019	Developing economies 2020	Developing economies 2021	Developing economies 2020–2021 growth rate (%)	Of which, LDCs 2019	Of which, LDCs 2020	Of which, LDCs 2021	Of which, LDCs 2020–2021 growth rate (%)
Total								
Value	**133 874**	**92 551**	**101 345**	**10**	**12 824**	**10 824**	**6 332**	**-41**
Number of projects	**1 686**	**1 147**	**1 277**	**11**	**114**	**85**	**69**	**-19**
Power [a]								
Value	18 484	10 841	4 169	-62	1 483	3 452	2 000	-42
Number of projects	45	22	20	-9	4	4	1	-75
Renewable energy								
Value	40 880	28 977	35 831	24	2 030	3 601	1 329	-63
Number of projects	241	190	144	-24	15	21	9	-57
Transport services								
Value	25 921	10 522	13 327	27	3 627	1 071	449	-58
Number of projects	321	182	269	48	36	17	22	29
Telecommunication [b]								
Value	18 285	25 756	26 125	1	255	2 112	1 717	-19
Number of projects	303	241	281	17	6	22	20	-9
Water, sanitation and hygiene (WASH)								
Value	1 819	633	4 119	551	61	-	136	..
Number of projects	17	7	19	171	1	-	1	..
Food and agriculture								
Value	21 700	11 347	11 847	4	4 812	477	421	-12
Number of projects	428	291	271	-7	30	12	7	-42
Health								
Value	5 556	3 618	4 805	33	419	77	172	123
Number of projects	256	151	188	25	14	5	3	-40
Education								
Value	1 228	858	1 121	31	137	33	109	229
Number of projects	75	63	85	35	8	4	6	50

Source: UNCTAD, based on information from Financial Times Ltd, fDi Markets (www.fdimarkets.com).
[a] Excluding renewable energy.
[b] Including information services activities.

The stronger growth performance of international project finance can be explained by loose financing conditions, infrastructure stimulus and significant interest of financial market investors in participating in large-scale projects. It is likely that international project finance will increasingly play the leading role in SDG investment, including by leveraging public investment through private finance participation.

The diverging trends between greenfield and international project finance investment are evident across several sectors. Greenfield investment in the power sector continued to decline in 2021 and remained at less than half the level of 2019. In contrast, international project finance activity recovered almost to its pre-pandemic level, and its value increased by 68 per cent, due to large deals such as the 1.5 GW Basra gas-fired power project in Iraq, estimated at about $10 billion.

Similarly, the number of greenfield investment projects in renewable energy remained continued to decline, although the value of such projects increased by 24 per cent, driven by a few large projects such as the Base-one project in Ceará, Brazil, valued at $5.4 billion. International project finance activity in renewables is booming, increasing both in numbers of projects and in values, confirming the shift in sources of investment. It is responsible for the bulk of overall growth in SDG investment.

Table I.10. International project finance deals in SDG sectors in developing economies
(Millions of dollars and per cent)

SDG-relevant sector	Developing economies 2019	Developing economies 2020	Developing economies 2021	Developing economies 2020–2021 growth rate (%)	Of which, LDCs 2019	Of which, LDCs 2020	Of which, LDCs 2021	Of which, LDCs 2020–2021 growth rate (%)
Total								
Value	**178 021**	**125 738**	**270 356**	**115**	**24 032**	**29 833**	**51 249**	**72**
Number of projects	**408**	**360**	**543**	**51**	**72**	**48**	**49**	**2**
Power[a]								
Value	29 452	21 758	36 490	68	8 267	3 910	970	-75
Number of projects	46	32	39	22	13	6	3	-50
Renewable energy								
Value	53 231	69 149	183 171	165	7 970	12 695	46 519	266
Number of projects	283	275	393	43	46	35	35	0
Transport infrastructure								
Value	36 092	22 605	22 995	2	7 164	12 849	3 135	-76
Number of projects	46	21	50	138	9	4	6	50
Telecommunication								
Value	55 127	9 826	16 875	72	320	-	410	..
Number of projects	10	13	31	138	2	-	2	..
Water, sanitation and hygiene (WASH)								
Value	3 398	1 339	536	-60	130	380	138	-64
Number of projects	15	14	10	-29	1	3	2	-33
Food and agriculture								
Value	562	1 034	8 155	688	181	-	-	..
Number of projects	4	3	10	233	1	-	-	..
Health								
Value	120	9	2 035	22 514	-	-	-	..
Number of projects	2	1	5	400	-	-	-	..
Education								
Value	40	18	100	473	-	-	78	..
Number of projects	2	1	5	400	-	-	1	..

Source: UNCTAD, based on data from Refinitiv SA.
[a] Excluding renewable energy.

The momentum in international project finance, specifically in renewables, shows that this form of investment is particularly suitable for the risk profile of such projects in developing economies. The large size of some individual projects makes risk-sharing arrangements more attractive. International project finance deals also make it easier for domestic capital or governments to participate in or initiate the project. In the non-renewable power sector, a similar trend can be observed. The appetite of international investors for fossil-fuel-based facilities is waning, and projects are increasingly initiated by domestic or State-owned enterprises, explaining the stagnant greenfield numbers and continued growth in international project finance, through which international investors can participate in domestic projects.

Project finance activity in transport infrastructure more than doubled in numbers, returning to the pre-pandemic level, although the increase in value was marginal. Most of the international project finance investments target critical infrastructure in roads, bridges and ports. For example, Nigeria introduced five projects for expanding, repairing and maintaining 884 km of toll road. In Kenya, four bridge projects will bring connectivity with remote areas. Of the 600 international projects in transport infrastructure and services (considering both greenfield and project finance) announced in 2021, 319 are in developing economies and more than half in Asia (232 projects).

LDCs account for a small share, with only 28 projects. The Berbera Port and Economic Zone project is ground-breaking for the Horn of Africa, as it is poised to provide a trade gateway for the countries surrounding it. Such projects in LDCs have the potential to address long-term challenges in access to markets and supply chain bottlenecks.

In the telecommunication sector, which contributes to SDG 9 on universal access to industry, innovation and infrastructure, large-scale private investment clearly outweighs public sector investment. The most relevant projects from an SDG perspective are those in low-income countries, including LDCs, where a large share of the population is still excluded from access to basic infrastructure and connectivity. For example, in the Democratic Republic of Congo, a fibre network estimated at $200 million will help to improve Internet access and connectivity for more than 30 million people across Central Africa. SDG-relevant greenfield activity in telecommunication picked up in 2021, also growing in value (1 per cent from a negative post-pandemic trend). International project finance activity in the sector more than doubled, with the value of deals also picking up (72 per cent). In LDCs, greenfield investment decreased in 2021 in comparison with 2020, and the level of project finance activity remains low.

Greenfield investments in WASH rallied in 2021. The value of announced investment increased six-fold, and the number of projects more than doubled. Yet project finance deals and activity in the sector continued to decline compared with pre-pandemic levels.

Investment in the food and agriculture sector also reversed the persistent negative trend and the pandemic shock. International project finance deals saw a recovery, both in value and in project activity in developing economies, although investment activity remains small, with only 10 projects in 2021. The large increase in value was driven by a $7 billion phosphates project in Algeria, sponsored by China – now particularly important in light of shortages in phosphorus-based fertilizers caused by the war in Ukraine. In LDCs, greenfield investments lagged, and no project finance activity was registered in 2021.

Greenfield investment in the health sector partially recovered in 2021. Investments included hospitals and several COVID-19-related projects such as vaccine production. The sharp rise in project finance values was due to a single $1.6 billion project involving the construction of a large hospital and subsidiary facilities in China. Out of 188 new greenfield projects in the health sector, only 3 were in LDCs. However, the total value of such investment in LDCs increased, driven by BioNTech (Germany), which will construct a vaccine production facility in Rwanda at a total estimated cost of $79 million.

International investment in the education sector has fully recovered from the pandemic-related decline. A number of education projects were announced in developing countries, including a significant expansion of rural secondary schools in Malawi (table I.11).

In LDCs, the SDG investment trend is less favourable than in other developing economies, and the detrimental impact of the pandemic persists. The share of total SDG investment in developing countries (both greenfield and international project finance values) that went to LDCs decreased from 19 per cent in 2020 to 15 per cent in 2021. Their share in the number of projects declined from 9 to 6 per cent.

Physical infrastructure and broader infrastructure industries (including utilities and power) are capital-intensive projects that are highly dependent on the long-term risk outlook. This can explain in part the stagnant trend in LDCs. In addition, the boost in infrastructure project finance in developed economies and high-income developing countries because of pandemic-related recovery packages risks drawing private project sponsors away from LDC markets (*WIR21*). The unfavourable trends in SDG-related investment in LDCs add to their structural handicaps and aggravate persistent challenges, including weak infrastructure, underdeveloped human capital and a narrow productive capacity base.

Table I.11. Examples of SDG-relevant investment projects in developing economies announced in 2021, by sector

SDG-relevant sector	Country	Project name	Total cost estimate (Millions of dollars)	Description
Renewable energy and power	Mauritania	30 GW Mauritania Power-to-X Hydrogen Project	40,000	PPP project in the Sahara sponsored by Australian developer CWP Global and the Government, generating wind and solar energy to power electrolysers to produce hydrogen
	Malaysia	20.76 MW Kulim Large-Scale Solar Photovoltaic Project	20,725	Build-own-operate project by Energy ES, an incorporated joint venture company of Savelite Engineering, Moderntent Development and Frasers Construction
	Viet Nam	3900 MW Hai Phong Offshore Wind Power Plant Project	11,900	A build-own-operate project funded by a joint venture between T&T Group and Orsted
Telecommunication	Nigeria	MTN Nigeria Network Infrastructure Project	1,460	A build-own-operate project, sponsored by MTN Nigeria Communications, to connect some 3,000 rural communities to the network
	Democratic Republic of Congo	Liquid Technologies and Facebook Fibre Network Project	202	Construction of a fibre network to help connect East and West Africa, enabling improved Internet access for more than 30 million people across Central Africa
	Sri Lanka	Axiata and Mavenir TIP Evenstar 4G Radio Project	154	Deployment and integration of Open vRAN in Sri Lanka, Malaysia and Indonesia to provide seamless service continuity, better mobile broadband experience and next-generation voice services
Transportation	Egypt	Bombardier Transportation Monorail Project	2,321	Construction of two monorails to connect the New Administrative City with East Cairo and 6th October City with Giza
	El Salvador	Tren Pacifico Rail PPP Project	450	A 555-km mass transit system under a PPP scheme, sponsored by Comisión Ejecutiva Portuaria Autonoma and the Central American Bank for Economic Integration
	Bangladesh	Bangladesh Dual-Gauge Railway Line Project	282	A build-own-operate project comprising construction of an 80-km mass transit system, with Bangladesh Railway and Rites Ltd as sponsors
Water, sanitation and hygiene (WASH)	Saudi Arabia	Solar-powered water desalination plant in Saudi Arabia	827	Construction of the largest solar-powered water desalination project, under a PPP scheme sponsored by Engie and Saudi Water Partnership, awarded as a build-own-operate contract, with commercial operation expected in 2024
	Egypt	Wastewater treatment plant (El-Hammam)	739	Construction of an agricultural waste managment plant with a capacity of 6 million cubic metres, in a joint venture with Hassan Allam, Arab Contractors and Orascom Construction
	Mozambique	Pemba Water Supply Center and Pipeline Network Project	134	A build-own-operate project including construction of a 172-km water pipeline; sponsored by Water Supply & Sanitation Service Improvement Project

/...

Table I.11. Examples of SDG-relevant investment projects in developing economies announced in 2021, by sector (Concluded)

SDG-relevant sector	Country	Project name	Total cost estimate (Millions of dollars)	Description
Health	Kazakhstan	RenEll Multidisciplinary Hospital PPP Project	303	Construction of several multidisciplinary hospitals in the cities of Kokshetau, Aktobe, Atyrau, Aktau, Taraz, Pavlodar, and Karaganda, sponosered by RenEll and provided for the State Programme for the Development of Health Care for 2020-2025
	Sri Lanka	Hambantota COVID-19 Vaccine Plant Project	154	Construction of a hospital in Hambantota in a deal allowing the facility to source up to 9 million COVID-19 vaccine doses
	Malaysia	Chukai Private Specialist Hospital Project	24	Construction of 100 beds on 2.2 hectares of land owned by the Kemaman Municipal Council in Kg. Jaya, Mukim Chukai, Kemaman that will give residents in the southern part of Terengganu access to high-quality health care and specialist treatment
Food and agiculture	Taiwan Province of China	Linkou District Wind-Powered Smart Farm Project	82	Construction of a demolition wind-powered smart farm, sponsored by Alternaturals Inc under a build-own-operate scheme
	South Africa	Pinetown Plant Upgrading Project	34	Construction of a flour mill by Tetra Pak Nordic Holding in a build-own-operate project that aims to have the world's most sustainable packaging made from renewable materials
	Maldives	Sustainable Economic Empowerment and Development (SEED) Project	2	Support for households affected by COVID-19 by assisting 2,000 MSMEs and 250 smallholder farmers through the Business Center Corporation's outreach initiatives, implemented in a build-own-operate mode, by the Government of Japan and the United Nations Development Programme, with enhanced private sector participation
Education	Malawi	Malawi Rural Secondary Education Expansion for Development (SEED) Project	78	Building of 38 schools in a partnership between the governments of the United States and of Malawi, funded through Basic Education and PEPFAR funds
	Malaysia	Sankyu Technical Academy	29	Building of the company's first human resources training centre outside of Japan, in the Medini Central Business District, under a build-own-operate scheme
	Peru	Colegio San Felipe, Escuela Nuestra Senora de La Visitacion, Jose de la Torre Ugarte, Jorge Basadre Grohman School Project	7	Building of 75 schools by a consortium of eight companies from the United Kingdom and Finland (Gleeds, Arup Group, 4Global, AFRY Group Finland, Lahdelma & Mahlamki Architects, Isku, Polar Partners and Mace)

Source: UNCTAD, based on data from Refinitiv SA.

The dependence of many developing economies, and particularly LDCs, on grain imports from the Russian Federation and Ukraine and their consequent vulnerability to the food crisis underscore the need to accelerate efforts to foster international private investment in food security and to diversify food supply chains. Despite the calls for increased investment as part of the effort to achieve SDG 2 on food security, investment in agriculture remains small, at less than 1 per cent of total FDI flows globally.

2. Climate change and investment

UNCTAD first reported on the investment gap in climate change mitigation and adaptation in *WIR14*, which analysed investment needs and investment levels across all SDG areas. Subsequently, the *SDG Investment Trends Monitor* and the *WIR* series have continued to report on trends in these two areas. In consideration of the growing urgency and renewed emphasis placed on the mobilization of financial resources for investment in combating climate change for COP27, this section on climate change and investment breaks down the aggregate figures on mitigation and adaptation provided in the SDG investment section. It also adds insights on other relevant sectors to provide a more granular view of investment trends related to climate change. The analysis focuses on cross-border private investment and reports mostly greenfield investment and international project finance trends. The data collection approach follows the same methodology used for the assessment of SDG investment trends (box I.3).

Box I.3. Measuring international private climate change investment

UNCTAD's data on climate change investment focus on direct investments in greenhouse gas (GHG) emission reductions and climate resilience activities. It includes greenfield investments (new projects and expansions by individual overseas investors) and project finance (large-scale projects, mostly in infrastructure industries, involving multiple investors and a significant debt component). Both greenfield investments and international project finance data are on an announcement basis.[a]

As in the case of UNCTAD's SDG *Investment Trends Monitor* and in line with the scope of the *World Investment Report*, the focus is on international investment, i.e. cross-border investment flows. For international project finance this implies that the project's sponsor is an international investor (although co-investors may include domestic financiers).[b]

International project finance investment flows are retrieved from Refinitiv SA and greenfield investments are sourced from fDi Markets. The sectoral breakdown distinguishes the following categories:

Climate change mitigation

Renewable energy. This includes investments in power generation projects from the following sources: biomass, geothermal, hydroelectric, solar, tidal or wave (marine) and wind. While energy from residual waste (excluding biomass) is only partially renewable due to the presence of fossil-based carbon in the waste, such projects are also included in this category. As hydrogen is a secondary source of energy, only projects producing hydrogen from the renewable energy sources listed above qualify as climate mitigation investments. Whenever the primary source of energy is not specified in the project, the project is not included in the renewable energy category.

Energy efficiency and emission reduction. Projects included in this category vary depending on the data available across data sets. Greenfield investment data distinguish electric vehicles and clean technologies, which include investments in the production of new materials used in developing renewable energy projects and other products that contribute to reducing greenhouse gases emissions. fDi Markets allows for the identification of such projects across standard industrial classifications through its project tags. International project finance further includes energy transmission lines, carbon capture and battery storage projects.

Low-carbon mobility. This category captures transport projects that contribute to a decrease in GHG emissions. They consist mostly of projects in public transport (trains, buses, municipal transport).

Climate change adaptation

Water management. This category includes investments in projects building resilience to climate related changes in the water cycle. Both fDi Markets and Refinitiv SA provide a sufficiently granular industrial breakdown to identify such projects.

Other adaptation projects. Several industry-wide projects fall into this category including investments that improve the climate resilience of existing infrastructure, as well as investments in climate-resilient agriculture and coastal protection. These projects are selected through manual screening of the database.

Source: UNCTAD.

[a] The value of such a project indicates the capital expenditure planned by the investor at the time of the announcement. Data can differ substantially from the official FDI data as companies can raise capital locally and phase their investments over time, and a project may be cancelled or may not start in the year when it is announced.

[b] UNCTAD's sectoral breakdown of international investment flows is based on the methodology in the Global Landscape of Climate Finance (Climate Policy Initiative, 2021) but adapted to the granularity and quality of data available for international project finance and greenfield investments.

Table I.12. Climate change investment categories

Sectors	Investment area
Climate change mitigation	
Renewable energy	• Power generation from: biomass, geothermal, hydroelectric, hydrogen, solar, tidal or wave, waste (excluding biomass), wind.
Energy efficiency/ emission reduction	• Energy provision efficiency transmission lines, battery storage, carbon capture. • Other investments in energy efficient technology or products: electric vehicles, clean technologies.
Low-emission transport	• Mass transit systems: rail, public transport systems.
Climate change adaptation	
Water management	• Investments on climate related changes in the water cycle: water pipelines, water supply, district cooling (i.e. deep ocean or lake water cooling systems), desalination, water storage, disposal and treatment.
Other adaptation	• Investments to improve the climate resilience of existing infrastructure, and coastal protection. • Climate resilient agriculture, such as flood / drought resistant crops.

Source: UNCTAD.

Climate change investments are broadly defined as *mitigation* investments in cleaner and/or more energy-efficient technologies supporting the reduction of greenhouse gas emissions, and *adaptation* investments, which are those in critical infrastructure, technologies and activities to improve resilience and help adapt to the consequences of climate change. Table I.12 shows the categorization adopted for the purpose of reporting international investment trends in this section. Combating climate change will require many other types of investment, including in research and development, energy-efficient buildings and means of production, green minerals and materials needed to produce batteries or clean energy technologies, as well as other, often yet unknown adaptation investments. The scope here is limited to the key areas in which international direct investors are active to date and for which it is possible to monitor discrete investment projects.

For international private investment, mitigation is far more important than adaptation. The attractiveness of the various categories of climate-relevant investment for the private sector depends on the existence of a clear revenue model and on project- and country-level risks (*WIR21*). Adaptation projects are often public goods, characterized by steep upfront costs, long investment timelines, lack of a clearly identifiable revenue stream or unattractive risk-return profiles. These categories necessarily rely on public investment (table I.13).

Looking at total climate change mitigation finance in 2019, 54 per cent was funded by private sources in 2019–2020.[2] For project finance, the share is even higher, with 85 per cent of mitigation investments (including domestic projects) in developed economies and 56 per cent in developing economies not requiring any public sector involvement (figure I.16).[3] In contrast, just over half of adaptation projects in developed economies and only 18 per cent in developing ones have no government involvement. For very large projects in mitigation, and in particular in developing economies, the involvement of multilateral development banks is often required to lower investment risk.[4]

Table I.13.	Adaptation and mitigation: the scope for private investment
Scope for private investment	**Example projects**
i. Projects that are pure public goods	Floodwalls, protection systems for dams, drainage systems, reforestation, mangrove protection, disaster prevention, early warning systems
ii. Projects that allow for PPP models or concessionary schemes (identifiable revenue stream)	Climate resilient infrastructure, green infrastructure, water management, public transportation
iii. Projects that can be privately financed but that may require incentives or subsidies to cover the additional cost of making them climate friendly or climate-change resilient	Agricultural investment in resistant crops, weather monitoring systems, clean technologies, carbon-neutral buildings, carbon capture
iv. Projects that can be purely privately financed	Renewable energy generation, electric vehicles, green minerals extraction

Source: UNCTAD.

Figure I.16. **Share of government participation in mitigation and adaptation project finance investments, 2011–2021**
(Per cent)

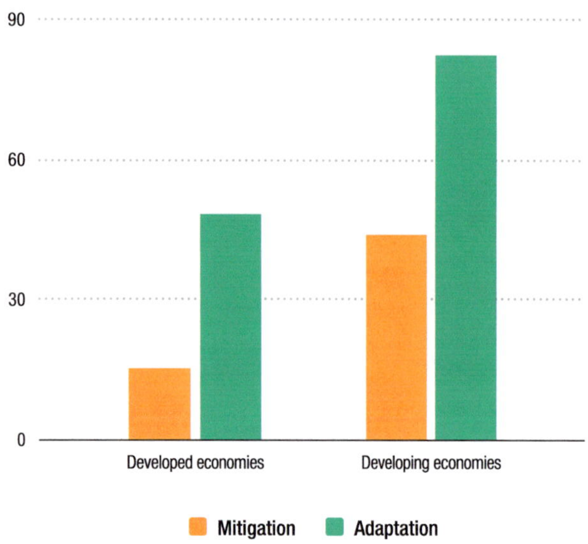

Source: UNCTAD, based on data from Refinitiv SA.
Note: The data include both domestic and international projects.

Categories that have higher shares of projects with public sector participation show a correspondingly lower share of internationally sponsored projects. In developing economies where the political and economic environment for investors is less predictable, government involvement – especially through equity participation – can reduce the perceived risk of the project. However, beyond a certain threshold, higher government equity shares can also discourage foreign investors, as they may fear public interference and governance issues (*WIR21*; Barclay and Vaaler, 2021).

In both developed and developing economies, fewer than a quarter of adaptation projects have a foreign sponsor, and nearly all of those are water management projects. Beyond water management, only a single adaptation project in resilient infrastructure had a foreign sponsor over the last decade: a $38 million project in the Marshall Islands to develop energy-efficient, disaster- and climate-resilient digital infrastructure across all 24 inhabited atolls and islands, announced in 2019.

Trends

Mitigation projects account for more than 95 per cent of international climate investments, with the remainder in adaptation. The vast majority is in renewables and, to a lesser extent, in energy efficiency projects (figure I.17). In developing regions, the share of adaptation projects is higher (12 per cent, compared with 1 per cent in developed economies) owing to the greater prevalence of international water management projects.

Climate investment showed an upward trend after the adoption of the SDGs in 2015, a trend that was interrupted by the pandemic but recovered strongly in 2021, with total project values at twice the pre-pandemic level of 2019. Mitigation investments funded through international project finance more than doubled in value. Adaptation project values increased almost three-fold, although project numbers remained low (table I.14).

Figure I.17. International mitigation and adaptation investment projects, 2011–2021 (Billions of dollars)

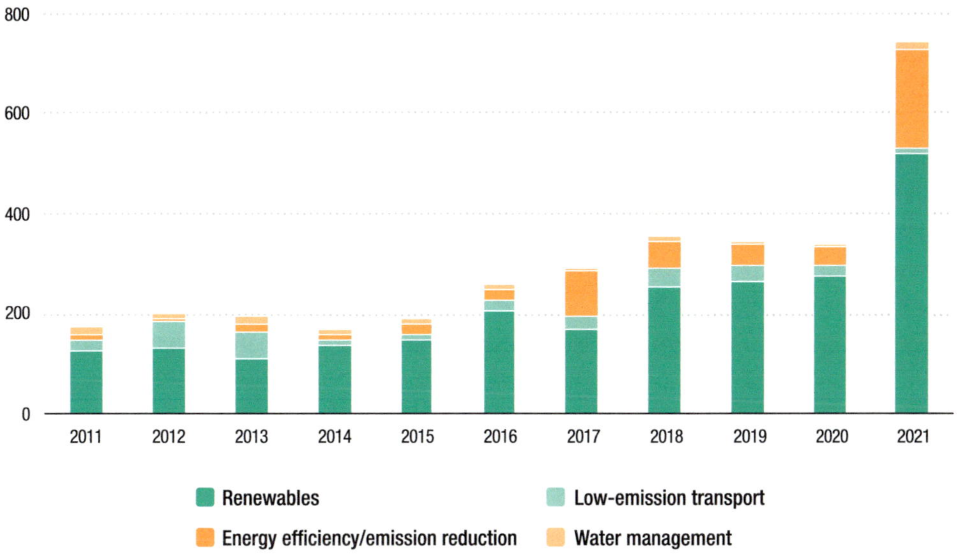

Source: UNCTAD, based on information from Financial Times Ltd, fDi Markets (www.fdimarkets.com) for greenfield projects and Refinitiv SA for international project finance deals.

Table I.14. Announced greenfield and international project finance deals in climate change sectors, 2019–2021 (Millions of dollars and per cent)

	Announced greenfield projects				International project finance deals			
Climate Change relevant sector	2019	2020	2021	2020–2021 growth rate (%)	2019	2020	2021	2020–2021 growth rate (%)
Total mitigation								
Value	**125 149**	**115 439**	**159 787**	**38**	**212 888**	**217 556**	**552 203**	**154**
Number of projects	**804**	**739**	**1 090**	**47**	**761**	**814**	**1 226**	**51**
Renewable energy								
Value	92 479	92 016	85 175	-7	170 835	185 225	418 306	126
Number of projects	520	524	467	-11	712	764	1 070	40
Energy efficiency or emission reduction								
Value	31 651	23 173	74 456	221	9 061	13 003	124 011	854
Number of projects	258	205	611	198	33	39	136	249
Low-emission transport								
Value	1 019	250	156	-37	32 991	19 328	9 886	-49
Number of projects	26	10	12	20	16	11	20	82
Total adaptation								
Value	2 316	716	4 412	516	4 383	3 358	9 305	177
Number of projects	35	15	30	100	21	21	19	-10
Water management								
Value	2 316	716	4 412	516	4 383	3 358	9 268	176
Number of projects	35	15	30	100	21	21	18	-14
Other adaptation								
Value	-	-	-	..	-	-	38	..
Number of projects	-	-	-	..	-	-	1	..

Source: UNCTAD, based on information from Financial Times Ltd, fDi Markets (www.fdimarkets.com) for greenfield projects and Refinitiv SA for international project finance deals.

Renewables and energy efficiency projects accounted for most of the growth in 2021. New projects included, for example, the Xlinks subsea transmission cables project in Morocco, which involves the construction of a 3,800 km transmission line with 3.6 GW of capacity (estimated at $20 billion) to enable solar energy from the Sahara and wind power off the Atlantic to be sent to the United Kingdom. Another example is the carbon capture and storage project at the Bayu-Undan offshore gas field in Timor-Leste waters, estimated to cost $1.6 billion. Other examples appear in table I.15.

Renewable energy project finance and greenfield investments represented 70 per cent of all international climate change investments in 2021, with projects in developed economies accounting for the lion's share (61 per cent). Europe alone accounted for almost half of renewables projects, followed by Latin America and the Caribbean, North America and developing Asia – each of which attracted about 200 projects in 2021 (figure I.18). The number of international projects in renewables in Africa doubled between 2011 and 2021, from 36 to 71, including several megaprojects such as the power-to-x project for the construction of a 30 GW hydrogen plant in Mauritania (estimated at $40 billion).

Within renewables, solar and wind accounted for more than three quarters of investments. They reached a peak share of 86 per cent in the years 2018 to 2020 (figure I.19). Historically, hydroelectric energy has always been important in renewables investment, with yearly investments of $15–20 billion. Other sources are slowly gaining importance, including biomass, with about $10 billion of investment in recent years; hydrogen, which boomed in 2021; and, especially in developed economies, waste-to-energy projects. After remaining stagnant in 2019 and 2020, international investments in renewables almost doubled in 2021, due to a 42 per cent increase in investments in solar and wind energy generation and a boom in green hydrogen energy.

Table I.15. Examples of international project finance deals in renewable energy, developing economies, 2021

Renewable energy[a]	Country	Project name	Value (Millions of dollars)
Biomass	Philippines	Prime Infrastructure Waste-to-Fuel Biorefinery Project	424
Geothermal	Nicaragua	San Jacinto-Tizate Geothermal Power Project	280
Green hydrogen	Brazil	Pecem Industrial Complex Green Hydrogen Project	2,000
Hydroelectric	Burundi	10.2 MW Mpanda Hydropower PPP Project	43
Residual waste (excluding biomass)	Kazakhstan	Kazakhstan Waste Incineration Power Plant Project	110
Solar	South Africa	Kenhardt Solar and Battery Project	1,000
Wind	Sri Lanka	200 MW Mannar Wind Power Project	93

Source: UNCTAD, based on data from Refinitiv SA.
[a] No tidal or wave (marine) projects have been reported in developing economies since 2015.

Figure I.18. **International investments in renewables, by region, 2011–2021**
(Number of projects)

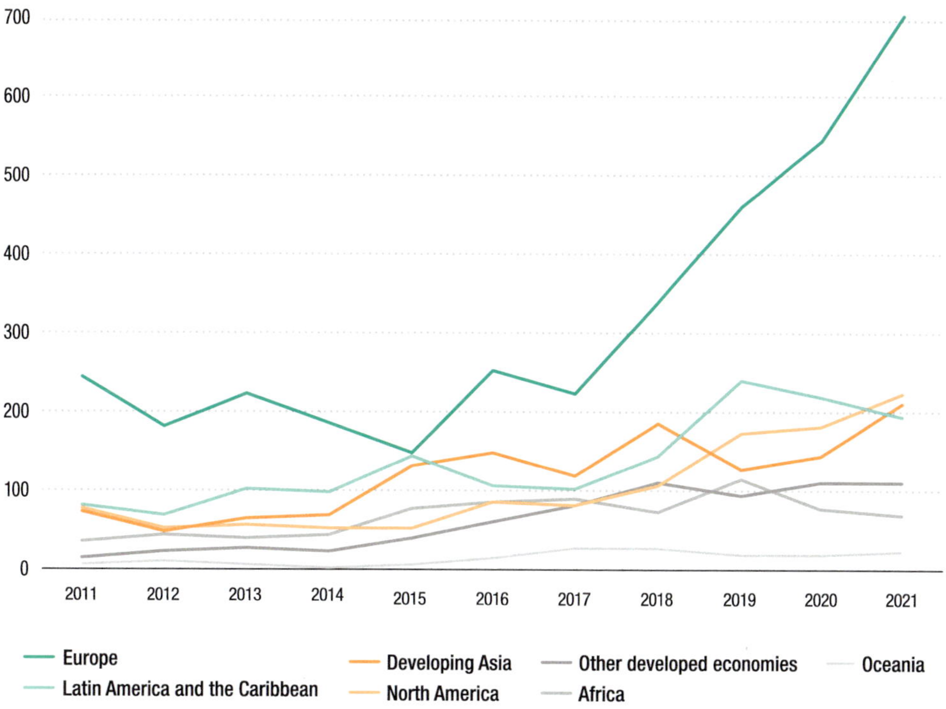

Source: UNCTAD, based on information from Financial Times Ltd, fDi Markets (www.fdimarkets.com) for greenfield projects and Refinitiv SA for international project finance deals.

Figure I.19. **Investment projects in renewables, by type, 2011–2021** (Billions of dollars)

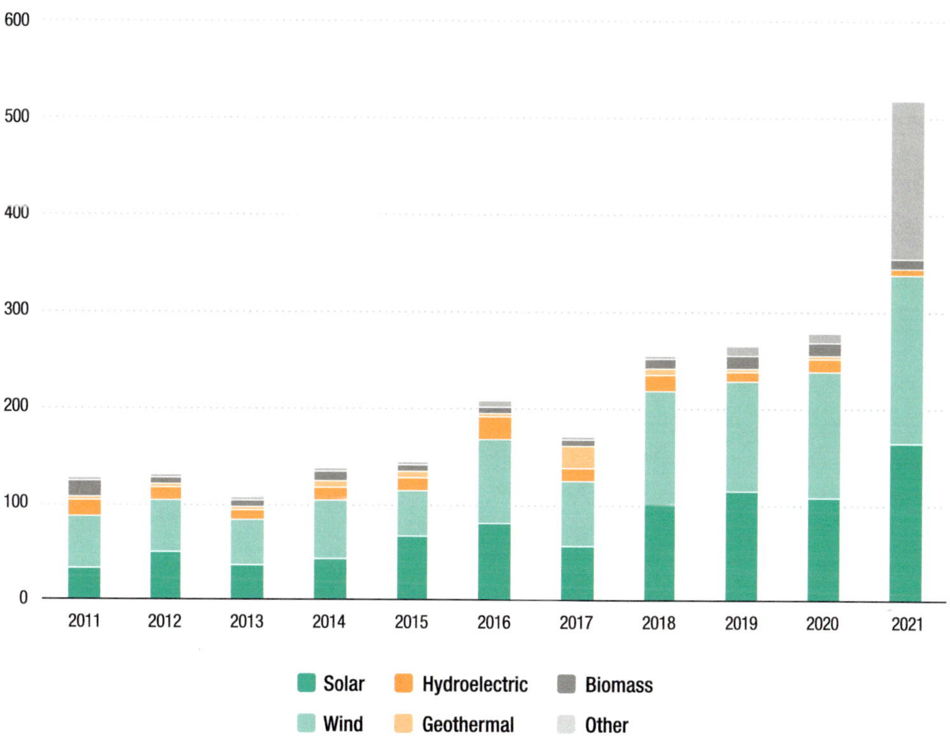

Source: UNCTAD, based on information from Financial Times Ltd, fDi Markets (www.fdimarkets.com) for greenfield projects and Refinitiv SA for international project finance deals.

The energy price shock caused by the war in Ukraine could have implications for international investment in the energy transition. On the one hand, a significant increase in oil and gas prices, as seen immediately after the start of the war (although mitigated since by policy action), could shift investment back into extractive industries and fossil-fuel-based energy generation, temporarily reversing the trend towards renewables documented over the past 10 years. In 2011–2013, when oil prices were last above $100 per barrel, the total value of investment projects in fossil fuels was almost a third higher on average than in the second half of the last decade. On the other hand, expectations are that the fuel crisis will also boost investment in renewable energy, especially in Europe. However, investment in renewables is already growing at high speed, and it is unclear if further stimulus could generate enough capacity in the short term to replace supplies by the Russian Federation.

C. INTERNATIONAL PRODUCTION

1. Key indicators of international production

International production gained further strength in 2021, with all indicators of FDI rising, albeit at different growth rates (table I.16). FDI stock reached a record $45 trillion, equivalent to almost half of global GDP. Therefore, the rate of return remained unchanged, at 4.9 per cent, despite the jump in corporate profits.

Table I.16. Indicators of FDI and international production, 2021 and selected years
(Billions of dollars)

Item	Value at current prices					
	1990	2005–2007 (pre-crisis average)	2018	2019	2020	2021
FDI inflows	205	1 425	1 448	1 481	963	1 582
FDI outflows	244	1 464	941	1 124	780	1 708
FDI inward stock	2 196	14 605	32 843	36 530	41 728	45 449
FDI outward stock	2 255	15 315	31 393	34 496	39 546	41 798
Income on inward FDI [a]	82	1 129	2 199	2 264	1 997	2 193
Rate of return on inward FDI [b]	*5.2*	*9.2*	*6.5*	*6.0*	*4.9*	*4.9*
Income on outward FDI [a]	128	1 243	2 128	2 259	2 041	2 131
Rate of return on outward FDI [b]	*8.4*	*10.5*	*6.5*	*6.6*	*5.4*	*5.3*
Cross-border M&As	98	729	816	507	475	728
Announced greenfield FDI projects	..	..	982	846	575	659
Sales of foreign affiliates	4 801	19 781	32 884	32 889	..	..
Value added of foreign affiliates	1 074	4 668	7 148	6 512	..	..
Total assets of foreign affiliates	4 649	47 124	96 130	92 235	..	..
Employment by foreign affiliates (thousands)	20 449	49 840	84 066	83 597	..	..
Memorandum:						
GDP[c]	23 475	52 481	86 085	87 536	85 239	96 293
Gross fixed capital formation[c]	5 838	12 477	21 908	22 488	22 028	24 902
Royalties and licence fee receipts	31	189	417	457	469	471

Source: UNCTAD.

Note: Not included in this table are the value of worldwide sales by foreign affiliates associated with their parent firms through non-equity relationships and of the sales of the parent firms themselves. Worldwide sales, value added, total assets and employment of foreign affiliates are estimated by extrapolating the worldwide data of foreign affiliates of MNEs from Australia, Austria, Belgium, Canada, Czechia, Finland, France, Germany, Greece, Israel, Italy, Japan, Latvia, Lithuania, Luxembourg, Portugal, Slovenia, Sweden, Switzerland and the United States for sales; those from Czechia, France, Israel, Japan, Portugal, Slovenia, Sweden and the United States for value added (product); those from Austria, Germany, Japan and the United States for assets; those from Czechia, Japan, Portugal, Slovenia, Sweden and the United States for exports; and those from Australia, Austria, Belgium, Canada, Czechia, Finland, France, Germany, Italy, Japan, Latvia, Lithuania, Luxembourg, Macao (China), Portugal, Slovenia, Sweden, Switzerland and the United States for employment, on the basis of three-year average shares of those countries in worldwide outward FDI stock.

[a] Based on data from 168 countries for income on inward FDI and 144 countries for income on outward FDI in 2021, in both cases representing more than 90 per cent of global inward and outward stocks.

[b] Calculated only for countries with both FDI income and stock data. The stock is measured in book value.

[c] Data from IMF (2022b).

2. Internationalization trends of the largest MNEs

The recovery after the first year of the pandemic enhanced the degree of internationalization of the top 100 MNEs but this was mostly limited to their sales (table I.17). Rescue and stimulus packages boosted revenues of companies in construction materials, mining, hydrocarbons, commodity trading and utilities (especially those with a greener energy portfolio). High demand for health-care products lifted revenues of pharmaceutical MNEs, almost doubling them for major vaccine providers. In some cases these higher sales, combined with low interest rates and high share prices, translated into foreign acquisitions and expansion of business lines abroad.

The largest deal was the acquisition by the pharmaceutical firm AstraZeneca (United Kingdom) of Alexion Pharmaceuticals (United States) for $40 billion. Perhaps an even bigger operation was a complex asset swap deal (the value of which was not fully disclosed) that started in 2018 and was completed in 2020; it brought RWE (Germany) into the upper half of the 2021 ranking by more than doubling its foreign assets.[5] The deal involved the acquisition of the international business of E.ON (Germany) with the objective to transform the vertically integrated utilities company and refocus it on renewables.

Automotive MNEs also enjoyed an increase in revenues, capturing some of the pent-up demand of 2020; however, they did not increase their foreign investment, having to concentrate on overcoming supply chain constraints. Similarly, light industry MNEs, despite the stabilization of consumer demand, mostly abstained from expanding their overseas operations.

Table I.17. Internationalization statistics of the 100 largest non-financial MNEs, worldwide and from developing economies (Billions of dollars, thousands of employees and per cent)

	100 largest MNEs, global					100 largest MNEs, developing economies		
Variable	2019[a]	2020[b]	Change, 2020–2019 (%)	2021[b]	Change, 2021–2020 (%)	2019[a]	2020	Change (%)
Assets (Billions of dollars)								
Foreign	9 322	9 591	2,9	10 092	5,2	2 479	2 642	6,6
Domestic	7 698	8 251	7,2	8 664	5,0	5 061	5 857	15,7
Total	17 021	17 842	4,8	18 756	5,1	7 540	8 499	12,7
Foreign as share of total (%)	55	54		54		33	31	
Sales (Billions of dollars)								
Foreign	5 982	5 196	-13,1	6 409	23,3	1 963	1 812	-7,7
Domestic	4 375	3 950	-9,7	4 720	19,5	3 155	3 041	-3,6
Total	10 357	9 146	-11,7	11 128	21,7	5 118	4 854	-5,2
Foreign as share of total (%)	58	57		58		38	37	
Employment (Thousands)								
Foreign	9 591	9 140	-4,7	9 157	0,2	4 359	4 150	-4,8
Domestic	10 396	10 192	-2,0	11 000	7,9	8 981	8 971	-0,1
Total	19 987	19 332	-3,3	20 157	4,3	13 341	13 121	-1,6
Foreign as share of total (%)	48	47		45		33	32	
Unweighted average TNI	61	62		62		50	48	
Median TNI	63	62		61		49	47	

Source: UNCTAD, FDI/MNE database (https://unctad.org/fdistatistics).
Note: Data refer to fiscal year results reported between 1 April of the base year and 31 March of the following year. Complete 2021 data for the 100 largest MNEs from developing economies are not yet available.
[a] Revised results.
[b] Preliminary results.

The aggregate transnationality index (TNI) of the top 100 MNEs was weighed down by corporate restructuring operations and reconfigurations carried out by several firms in the ranking. For example, the spin-off of its truck unit by Daimler (Germany) led to a 17 per cent decrease in its foreign assets. Daimler had restructured into a holding company containing a car division, a truck unit and a financial services arm in 2019, but weak synergy between the two manufacturing businesses and a diverging geographical focus led to the spin-off. General Electric (United States) continued its decade-long restructuring, selling its Capital Aviation Services to AerCap (Ireland) for $30 billion and announcing it will further split into three companies focused on health care, energy and aviation.

The top developing-country MNEs resumed overseas investment activity in 2021, especially in the services industries. Among the largest deals were the continued expansion of State Grid (China) in the Chilean energy provision market with the acquisition of Cia General de Electricidad for $3.1 billion; the South African digital MNE Naspers' acquisition of Stack Exchange (United States), a provider of knowledge-sharing and management platforms, for an estimated $1.8 billion; and the purchase by logistics company DP World (United Arab Emirates) of Syncreon NewCo (United States), a provider of long-distance freight trucking services, for $1.2 billion.

The second year of the pandemic continued to buoy tech MNEs but not equally across different segments of the industry. Competition in the software and IT services industry depressed revenues and led IBM (United States) to spin off the IT services business Kyndryl. In contrast, consolidation and support through national industrial policies gave a big push to semiconductor companies; e.g. Micron Technology (United States) joined the top 100 ranking. Together with the return to the ranking of Oracle (United States), this brings the total number of tech and digital MNEs to 15.[6] In comparison with five years ago, the list also includes two Chinese hardware producers, Legend and Huawei, while the semiconductor producer Broadcom (United States) and the hardware company Nokia (Finland) have dropped off the list.

Tech MNEs have an international footprint that differs fundamentally from that of other MNEs because, with their many digital services, they can often reach foreign markets without making large investments in overseas assets (*WIR17*). Figure I.20 depicts the recent evolution of tech MNEs' share of assets and sales in the top 100 ranking. Tech MNEs have gained increasing weight in the ranking in terms of number of companies and also in terms of their share in total assets and sales. Sales have been growing at an annual rate of 19 per cent since 2016, compared with about 4 per cent for the rest of the MNEs in the ranking. The pandemic has further accelerated this trend, so that tech MNEs' revenues now account for more than 20 per cent of the ranking's total sales.

Figure I.20. **Evolution of tech MNEs in UNCTAD's ranking of the top 100 MNEs, 2016 – 2021** (Number and per cent)

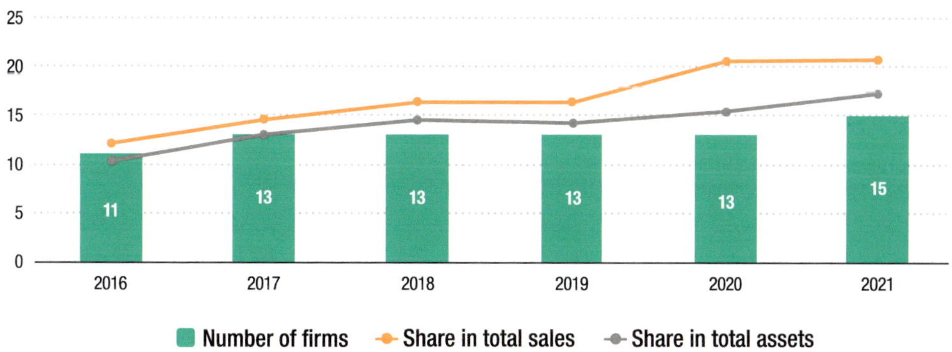

Source: UNCTAD FDI/MNE database (https://unctad.org/fdistatistics).

3. Internationalization trends of digital MNEs

To assess the potential impact of digitalization on international production, *WIR17* analyzed and provided a ranking of the top 100 digital MNEs. An update of this ranking provides evidence of their growing importance in the economy (box I.4).

The inherent dynamism of digital companies, coupled with the pandemic-induced acceleration in the adoption of digital solutions, is reflected in a significant number of new companies (39) in the ranking of the top 100 digital MNEs. The segments that saw the highest relative number of new entrants were Internet platforms (9 out of 15) and e-commerce (9 out of 21), with the initial public offerings of relevant digital companies that were private during the compilation of the first top digital ranking, such as Airbnb (United States), Didi Global (China), Uber (United States) and WeWork (United States). In both segments new entrants represent almost half of the companies in the group. In absolute terms the digital solution category had the highest number of new entrants (14). With respect to the companies that fell out of the ranking, almost a third (14) were acquired by others. This is the case of LinkedIn (acquired by Microsoft), Priceline (by Booking Holdings (United States)), Viacom (by National Amusement (United States)) and Sky (by Comcast (United States)), among others. Another third of the companies that fell out of the ranking (14) were simply outranked by other companies.

Despite the high number of new companies, the ranking is still dominated by companies from developed economies, mostly from the United States (59) followed by other developed economies (32). Nonetheless, MNEs from South-East Asia and Latin America are gaining global relevance, e.g. Mercado Libre (Argentina), and Joyy and SEA (both Singapore).

Especially for e-commerce MNEs, local knowledge is proving an important factor, as shown by the large share (two thirds) of non-United States MNEs. Geographical diversity also increased in the internet platforms segment with the entry of companies from China, Singapore and Europe. In particular, the Chinese search engine Baidu has expanded its foreign operations since 2016, including by entering a partnership with the social network company Snap (United States). Despite their economic importance, preeminent Chinese digital companies (such as Meituan and JD.com) are not represented in the ranking owing to their focus on the large domestic market.

The overall FDI lightness – the ratio of the foreign share of sales to the corresponding share of assets – of the new ranking is higher than that of the 2017 ranking. This is partly because the new entrants were on average 30 per cent lighter than the companies that continued in the ranking. Digital solution entrants were two times lighter than the companies that carried over from the previous ranking.

Overall, for digital MNEs, the ratio between the share of sales generated by foreign affiliates and the corresponding share of foreign assets (the FDI lightness index) is very high compared with that of UNCTAD's top 100 MNE ranking, with the exception of the tech group in that broader ranking (table I.18).[7] Between 2016 and 2021, the sales of traditional MNEs in UNCTAD's top 100, excluding technology MNEs, increased at a much slower pace than those of top digital companies, further accentuating the difference between digital and traditional MNEs.

Foreign asset lightness varies between segments of the digital economy, which highlights the different underlying business models within this group of MNEs. Internet platforms and digital solutions have the lightest ratios. Their business model is easily scalable internationally; it does not necessarily require physical capital investment in each of the markets where they generate sales. In contrast, e-commerce and digital content MNEs are more similar to traditional MNEs. Global e-commerce firms rely on their own large-scale distribution centres across the world, while many digital content MNEs are traditional firms that have transformed or expanded into digital markets ("gone digital" rather than "born digital"). They often still engage in the physical production of their content and maintain a relatively higher share of foreign assets. This is also confirmed by their engagement in equity acquisitions and greenfield investments.

Box I.4. UNCTAD's top 100 digital MNEs

The *World Investment Report 2017* introduced the first ranking of the top 100 digital MNEs and investigated the effect of digitalization on global investment patterns. Recently, a Special Issue of the *Global Investment Trends Monitor* (UNCTAD, 2022) and a related UNCTAD Insights research note in *Transnational Corporations* (Trentini et al., 2022) presented an updated of the ranking and of the investment footprint of digital MNEs.

The update is timely because (i) a five-year timespan is sufficient to look at evolutionary trends; (ii) the five years include the COVID-19 pandemic period, which has provided a huge boost to digital activities; and (iii) recent international policy developments – including Pillar I of the G20/OECD Base Erosion and Profit Shifting (BEPS) project and the Digital Services Act of the European Union – make it interesting to assess which firms and activities will be most affected.

The updated ranking closely follows the methodology established in *WIR17* (and explained in Casella and Formenti, 2018). The compilation of data for the new ranking started from the original ranking, updating the underlying statistics – operating revenues, sales and assets. Additional companies were selected using the same criteria as in *WIR17*: (i) listed companies with total revenues above $1 billion, reporting information on foreign business (i.e. foreign sales and foreign assets, or at least one of the two), and (ii) relevant core industry or activity. Companies were selected by screening a sample of large public companies in tech or consumer-facing[a] industries on the basis of activity codes, business description and financial reporting to determine their core activity.

As in *WIR17*, digital MNEs are classified into four main types:

(i) Internet platforms: born digital, and operated and delivered through the Internet, such as search engines, social networks and other platforms and shared-economy companies (e.g. ride-hailing companies Uber (United States) and Didi Global (China), and shared accommodation platform Airbnb (United States)).

(ii) Digital solutions: other Internet-based players and digital enablers. This category is expanded to include providers of software as a service (SaaS) and fintech, in addition to e-payment solutions. Fintech has a broader range of services: brokers, banking and finance.

(iii) e-Commerce: online platforms that enable commercial transactions. This category includes e-retailers and the new delivery group (mostly food delivery and mobile apps) which gained significant relevance during the pandemic.

(iv) Digital content: producers and distributors of goods and services in digital-format media, including games as well as data and analytics.

The digital MNEs were matched to investment project data, in particular data on M&As and greenfield investments from Refinitiv and fDi Markets, to provide an assessment of digital FDI. These data provide information on the geography and industry of investments.

Source: UNCTAD.

[a] In the initial sample, consumer-facing companies were included and screened if they have a significant digital offering (for goods companies) or product (mostly services companies that could digitalize).

Table I.18. Sales growth rates and FDI lightness: comparison between traditional top 100 MNEs, tech MNEs and top digital MNEs

	Total sales increase (%)	FDI lightness		
	2016–2021	2016	2021	Change (%)
Traditional MNEs	36	1.00	1.01	2
Tech MNEs (from top 100)	73	1.50	1.45	-3
Top digital MNEs	**159**	**1.37**	**1.58**	**15**
Internet platforms	212	2.25	2.32	3
Digital solutions	110	1.85	2.21	20
E-commerce	225	1.03	1.21	17
Digital content	68	1.32	1.12	-15

Source: UNCTAD FDI/MNE database (https://unctad.org/fdistatistics).

The overall lightness of the top 100 digital MNEs increased by 15 per cent since 2016. Digital solutions MNEs increased their asset lightness the most, pushed by fast-growing foreign sales during the pandemic. Similarly, e-commerce companies benefitted from the heightened demand for delivery services during lockdown periods. Digital content MNEs became asset heavier.

Internet platforms increased their already high lightness index only marginally. One explanation for this relative slowdown lies in the vertical integration being pursued by major platforms and their expansion across business segments. For example, Alphabet (United States) decreased its asset lightness ratio from 2.2 to 2 over the period, as it increased physical asset investments overseas to support international growth.

The different international asset footprints are also evident in diverging investment patterns since 2016. Traditional top manufacturing MNEs engage almost exclusively in greenfield investment, with a share of about 90 per cent of greenfield investment projects over their total number of foreign investment projects. In contrast, digital MNEs typically engage less in greenfield investment; most of their investment abroad relates to acquisitions of competitors or valuable start-ups and sales support activities. E-commerce companies are the exception, because they need to set up their networks of warehouses and distribution facilities, accounting for more than two thirds of all projects. The soaring e-commerce activity induced by the pandemic translated into an increase in greenfield investments (mostly in logistics and sales-related projects) of 120 per cent in 2020 and a further 10 per cent in 2021 (figure I.21). Much of that increase was accounted for by e-commerce giant Amazon. Before the pandemic, the increase was due largely to coworking space provider WeWork (United States), which invested heavily to expand its real estate portfolio.

Figure I.21. **Greenfield investment projects of top 100 digital MNEs, by segment, 2016–2021** (Billions of dollars)

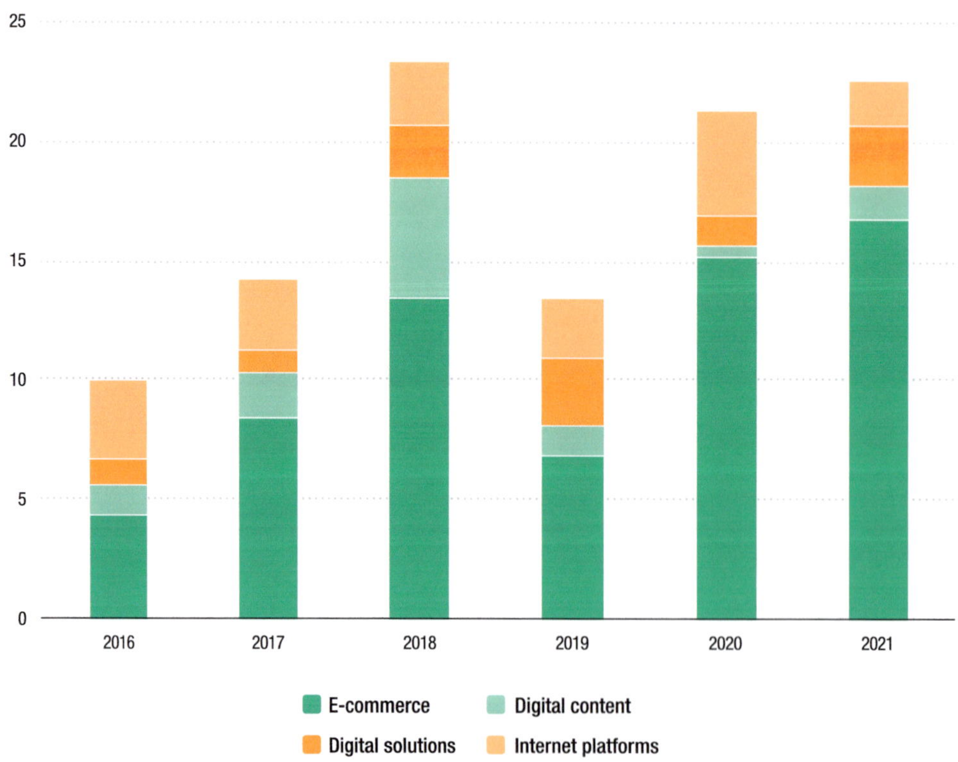

Source: UNCTAD, based on Financial Times Ltd, fDi Markets (www.fdimarkets.com).

In addition to logistical and sales support points (accounting for 42 per cent of the projects), digital MNEs also set up professional services offices (24 per cent of their greenfield investment projects), research and development (R&D) centres (14 per cent) and ICT and internet infrastructure (10 per cent). The relative importance of R&D and ICT investments for digital MNEs is significantly higher than for traditional MNEs, for which investments in R&D centres account on average for only 6-7 per cent and those in ICT and Internet infrastructure about 2–3 per cent of the total number of greenfield projects. The share of investment in these two activities varies across segments, with digital content companies devoting more than a third (35 per cent) of their projects to R&D centres, while digital solutions providers devote a slightly lower share (31 per cent) to internet infrastructure. Also, almost half of all R&D and two thirds of ICT and Internet infrastructure investments are made by the largest 10 digital MNEs in terms of assets: Amazon, Alphabet (both United States), Alibaba Group and Tencent (both China), Walt Disney, Meta Platform (both United States), Rakuten (Japan), and Salesforce, FIS and Fiserv (all United States).

More than 60 per cent of greenfield investments are in developed economies (table I.19.), especially in Europe (45 per cent). The geographical focus differs by segment. R&D projects concentrate in developed countries, with Canada, the United Kingdom and Spain among the top recipients; of R&D investment in developing economies, India captures almost half of all projects. Professional services seem to be the most geographically spread out, with almost half of such projects flowing to developing countries, especially in Asia and in Latin America.

Foreign acquisitions also show different profiles for the various categories. E-commerce MNEs and Internet platforms are less active in this case (figure I.22). Digital content and digital solutions providers accelerated their acquisitions in 2021, increasing their deals by 48 and 70 per cent respectively, pushed by heightened demand for their services in the second year of the pandemic.

Table I.19. **Top 100 digital MNEs' greenfield investment projects: geographical distribution by activity** (Number and per cent)

	Logistics and sales	Professional services	R&D	ICT and Internet	Other[a]	Total
Total number of projects	*905*	*520*	*294*	*219*	*227*	*2165*
Developed economies	**69**	**53**	**68**	**60**	**55**	**63**
Europe	56	30	43	42	43	45
North America	9	5	18	4	5	8
Other developed economies	5	18	7	15	7	9
Developing economies	**31**	**47**	**32**	**40**	**45**	**37**
Africa	2	1	2	3	4	2
Asia	19	29	24	26	25	23
China	2	15	2	1	2	5
India	8	2	13	5	2	6
Latin America and the Caribbean	10	17	7	11	16	12
Brazil	4	5	2	5	2	4
Mexico	3	5	1	..	1	2

Source: UNCTAD, based on information from Financial Times Ltd, fDi Markets (www.fdimarkets.com).
[a] Other includes, in order of importance, headquarters, customer care services, technical support, manufacturing, construction, maintenance and electricity.

Figure I.22. **International equity acquisitions of top 100 digital MNEs by segment, 2016–2021** (Number)

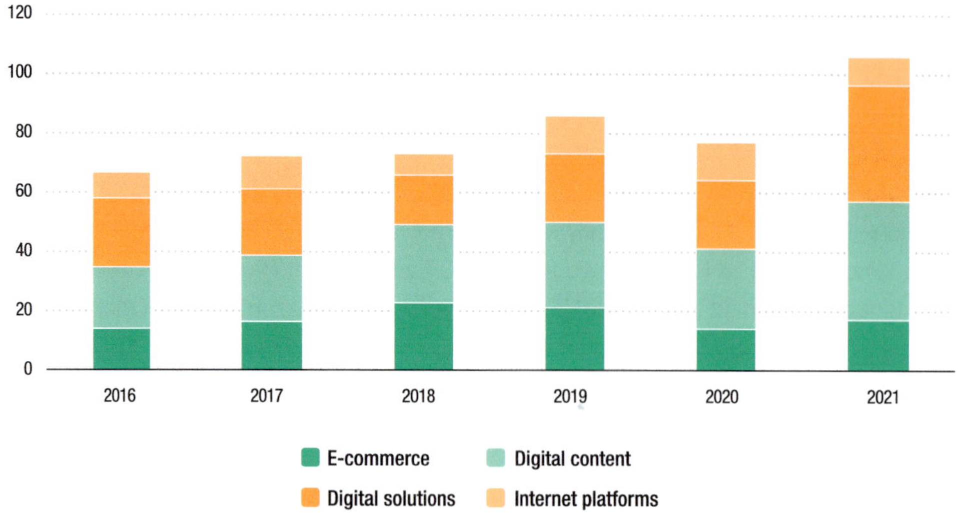

Source: UNCTAD, based on data from Refinitiv SA.

Note: The figure reports numbers of deals instead of volumes because of the high quantity of deals for which values were not disclosed. Equity acquisitions include minority stakes.

The most common acquisition targets are software, IT consulting and online services (platform) companies, which account for 48 per cent of deals by digital MNEs. Other industries in which digital MNEs regularly acquire firms are professional services, publishing and broadcasting (for digital content MNEs), financial services (for digital solutions providers), retail and business-to-business services (for e-commerce companies), and travel services and audiovisual services (for Internet platforms).

Thus, the international expansion of digital MNEs through acquisitions occurs both horizontally (within the same industry) and vertically (in different industries). Some digital MNEs can expand their business across segments, bundling multiple services into their applications; e-commerce and e-payments are typically combined in the same app, to which – in an effort to leverage synergies and network effects – new digital companies often add much more (e.g. ride-hailing, social networking, streaming). Confirming this logic, Internet platforms typically invest in vertical deals; they buy companies in the same industry in only 13 per cent of cases. In contrast, digital solutions MNEs engage mostly in horizontal deals, expanding in foreign markets by acquiring overseas direct competitors to quickly gain local knowledge and customer relationships. E-commerce and digital content MNEs lie between these two extremes, with a share of horizontal deals of about 23 per cent.

For the many firms new to this year's top 100 ranking of digital MNEs, their investment profile differs from that of well-established MNEs. Large digital MNEs are already globally dominant players, and their investment decisions are mostly motivated by the need to protect business and to secure the next innovation, rather than to reach foreign customers. The top 10 MNEs by assets in the ranking account for a fifth of the deals (and almost half of the greenfield projects) mostly in innovative start-ups in other developed economies or segments of their supply chain (ICT and infrastructure). More than 80 per cent of the foreign equity acquisitions of digital MNEs are in other developed economies, with European firms the target of almost half (48 per cent) of all deals. Among developing economies, digital MNEs targeted firms in India firms in a sizeable share of deals (7 per cent), because of its thriving tech start-up scene.

Digital MNEs from the United States accounted for 53 per cent of all deals, targeting in more than half of the cases (53 per cent) companies from European countries – in particular, the United Kingdom (23 per cent). In developing economies, United States MNEs targeted India in 8 per cent of deals, mostly buying minority stakes to gain access to the market and to local innovative solutions. For example, eBay (United States) jointly with Microsoft (United States) and Tencent (China), acquired an undisclosed minority stake in online retailer Flipkart (India), for $1.4 billion in 2017. Similarly, Paypal (United States) acquired undisclosed minority stakes in a range of Indian companies across several industries, including software providers, online brokerage systems, professional services and electronic payments (Moshpit Technologies, Speckle Internet Solutions, Scalend Technologies, Freecharge Payment Technologies).

European digital companies (of which there are 22 in the ranking) accounted for a quarter of foreign equity acquisition deals, of which more than half were in other European countries (54 per cent), in search of opportunities to consolidate operations with competitors. Another quarter were in the United States. One example of the first type of deals is the 2020 merger of two delivery companies, Takeaway (The Netherlands) and Just Eat (United Kingdom), a deal valued at $8 billion. Music streaming company Spotify (Luxembourg) was one of the most active buyers in the United States, where its acquisitions included the Internet software and services companies Podz and Betty Labs (for undisclosed value) in 2021.

The four Chinese companies in the ranking accounted for 11 per cent of the deals and invested a relatively higher share in developing-economy MNEs (34 per cent) than their developed counterparts did. They invested especially in Asia, with shares divided equally between India and South-East Asia. Across developed economies, 41 per cent of their acquisitions were in Europe and 12 per cent in the United States. Most of the deals involved an undisclosed minority participation, often as part of a group of international investors. The only majority acquisition was the purchase by Alibaba (China) of e-commerce company Lazada (Singapore) – which has been occurring in several tranches with one still pending – for a total of $4 billion.

Digital MNEs' engagement in international project finance deals is limited. Only the very top digital MNEs have now started investing overseas, especially in ICT infrastructure. For example, Alphabet (United States) is among the sponsors of one of the largest project finance deals in the telecommunication sector in Africa; a $47 billion project announced in 2019 to construct a subsea internet cable running from Portugal to South Africa, resulting in improved high-speed and affordable Internet access for West Africans. Amazon (United States) in addition to establishing data centres in different regions, has recently been sponsoring renewable energy projects.

4. Internationalization trends of SMEs

Small and medium-sized enterprises (SMEs) – defined as firms with revenues below $15 million and fewer than 300 employees – are the backbone of most economies and contribute significantly to growth and development (box I.5). Only the most productive and dynamic SMEs engage in international business activity through trade and investment. Few invest in physical assets abroad.

Predictably therefore, FDI by SMEs is small. Moreover, SME investment activity has shown a downward trend since 2015 (figure I.23). The number of FDI projects by SMEs fell from 880 in 2015 to 195 in 2021, and the share of SMEs in total greenfield investment projects declined from 5.7 to 1.3 per cent. The decline in 2020 can be explained by the economic fallout from the COVID-19 pandemic, which hit small businesses disproportionally;

Box I.5. Foreign direct investment by multinational SMEs

A new UNCTAD research project examines the internationalization process of SMEs, with a focus on FDI by SMEs from and to developing economies. A novel aspect of the research is the analysis of the role of SMEs in South–South and intraregional FDI. The objective is to evaluate the importance of SME international expansion, particularly through FDI, for the economies of both home and host countries.

UNCTAD first published a study on FDI by SMEs in 1998 (UNCTAD, 1998), focusing on developing economies in Asia. In the intervening quarter-century, the growing importance of global value chains, the continued rise of emerging-market players and the new industrial revolution have changed the landscape. In addition, the more difficult international policy environment for international investment in recent years and the economic fallout from the pandemic have both had disproportionately negative effects on SMEs. This makes it imperative to take a fresh look at FDI by SMEs.

UNCTAD's research project will bring together empirical evidence on FDI by SMEs covering all developing regions and cutting across industries. It will include firm-level evidence and case studies on Argentina, Brazil, Colombia, Ghana, Peru, Thailand, Turkey and Viet Nam. This project will also contribute to realization of the BAPA+40 outcome of "More than 40 entities participating in the UN mechanism for the implementation of this resolution will welcome data on South-South investment by SMEs".[a]

A fundamental driver for the project is the perception that in many economies policy tools and institutions for promoting international investment are mostly geared towards attracting large-scale industrial projects by major MNEs, and that investment promotion agencies, special economic zones and other home- and host-economy institutions have often not paid sufficient attention to the needs of SME investors. The project will aim to provide clear policy recommendations to strengthen the investment environment and investment facilitation for multinational SMEs.

Source: UNCTAD.
[a] Official Records of the General Assembly, Seventy-third Session, Resolution 73/291 24*(m)*.

however, the decline before the pandemic indicates that longer-term factors hinder SME internationalization. These factors include unequal access to finance, the growing digital gap between SMEs and larger companies, continued concentration in international business and, from a policy perspective, a lack of investment promotion and facilitation measures targeted to SMEs. The deteriorating international policy environment for trade and investment, especially the trade tensions after 2017, are also likely to have discouraged SMEs more than large MNEs. Looking ahead, the potential role of SMEs in South–South and intraregional FDI could provide some impetus to reverse the downward trend, as regional economic cooperation among developing economies takes hold.

Figure I.23. Greenfield projects by SMEs, 2015–2021 (Number and per cent)

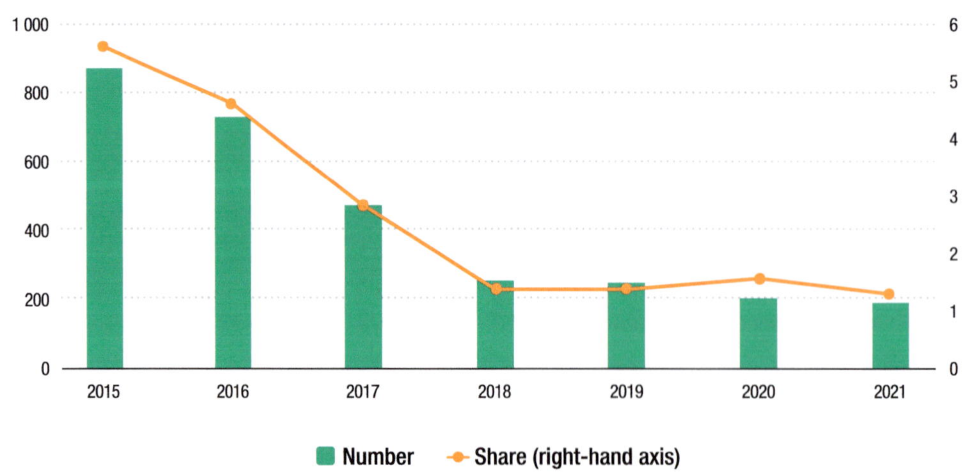

Source: UNCTAD, based on information from the Financial Times Ltd, fDi Markets (www.fDimarkets.com).

Foreign investment by SMEs from developing economies represented only 6 per cent of all SME greenfield investment projects in 2021. This contrasts with the 39 per cent share of developing economies in total outward investment. SME outward investors are predominantly from upper-middle-income developing economies; for example, SMEs from China, India and Turkey are relatively active. Home-country economic conditions are clearly a key factor in the internationalization of SMEs.

SMEs invest relatively more within their own regions than MNEs do (figure I.24). This holds for both developed and developing economies, and for almost all regions except for developing Asia, where the data are skewed by the large numbers of Chinese SMEs, which are highly active in Africa, and by Turkish SMEs, which invest almost exclusively in Europe.

A more nuanced picture emerges when looking at bilateral investment links, confirming that SMEs are more likely to invest within their region than large MNEs. The average distance to the host economy of greenfield investments by MNEs is about 4,000 km, whereas for SMEs it is about 3,500 km. Moreover, SMEs have a higher average share of greenfield investment in neighbouring countries (19 per cent) than do all firms (14 per cent).

In addition to their tendency to invest regionally, SMEs are more likely to invest in economies at a similar level of development as their home economy. SMEs from developed economies tend to invest in developed economies – irrespective of the region – whereas SMEs from developing economies target investment projects in other developing economies.

Overseas investment by SMEs tends to concentrate in industries that do not require high set-up (or fixed) costs, such as services and some specialized and light manufacturing. SMEs in information and communication services and those in professional services activities together account for more than half of all foreign investment projects (figure I.25). Within information and communication services, more than three quarters of projects are in software and information technology services, highlighting the importance of the digital economy for the development of a dynamic SME sector.

Figure I.24. **Shares of regional greenfield projects, SMEs and total, by region**
(Per cent)

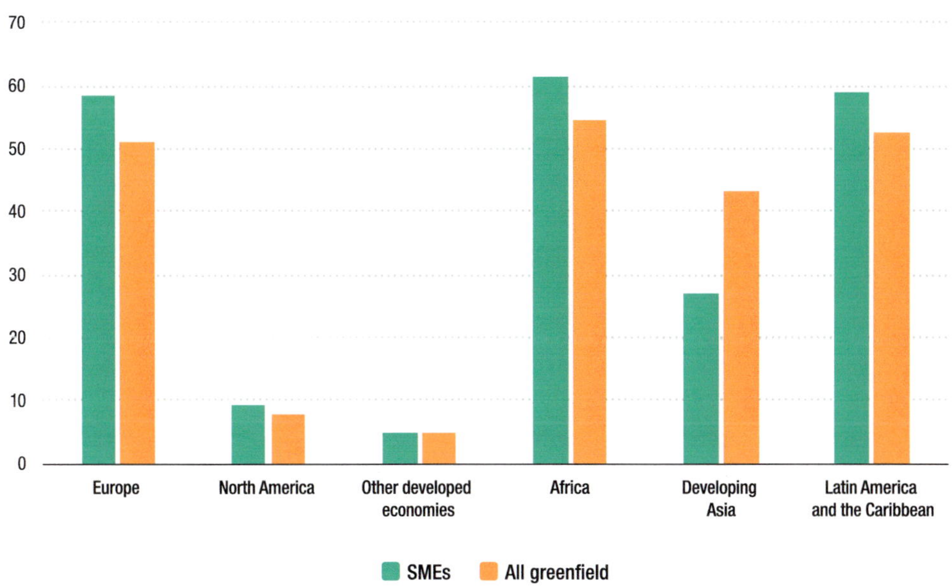

Source: UNCTAD, based on information from the Financial Times Ltd, fDi Markets (www.fDimarkets.com).

Figure I.25. **Top sectors of greenfield projects, SMEs and total, 2015–2021** (Per cent)

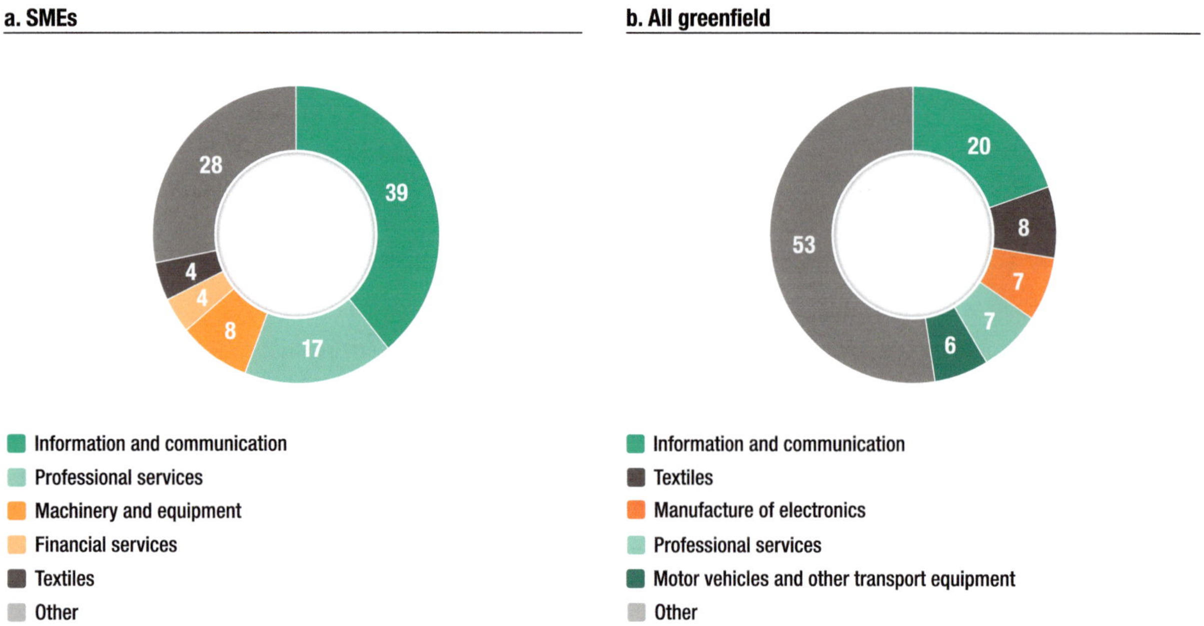

Source: UNCTAD based on information from the Financial Times Ltd, fDi Markets (www.fDimarkets.com).

NOTES

[1] For the list of LDC, LLDCs and SIDS, please see footnotes e,f,g of annex table I. The category of LDCs overlaps partly with that of LLDCs and SIDS. There are 17 economies that are both LDCs and LLDCs, and 6 that are both LDCs and SIDS.

[2] See also the report on the Global Landscape of Climate Finance 2021 by Climate Policy Initiative (CPI, 2021).

[3] Government involvement includes any form of support through grants, guarantees, loans, equity participations, subsidies, tax breaks, and ancillary infrastructure improvements.

[4] According to the *Joint Report on Multilateral Development Banks' Climate Finance*, the multilateral development banks collectively committed $66 billion in 2020 – $50 billion, or 76 per cent, for mitigation and $16 billion, or 24 per cent, for adaptation. Of the total, 58 per cent was committed to low- and middle-income economies (AfDB et al., 2020).

[5] Although the deal was completed in 2020, it affected financial accounts only in fiscal year 2021, with RWE's total assets increasing by 113 and its foreign ones by 130 per cent.

[6] In 2017, Hitachi (Japan) was categorized as tech company because its core industry was historically defined as manufacturing of computers; however, in consideration of the expansion of its business in many new areas including electric grids, automotive and railways it is now categorized as conglomerate. In addition, the preliminary ranking for *WIR17* included Oracle (United States), which ultimately joined the ranking only in the following year, replacing Broadcom (United States).

[7] Three MNEs are in both the broader UNCTAD ranking of the top 100 MNEs and the UNCTAD ranking of the top 100 digital MNEs: Alphabet and Amazon (both United States) and Tencent (China).

CHAPTER II

RECENT POLICY DEVELOPMENTS AND KEY ISSUES

INTRODUCTION

In 2021, the number of investment policy measures returned to pre-pandemic levels (109), decreasing by 28 per cent compared with 2020, signalling an end to the emergency investment policymaking that characterized the first year of the COVID-19 pandemic. The pandemic nevertheless continued to affect the nature of investment policy measures adopted in 2021. Developed countries, in particular, expanded the protection of strategic companies from foreign takeovers, in a continuation of a trend towards tighter regulation of investment, which brought the ratio of measures less favourable to investment over those more favourable to an all-time high (42 per cent). Conversely, developing countries continued to adopt primarily measures to liberalize, promote or facilitate investment, confirming the important role that foreign direct investment (FDI) plays in their economic recovery strategies. Investment facilitation measures constituted almost 40 per cent of all measures more favourable to investment, followed by the opening of new activities to FDI (30 per cent) and by new investment incentives (20 per cent) (section A).

The first quarter of 2022 saw a dramatic increase in the adoption of investment policy measures (75 – a record for a single quarter), largely because of the war in Ukraine. Sanctions and countersanctions affecting FDI to and from the Russian Federation, Belarus and the non-Government controlled areas of eastern Ukraine, constituted 70 per cent of all measures adopted in Q1 2022. The balance points to the continued adoption of measures more favourable to investment in developing countries (13 out of 14) and more restrictive measures in developed ones (5 out of 8).

At the international level, several notable developments in 2021 and 2022 accelerated the trend towards reform of the international investment agreements (IIA) regime. These include the conclusion of new-generation megaregional economic agreements, the termination of bilateral investment treaties (BITs) and multilateral discussions on the reform of investor–State dispute settlement (ISDS) mechanisms. At the same time, greater policy attention to investment facilitation, climate change and human rights is set to recalibrate international investment governance (section B).

Tax policy is one of the key instruments utilized around the world to promote investment, and the pandemic has accentuated the importance of tax incentive and relief efforts in economic recovery and resilience packages adopted worldwide. The ongoing reform of the international tax system may affect the capacity of countries to continue relying on certain types of tax incentives to promote FDI. In this context, section C of this chapter highlights key trends in the taxation of investment. Statutory corporate income taxes have dropped in all regions since 1980, as countries have increasingly engaged in tax competition to promote investment regardless of their size or level of development (section C.1). Beyond reducing the statutory corporate tax rates, countries rely on investment incentives, mainly in the form of tax holidays or reduced corporate tax rates, to attract investors to priority sectors or regions, as highlighted by analysis of tax-related investment policy measures adopted worldwide in the last decade (section C.2).

With respect to tax policy, IIAs impose obligations on States that can create friction with taxation measures taken at the national level. The actions of tax authorities, as organs of the State, and tax policymaking more generally can potentially engage the international responsibility of a State under an IIA when they adversely affect foreign investors and investment. It is therefore important to enhance cooperation between investment and tax policymakers. The joint expertise of these two policy communities can help improve the coherence between tax and investment policymaking. Equally important is the need to minimize the risk of friction between the IIA regime and the global tax treaty network, with more than 3,000 agreements each (section C.3).

A. NATIONAL INVESTMENT POLICIES

1. Overall trends

The number of investment policy measures adopted in 2021 returned to pre-pandemic levels (109), decreasing by 28 per cent from the number in 2020. However, the trend towards tighter regulation of investment continued, and the ratio of measures less favourable to investment over those more favourable was the highest on record (42 per cent, a point higher than in 2020).

Fifty-three economies introduced an aggregate 109 policy measures affecting foreign investment in 2021 – a decrease of approximately 28 per cent compared with 2020, as the haste to adopt emergency pandemic-related measures has subsided and the total number of investment policy measures has returned to pre-pandemic levels (figure II.1).

Although the number of new measures less favourable to investment declined by 20 per cent (from 50 in 2020 to 40 in 2021), they reached the highest proportion ever recorded (42 per cent of non-neutral measures), as several countries reinforced their screening regimes for investment or extended the temporary regimes introduced in reaction to the pandemic (figure II.2).[1] This surge in measures to tighten control over investor entry and operation continues the policy trend observed since the global financial crisis, which the pandemic accentuated. It started in developed countries but is increasingly extending to developing ones (section A.2).

Figure II.1. | **Changes in national investment policies, 2003–2021** (Number of measures)

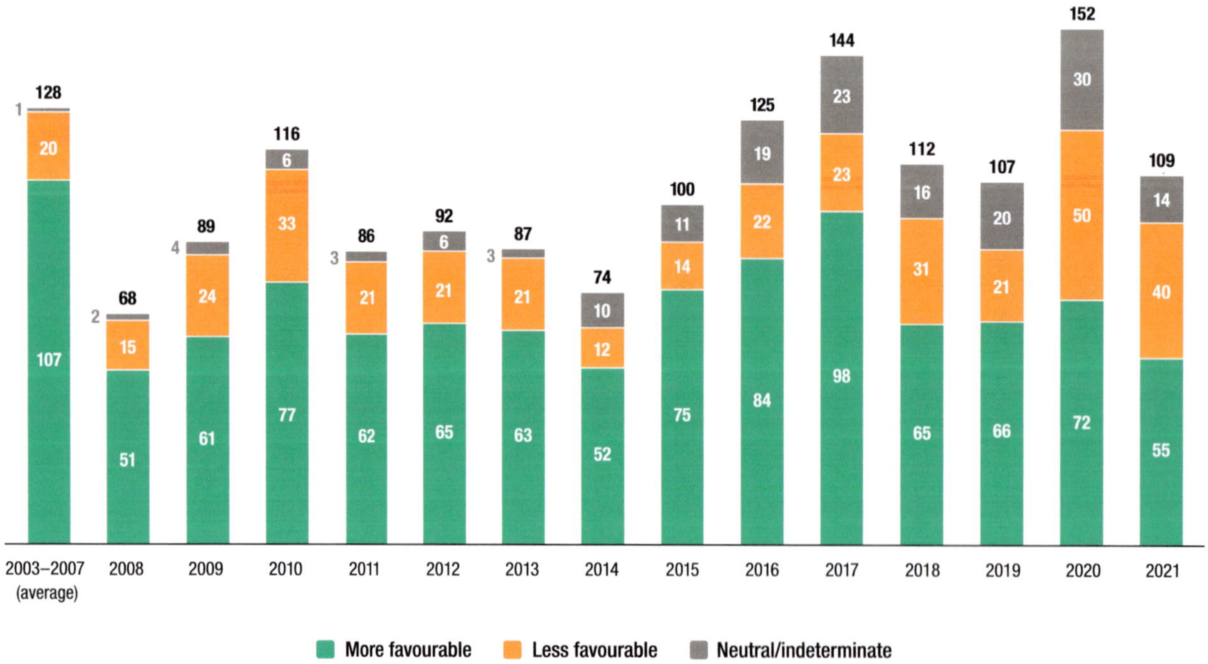

Source: UNCTAD, Investment Policy Monitor.

The number of measures more favourable to investment (55) declined by almost 24 per cent to reach the lowest share on record (58 per cent). The large majority of these measures (48, or 87 per cent) were undertaken in developing countries, highlighting that investment attraction remains a key element in these countries' economic recovery strategies. Many countries took further steps towards investment facilitation by simplifying or streamlining administrative procedures, and several others expanded their investment incentive regimes to attract more foreign investment (see section 1.b). The remaining 14 measures were of a neutral or indeterminate nature (figure II.1).

Figure II.2. **Changes in national investment policies, 2005–2021** (Per cent)

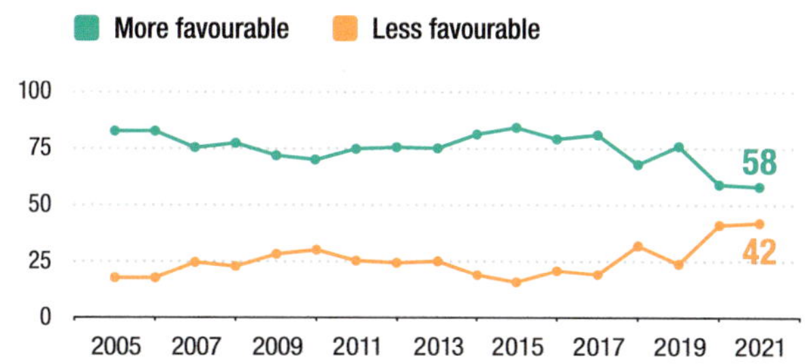

Source: UNCTAD, Investment Policy Monitor.

In regional terms, developing countries in Asia once again led the adoption of new investment policy measures (40), followed by countries of Latin America and the Caribbean (18) and Africa (17). Among developed regions, European countries continued to adopt the largest number of measures (19), although these declined by 30 per cent compared with 2020 – a year in which many of them implemented the European Union (EU) regulation on FDI screening of 2019. The number of measures adopted in North America and other developed regions remained stable compared with 2020 (figure II.3).

Overall trends mask important regional differences in the nature of the measures introduced. Almost two thirds of the measures adopted in developing economies, including in developing Asia, Africa, and Latin America and the Caribbean, were meant to promote or facilitate investment, continuing a well-established trend (64 per cent, or 77 per cent when excluding policies of neutral nature). In contrast, the majority of the measures adopted

Figure II.3. **Regional distribution of national investment policy measures in 2021** (Number of measures)

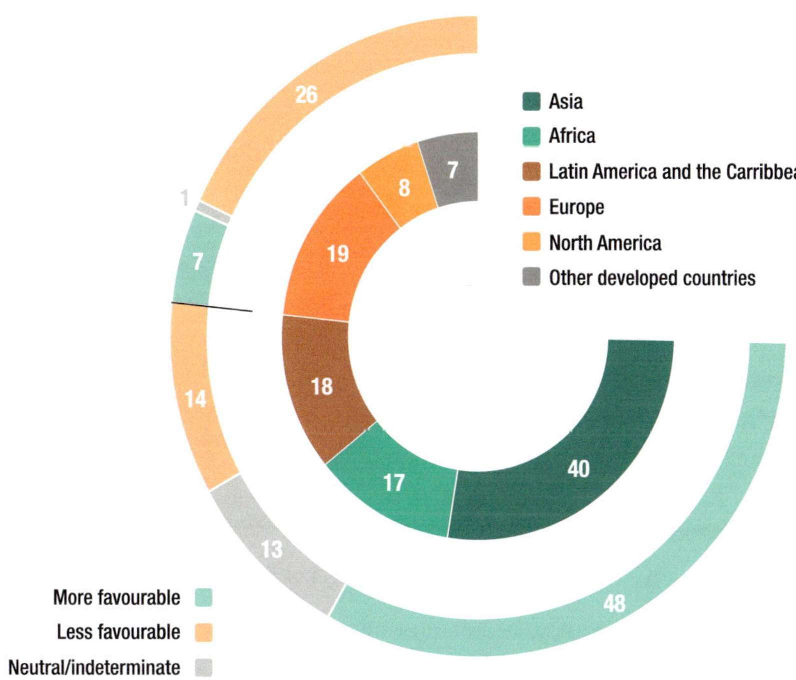

Source: UNCTAD, Investment Policy Monitor.

by developed countries introduced or reinforced investment restrictions (76 per cent, or 79 per cent when excluding policies of neutral nature). All of them related directly or indirectly to national security concerns about foreign ownership of critical infrastructure, core technologies or other sensitive domestic assets. Often, these measures were an extension of the restrictions introduced in the midst of the pandemic and motivated by the desire to protect sensitive domestic businesses against foreign takeovers (section 1.a).

The first quarter of 2022 saw a dramatic expansion in investment policymaking around the world, largely as the result of the war in Ukraine and the flurry of sanctions and countersanctions adopted by several countries. Twenty-seven countries and the EU introduced 75 policy measures affecting foreign investment, the highest level ever recorded in a quarter. Seventy per cent of them (52 measures) represented sanctions adopted in the context of the war in Ukraine. These include primarily measures targeted at prohibiting or otherwise limiting FDI to and from the Russian Federation, Belarus and the non-Government controlled areas of eastern Ukraine, as well as countersanctions adopted by the Russian Federation to impose restrictions on transnational business activities.[2]

Beyond sanctions that impose outright prohibitions or limitations on FDI, several measures that aim to interrupt a broad range of foreign transactions also have an impact on investment activities. Among them are sanctions targeting Russian banks and their subsidiaries; trade restrictions on inputs, goods, software and technology; and blocking sanctions that target transport companies, which have a significant impact on supply chains for foreign manufacturers in several sectors. Finally, travel bans and asset freezes affecting hundreds of individuals and entities targeted by sanctions have impacts on a broad range of foreign investment.

Among the 23 investment policy measures adopted in the first quarter of 2022 unrelated to sanctions, 60 per cent were adopted by developing countries. All but one aimed to facilitate or attract FDI. Conversely, among the remaining eight measures adopted by developed countries, five aimed to tighten control on FDI. One measure was of neutral nature.

a. Developed countries continued increasing FDI scrutiny for national security concerns

The trend towards increased FDI screening intensified in 2021, with at least four more countries adopting new FDI screening mechanisms and at least twice as many tightening existing mechanisms.

Two thirds of the policy measures less favourable to investment adopted in 2021 concerned the introduction or tightening of national security regulations affecting FDI. Nearly all of them were adopted by developed economies. In particular, at least four additional countries introduced FDI screening mechanisms, including three European countries (Czechia, Denmark and Slovakia) and Saudi Arabia. This brought the total number of countries conducting FDI screening for national security to 36. In addition, at least eight countries and the EU reinforced existing screening regimes for foreign investment. Together, countries that conduct FDI screening account for 63 per cent of global FDI flows and 70 per cent of FDI stock (up from 52 and 67 per cent respectively in 2020).

For example,

- *Australia* amended the Foreign Acquisitions and Takeovers Act to permanently lower to $0 the monetary threshold for mandatory screening of sensitive national security projects. Accordingly, foreign investors require approval for all investments in land or businesses that are sensitive to national security, regardless of the amount invested.

- *Canada* lowered slightly the thresholds that trigger FDI screening[3] and strengthened its scrutiny of foreign investment in four areas of heightened risk: sensitive personal data, specified sensitive technology areas, critical minerals and investments by State-owned or State-influenced foreign investors.
- *Czechia* introduced a new FDI screening mechanism in line with the EU Guidance on FDI screening. According to the new law, any non-EU investor must obtain a permit prior to acquiring effective control of a company in the country.
- *Denmark* introduced an FDI screening mechanism through the Investment Review Act. It requires foreign investors to obtain prior governmental approval for an acquisition of at least 10 per cent of shareholding in a Danish company, as well as for establishing a new company in selected sectors.
- *France* included technologies related to renewable energy production in the list of sectors and key technologies subject to the FDI review mechanism.
- *Germany* added 16 high-tech activities to the list of activities covered by the FDI review mechanism, bringing the total to 43, and changed the thresholds that trigger investment screening for different types of acquisitions, depending on their sectors.
- *Italy* expanded the scope of the procedures that require prior government approval for foreign investors to acquire assets strategically important to the national interest. The amendments concern ports, airports, motorways of national interest, national spaceports, railway network within the trans-European network, and broadband and ultrabroadband services.
- *Japan* added a requirement that foreign investors in 34 rare earth metals obtain prior government approval. Accordingly, foreigners who wish to acquire more than 1 per cent of the stock of a listed company or more than one share of the stock of an unlisted company are required to notify the Bank of Japan.
- *Saudi Arabia* established a Standing Ministerial Committee for Foreign Investment Investigation, tasked with identifying sensitive and strategic sectors or companies in which foreign investment might affect national security or public order. Foreign investments in those sectors will be subject to examination and potentially restrictions.
- *Slovakia* established an investment screening mechanism according to which any acquisition of more than 10 per cent of shares or voting rights in an operation of critical infrastructure may be subject to review in light of possible disruption of public order or national security. The governmental power to block acquisitions applies to a list of sectors that includes transport, information and communication technology, energy, mining, postal services, pharmaceuticals and chemicals, metallurgy, health care, water, finance and agriculture.
- *Spain* extended the suspension of the FDI liberalization regime until 31 December 2022. Therefore, investors from the EU or the European Free Trade Association (FTA) buying at least 10 per cent of a Spanish company must notify the Spanish authorities and await approval. This temporary scheme applies if the acquisition or investment in publicly traded companies operating in the strategic sector exceeds €500 million.
- *The United Kingdom* introduced a stand-alone screening regime separate from the merger control regime, to address acquisitions of British companies and assets by both domestic and foreign investors. The screening procedure focuses on evaluating risks to national security associated with such acquisitions. The law introduces a mandatory notification of the Minister for Investment prior to gaining control over a company or an asset.
- *The United States* prolonged the prohibition for its citizens of investing in companies related to China's defence and surveillance technology sector by one year (until 12 November 2022) and extended the ban to eight new companies.

- At the regional level, the *European Commission* expanded the list of projects and programmes of "Union interest" to include investments related to the Space Programme, the Digital Europe Programme and the European Defence Fund, as well as the Europe4Health Programme. Accordingly, the Commission may issue an opinion if it considers that such investments pose a threat to the security and public order of more than one Member State or the Union as a whole.

b. Developing economies aimed at reducing the risks of crowding out and increasing FDI's contribution to local economic development...

In developing countries, most restrictions on FDI are aimed at protecting domestic companies, including SMEs or companies operating in strategic sectors and activities, as well as increasing local content.

For example,

- *Burundi* has introduced an eligibility threshold of $500,000 for foreign investment that seeks to benefit from incentives under the Investment Code.
- *Indonesia* required foreign investors in a non-bank payment services provider to guarantee a minimum of 15 per cent Indonesian shareholding, with 51 per cent of the voting rights to be held by Indonesian investors.
- *Mauritius* extended the scope of restrictions on the ownership of property by non-citizens. A requirement for prior approval by the Office of the Prime Minister on holding, purchasing or acquiring property was extended to property disposal, which includes burdening a property with a mortgage or charge.
- *Mexico* amended the Hydrocarbon Act to grant the State new powers to exercise regulatory controls over the distribution, storage, import and export of fuels and oil produced by the country.
- *Mozambique* increased the minimum capital requirement for foreign investors to be able to freely repatriate profits and investment capital from $45,000 to $130,000.
- *Namibia* amended the rules regarding the transfer, cessation and assignment of mineral licences to foreign companies, requiring the local retention of at least 15 per cent interest in the company.
- *Nepal* required foreign investors to transfer at least 70 per cent of the proposed investment capital before starting a business, and the balance within the following two years.
- *South Africa* introduced a new requirement under which private security companies must be at least 51 per cent owned and controlled by South African citizens.

c. ...but largely continued to embrace policies to promote or facilitate investment

At least 30 developing countries implemented various promotion and facilitation measures in 2021, hoping to attract additional FDI and help overcome the economic crisis caused by the pandemic. Investment facilitation measures accounted for almost 40 per cent of all measures more favourable to investment.

(i) New investment facilitation measures

Many new measures concerned the simplification of administrative procedures for investment. For example,

- *Angola* amended the Private Investment Law to introduce several facilitation mechanisms. For instance, investors who obtain a Private Investment Registration Certificate are now exempt from obtaining provisional licences and other authorizations from public administration bodies.
- *China* simplified the documentation required for company registration in the Shenzhen Special Economic Zone. Applicants can simply provide documents and information when they file applications online.
- *Fiji* introduced a broader range of treatment and protection guarantees for foreign investors and removed the requirement to apply for a Foreign Investor Registration Certificate. It also harmonized reporting obligations on foreign and local investors.
- *India* launched the National Single-Window System, which will become a one-stop shop for approvals and clearances needed by investors, entrepreneurs and businesses.
- *Indonesia* eased the employment licensing process for tech-based start-ups seeking to hire foreign workers by waiving the Foreign Worker Utilization Plan requirement for contracts shorter than three months.
- In the *United Arab Emirates*, Abu Dhabi launched the Virtual Licence, allowing non-resident foreign investors to obtain an economic licence for doing business in Abu Dhabi without any prior residence procedures and from any location outside the United Arab Emirates.

(ii) New investment incentives

At least 15 countries introduced new incentives for investors, most of them in the form of new fiscal benefits for priority sectors or through the institution of special economic zones (SEZs). For example,

- *Angola* introduced the Free Zones Act, focused on developing the agricultural and industrial sectors, labour-intensive industries and high-tech industries. The Act grants a range of tax incentives to companies established in the free zones.
- *Botswana* announced that, in addition to other commercial and fiscal incentives, income accruing to an investor or developer from SEZ-licensed operations is to be taxed at a special rate of 5 per cent for the first 10 years of operation in an SEZ and 10 per cent thereafter.
- *Honduras* created a general rebate of the airport tax for new low-cost operators as well as rebates ranging from 75 to 100 per cent of take-off and landing charges for certain domestic airports.
- *Mauritius* introduced several new tax incentives for investment, including double tax deduction on expenditure incurred for research and development targeting the African market and the acquisition of specialized software and systems, 10 years carry-forward of unrelieved investment tax credit for manufacturing companies and an 8-year tax holiday for new companies in prescribed sectors and activities.
- *Uzbekistan* introduced new tax and customs incentives for both national and foreign investors in capital-intensive sectors including oil, natural gas, gold, copper, tungsten and uranium. The incentives include reduced taxes on subsoil use and customs duty exemptions on equipment, material and technical resources and special equipment not produced in the country.
- *Zambia* reduced the general corporate income tax rate from 35 to 30 per cent and extended the 15 per cent corporate income tax rate for hotel income from lodging and food services through 2022. It also made the mineral royalty levy deductible for corporate income tax purposes.

(iii) Other legal and institutional reforms to promote FDI

Several countries adopted new or enhanced legal and institutional mechanisms to promote FDI in 2021. For example,

- *Cambodia* adopted a new Law on Investment, offering a range of new investment incentives, new investor guarantees (including non-discrimination, guarantees against nationalization and arbitrary expropriation) and improved registration procedures.
- *Ecuador* signed the Convention on the Settlement of Investment Disputes between States and Nationals of Other States, thereby opening the process of Ecuador's return to the multilateral dispute settlement mechanism.
- *Indonesia* established a new Ministry of Investment, thus upgrading the status of the Indonesian Investment Coordinating Board. A key goal of the reform is to enhance the ease of doing business in the country.
- *Panama* created a new Export and Investment Promotion Agency (ProPanamá).
- *Sudan* passed the Public Private Partnership Law, aimed at encouraging private entities to invest and participate in projects alongside public entities.

d. FDI liberalization

Thirty per cent of the policy measures more favourable to FDI introduced in 2021 concerned partial or full liberalization of investment in a variety of industries, including in particular utilities (e.g. telecommunications, electricity), but also transportation, insurance and several manufacturing activities. As in previous years, developing economies in Asia were the most active in liberalizing foreign investment.

For example,

- *Angola* authorized the privatization of 51 per cent of the capital held by MS–TELCOM in NetOne Telecomunicações, SA, through a limited tender by prior qualification open to national and international investors.
- *Brazil* allowed a partial privatization of the electricity company EletroBras. Accordingly, the State's stake in the company is expected to be reduced from approximately 61 to 45 per cent.
- *China* continued to open its economy to FDI. Among the main measures: the number of sectors restricted or prohibited for foreign investors was reduced from 33 to 31; comprehensive pilot programmes were approved on the opening of 12 services sectors to FDI in the Tianjin, Shanghai and Chongqing municipalities and in Hainan Province; and foreign investors are now encouraged to establish regional headquarters in China for fund management, procurement and sales.
- *India* shifted to allow 100 per cent foreign participation in the telecommunication services industry, including all services and infrastructure providers, through the Automatic Route. Thus, non-resident investors or Indian companies do not require any approval from the Government of India for the investment. The FDI ceiling in insurance companies was also raised, from 49 to 74 per cent.
- *The Philippines* shifted to allow 100 per cent foreign ownership of select public services, including telecommunications, airlines, shipping and railways and up to 40 per cent in the operation of a public utility, including electricity distribution and transmission, airports, seaports, water pipeline distribution and sewerage, tollways and expressways, and public utility vehicles. The Government also reduced the minimum paid-up capital requirements for foreign retail enterprises from $2.5 million to $1 million and

removed the pre-qualification requirements for foreign retailers of having engaged in the retailing industry for the preceding five years or of holding at least five retailing branches in the world.

2. M&A controls affecting foreign investors

In 2021, the number of merger and acquisition (M&A) deals valued at over $50 million that were withdrawn by the parties for regulatory or political concerns remained stable (14 deals), but their value quadrupled, to over $47 billion.

At least 14 large M&A deals were terminated by the parties in 2021 for regulatory or political reasons. While the number of such deals remained stable (15 were terminated in 2020), their aggregate value almost quadrupled, from $12.4 billion in 2020 to $47.1 billion in 2021. The terminated deals concerned a variety of industries, including extractive industries, semiconductors, automotive and aviation, financial services, trading and media (table II.1).

Table II.1. Foreign acquisitions withdrawn for regulatory or political reasons in 2021 (Illustrative list)

	For national security reasons
Shandong Gold Mining Co Ltd – TMAC Resources Inc	On 5 January 2021, Shandong Gold Mining (China) withdrew from its definitive agreement to acquire the entire share capital of TMAC Resources Inc. (Canada) for $144 million. The Canadian Government blocked the sale of TMAC Resources and its Hope Bay gold-mining project to Chinese State-owned company Shandong Gold following a national security review under the Investment Canada Act.
TMH International AG – Bergen Engines AS	On 25 March 2021, TMH International (Switzerland), a unit of Transmash Holding JSC (Russian Federation), cancelled its plans to acquire Bergen Engines, based in Norway and owned by Rolls-Royce (United Kingdom), for $180 million, after indication from the Norwegian Government that the deal would be blocked on national security grounds, on the basis of concerns that the engine maker would have been of significant military strategic interest to the Russian Federation.
China Oceanwide Holdings Group Co Ltd – Genworth Financial Inc	On 6 April 2021, China Oceanwide Holdings Group (China) withdrew its bid to acquire the entire share capital of life insurance company Genworth Financial (United States) for an estimated $2.7 billion, fearing that the United States might stall it over concerns about Chinese access to sensitive data of United States citizens.
TransDigm Group Inc – Meggitt PLC	On 7 September 2021, TransDigm Group (United States) announced the cancellation of its plans to acquire the entire share capital of the aerospace and defence company Meggitt (United Kingdom) for $9.7 billion, over concerns of increased scrutiny by the Government of the United Kingdom of defence company takeovers after a flurry of M&As in the sector.
Alimentation Couche-Tard Inc – Carrefour SA	On 16 January 2021, Alimentation Couche-Tard (Canada) decided to drop its merger plan for $19.7 billion with the food retail corporation Carrefour (France), because the French Finance Minister had voiced objection to the deal on the grounds that it would present risks to France's food sovereignty.
	For competition reasons
Kina Securities Ltd – Fiji business of Westpac Banking Corp	On 22 September 2021, Kina Securities (Papua New Guinea) abandoned its plans to acquire the entire share capital of the Fiji business of the bank and financial services corporation Westpac Banking Corp (Australia), following a decision by Papua New Guinea's Independent Consumer and Competition Commission to deny authorization for the proposed acquisition.
Aquiline Capital Partners LLC – Aon PLC	On 26 July 2021, Aquiline Capital Partners (United States) withdrew its bid to acquire the United States retirement business of Aon PLC (United Kingdom), concerned that the Justice Department of the United States had filed a lawsuit aimed at stopping insurance broker Aon's $30 billion acquisition of Willis Towers Watson because it would reduce competition and could lead to higher prices.
Arthur J Gallagher & Co – Willis Towers Watson PLC	On 26 July 2021, Arthur J. Gallagher (United States) terminated its plans to acquire the reinsurance brokerage business of Willis Towers Watson (United Kingdom), after the planned merger of Aon PLC and Willis Towers Watson was scrapped. Willis Towers Watson agreed to divest Willis Re Ltd and certain corporate risk, broking, and health and benefits businesses to Gallagher for $3.6 billion to allay competition concerns about its terminated merger with Aon.

/...

Table II.1.	Foreign acquisitions withdrawn for regulatory or political reasons in 2021 (Illustrative list) (Concluded)
	For other regulatory reasons
Chijin International Ltd – Mensin Bibiani Pty Ltd	On 23 April 2021, Chijin International (Hong Kong, China), a unit of Chifeng Jilong Gold Mining Co Ltd (China), withdrew from its agreement to acquire the entire share capital of Mensin Bibiani, a gold ore mine operator based in Ghana, from Resolute Mining Ltd (Australia) for $108.9 million. In a filing, Chifeng Jilong said that Resolute did not disclose that the Ministry of Lands and Natural Resources of Ghana had terminated the mining lease.
VI Investment Corp – JT Savings Bank Co Ltd	On 31 March 2021, VI Investment Corp (Republic of Korea) abandoned its proposed acquisition of the entire share capital of J Trust Savings Bank (Japan) for $129 million, as it failed to get approval from the Financial Supervisory Service of the Republic of Korea.
Remus Horizons PCC Ltd – FAR Ltd	On 21 April 2021, private investment fund Remus Horizons (United Kingdom) withdrew its tender offer of $158.8 million for the entire share capital in oil and gas exploration company FAR (Australia), because Remus had its registration as a private investment fund suspended by the Guernsey Financial Services Commission.
Pershing Square Tontine Holdings Ltd – Universal Music Group BV	On 19 March 2021, Pershing Square Tontine (United States) walked away from its plans to acquire a 10 per cent stake in Universal Music Group (France) for $4 billion, after the Securities and Exchange Commission of the United States raised issues with several elements of the proposed transaction – in particular, whether the structure of the initial business combination qualified under New York Stock Exchange rules.
	While waiting for host-country approval
Applied Materials Inc – Kokusai Electric Corp	On 29 March 2021, Applied Materials (United States) cancelled its plans to acquire the entire share capital of semiconductor manufacturing company Kokusai Electric (Japan) for $3.5 billion, announcing that the amended Kokusai Electric Corporation share purchase agreement with KKR HKE Investment LP was terminated as of 19 March 2021 as Applied Materials did not receive confirmation of timely approval from the regulator in China.
Wise Road Capital Ltd – Magnachip Semiconductor Corp	On 13 December 2021, Wise Road Capital Ltd (China) withdrew its bid for power and display chipmaker Magnachip Semiconductor Corp (Republic of Korea). Wise Road offered $1.4 billion in cash in March 2021. According to Magnachip, the offer was withdrawn because after months of effort the companies had failed to obtain approval of the merger by the Committee on Foreign Investment in the United States. The company also withdrew the application for approval of the merger submitted to the Korean Ministry of Trade, Industry and Energy.

Source: UNCTAD, based on media and company reports.

At least five deals were formally prohibited by the host country for national security reasons, up from three in 2020, confirming that national security concerns underpin increased screening of foreign investment. Such deals concerned the defence sector, involving the manufacturing of aircraft parts and auxiliary equipment (United States); food trading, raising the issue of food sovereignty (France); life insurance, mortgage financing and investment services, raising concerns related to access to sensitive data of host-country citizens (United States); the maritime industry, aimed at avoiding foreign influence in maritime engine making (Norway); and the mining sector, highlighting risks of increased foreign influence in the Arctic (Canada).

At least three deals were discontinued because of concerns from competition authorities in the industries, including denial of banking business by a foreign entity (Papua New Guinea), and withdrawal of plans to acquire businesses in the insurance industry (United States). Another four deals were withdrawn for various regulatory reasons, and one planned acquisition was terminated because of delays in receiving approval from the host country (China).

It should also be noted that the actual number and value of deals screened out by governments worldwide for national security reasons, though not available, is likely to be significantly higher, particularly in light of the extended adoption of FDI screening mechanisms discussed in the previous section. The adoption or announcement of tighter screening of M&A deals is also likely to have had a chilling effect on the number of deals in a number of strategic sectors.[4]

B. INTERNATIONAL INVESTMENT POLICIES

1. Trends in IIAs: new treaties and other policy developments

Several notable developments in 2021 and 2022 accelerated the trend towards reform of the international investment agreement (IIA) regime. These include the conclusion of new-generation megaregional economic agreements, the termination of bilateral investment treaties (BITs) and multilateral discussions on the reform of investor–State dispute settlement (ISDS) mechanisms. At the same time, greater policy attention to investment facilitation, climate change and human rights is set to recalibrate international investment governance.

a. Developments in the conclusion and termination of IIAs

In 2021, countries concluded 13 IIAs. As in 2020, the number of effective treaty terminations exceeded that of new IIAs, with 86 terminations.

In 2021, countries concluded at least 13 new IIAs: 6 BITs and 7 treaties with investment provisions (TIPs). This brought the size of the IIA universe to 3,288 (2,861 BITs and 427 TIPs).[5] In addition, at least 13 IIAs entered into force in 2021, bringing the total of IIAs in force to at least 2,558 by the end of the year (figure II.4).

The number of terminations in 2021 exceeded the number of newly concluded IIAs: At least 86 IIA terminations entered into effect ("effective terminations"), of which 75 were terminations by mutual consent, 4 were unilateral terminations, 4 were replacements (through the entry into force of a newer treaty), and 3 expired. Of the 75 terminations by mutual consent, 74 were based on the agreement to terminate intra-EU BITs; the remaining termination concerned the BIT between Malta and the United Kingdom. By the end of the year, the total number of effective terminations reached at least 483, with 69 per cent of them terminated in the last decade (figure II.5).

Figure II.4. Number of IIAs signed, by decade, 1961–2021

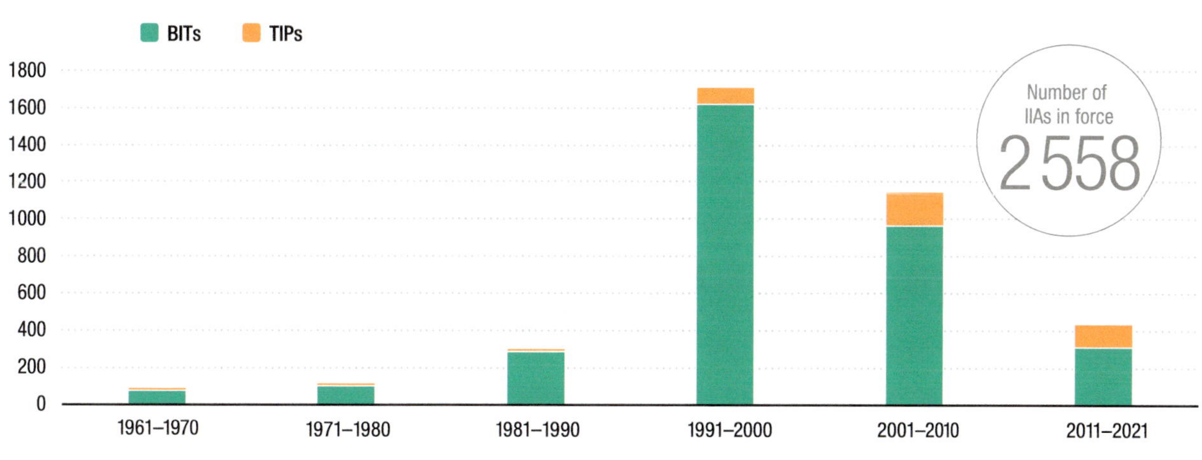

Source: UNCTAD, IIA Navigator.

Figure II.5. **Number of terminated IIAs, by decade, 1991–2021**

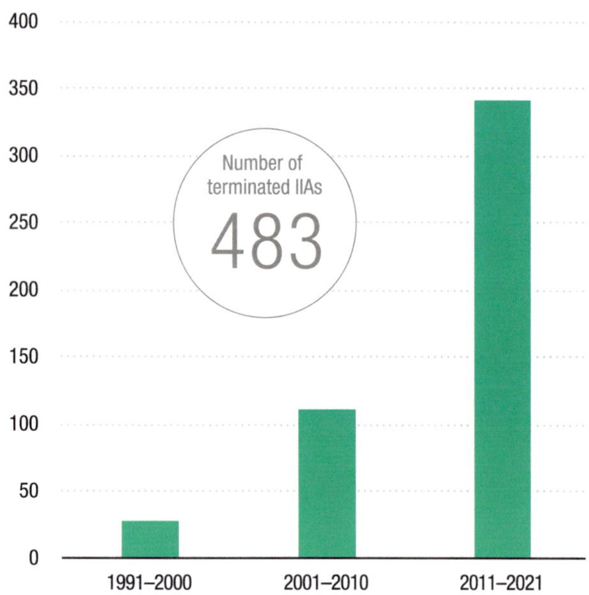

Source: UNCTAD, IIA Navigator.

The TIPs concluded in 2021 can be grouped into two categories:

1. Agreements with obligations commonly found in BITs, such as substantive standards of investment protection:

- Australia–United Kingdom FTA
- Israel–Republic of Korea FTA

2. Agreements with limited investment provisions (e.g. market access, national treatment (NT) and most-favoured-nation treatment (MFN) with respect to commercial presence, an institutional framework to promote and cooperate on investment) but do not contain substantive investment protection provisions:

- Cambodia–Republic of Korea FTA
- Cameroon–United Kingdom Economic Partnership Agreement
- Chile–Paraguay FTA
- Ghana–United Kingdom Interim Trade Partnership Agreement
- India–Mauritius Comprehensive Economic Cooperation and Partnership Agreement

The four substantive IIAs concluded in 2021 for which texts are available feature many reformed provisions aimed at preserving regulatory space while granting investor protection.[6] All four clarify the fair and equitable treatment (FET) standard and the scope of indirect expropriation. Three IIAs contain general exceptions for the protection of human, animal or plant life or health (Australia–United Kingdom FTA, Georgia–Japan BIT, Israel–Republic of Korea FTA). All four include clauses on "not lowering of standards" (e.g. for laws or measures related to labour and the environment) and two of them also incorporate provisions on the promotion of corporate social responsibility standards (Australia–United Kingdom FTA, Colombia–Spain BIT). Three IIAs provide for ISDS subject to certain limitations, e.g. in the form of limited periods in which to submit claims (Colombia–Spain BIT, Georgia–Japan BIT, Israel–Republic of Korea FTA); one IIA omits ISDS altogether (Australia–United Kingdom FTA). One, the Australia–United Kingdom FTA, contains a dedicated chapter on gender equality and women's economic empowerment in the context of trade and investment.

b. Other developments relating to investment rulemaking

Other notable developments continued the trends towards reform of the international investment regime. This includes greater attention to investment facilitation, climate change, anti-corruption, due diligence and human rights.

African Continental Free Trade Area negotiations on the Investment Protocol: The negotiations on investment of the African Continental Free Trade Area (AfCFTA) commenced in March 2021, and subsequent rounds of discussions started in March 2022. The AfCFTA Protocol on Investment will aim at promoting, facilitating and protecting intra-African investment that fosters sustainable development while safeguarding the State Parties' right to regulate. The Negotiating Principles for the Protocol recognize UNCTAD's work on IIA reform and refer to its Investment Policy Framework for Sustainable

Development (UNCTAD, 2015) and its IIA Reform Accelerator (UNCTAD, 2020b). UNCTAD continues to provide technical support to the African Union and the AfCFTA Secretariat in the process leading to the conclusion of the Protocol. The Investment Protocol is expected to be finalized and adopted in September 2022.

EU agreement for the termination of intra-EU BITs: The termination agreement entered into force for 19 EU member States and effectively terminated over 110 intra-EU BITs as of March 2022.[7] The termination agreement was signed by 23 EU member States on 5 May 2020 and came into effect on 29 August 2020, following receipt by the Depository of the second instrument of ratification.

EU corporate sustainability due diligence directive: On 23 February 2022, the European Commission adopted a proposal for a directive on corporate sustainability due diligence, which has been submitted to the European Parliament and the Council for approval.[8] The proposed directive aims to foster sustainable and responsible corporate behaviour and to anchor human rights and environmental considerations in companies' operations and corporate governance. Under the new due diligence rules, certain groups of EU and non-EU companies will need to address adverse impacts of their activities, including in their value chains inside and outside the EU. The proposal builds on concepts set out in the Organisation for Economic Co-operation and Development (OECD) Guidelines for Multinational Enterprises and the United Nations Guiding Principles on Business and Human Rights. Encouraging corporate social responsibility and responsible business practices also plays a role in EU investment policymaking and related negotiation processes, including the modernization of the Energy Charter Treaty (ECT).

International Centre for Settlement of Investment Disputes approves amended rules: On 21 March 2022, ICSID member States approved the amended rules of the International Centre for Settlement of Investment Disputes (ICSID). The amendments reflect extensive dialogue with ICSID's membership and the public. ICSID launched the amendment process in 2016 and published proposals in a series of six working papers. The updated rules incorporate greater transparency in the conduct and outcome of proceedings, new disclosure requirements for third-party funding, expedited arbitration rules for parties wishing to shorten further the procedural calendar, and broadened access to ICSID's procedural rules and administrative services.[9] The updated rules will come into effect on 1 July 2022.

Investment Facilitation for Development negotiations at the World Trade Organization: Over 110 members of the World Trade Organization (WTO) are participating in the Joint Initiative on Investment Facilitation for Development. On 25 September 2020, participants in the structured discussions on investment facilitation for development began formal negotiations. On 10 December 2021, members drafted the Joint Statement on Investment Facilitation for Development, which sets the goal to finalize an agreement by the end of 2022.[10] In February 2022, participants agreed to establish a Working Group of international organizations that work on investment facilitation (including UNCTAD) to develop a Self-Assessment Guide to help developing and least developed countries assess their needs in terms of implementing the future agreement. A negotiating meeting on 15–16 March 2022 focused on definitions of "authorization", the provisions on MFN treatment/non-discrimination, responsible business conduct, and special and differential treatment, among other topics.

Modernization of the ECT: Six rounds of negotiations on the modernization of the ECT were held in 2021. The Modernization Group held its 11th round of negotiations on 1–4 March 2022, making progress on investment protection (e.g. denial of benefits, MFN clause, right to regulate), dispute settlement (e.g. frivolous claims, third-party funding, valuation of damages), sustainable development and corporate social responsibility.

The negotiations also addressed the principle of flexibility in the definition of "economic activity in the energy sector". Two more rounds of negotiations are scheduled in 2022, with the objective of reaching an agreement in principle.

OECD work programme on the future of investment treaties: In March 2021, the OECD launched a two-year work programme on the future of investment treaties, to address issues relating to climate change, the pandemic and digital transformation, with concerns about the climate crisis at its core. The work programme has discussions in two tracks: Track 1 addresses challenges facing future IIAs and changes to the current treaty regime, and Track 2 discusses the possible modernization of provisions found in old-generation IIAs (Gaukrodger, 2021).

UNCITRAL Working Group III on investor–State dispute settlement reform: In February 2021, Working Group III of the United Nations Commission on International Trade Law (UNCITRAL) held its 40th session in Vienna, Austria and then resumed virtually on 4–5 May 2021. Discussions revolved around establishing a workplan for the next five to six years. The Working Group held its 41st session in Vienna on 15–19 November 2021. In this session, the Working Group deliberated on the draft code of conduct for adjudicators in international investment disputes and the working agenda on the draft provisions in 2022. The 42nd session took place on 14–18 February 2022 in New York. Topics discussed at this session included the multilateral advisory centre, the standing multilateral mechanism (selection and appointment of ISDS tribunal members and related matters) and the draft code of conduct for adjudicators in international investment disputes (UNCITRAL, 2022).

UNCTAD Annual IIA Conference: On 19 October 2021, UNCTAD held its annual IIA Conference as part of the World Investment Forum 2021, gathering high-level representatives from government, the private sector, civil society and academia. Experts took stock of IIA and ISDS reform efforts and agreed on the need to accelerate IIA reform in the public interest. The IIA Conference 2021 provided a platform to engage in IIA reform and made concrete steps toward a more coherent and consolidated process of modernizing old-generation IIAs.

United Nations Working Group on Business and Human Rights: In its 2021 report to the United Nations General Assembly (United Nations, 2021), the United Nations Working Group on Business and Human Rights highlighted the imbalances of the IIA regime. The report urges States to ensure that all existing and future IIAs are compatible with their international human rights obligations. Building on recommendations made by UNCTAD and other organizations, the Working Group outlines five reform pathways for States to harness the potential of IIAs in encouraging responsible business conduct on the part of investors, in line with the United Nations Guiding Principles on Business and Human Rights. In its 10th Annual Forum on Business and Human Rights, the United Nations Working Group included a session dedicated to the reform of the IIA regime.[11] The session presented the recommendations made in the 2021 report and discussed the role of UNCTAD and other international and regional organizations in supporting States in carrying out structural and systemic reform of the international investment regime.

United Nations Office on Drugs and Crime–UNCTAD work on Corruption and International Investments: In December 2019, the Conference of the States Parties to the United Nations Convention against Corruption adopted Resolution 8/9, in which it noted "the positive role of international investments and the importance of minimizing opportunities for corruption and transfer of proceeds of crime". In this context, the United Nations Office on Drugs and Crime (UNODC) partnered with UNCTAD in May 2021 to organize an Expert Group Meeting on Corruption and International Investments. Participants in the meeting called for strong and coherent anti-corruption provisions in IIAs and a better balance between the interests of investors and host States, to enable host States to regulate for the public interest, including preventing and fighting corruption. In December 2021, UNODC and UNCTAD organized an expert-level event during the Conference of the States Parties to the United Nations Convention against Corruption, which took place in Sharm el-Sheikh, Egypt. Participants reported to the Conference on the activities and progress made by the Expert Group Meeting on Corruption and International Investment.

2. Key investment-related issues in megaregional agreements

Megaregional agreements have been proliferating, covering a broad range of economic issues beyond investment disciplines. These agreements' comprehensive nature and geostrategic relevance are increasingly shaping international investment rulemaking and policy.

Megaregional agreements are broad economic agreements among a group of countries that together carry significant economic weight and in which investment is only one of several subjects addressed. Among the other subjects are, for instance, trade in goods and rules of origin, trade in services, competition, e-commerce, intellectual property (IP), public procurement, regulation of State-owned enterprises (SOEs) and small and medium-sized enterprises (SMEs). The multitude of economic issues covered in megaregional agreements may have a more substantial positive impact on FDI flows and greater geopolitical relevance than BITs (table II.2). Most megaregional agreements liberalize market access and, more generally, foster regional integration among the contracting parties, stimulating additional investment flows.

Table II.2. Selected recent megaregional agreements at a glance

Megaregional IIA	Selected provisions with impact on investment (other than the investment chapter)
AfCFTA	• Protocols on competition, IP rights and investment are under negotiation • ROOs to be harmonized across the continent • Pan-African Payments and Settlements System operational • Will cater to African SMEs • Liberalization of services sector, which accounts for 75 per cent of greenfield investment in Africa, with specific commitments to be concluded in 2022 • Trade and investment facilitation measures to be concluded in 2022
CPTPP	• Regulatory coherence and business facilitation (e.g. implementation mechanisms, simplified customs procedures) • E-commerce (e.g. validity of e-signatures, prohibition of data localization and requirements to disclose software source codes, customs exemptions for digital products, online consumer protection) • SMEs (e.g. special committee, dialogue mechanism, transparency and information-sharing) • IP rights (e.g. goes beyond TRIPS, regulates criminal procedures and remedies, regulates geographical indications) • SOEs (progressive provisions aimed at reducing unfair competition) • Innovative regulation of the ROOs (designed specifically for each tariff line to allow for less costly and more integrated regional value chains) • Liberalization of services (uses negative list with two types of measures) • Public procurement (e.g. increased transparency, clear criteria for selection procedures, reduced barriers to foreign bidders) • Environmental and labour standards (comprehensive e.g. to adopt and maintain laws and practice governing "acceptable conditions of work"; obligation to combat the illegal take of, and trade in, wild flora and fauna)
EU–UK TCA	• Investment liberalization (e.g. similar to the WTO, based on national treatment and MFN; various sectoral carve-outs; no automatic access to the EU single market; no country-of-origin principles and passporting; removal of the economic-needs test and quantitative restrictions; four modes of market access) • State aid, labour and environmental standards (e.g. streamlined procedure for countermeasures, progressive provisions on the environment and labour) • Competition (e.g. requirement of similar standards in labour, environment, tax and State aid) • Public procurement (e.g. accessibility to public procurement markets, including for smaller contracts) • Digital trade (e.g. prohibition of data localization; high consumer protection)

/...

Table II.2.	Selected recent megaregional agreements at a glance (Concluded)
Megaregional IIA	**Selected provisions with impact on investment (other than the investment chapter)**
RCEP	• ROOs harmonized across the member States (threshold for regional value content is approximately 40 per cent; gradual move towards self-certification) • Liberalization of services (combined positive and negative lists; commitments in financial, telecommunication and professional services) • IP rights (comprehensive coverage, e.g. enforcement against pirate and counterfeit goods by allowing rights holders to apply for suspension of the release of suspicious goods) • E-commerce (e.g. validity of e-signatures, removal of customs duties for electronic transmissions, limited prohibition of data localization) • Competition, SMEs and public procurement (e.g. transparency in procurement regulations and tenders)
USMCA	• ROOs commitments with a threshold for regional value content at 60 per cent as a general rule and 75 per cent in the automotive industry and other thresholds for specific product lines • Provisions on labour costs ("high-wage factory" requirement for tariff-free qualification) • Liberalization of services (e.g. expanded market access in agriculture and financial services) • Increase in de minimis value for tariff-free imports • Streamlined customs procedures • E-commerce provisions (e.g. prohibits data localization and requirements to disclose software source codes, offers customs exemptions for digital products, provides protection from lawsuits related to content posted on digital platforms) • IP rights (strong and extensive protections) • Labour (complex provisions, e.g. Rapid Response Labour Mechanism to address complaints related to violation of labour rights) • Special provisions on SMEs • Currency regulation (e.g. reaffirms market-determined exchange rates and prohibits currency manipulation)

Source: UNCTAD.
Note: IP = intellectual property, MFN = most-favoured nation, ROOs = rules of origin, SMEs = small and medium-size enterprises, TRIPS = Trade-Related Aspects of Intellectual Property Rights, WTO = World Trade Organization.

The following sections summarize selected key non-investment provisions found in five recently concluded megaregional agreements that indirectly affect investment flows and policy. The five agreements are the following:

- African Continental Free Trade Agreement (AfCFTA), in force since 30 May 2019
- Comprehensive and Progressive Agreement for Trans-Pacific Partnership (CPTPP), in force since 30 December 2018
- EU–United Kingdom Trade and Cooperation Agreement (EU–UK TCA), in force since 1 May 2021
- Regional Comprehensive Economic Partnership Agreement (RCEP), in force since 1 January 2022
- United States–Mexico–Canada Agreement (USMCA), in force since 1 July 2020

The investment chapters of these megaregional agreements were discussed in the *World Investment Report 2021*.

Liberalization of trade in services

Services liberalization may affect investment inflows. It may induce investors in the services sector to establish their presence in host countries and by lowering or removing regulatory barriers may provide new opportunities for firms to offer services. Compared with regulations in the General Agreement on Trade in Services (GATS), the services regulations in the new megaregional agreements provide a broader set of disciplines (e.g. investment liberalization, domestic regulation, competition policy). They generally provide additional levels of market access and NT commitments, either covering additional sectors or deepening GATS obligations in this area.

The megaregional agreements approach the regulation of services in various ways, and the level of access depends on how the service is supplied. For instance, the CPTPP is based entirely on a negative list, such that all services, except those specifically excluded, are liberalized. The negative list contains two types of exclusions (non-conforming measures): (i) a standstill and ratchet mechanism, which covers areas that cannot become more restrictive in the future and, once liberalized, cannot be reversed; and (ii) reservations, under which member States have complete discretion to regulate and are free to change domestic liberalization measures. The EU–UK TCA contains four modes of service provision with concomitant regulations. In Mode 1, the service crosses the border (e.g. Internet); in Mode 2, a consumer uses the service while abroad (e.g. a tourist purchasing service in another country); in Mode 3, a company establishes a branch to supply services in another country; and Mode 4 refers to the mobility of professionals for business purposes. The RCEP uses both positive and negative lists, depending on the Contracting Party. The AfCFTA uses a positive list, with schedules that are to be completed in 2022.

Regarding the sectors covered, the services liberalization commitments commonly found relate to telecommunications (RCEP, USMCA), financial services (CPTPP, EU–UK TCA, RCEP, USMCA), energy (EU–UK TCA) and professional services (CPTPP, EU–UK TCA, RCEP). Modern megaregional agreements often include specific regulations on digital services as well.

Supply chains and the rules of origin

The megaregional agreements under review aim at making global and regional supply chains more effective by simplifying and harmonizing the rules of origin (ROOs). The ROOs in these agreements regulate the regional value content required for goods to qualify for tariff-free (or lower-tariff) treatment, and they facilitate the administrative procedures connected with cross-border trade. In this way, the agreements have an important effect on investment flows between the parties.

For example, the RCEP harmonizes ROOs across its 16 member States, which are at different levels of economic development. They include import- and export-oriented economies, services- and goods-based economies, and landlocked and island States, as well as countries with large differences in population. The RCEP ROOs set a relatively low threshold for regional value content (40 per cent), which, in combination with the move towards self-certification of origin, removal of non-tariff barriers and other trade facilitation measures, is likely to boost the integration of global supply chains across the region. This may contribute to encouraging foreign investment inflows. The USMCA ROOs, by contrast, include a relatively high threshold for regional value content (60 per cent as a general rule and 75 per cent for the automotive industry), incentivizing companies to locate their production facilities in the region. This is complemented by a provision requiring that 40–45 per cent of the parts of any tariff-free vehicle must come from a "high-wage factory"' (i.e. pay a minimum of $16 per hour on average). The CPTPP uses an innovative approach to ROOs, which are designed specifically for each tariff line. This makes trade easier, as once the ROOs are satisfied for one product tariff line, there is no need for further modifications. For instance, the CPTPP regulates smartphone supply chains that cover components and materials sourced in many countries.

Competition

Competition policies are also likely to have an impact on foreign investment. The new megaregional agreements commonly include chapters that regulate competition. These provisions generally require parties to adopt and maintain laws and procedures against anti-competitive activities, and enforce those laws accordingly, generally through a competition authority (e.g. RCEP Chapter 13, CPTPP Chapter 16, USMCA Chapter 21). Moreover, other provisions affect competition; for instance, the requirement for similar standards in labour, environment, tax and State aid. For the AfCFTA, negotiations on the Competition Protocol are under way and will continue into 2022.

Regulating competition will be particularly important for African SMEs (90 per cent of African businesses). UNCTAD has been highlighting the linkage between investment, competition and industrial policies in Africa (UNCTAD, 2021a). Competition policies protect market participants, including SMEs, from monopolies and other anti-competitive practices and by facilitating access to credit they increase productivity, among other benefits.

E-commerce and the digital economy

The new agreements reflect the continuing turn towards a digital economy. Although they regulate e-commerce through specially dedicated chapters, their provisions on services liberalization and investment are equally relevant for a digital economy. Their provisions on e-commerce regulate various aspects of trade in data, such as prohibition of data localization measures, commitments to allow cross-border data transfers, protection of online consumers, regulations on customs duties, and fees and other charges on electronic transmissions and digital products (e.g. CPTPP Chapter 14, USMCA Chapter 19, EU–UK TCA Part Two Title III). In addition, some of these agreements protect businesses by prohibiting the disclosure of software source code as a condition for the import, sale, or use of the software (e.g. CPTPP, USMCA). Some agreements, while regularizing cross-border transfer of data, do not include a general prohibition of data localization requirements (e.g. RCEP). Finally, some protect online platforms from lawsuits related to content posted on the online platforms (e.g. USMCA).

IP rights

The new megaregional agreements strengthen the protection of IP rights. Strong IP rights may influence investment decisions, especially for knowledge-based FDI and projects with high research and development components. By and large, the IP commitments in these agreements go beyond the WTO's Agreement on Trade-Related Aspects of Intellectual Property Rights. The new megaregional agreements, for example, extend the time frame of copyright protection (e.g. USMCA), provide for procedures and remedies for enforcement of IP rights against pirate and counterfeit goods (e.g. RCEP, CPTPP, USMCA), and contain extensive protections for a wide variety of IP rights including comprehensive coverage of geographical indications (e.g. CPTPP).

Public procurement

Megaregional agreements may affect investment by opening government procurement markets to economic actors from other contracting parties. Their commitments generally require fair and transparent selection procedures, such as making laws and regulations on procurement publicly available (e.g. RCEP, CPTPP, USMCA), and may cover small government contracts as well (e.g. EU–UK TCA). Transparent and non-discriminatory government procurement policies in megaregional agreements can also lead to greater competition between domestic and foreign investors for government procurement contracts and fewer market distortions leading to economic inefficiencies, and more generally to a more favourable, transparent and attractive investment environment for foreign investors.

Small and medium-size enterprises

The new agreements will also affect the business environment and investment in the contracting parties, as they include specific chapters on SMEs. These provisions aim to make it possible for SMEs to take full advantage of the opportunities that the agreements create. Generally, they do so by fostering cooperation and collaboration to promote SMEs, through information-sharing tools, rules on transparency that reduce administrative costs, and exchange of best practices related to such concerns as access to capital and credit.

For instance, the USMCA and the CPTPP include chapters on SMEs that create SME committees and dialogue mechanisms (USMCA Chapter 25, CPTPP Chapter 24).

The RCEP contains provisions on information-sharing and creates contact points to facilitate cooperation and information-sharing related to the Agreement (RCEP Chapter 14). In addition, various provisions on regulatory coherence, trade facilitation, public procurement and business facilitation further assist SMEs in taking full advantage of the opportunities that these agreements create and making supply chains less costly.

State-owned enterprises

The new megaregional agreements also regulate SOEs to address the risks of unfair trade practices, unfair competition and obstacles to trade. The commitments require SOEs to act according to commercial considerations. Complex regulations of SOEs can be found in the USMCA and the CPTPP; they include traditional non-discrimination and commercial considerations disciplines from the General Agreement on Tariffs and Trade but also a legal framework on Non-Commercial Assistance (USMCA Chapter 22; CPTPP Chapter 17). The framework addresses effects that are adverse to the interest of other State parties because of the advantages that SOEs may gain through their government relationships.

3. Trends in ISDS: new cases and outcomes

The total ISDS case count had reached 1,190 by the end of 2021, with at least 68 new arbitrations initiated in 2021. Two IIAs signed in the 1990s – the ECT and NAFTA – continued to be the instruments invoked most frequently.

a. New cases initiated in 2021

In 2021, at least 68 new treaty-based ISDS cases were initiated. Five countries faced their first known ISDS claims.

In 2021, investors initiated 68 publicly known ISDS cases under IIAs (figure II.6). As of 1 January 2022, the total number of publicly known ISDS claims had reached 1,190. As some arbitrations can be kept confidential, the actual number of disputes filed in 2021 and in previous years is likely higher. To date, 130 countries and one economic grouping are known to have been respondents to one or more ISDS claims. In 2022, the war in Ukraine brought into the spotlight past and potential future ISDS claims relating to armed conflict (box II.1).

Figure II.6. Trends in known treaty-based ISDS cases, 1987–2021

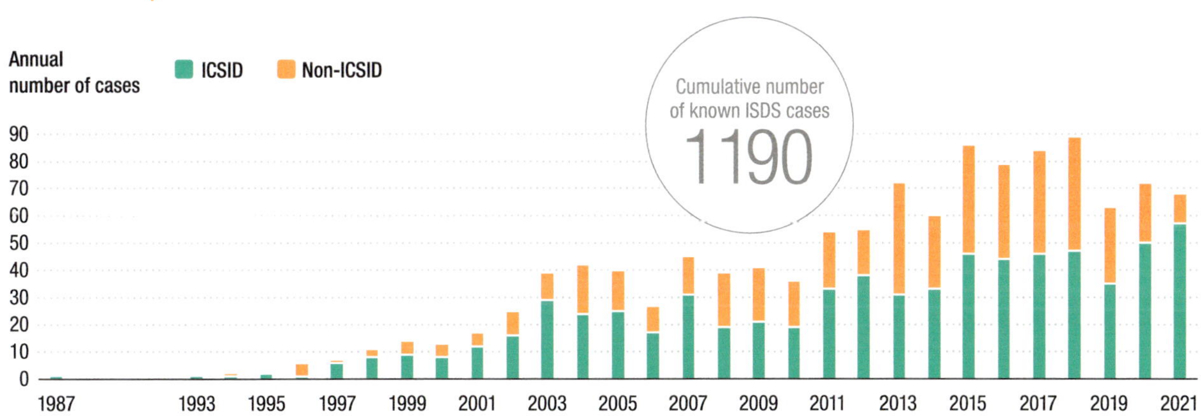

Source: UNCTAD, ISDS Navigator.
Note: Information has been compiled from public sources, including specialized reporting services. UNCTAD's statistics do not cover investor–State cases that are based exclusively on investment contracts (State contracts) or national investment laws, or cases in which a party has signalled its intention to submit a claim to ISDS but has not commenced the arbitration. Annual and cumulative case numbers are continually adjusted as a result of verification processes and may not match exactly case numbers reported in previous years.

Box II.1. IIA-based ISDS cases related to war and armed conflict: facts and examples

ISDS cases can arise out of events related to war and armed conflict. In the past, at least 30 ISDS cases brought against States arose out of destruction or harm caused to investments in the context of war, armed conflict, military operations and civil unrest. This includes the first known ISDS case based on an IIA brought in 1987: *AAPL v. Sri Lanka*, which arose out of the alleged destruction of the claimant's investment during a military operation conducted by Sri Lankan security forces.

International courts and tribunals (e.g. the International Court of Justice and the International Criminal Court) may weigh in on specific elements of armed conflicts. Disputes may also occur in the trade context and at the WTO through the State–State dispute mechanism.

The stock of IIAs in force commonly protects covered investments in cases of direct and indirect expropriation, impairment and losses owing to war or armed conflict. They also include other substantive protection standards such as full protection and security, and FET. While most of these treaties grant foreign investors direct access to international arbitration in case of treaty violations and the possibility of treaty shopping, some of them include exceptions that could allow countries to avoid facing ISDS claims in emergency situations. Generally, ISDS tribunals have not pronounced on the legality of the use of force; instead, they have limited their assessments to the question of State responsibility for breaches of IIAs. The underlying events giving rise to ISDS claims related to armed conflicts are multifaceted and multi-layered.

Out of the 30 ISDS cases identified in this context, the Russian Federation and Libya were the most frequent respondents, with 10 cases each. The cases against the Russian Federation related to the events in Crimea in 2014, including nationalizations in different economic sectors. Ukrainian companies and businesspeople invoked the Russian Federation–Ukraine BIT (1998), alleging expropriation of assets by the Russian Federation (e.g. *Ukrenergo v. Russia; Oschadbank v. Russia; Naftogaz and others v. Russia*). The cases against Libya mostly related to the alleged failure to protect foreign investments during times of war and civil unrest in the country (e.g. *Trasta v. Libya; Cengiz v. Libya*). In addition, several ISDS cases have related to economic sanctions and the suspension of diplomatic relations (e.g. *Qatar Pharma and Al Sulaiti v. Saudi Arabia; beIN v. Saudi Arabia*).

Source: UNCTAD.
Note: The ISDS cases related to war and armed conflict were identified on the basis of UNCTAD's ISDS Navigator and information from other public sources, including notices of arbitration, arbitral decisions and specialized reporting services.

(i) Respondent States

The new ISDS cases in 2021 were initiated against 42 countries. Peru was the most frequent respondent, with six known cases, followed by Egypt and Ukraine with four known cases each. Five countries – Cambodia, the Republic of Congo, Finland, Malta and the Netherlands – faced their first known ISDS claims. As in previous years, the majority of new cases (about 65 per cent) were brought against developing countries.

(ii) Claimant home States

Developed-country claimants brought most – about 75 per cent – of the 68 known cases in 2021. The highest numbers of cases were brought by claimants from the United States (10 cases), France (5 cases), the Netherlands (5 cases) and the United Kingdom (5 cases).

(iii) Applicable investment treaties

About 75 per cent of investment arbitrations in 2021 were brought under BITs and TIPs signed in the 1990s or earlier. The ECT (1994) was the IIA invoked most frequently in 2021, with seven cases, followed by the North American Free Trade Agreement (NAFTA) (1992) in combination with the USMCA (2018), with four cases.[12] Overall (1987–2021), about 20 per cent of the 1,190 known ISDS cases have invoked the ECT (145 cases), NAFTA (76 cases) or the OIC Investment Agreement (16 cases).

b. ISDS outcomes

(i) Decisions and outcomes in 2021

In 2021, ISDS tribunals rendered at least 54 substantive decisions in investor–State disputes, 31 of which were in the public domain at the time of writing: 11 of the public decisions principally addressed jurisdictional issues (including preliminary objections), with 4 upholding the tribunal's jurisdiction and 7 declining jurisdiction. The remaining 20 public decisions were rendered on the merits, with 12 holding the State liable for IIA breaches and 8 dismissing all investor claims.

In addition, six publicly known decisions were rendered in annulment proceedings at the ICSID. Ad hoc committees of the ICSID rejected the applications for annulment in five cases; in one case, the award at issue was partially annulled.

Figure II.7. Results of concluded cases, 1987–2021 (Per cent)

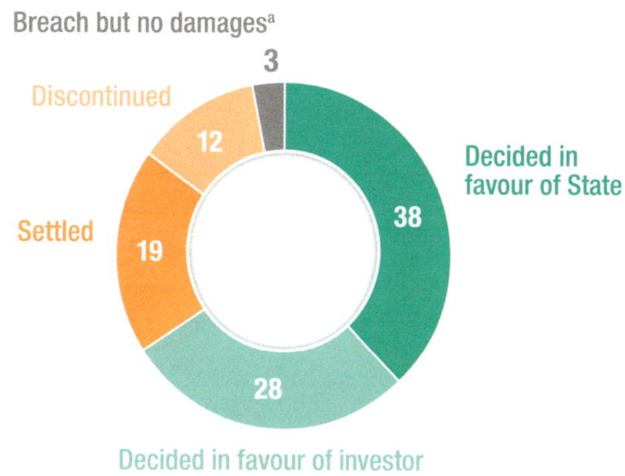

Source: UNCTAD, ISDS Navigator.
[a] Decided in favour of neither party (liability found but no damages awarded).

(ii) Overall outcomes

By the end of 2021, at least 807 ISDS proceedings had been concluded. The relative share of case outcomes changed only slightly from previous years (figure II.7).

C. KEY TRENDS IN TAXATION OF INVESTMENTS

Foreign investors base their decision to enter a country on many factors, including political stability, economic potential, natural resources, transparency and efficiency of regulatory regimes and the level of infrastructure and skills. The tax regime is also a factor in investment decisions, and although tax incentives are frequently far from being the most important one,[13] they have traditionally been one of the most widespread policy tools to attract and retain foreign investment. The pandemic has accentuated the importance of incentives and tax relief efforts as part of the economic recovery and resilience packages adopted worldwide.[14]

This section highlights key trends in the taxation of investment by analysing the evolution of corporate income taxes (CITs) across the world (section C.1), as well as country efforts to attract investments through tax incentives (section C.2). It highlights how, beyond engaging in tax competition for investment by lowering the statutory CITs, countries rely on a wide array of investment incentives to attract investors to priority sectors or regions. Section C.3 highlights how IIAs impose obligations on States that can create friction with taxation measures and sheds light on the interplay between the international tax system, double-taxation treaties (DTTs) and investment policymaking.

The analysis of the tax incentives for investment is based on review of tax-related investment policy measures adopted worldwide in the last decade. The chapter also examines the treatment of tax incentives in investment laws, which often constitute the legal basis for their adoption, and in industrial policies, which generally provide their broader policy background or motivation.

For the purpose of this analysis, tax incentives are categorized into CIT-based and other incentives. CIT-based incentives include two kinds:

(i) Profit-based incentives, i.e., those determined as a percentage of profit, including tax holidays, reduced CIT or loss carry-forward or carry-back to be written off against profits earned later

(ii) Expenditure-based (or capital investment-based), i.e., those that reduce the after-tax cost of capital investment expenditure, including investment allowance, accelerated depreciation, tax credits and the like[15]

Profit-based incentives provide tax relief based on earnings and not on new investment. In this regard, they are particularly attractive to mobile FDI. Expenditure-based incentives, by contrast, tend to promote reinvestment and therefore further integration into the local economy. In addition, expenditure-based incentives typically target specific types of capital investment or activities that can be associated with countries' sustainable development objectives, such as skills development and low-carbon transition. Other tax incentives include reduced rates on indirect taxes (e.g. value added tax (VAT), duties and tariffs), taxes on labour and land, social security contributions and other payments.

The analysis confirms that countries rely intensively on tax incentives for investment and that profit-based incentives are among the most widespread and frequently adopted ones (see chapter IV).

1. Evolution of corporate income tax rates

CIT rates have gradually declined throughout the world since the 1980s, as countries have increasingly engaged in tax competition to promote investment. Declines have been seen in all geographical regions and in an overwhelming majority of economies, regardless of their size or level of development.

In 1980, the worldwide CIT rate averaged 39.3 per cent, and 80 per cent of the jurisdictions for which data on CIT rates are available imposed rates of 30 per cent or higher. A steady decline was observed globally until 2010, when the number of economies charging CIT at or above 30 per cent decreased to 67 and the worldwide average CIT rate fell to 23.7 per cent. Since then, the average rate has practically stabilized at the current level of 22.7 per cent (figure II.8). In 2021, fewer than one third of all countries applied CIT at 30 per cent or above.[16]

The largest downswing has occurred in developed regions, where the average CIT rate more than halved between 1980 and 2021 (from 41.8 per cent to 19.9 per cent) (see figure II.8). The average rate for developing regions, which contain 75 per cent of the world's economies, has been very close to the worldwide average. Nevertheless, 105 developing economies (some 65 per cent) still have CIT rates above the world average. The average CIT rate for the least developed countries (LDCs) has followed the common downtrend but has been characterized by more volatility and the highest values among the three groups. Although the average rate in LDCs has dropped from 44.3 to 28 per cent over the last four decades, in half of these countries it remains at the level of 30 per cent or above. Whereas in many developing economies reducing the corporate tax became possible because of a shift from direct to indirect taxes in the structure of fiscal income, this was not the case for several LDCs, which rely much less on other sources of fiscal revenue than on CIT.[17]

In 2021, Europe, which has seen the largest reduction in CIT rates of all regions, had the lowest regional average rate, at 19.1 per cent, followed by Asia at 19.3 per cent. In contrast, Africa had the highest regional average statutory rate, at 28.2 per cent. Countries in Latin America and the Caribbean also tend to have higher corporate tax rates than do Asian and European economies, and in Oceania and North America corporate tax rates align closely to the world average at 22.9 and 23.3 per cent, respectively (figure II.9).

Figure II.8. **Statutory CIT rates, regional and world averages, 1980–2021**
(Per cent)

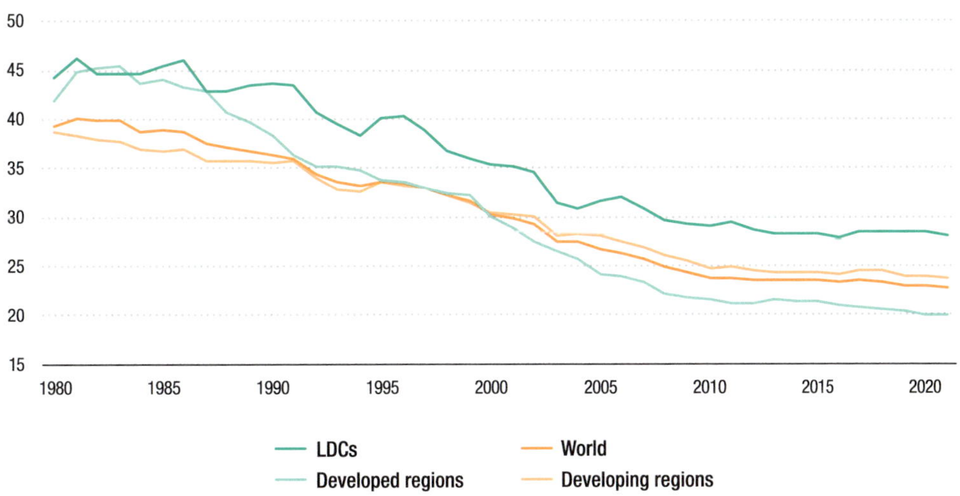

Source: UNCTAD, based on Tax Foundation.

Figure II.9. | **Average statutory CIT rate by region, 1980 and 2021** (Per cent)

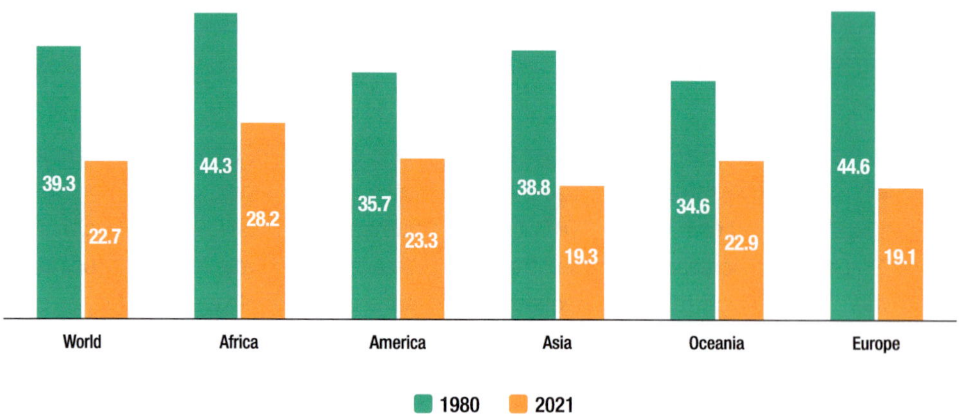

Source: UNCTAD, based on Tax Foundation.

2. Tax incentives for investment

a. Recent trends in investment policy measures related to taxation

National investment policy measures adopted in the past decade reveal widespread use of investment tax incentives across all regions. Profit-based incentives, including tax holidays and reduced CIT, are the most frequently used, with lower emphasis on expenditure-based and other tax and non-tax incentives for investment. Most tax incentives target specific sectors or policy objectives. In Africa and Asia, the majority are not time-bound.

This section highlights key trends in the taxation of investment, on the basis of a review of headline investment policy measures related to taxation adopted worldwide from January 2011 to December 2021, as recorded by UNCTAD in its Investment Policy Monitor.[18] It reveals the continued and extensive use of tax incentive schemes by countries around the world as a tool for promoting and attracting FDI. In that period, of 100 countries adopting measures related to taxation, 90 lowered taxes, introduced new tax incentives or made existing incentives more generous. Of all tax measures adopted, only 17 per cent were specifically directed at foreign investors, while 83 per cent targeted both domestic and foreign investors.

Investment-related tax measures adopted globally during the last decade were overwhelmingly more favourable to investment – 83 per cent introduced new incentives or made existing incentives more generous across the economy or in selected sectors. This trend held for all levels of development (84 per cent in developing countries, 82 per cent in LDCs and 81 per cent in developed countries) and all regions, though it is particularly strong in Asia (figure II.10).

Figure II.10. | **Tax-related investment policy measures more favourable to investment by region** (Per cent)

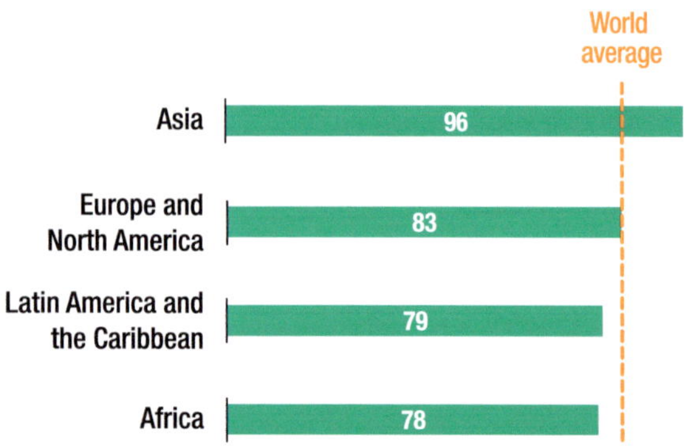

Source: UNCTAD, Investment Policy Monitor.

Among tax measures less favourable to investment, three out of four consisted of an increase in tax rates (e.g. CIT or VAT) or the establishment of new taxes (e.g. mining royalties or other sector-specific taxes). The remainder involved the outright elimination of an incentive scheme. Almost half of all tax measures less favourable to investment were adopted in Africa (19 measures), one third in Latin America and the Caribbean (12 measures), with the balance split between Europe and North America (7 measures in all) and Asia (2 measures).

(i) A strong reliance on profit-based tax incentives for investment

Jointly considered, CIT-based instruments are the most prevalent form of investment incentive introduced over the last decade across the globe (49 per cent of all new incentives) (figure II.11). Their share in all investment incentives is evenly distributed between all regions (51 per cent in Europe and North America and Latin America and the Caribbean, 48 per cent in Africa, 47 per cent in Asia).

Focusing specifically on fiscal incentives, 39 per cent of those adopted globally since 2011 were profit-based. Tax holidays were used by the largest number of countries (55). By themselves, they represent about 20 per cent of all fiscal incentives introduced worldwide (22, 19 and 17 per cent of all incentives adopted respectively by LDCs, developing and developed countries). Tax holidays are also the main profit-based incentive used by African and Asian countries (accounting for 21 and 23 per cent of all tax incentives respectively), while reduced CIT is the most frequent profit-based incentive in Latin American and Caribbean countries (18 per cent) and European and North American countries (20 per cent) (figure II.12).[19]

Tax holidays of up to five years are the incentive most utilized worldwide (figure II.13). This overall trend is largely influenced by African countries, which overwhelmingly favour the use of short-term tax holidays (75 per cent). By contrast, longer tax holidays of up to 10 years are the most common among countries of Latin America and the Caribbean (62 per cent). Tax holidays of over 10 years are much less common in developing countries (20 per cent) and LDCs (11 per cent), than in developed countries (40 per cent).

Figure II.11. **New investment incentives by main type and region, 2011–2021**
(Number of incentives)

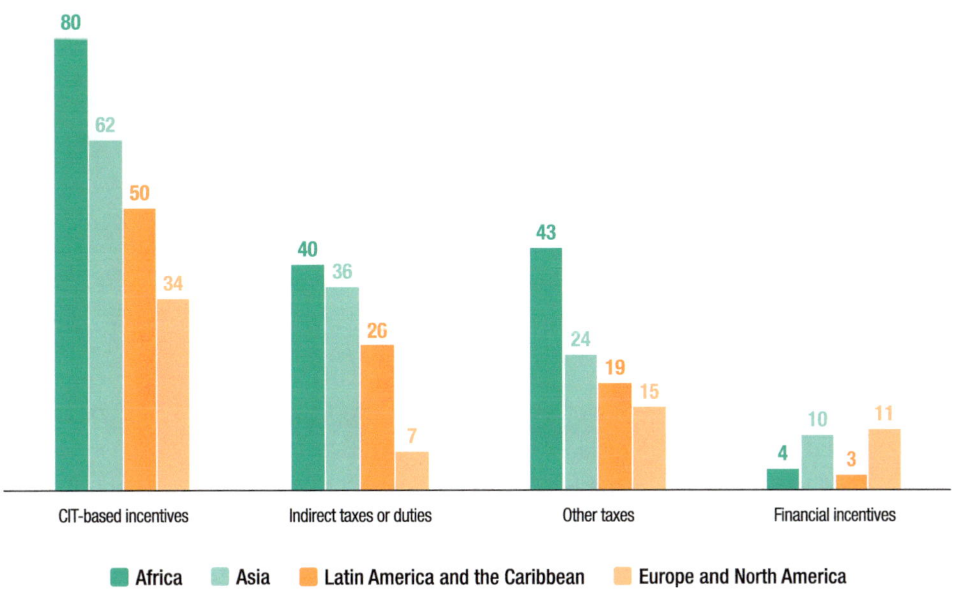

Source: UNCTAD, Investment Policy Monitor.

Figure II.12. New CIT-based investment incentives by type and region, 2011–2021
(Number of incentives)

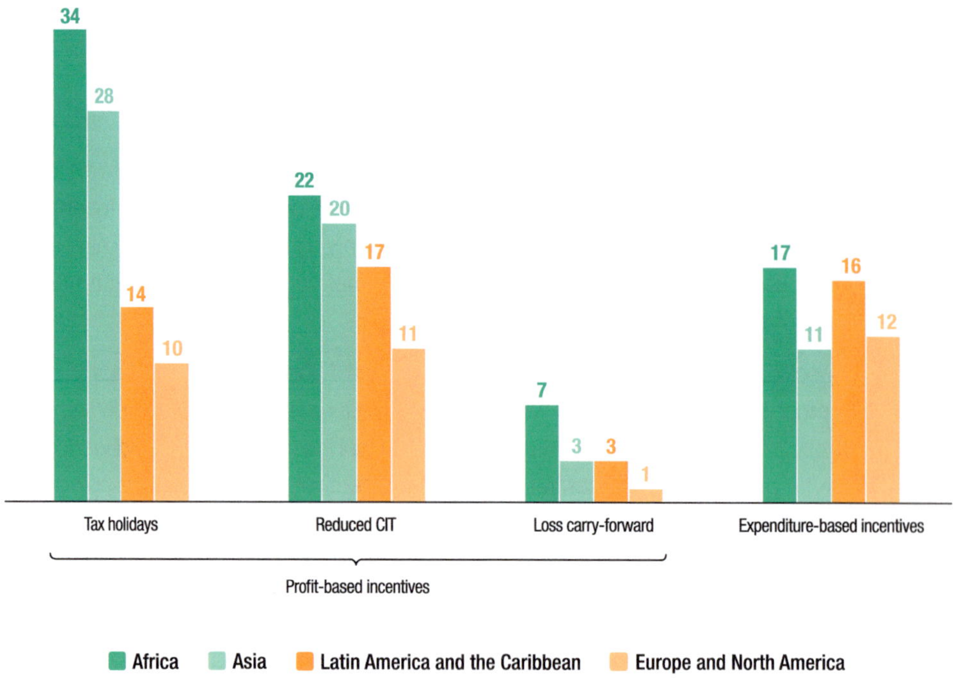

Source: UNCTAD, Investment Policy Monitor.

Figure II.13. Investment-related tax holidays by duration, by region and world
(Per cent)

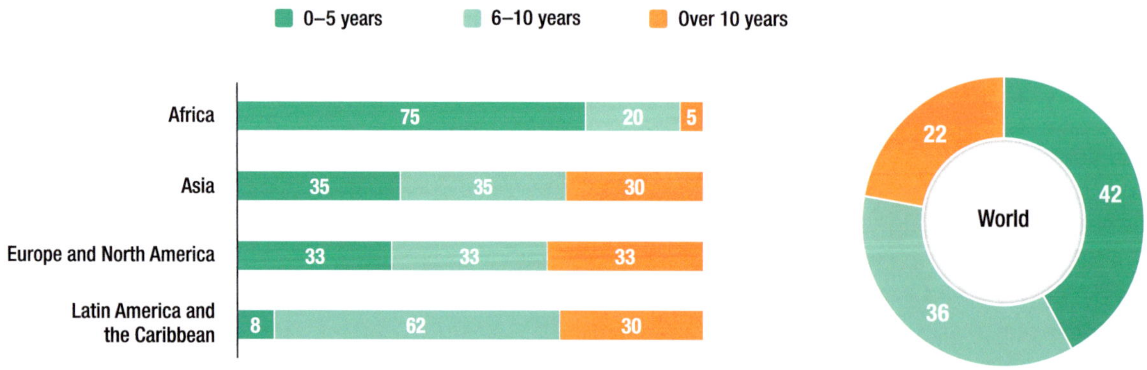

Source: UNCTAD, Investment Policy Monitor.

Reductions of the CIT rate (across all sectors or in selected sectors) accounted for 16 per cent of all tax incentives introduced worldwide since 2011 (42 countries). Their weight in the overall incentives landscape is higher in developed countries (21 per cent) than in developing ones (16 per cent) and in LDCs (14 per cent).

In contrast, the use of loss carry-forward provisions was much less widespread (accounting for 3 per cent of all new tax incentives). Almost 30 per cent of loss carry-forward provisions are included in incentive packages for SEZs.

(ii) With lower emphasis on expenditure-based incentives

Expenditure-based incentives represent 13 per cent of all tax incentives for investment introduced over the last decade. They mainly consist of schemes to provide accelerated depreciation for fixed assets, investment allowances and/or tax credit mechanisms. This type of fiscal incentive was adopted by 39 countries worldwide (14 in Africa, 10 in Latin America and the Caribbean, 8 in Asia and 7 in Europe and North America). Over 55 per cent of expenditure-based instruments were adopted in conjunction with a tax holiday or a CIT reduction.

(iii) And frequently in combination with other tax and non-tax incentives for investment

Both expenditure-based and profit-based incentives for investment are often combined with additional fiscal benefits in the form of tax breaks for indirect taxes and duties, such as VAT or import tariffs. These accounted for about 30 per cent of all tax incentives introduced in Asia and in Latin America and the Caribbean. They were also frequently utilized in Africa (24 per cent of all tax incentives), but far less common in Europe and North America (13 per cent). They can be found in virtually every tax scheme for the establishment of an SEZ across all regions.

Deductions and exemptions for taxes on labour and land and other payments are also used extensively as tax incentives for investment. They accounted for over a quarter of all tax incentives in Africa and in Europe and North America (adopted by 25 and 11 countries respectively). They are also relatively frequently used in Asia and in Latin American and the Caribbean, where they represented 20 per cent of all new tax incentives in the past decade.

In addition, several non-tax instruments to promote investment were introduced jointly with the tax reform initiatives over the last 10 years. They include financial incentives (e.g. grants, loans or State subsidies supporting salaries or production output), relaxed restrictions on foreign ownership and business facilitation measures (such as simplified import and export procedures, single-window mechanisms for permits and licences, and streamlined procedures for employment visas). Business facilitation measures are particularly noteworthy and represent the most significant non-tax promotion instrument adopted in every region of the globe (62 per cent of all non-tax promotion instruments in Africa, 57 per cent in Europe and North America, 56 per cent in Latin America and the Caribbean, 46 per cent In Asia).

(iv) Target sectors change by region and level of development

Globally, 57 per cent of all tax-related investment policy measures more favourable to investment are sector-specific. In particular, developing countries (70 per cent) and LDCs (55 per cent) often implement reduced-CIT incentives that are based exclusively on sectoral requirements. In contrast, almost two thirds of reduced-CIT incentives adopted by countries in Europe and North America are granted fully or partially on the basis of minimum investment thresholds.

Most sector-specific tax incentives for investment introduced in the last decade target manufacturing and services (figure II.14). Tax incentives for the services sector are particularly relevant in Europe and North America (53 per cent of all incentives), and Latin America and the Caribbean (38 per cent) and fairly relevant in Africa (28 per cent). In contrast, Asian countries adopted more tax incentives for investment in the manufacturing industry than for all other sectors combined (52 per cent). Notably, all tax incentives specifically targeting the agricultural and extractive sectors are concentrated in developing countries and LDCs.

Figure II.14. **Sectoral distribution of new tax incentives for investment, by region and world, 2011–2021** (Per cent)

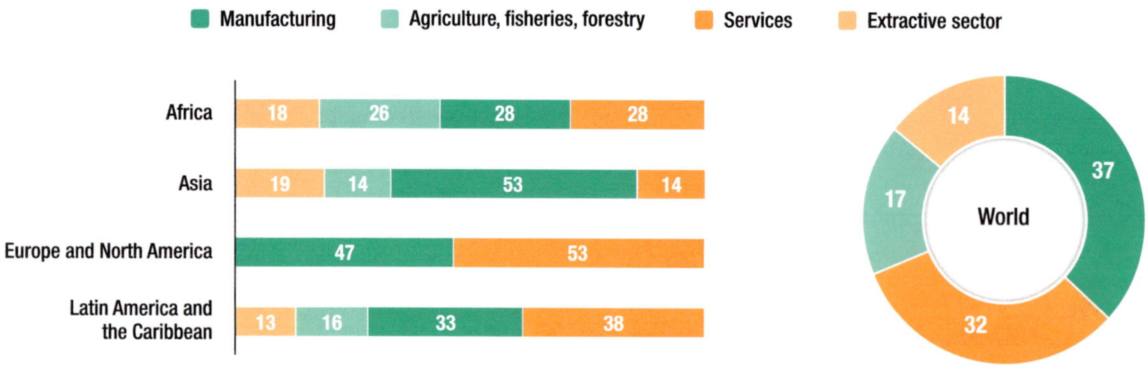

Source: UNCTAD, Investment Policy Monitor.

Tax incentives that specifically target manufacturing industries for the most part have been designed to apply horizontally across all manufacturing activities (79 per cent). The balance reveals a substantial share of incentives aimed at the manufacturing of transport equipment (44 per cent), the production of computer and electronic equipment (33 per cent) and the production of pharmaceuticals (22 per cent). Zooming in on tax incentives that specifically target services, 73 per cent apply to the whole sector. The rest reflect a policy focus on information technology (32 per cent), tourism (27 per cent) and transport (22 per cent).

(v) Specific policy objectives are often associated with new incentives

Over 60 per cent of tax-related measures more favourable to investment introduced over the last decade are associated with the pursuit of one or more policy objectives, such as the development of specific regions within a country (e.g. priority development areas or rural areas), the promotion of exports, the reduction of unemployment or the upgrading of skills, the promotion of research and development and the transfer of innovative technologies (figure II.15). Individually considered, tax incentives that aim at regional promotion are the most recurrent globally (24 per cent), in Africa (33 per cent) and in Asia (27 per cent). Among these incentives, 70 per cent aimed at promoting the development of an SEZ and 30 per cent targeted the development of a specific location within the country. Employment promotion is the most recurrent policy objective associated with incentives in Europe and North America (35 per cent), and in Latin America and the Caribbean (33 per cent).

Figure II.15. **Policy objectives associated with new tax incentives for investment, 2011–2021** (Per cent)

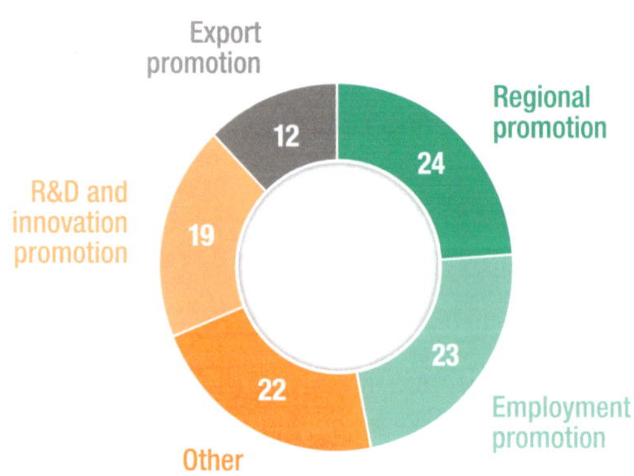

Source: UNCTAD, Investment Policy Monitor.
Note: "Other" includes various policy objectives including the expansion of health-care and education markets, the internationalization of national enterprises and support for the generation of domestic added value.

(vi) Only about half of new incentives worldwide and one third in Africa are time-bound

About half of all tax incentives for investment introduced worldwide over the last decade were time-bound (48 per cent), but the share is lower in

Africa (35 per cent) and in Asia (40 per cent), with important implications in terms of forgone revenue, impact assessment and distortions in the market. Conversely, time-bound incentives are more frequently used in Latin American and Caribbean countries (60 per cent) and particularly significant in European and North American countries (79 per cent).

(vii) Investment laws are among the main instruments to introduce tax incentives for investment

Investment laws and the associated secondary legislation were the primary legal basis for the introduction of tax incentives in LDCs (55 per cent), followed by tax codes or budget laws (16 per cent), ad hoc decrees (10 per cent) and other policy instruments (19 per cent). African countries also enacted tax-related investment incentives mostly through introducing or revising national investment laws (39 per cent) or through enacting budgetary or taxation legislation (33 per cent). The use of ad hoc decrees for adoption of tax-related incentive schemes is minimal in Africa, whereas it is very significant in Latin America and the Caribbean (84 per cent of all measures) and in Europe and North America (71 per cent) and remains substantial in Asia (45 per cent).

b. Tax incentives in investment laws

Over half of the investment laws worldwide contain tax incentives for investment, including three quarters of investment laws in LDCs. In only 30 per cent of the laws, incentives are granted on the basis of measurable criteria, and allocation decisions can involve several stakeholders, including investment promotion agencies.

Of 126 investment laws in UNCTAD's Investment Law Navigator,[20] 68 laws (54 per cent) dedicate a section to the treatment of tax incentives for investment. LDCs lead the trend, with three quarters of their investment laws including provisions on tax incentives, followed by developing and developed countries (46 and 36 per cent of all investment laws, respectively).

On a regional basis, almost two thirds of investment laws in Africa and Asia include a section on tax incentives. In other regions, the treatment of tax incentives in investment laws is less prominent (44 per cent in Latin America and the Caribbean, 42 per cent in Europe and 10 per cent in Oceania).

One third of the investment laws dealing with taxation selectively reproduce or illustrate incentives that are regulated by separate legislation (e.g. tax, customs or sectoral). This is the case, notably, for all developed countries that deal with incentives in their investment law (Bulgaria, Lithuania, Russian Federation, Serbia), but also of some developing countries (the Plurinational State of Bolivia, Guyana, the Republic of Moldova, Qatar, Tajikistan, the United Republic of Tanzania and Turkmenistan). However, the remaining two thirds of investment laws (43 laws) are themselves the legal basis for the introduction of special tax regimes for investment. This includes almost 50 per cent of investment laws in Africa, 38 per cent in Asia, 22 per cent in Latin America and the Caribbean and 10 per cent in Oceania. These are the laws considered in the following analysis.

(i) Profit-based incentives are prevalent also in investment laws

Although there are significant differences in the range of incentives offered, over 80 per cent of all investment laws dealing with tax incentives utilize profit-based incentives to promote investment. In particular, tax holidays are offered in the investment laws of 31 countries (16 countries in Africa, 12 in Asia, 3 in Latin America and the Caribbean), and reduced CIT in those of 15 countries (9 countries in Africa, 4 in Asia, 2 in Latin America and the Caribbean).

Expenditure-based incentives can be found in more than 60 per cent of investment laws dealing with tax incentives (27 investment laws), including those of 17 countries in Africa, 6 in Asia, 3 in Latin America and the Caribbean, and 1 in Oceania, with an almost equal distribution among developing economies and LDCs (12 and 15 countries respectively).

Among incentives not based on CIT, the ones most frequently used are exemption from customs duties on goods imported and directly involved in realizing the investment (86 per cent), exemption from VAT (37 per cent), exemption from land taxes (26 per cent) and exemption from stamp duty (16 per cent).

(ii) The governance of incentives varies greatly across countries

In only about 30 per cent of investment laws, investors are automatically eligible for incentives based on measurable criteria, such as the invested amount, the volume of employment generated or the location of the investment. In all other cases, the provision of tax incentives and their scope and duration depend on the discretion of the authorities. These are often the ministries of finance, industry or both. The process of approval can also require an expert opinion of several governmental institutions (box II.2). These findings were confirmed by the investment promotion agencies (IPAs) that responded to UNCTAD's Annual Survey of Investment Promotion Agencies for 2022. Of 126 respondents to the survey, only 29 per cent indicated that incentives in their country are granted automatically on the basis of objective criteria, whereas the large majority (63 per cent) indicated that incentives are allocated on the basis of an assessment process that involves criteria that may or not all be public. In all other cases, incentives are granted on an ad hoc basis through negotiation with investors (8 per cent).

IPAs are also actively involved in the provision of tax incentives. Their role varies from facilitating investment to actively participating in the allocation of incentives (figure II.16). All respondents to the UNCTAD survey stated that their agency provides information to investors on available incentives and the application processes. Most IPAs also act as advisory agents by issuing recommendations to decision-making entities. Another core function of IPAs is to support their clients in administrative tasks, such as collecting and processing applications for incentives. Finally, almost one third of the IPAs actively participate in decisions regarding the allocation of tax incentives. This can create conflicts of interest, particularly when the IPA's performance is assessed on the basis of the investment volumes it helps to generate.

Figure II.16. | Role of IPAs in the provision of tax incentives (Per cent of respondents)

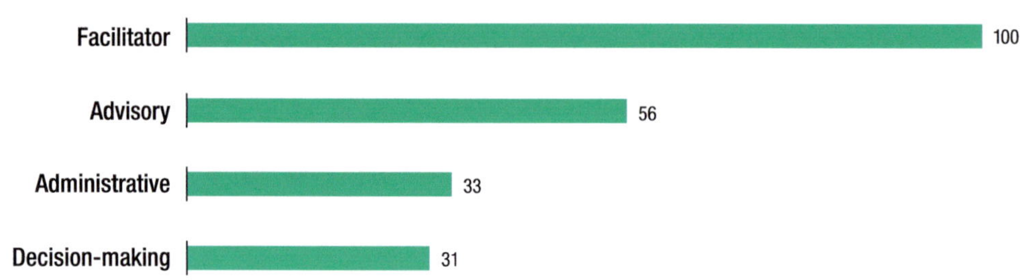

Source: UNCTAD.

Box II.2. Governance of tax incentives in investment laws (illustrative list)

Incentives granted on the basis of automatic criteria

In *Algeria*, investments registered with the National Agency of Investment Development automatically benefit from the tax incentives described in the investment law, including exemption from custom duties, exemption from VAT and exemption from CIT for up to three years during the operational phase.

In *Mali*, depending on the amount invested, investment projects can automatically benefit from a set of tax incentives that include exemption from import duties and VAT, and reduction of CIT.

In *Rwanda*, a package of tax incentives is available to registered investors that meet the requirements set forth in the Annex to the Law on Investment Promotion and Facilitation. Such investors are entitled to preferential CIT rates or tax holidays of up to seven years.

Incentives subject to approval by the IPA

In *Kuwait*, investors apply to the Direct Investment Promotion Authority for all or part of the incentives described in the investment law. The Authority, in line with the approved general policy of the State and economic development plans, defines the value, type and duration of incentives and exemptions granted.

In *Libya*, the IPA may offer additional advantages beyond those applicable under the standard tax incentive regime, for those investment projects that contribute to the achievement of food security, regional development, environmental protection or the development of energy and water infrastructure.

In *Myanmar*, the Myanmar Investment Commission, in charge of investment promotion activities, is responsible for granting and defining the scope of available tax exemptions or relief for investors that apply for preferential treatment.

Under the investment laws of *Senegal and Togo*, the IPA defines the scope of the tax incentives and advantages granted. In case of refusal, the IPA is required to provide justification.

Subject to approval by other authorities

In *Burkina Faso* and *Niger*, the preferential tax regimes are granted by joint decree of the ministers in charge of industry and finance.

In *Benin*, approval for preferential treatment for investments is given by the Government on the proposal of the Minister of National Planning and following the opinion of the Technical Commission on Investments.

Cameroon may provide investors with tax incentives upon approval by the Minister in charge of private investment, with the assent of the Minister of Finance.

Source: UNCTAD, Investment Laws Navigator.

c. Tax incentives in industrial policies

Most recent industrial policies call for the introduction of new tax incentives for investment (61 per cent), while only few call for their review or streamlining (15 per cent). The most recurrent motivations for introducing tax incentives in industrial policies are reducing the cost of doing business, supporting innovation, stimulating local production and developing SMEs.

Introduced under various names, such as strategic development plan, vision, industrial strategy, five-year plan or economic development policy, industrial policies remain widely employed around the world to impel long-term structural transformation and promote sustainable development objectives. Tax incentives are often a key element in the policy toolkit put forward by these documents.

Of 103 industrial policies implemented across the globe between 2011 and 2022 and reviewed by UNCTAD, 61 per cent mention tax incentives, 10 per cent mention only non-tax incentives (such as preferential loans, grants, export subsidies and credit guarantees), and 29 per cent do not refer to incentives at all. LDCs are more prone to utilize tax incentives in industrial policies (they appear in 68 per cent of them), followed by developing countries (61 per cent) and developed ones (56 per cent).

Unlike many investment laws, industrial policy documents are typically not the legal basis for the adoption of incentives, but they often provide a motivation for their introduction. As such, they are generally less detailed about the proposed nature of the tax incentives they contain, particularly in developing countries, where less than one fifth of industrial policies spell out the nature of the planned incentives, compared with one third of the industrial policies in developed countries.

One third of the tax incentives in industrial policies worldwide have no other policy objective than promoting investment by reducing the cost of doing business. The rest target one or more development goals. Chief among them are promoting R&D and innovation (24 per cent), promoting local production (19 per cent) and promoting SMEs and start-ups – also often considered an avenue for encouraging innovation (13 per cent), exports (13 per cent) and employment (9 per cent).

Other objectives pursued through tax incentives in industrial policies include goals as diverse as avoiding capital flight, promoting digitalization, developing e-commerce, increasing domestic savings or improving productivity, creating value, renewing equipment, taking countercyclical actions, promoting migration from the informal to the formal sector, and combating climate change.

Yet not all industrial policies call for the introduction of new incentives. About 15 per cent of them seek to review, streamline or ensure that the existing fiscal rebates produce the desired effects (box II.3).

Box II.3. Industrial policies calling for streamlining and rationalizing incentives (illustrative list)

Several countries have stressed the need to streamline, rationalize and review the tax incentives for investment in their industrial policy documents. Some examples:

Belize – Growth and Sustainable Development Strategy 2016–2019: "Action 4: The [Ministry of Investment, Trade and Commerce], in collaboration with the [Ministry of Economic Development], will lead efforts to review the incentive regime (tax and non-tax incentives) aimed at attracting investments, to take account of the need to minimize the provision of incentives to those who are not taking commensurate risks, balanced against the need to provide appropriate incentives on a timely basis in areas where they could be most effective" (p. 22).

Cameroon – National Development Strategy 2020–2030: "It will also have to do with strengthening the policy of mobilizing budgetary revenues by: (i) auditing tax exemptions in order to maintain only those with a proven positive impact on the economy" (p. 130).

Jordan – Economic Growth Plan 2018–2022: "Implementation of this policy requires: Adopting the principle of linking the increase in tax revenues to economic growth, addressing tax distortions, raising the efficiency of collections, and rationalizing unwarranted tax exclusions and exemptions" (p. 29).

Liberia – Industry for Liberia's Future (2011): "Policy 8: The Government will use incentives to promote investment in industrial activities and capabilities, and it will track and measure the impact incentives granted have to ensure the use of incentives is done in a transparent manner and serves the Government's strategic goals of generating investment, promoting sustainable economic growth, diversifying economic activities and expanding the private sector" (p. 26).

Malawi – National Industrial Policy (2016): "3.2.3 Taxation. The Government will: Monitor implementation of the Industrial Rebate Scheme to avoid misuse of the facility" (pp. 6-7).

Sri Lanka – Vision 2025: "We will rationalize the tax system by minimizing exemptions, holidays and special rates, towards a fair and effective tax administration" (p. 17.) "We will clarify and reform investment incentive policies to improve investment policy predictability. We propose to phase out tax holidays, which have been the main traditional incentive offered to investors, and switch to other forms of efficiency improving incentives" (p. 20).

/...

Box II.3.	**Industrial policies calling for streamlining and rationalizing incentives** (illustrative list) (Concluded)

Turkey – The Medium-Term Programme 2022–2024: "8. Efforts to review tax incentives, exceptions and exemptions by considering the efficiency principle will continue."

United Republic of Tanzania – National Five-Year Development Plan 2016/17–2020/21: "The Government needs to close loopholes leading to revenue leakages (...). This will involve measures geared to: (...) (viii) Reviewing tax holidays, tax exemptions and tax relief systems as incentives to investors in order to minimize their abuse and thus increase tax collection. (...) efforts will further be directed at minimizing the application of tax exemptions, building on existing reforms" (p. 91).

Source: UNCTAD, based on the documents listed in this box.

3. Taxation measures and international investment policies

a. IIA provisions and taxation measures

IIAs impose obligations on States that can create friction with taxation measures undertaken at national level. The actions of tax authorities, as organs of the State, and tax policymaking more generally can potentially engage the international responsibility of a State under an IIA when they adversely affect foreign investors and investments.

Some 2,500 old-generation IIAs are in force today. They typically feature broad provisions and include few exceptions or safeguards. Tax provisions do not usually form a principal part of IIAs, in part owing to the existence of DTTs. Most IIAs do not exclude taxation from their scope, which means that they cover a wide range of tax-related measures, whether of general or specific application. They can expose States to tax-related claims brought under the ISDS mechanism. Overall, investors have brought close to 1,200 ISDS cases based on IIAs against 130 countries. UNCTAD data suggest that in some 160 of these cases, investors have challenged tax-related measures undertaken by developed and developing countries (box II.4).

Box II.4.	**Tax-related ISDS cases based on IIAs: facts and numbers**

Investors have challenged tax-related measures in 165 ISDS cases based on IIAs. Tax-related claims accounted for about 15 per cent of the 1,190 publicly known ISDS cases filed overall as of the end of 2021.

Sixty per cent (99 cases) of the tax-related cases were brought against developed countries; the remaining 40 per cent (66 cases) were directed at developing countries. Spain was the most frequent respondent with 42 cases (about 25 per cent of all tax-related ISDS cases), followed by Ecuador and Italy with 10 cases each. Overall, 47 respondent States have faced at least one known tax-related ISDS claim.

Developed-country investors brought over 90 per cent of tax-related IIA claims. The highest numbers of such cases were initiated by investors from the Netherlands (30 cases), the United States (26) and Germany (24).

About 40 per cent of all such cases were intra-EU disputes between EU investors and EU member States (63 cases).

The ECT (1994) was the IIA invoked most frequently in tax-related ISDS cases, with 68 cases, followed by NAFTA (1992) with 12 cases and the Ecuador–United States BIT (1993) with 6 cases.

/...

Box II.4. Tax-related ISDS cases based on IIAs: facts and numbers (Concluded)

Several tax-related ISDS cases and awards have attracted public attention. High-profile examples include cases challenging the following types of State conduct:

- Imposition of capital gains taxes *(Vodafone v. India (I) and (II), Cairn v. India)*
- Initiation of tax investigations and large tax assessments *(Hulley Enterprises v. Russia, Veteran Petroleum v. Russia, Yukos Universal v. Russia)*
- Increases in windfall profit taxes and royalties *(Burlington v. Ecuador, ConocoPhillips v. Venezuela)*
- Legislative reforms in the renewable energy sector related to feed-in tariffs and incentives for solar energy *(The PV Investors v. Spain, Charanne and Construction Investments v. Spain)*
- Withdrawal of subsidies or tax exemptions *(Micula v. Romania (I))*

Source: UNCTAD.
Note: These 165 cases were identified on the basis of UNCTAD's ISDS Navigator and information from other public sources, including notices of arbitration, arbitral decisions and specialized reporting services.

IIA provisions – particularly the unreformed clauses prevalent in old-generation IIAs – can have a variety of implications for tax policymaking and tax-related measures (table II.3).

Definitions of investment and investor. Old-generation IIAs frequently rely on broad definitions, covering an open-ended list of assets held by foreign investors. A major challenge for host governments is to know whether an investment is foreign investment and by which (if any) IIA relationships it could be covered. The ownership chains behind a local investment may be complex and designed to access IIA benefits through indirect ownership stakes. This means that tax administrations and policymakers may not be able to determine whether certain actions or measures affect a foreign investor covered by an IIA.

Substantive scope of IIAs. Most old-generation IIAs do not contain exclusions from their substantive scope for taxation, which means that tax-related measures, whether of general or specific application, are covered by such IIAs. This includes tax measures that fall within the scope of a DTT between the two countries. Even where exclusions exist, ISDS tribunals adopt their own interpretation or definition of "taxes" and do not necessarily rely on domestic law guidance or international best practices.

Temporal scope of IIAs. Old-generation IIAs frequently extend treaty protection to investments made before the agreement's entry into force. A taxation measure that was taken prior to the entry into force of the IIA but with "lasting effects" on such investments could, under certain circumstances, give rise to ISDS proceedings, creating uncertainties for tax policymakers.

National treatment. The NT provisions of IIAs cover de facto and de jure discriminatory treatment. Distinctions based on residence are not specifically safeguarded under NT in IIAs. Preferential treatment exclusively granted to national investors, such as tax exemptions, may be challenged under IIAs even where this treatment is in accordance with the host State's legislation.

Most-favoured-nation treatment. Investors have rarely invoked the MFN standard to challenge the actual level of material treatment of foreign investors from third States. More frequently, investors have invoked the MFN clause to import more investor-friendly provisions from the host State's IIAs with third States, thereby "cherry-picking" advantageous IIA standards. For example, investors can attempt to circumvent tax exceptions in the IIA under which the ISDS case is brought, on the basis that another IIA signed by the host country does not contain them.

Table II.3.	IIAs and their implications for tax policymakers	
Selected IIA issue or provision	**Description**	**Implications for tax measures**
Definitions of investment and investor	• Old-generation IIAs frequently rely on broad definitions, covering an open-ended list of assets. Ownership chains behind a local investment may be complex and designed to access IIA benefits through indirect ownership stakes.	• Tax administrations and policymakers may not be able to determine whether certain actions or measures affect a foreign investor covered by an IIA.
Substantive scope	• Most old-generation IIAs do not contain exclusions from their substantive scope for taxation.	• Tax-related measures are covered by most old-generation IIAs.
Fair and equitable treatment	• ISDS tribunals' interpretations of fair and equitable treatment have expanded and covered expectations of regulatory stability and compliance with the investor's legitimate expectations, expectations of transparency and participation in governmental decision-making, and proportionality tests for State measures.	• For tax administrations and policymakers working in an environment of evolving tax regulations, FET concepts can create important challenges and potentially involve ISDS claims.
Indirect expropriation	• Most old-generation IIAs include protection in case of indirect expropriation, without explicit safeguards for non-discriminatory regulatory actions in the public interest. Tax measures with the effect of (substantially) depriving the investor of the value of their investment are vulnerable to challenge.	• There is no bright line separating permissible tax measures from tax measures that amount to confiscation or expropriation of investment and require compensation.
Investor–State dispute settlement	• Most IIAs provide for States' advance consent to international arbitration proceedings between an investor and the host State. Recourse to domestic courts or exhaustion of local remedies is not required under most IIAs. Tax matters are generally not excluded from ISDS.	• The types of tax-related claims that have arisen under IIAs have been diverse and often intertwined with non-tax measures.

Source: UNCTAD.

Fair and equitable treatment. FET is the clause most frequently invoked by investors in ISDS cases. Old-generation IIAs typically include an FET provision drafted in a minimalist, open-ended way. ISDS tribunals' interpretations of FET have expanded over time and have covered expectations of regulatory stability and compliance with the investor's legitimate expectations, expectations of transparency and participation in governmental decision-making and proportionality tests for State measures. For tax administrations and policymakers working in an environment of evolving tax regulations, these FET concepts can create important challenges and potentially involve ISDS claims.

Full protection and security. Many old-generation IIAs contain a full protection and security clause that does not include clarifications. ISDS tribunals have, in some cases, extended the scope of full protection and security to legal, economic or commercial, or other security aspects. Notions and concepts such as stability of the tax framework, stability of the commercial environment and protection against economic impairment of an investment can be relevant under this provision.

Expropriation. The expropriation provision protects foreign investors in case of dispossession of their investments by the host country. Most old-generation IIAs equally include protection in case of indirect expropriation, without explicit safeguards for non-discriminatory regulatory actions in the public interest. Tax measures with the effect of (substantially) depriving the investor of the value of their investment are vulnerable to challenge.

Expropriation clauses constitute a source of uncertainty for States and tax authorities. There is no bright line separating permissible tax measures from tax measures that amount to confiscation or expropriation of investment and require compensation.

Transfer-of-funds obligation. The transfer-of-funds provision grants the right to free movement of investment-related financial flows into and out of the host country. Many old-generation IIAs contain a transfer-of-funds provision without exceptions. In most IIAs, no explicit guidance is provided on the types of restrictive measures that may be permitted or conditions for their application. While the good faith application of tax measures is unlikely to violate this standard, including clear guidance in IIA texts can provide certainty to tax policymakers and investors and limit arbitral tribunals' discretion in ISDS cases.

"Umbrella" clause. An umbrella clause establishes a commitment on the part of the host State to respect its obligations regarding specific investments, for example, those arising from contractual arrangements. Revising or withdrawing bilateral (and potentially unilateral) commitments the host State entered into with respect to a foreign investor, such as tax stabilization clauses in investment contracts or tax rulings, can come within the ambit of the IIA. Through the umbrella clause, contractual obligations or unilateral commitments could thus be elevated to IIA obligations and lead to ISDS proceedings.

Public policy exceptions. Largely absent from old-generation IIAs, public policy exceptions permit measures otherwise inconsistent with the IIA to be undertaken under specified circumstances. They can provide a higher degree of flexibility in implementing tax measures when these are justified with respect to specific policy objectives (e.g. protecting the environment or public health) and can have implications for the outcomes of tax-related ISDS cases.

Investor–State disputes. About 95 per cent of IIAs provide for States' advance consent to international arbitration proceedings between an investor claimant and the respondent State. Investors can directly challenge State measures before an ISDS tribunal. Recourse to domestic courts or the exhaustion of local remedies is not required under most IIAs. Tax matters are generally not excluded from ISDS. The types of tax-related claims that have arisen under IIAs were diverse (e.g. withdrawal of incentives, increases in windfall profit taxes). They were often intertwined with non-tax measures (e.g. forced liquidation, interference with or termination of contracts). Such claims can but do not necessarily overlap with the subject matter covered by DTTs and mutual agreement procedures.

b. IIA reform and taxation measures

The broad clauses of unreformed IIAs can expose States to legal challenges when raising tax revenue or preventing tax avoidance or evasion. During the last decade, investment policymakers worldwide have reassessed the role of IIAs in national development plans and weighed the pros and cons of signing them. Many countries have embarked on reform of the IIA regime to address challenges for public policymaking that arise from broad and vague substantive protection standards coupled with wide access to investor–State arbitration in IIAs. IIA reform efforts aimed at refining and limiting the scope of the key standards have a direct bearing on taxation measures. These efforts can ensure that countries can implement legitimate, non-discriminatory taxation measures while minimizing the risk of ISDS claims. Since 2012, more than 80 countries and regional economic integration organization have benefited from UNCTAD support in developing reform-oriented model BITs and IIA reviews (*WIR19*). More than 1,000 government officials have been trained on key issues in IIAs and ISDS.

The strongest safeguard for tax policymaking would perhaps be a complete and unambiguous tax carve-out from the scope of an IIA (e.g. accompanied by a mechanism that gives the host State discretion to determine whether the carve-out applies in a specific dispute or that gives the competent authorities the power to decide). If the State parties negotiating or renegotiating an IIA do not desire or cannot agree on a complete tax carve-out, other options are available to limit a State's exposure to ISDS claims and safeguard the right to regulate in the public interest. Reform options can clarify and limit the scope of IIA provisions, narrow the interpretive discretion of ISDS tribunals and give respondent States a stronger legal basis in the IIA to defend themselves more effectively. In 2021, UNCTAD released a guide for tax policymakers on IIAs and their implications for tax measures (UNCTAD, 2021b). The guide was produced in cooperation with the WU Global Tax Policy Centre of the Vienna University of Economics and Business, Institute for Austrian and International Tax Law. It seeks to stimulate interaction between tax policymakers and IIA negotiators and provides policy recommendations on minimizing the risks of taxation-based ISDS claims.

c. Developments in the international tax system, DTTs and investment policymaking

The Base Erosion and Profit Shifting (BEPS) Project was launched in 2013 by the OECD and G20 to address tax planning strategies used by multinational enterprises (MNEs) to avoid paying taxes. Tax-planning strategies exploit loopholes and mismatches between national tax rules. Despite having done significant work to reduce opportunities for tax arbitrage, countries – particularly developing countries – have continued to raise concerns that increasing tax competition to attract FDI has frustrated revenue mobilization efforts. Furthermore, the rise of the digital economy has also challenged traditional tax rules, which generally attribute profits on the basis of physical presence in a jurisdiction. Combined, these developments have reignited reform in the international tax system not only to address the tax challenges arising from digitalization of the economy, but also to restore stability to the international tax framework and prevent uncoordinated unilateral tax measures (OECD, 2020b). A consensus-based response has been the primary focus of the two-pillar solution developed by the OECD Inclusive Framework on BEPS. The BEPS Project and other developments in this area shed light on the interplay between the international tax system, DTTs and investment policymaking (table II.4).

Among the key reform proposals, the members of the Inclusive Framework are negotiating the adoption of a minimum tax for the largest MNEs (commonly referred to as Pillar II). This reform is expected to dissuade MNEs from shifting profits and tax revenues to low-tax jurisdictions and minimize the race to the bottom between countries, particularly developing ones. Pillar II includes a Subject to Tax Rule that would be introduced by way of a bilateral agreement between States and would allow them to tax certain intragroup outbound payments such as interest and royalties if the residence country of the investor does not tax the respective income up to a minimum predetermined rate. The minimum taxation idea incorporated in Pillar II can have a profound impact on certain domestic tax incentives; e.g. the benefit of tax holidays or SEZs to investors might be eliminated or reduced when their application leads to an effective tax rate below a certain threshold for large-scale MNEs. Other tax developments, related to Pillar I of the BEPS Project, provide newly created taxing rights for market jurisdictions. Although these reforms are forward-looking, a significant number of DTTs between countries have already had a demonstrated impact on investment decisions.

Table II.4.	Developments in the international tax system and their implications for investment policymakers
Selected international tax development	**Implications for investment policymaking**
Base Erosion and Profit Shifting (BEPS) Tax planning and tax avoidance	• Reduces regulatory scope for tax avoidance • Aims to decrease for tax competition • Addresses situations in which no tax is paid, especially in the context of applying DTTs
BEPS Inclusive Framework Minimum tax for largest MNEs (Pillar II)	• Expected to dissuade large MNEs from shifting profits and tax revenues to low-tax jurisdictions and minimize the race to the bottom • Affects tax incentive schemes for foreign investment • Creates a minimum tax on foreign profits generated by large MNEs
Double-taxation treaties (DTTs) Functions, effects and challenges	• Focus on the interaction between and overlap of tax rules in two (or more) jurisdictions – i.e. the cumulative tax result – and aim to avoid double taxation and double non-taxation arising from the tax jurisdiction overlap • Affects FDI depending on how favourable a country's DTT network is • Attribute taxing rights based either on country of source or country of residence, definitions that are challenged by digital economy activities • Provide a set of tools to avoid tax abusive conduct (e.g. denial of benefits, beneficial ownership test) • Cover taxes on income and capital, leaving other charges, such as VAT or social security contributions, outside their scope • Face particular challenges in taxing income from intellectual property • Generally contain mutual agreement procedures, which provides for a best-efforts obligation to find a solution to a DTT tax dispute

Source: UNCTAD.

DTTs are aimed at improving the conditions for cross-border trade and investment. Whereas IIAs may come into play when actions of a given State or State agency (e.g. through domestic tax policy measures) adversely affect an international investment and give rise to international responsibility, DTTs tackle different barriers to cross-border activities. DTTs are not primarily focused on the unilateral tax rules in a given jurisdiction but rather on the *interaction and overlap* of these rules between two (or more) jurisdictions, each set of rules producing equitable and non-discriminatory results if taken in isolation. DTTs address the cumulative tax result of the overlapping domestic frameworks of the contracting parties. They aim to prevent this overlap leading to international double taxation as well as double non-taxation.

The underlying premise of DTTs is that double taxation is an impediment to cross-border activities, including investment, since it puts such activities at a double burden as compared to purely domestic situations. DTTs aim to prevent this double burden by attributing the taxing rights between jurisdictions for activities with a cross-border element. They determine which of the jurisdictions involved will have the right to tax the given income, thereby limiting the taxing rights of the other jurisdiction. The following section highlights key provisions in DTTs aimed at achieving this objective. Where one jurisdiction either cedes the right to tax or agrees to tax at a reduced rate, there is a possibility that, because of BEPS structures, the transaction is not taxed or is taxed at below a minimum rate in the other jurisdiction. The BEPS Project aims to prevent no taxation from occurring in case of tax avoidance. The goal of the most recent reforms revolving around Pillar II is to make sure that all profits generated by MNEs are taxed at a minimum rate, no matter how DTTs attribute the taxing rights or whether an arrangement can be classified as tax avoidance legally.

Personal scope. Just as IIAs determine their scope by defining which investors are covered, DTTs do the same by defining which taxpayers are within their scope. Tax residence under DTTs is mainly determined on the basis of *factual* ties, such as place of effective management for companies and domicile for individuals. Although the factual ties requirement makes treaty shopping relatively less straightforward, as it requires developing an objective link with a jurisdiction, the phenomenon still exists and is at the centre of a number of provisions and principles underpinning DTTs and broader international tax reforms. Research confirms that the effect of a DTT on FDI depends on whether a newly agreed DTT introduces any further benefits to the DTT network that a country already has (Petkova et al., 2018). Due to treaty-shopping structures, FDI would generally flow through the jurisdiction that offers the most favourable bilateral DTT with the targeted jurisdiction. Empirical observation demonstrates that one particularly advantageous DTT has the potential to substantially distort the FDI picture. A prominent example in this regard is the DTT between India and Mauritius, signed in 1982 and later amended by way of a protocol in 2016, which caused about one third of all FDI flows into India between 2000 and 2016 to come from the small island country (Kotha, 2017).

Denial of DTT benefits. DTTs provide a set of tools that domestic authorities may rely upon when a treaty has been invoked by a private party for abusive ends, including in case of treaty-shopping structures. These tools might be of a different nature: some address entitlement to the provisions of the DTT in general by allowing denial of benefits when the principal purpose of an arrangement is a tax benefit rather than a valid business rationale. Others, such as the beneficial ownership test, look at specific streams of income (e.g. dividend, interest, or royalties) and ask whether the recipient entity is the ultimate beneficiary of the payment. Moreover, DTTs generally allow contracting States to rely on their domestic anti-tax avoidance provisions for the purposes of denying DTT benefits.

Finding the right balance between allowing investors to take advantage of the most beneficial legal framework available to them and determining when their behaviour can be classified as abusive has been a challenge. Different jurisdictions have adopted different approaches to finding this balance, leading to diametrically different legal qualifications of the same underlying facts. For example, while some jurisdictions apply an economic substance test to determine the beneficial owner of a transaction, others focus on the existence of a legal obligation to pass on the income. Having vague and broad anti-avoidance rules such as the principal purpose test introduced in DTTs is beneficial to the tax authorities that are applying them as such rules require relatively limited administrative capacity. While favoured by developing countries for this reason, broad anti-avoidance rules undermine legal certainty and potentially open possibilities for arbitrary administrative practices. More specific anti-avoidance rules, by contrast, not only require substantial resources of the tax administrations but are also somewhat easier to circumvent as private parties can be well advised about the specific requirements of such rules. Thus, more recently the international tax landscape has seen a move away from introducing an ever-increasing number of anti-avoidance provisions and towards more general measures, such as a minimum tax for certain MNEs. These measures focus on creating a level playing field that may minimize the incentive to engage in tax avoidance practices rather than on filling the loopholes in a distortive international tax system.

Substantive scope of DTTs. DTTs generally include in their substantive scope only taxes on income and capital. This leaves some taxes, such as VAT, and other public liabilities, such as social security contributions, clearly outside their scope. However, there is no uniform view on whether other taxes such as direct turnover taxes or digital levies fall within the scope of DTTs. As some jurisdictions consider such taxes to fall outside the scope of DTTs, they apply unilateral tax measures in their tax framework that might result in double taxation for MNEs and potentially reduce FDI flows to the jurisdiction that levies them.

Attribution of taxing rights and active business income. Traditionally, DTTs attribute taxing rights to source countries only as long as the foreign tax resident has a "permanent establishment" on the territory of the source country. When a permanent establishment is missing, the income is taxed only in the country of residence. A permanent establishment, under its current definition, presupposes some form of a physical presence in the source country either through a fixed place of business or through a representative such as a dependent agent. This substantially restricts the possibility of the source country taxing income realized by digital business activity that requires no physical presence. International tax reform in the past several years has centred on changing this imbalance between the attribution of taxing rights between the source and residence countries for activities that are directed at the market of the source country, where the foreign resident has a significant digital presence in that market but does not meet the permanent establishment definition. The UN Model Convention introduced the concept of a services permanent establishment to enable source jurisdictions to establish a taxable presence.

The arm's length principle. Many MNEs operate a number of subdivisions in a global value chain, with the jurisdiction of each subdivision having taxing rights over a portion of the total income realized. The attribution of this income cannot be left to the sole discretion of the MNE, as it could opt to shift all profits to the country where the effective tax rate is lowest, by engaging in intragroup transactions. Here, the arm's length principle comes into play, introducing a transfer-pricing rule. When the subdivisions of an MNE transact with one another, they must valuate these transactions for tax purposes at market prices. As with anti-avoidance rules, application of this provision has proven difficult, especially for transactions that do not have meaningful free market comparators such as unique intellectual property rights. Thus, MNEs can engage in profit-shifting activities, sometimes with the active endorsement of the tax authorities of some jurisdictions that aim to provide favourable transfer-pricing administrative practices for the purposes of attracting investment. The result is to shift taxable base from both developed and developing countries into low-tax jurisdictions or in some instances, where specific legal forms are utilized, to a loophole referred to as "nowhere".

Attribution of taxing rights and passive business income. The principle under DTTs is that passive business income – dividends, interest and royalties – can be taxed also by the source country without a permanent establishment of the foreign resident on its territory. However, usually DTTs limit the taxing rights of the source country to a certain maximum percentage (e.g. not more than 10 per cent on the gross amount of the interest). Different DTTs contain different maximum percentages (or in some circumstances eliminate the taxing powers of the source country altogether), often triggering treaty-shopping structures where an investor chooses the cheapest tax route for repatriating the profits realized (looking at the dividend tax rates under different DTTs) or for financing activities (looking at the interest tax rates under different DTTs).

A common issue under DTTs is the treatment of royalty income from intellectual property. On the one hand, although the OECD Model attributes the exclusive taxing rights of royalty income to the State of residence, many DTTs (especially with developing countries) follow the UN Model, which provides limited taxing rights also to the source country. However, if the limited taxing rights of the source country go hand in hand with a beneficial intellectual property box regime in the country of residence, whereby royalty income is taxed at a favourable rate, the overall level of taxation of intellectual property income might be especially low. At the same time, intellectual property income is often at the core of excess profits generated by MNEs. The domestic minimum tax under Pillar II and the Subject to Tax Rule might contribute to ensuring at least a minimum level of taxation of intellectual property income.

Elimination of double taxation, capital import neutrality and capital export neutrality. Attributing taxing rights to a source country under a DTT does not automatically mean that the residence country is prevented from exercising taxing rights; it only means that the residence country is under an obligation to alleviate any double taxation. DTTs provide for two ways for residence countries to eliminate double taxation: the exemption method and the credit method. The exemption method is based on the idea of capital import neutrality, namely that all investment in a given jurisdiction must be subjected to the same level of taxation irrespective of where the investor is resident. Under the exemption method, therefore, the residence country exempts the foreign income from its tax base. Capital import neutrality would generally favour FDI outflows to lower tax countries. The credit method, by contrast, is based on the idea of capital export neutrality, namely that all domestic investors must be subjected to the same level of taxation no matter whether they have invested domestically or abroad. Under the credit method, therefore, the residence country recognizes (and gives credit for) all taxes paid in the source country but then also taxes the income up to its domestic corporate tax rate for the difference.

Tax disputes. DTTs contain a system for dispute settlement that differs from the ISDS mechanism used in IIAs. First, taxpayers are never direct participants in the international resolution of disputes and, therefore, the disputes are at the level of jurisdictions and never between an investor and a jurisdiction directly. Second, only a handful of DTTs contain an arbitration clause that can lead to a binding outcome in a State–State dispute. A number of countries have been opposing such binding arbitration. The vast majority of DTTs contain only the mutual agreement procedure, which provides for a best effort obligation rather than a requirement to find a solution for any taxation that has allegedly occurred not in accordance with the DTT in question. In principle, therefore, the first course of action for taxpayers is usually to seek recourse before the domestic courts of the jurisdiction involved. Tax-related disputes have also been brought to international arbitration under IIAs. IIAs cover a wide range of State conduct across economic sectors, including tax matters. The types of tax-related ISDS claims that have arisen under IIAs are diverse (e.g. withdrawal of incentives, increases in windfall profit taxes) and often intertwined with non-tax measures (e.g. forced liquidation, interference with or termination of contracts). They can, but do not necessarily, overlap with the subject matter covered by DTTs and the mutual agreement procedure.

Finally, it must be noted that DTTs form a rather consistent network with similar provisions. Therefore, international tax reform has seen instances where the whole system of DTTs has been amended simultaneously so that a recurring problem is addressed comprehensively. An example in this respect would be the multilateral instrument to prevent the use of DTTs for tax avoidance purposes, which covers DTTs between nearly 100 national jurisdictions around the globe.[21] Moreover, DTTs operate alongside other international agreements in the tax area, such as tax information exchange agreements. Whereas countries would generally be reluctant to conclude DTTs with offshore jurisdictions, tax information exchange agreements offer the greatly needed transparency regarding tax-relevant information held by such jurisdictions without involving the restriction on taxing rights that DTTs entail.

* * *

It is important to enhance cooperation between investment and tax policymakers to avoid the formulation of investment and tax policymaking in vacuums. The joint expertise of these two policy communities can help improve the coherence between tax and investment policymaking. Equally important is the need to minimize the risk of friction between the IIA regime and the global tax treaty network, with more than 3,000 agreements each. IIA reform efforts require broad internal policy coordination, which can benefit from the involvement of tax policymakers. Tax policymakers can provide information on past or planned tax measures relevant to commitments under existing IIAs or IIAs under negotiation and contribute to assessing the interaction between IIAs and DTTs. For example, special agencies or interministerial task forces with a mandate to coordinate investment policy-related work can provide a formal setting in which tax policymakers can share their expertise (UNCTAD, 2018b).

Looking ahead, a key emerging issue that merits major efforts for policy research and policymaking is the ever-growing interaction between industrial policy and trade, investment and tax policy regimes. The worldwide proliferation of industrial policy has intensified such interactions. According to the *World Investment Report 2018*, more than 100 countries have put in place some sort of industrial policy package, 80 per cent of which were formulated only in recent years. This has triggered extensive realignments between trade, investment, and tax policies, as well as with the newly established industrial policies and strategies. Although industrial policy may contribute to the sustainable development and inclusive growth of individual countries, it may also pose challenges and opportunities for the effort towards a coherent international approach to trade, investment, and tax policies (Owens and Zhan, 2018). This will undoubtedly exert significant and far-reaching impacts on tax regimes and reforms, as well as IIA regimes and reforms in the years to come.

NOTES

[1] Less favourable measures include those introducing limitations on the establishment of foreign investment or new obligations for established investment, be it domestically controlled or foreign-controlled. More favourable measures include those that aimed at liberalizing, promoting or facilitating investment.

[2] For details on the nature of the measures adopted, see UNCTAD's Investment Policy Monitor, at https://investmentpolicy.unctad.org/investment-policy-monitor

[3] The threshold for direct acquisition of control by foreign investors was reduced from $1.075 billion to $1.043 billion for investors from countries that are members of the WTO; from $1.613 billion to $1.565 billion for investors from countries that are members of a trade agreement with Canada.

[4] For instance, in March 2021, the Federal Trade Commission in the United States joined with its EU, United Kingdom and Canadian counterparts to announce that they would rethink their approach to M&As by Big Pharma, noting the high volume of recent deals and fast-rising drug prices. See J. Smyth, "Pharma dealmaking hit by greater scrutiny of prices and competition", *Financial Times*, 28 February 2022, https://www.ft.com/content/697f27b3-6b23-4326-95b5-02c25623eee2.

[5] The total number of IIAs is revised in an ongoing manner as a result of retroactive adjustments to UNCTAD's IIA Navigator.

[6] The substantive IIAs for 2021 with texts available are: Australia–United Kingdom FTA, Colombia–Spain BIT, Georgia–Japan BIT and Israel–Republic of Korea FTA. The scope and depth of commitments in each provision varies across these IIAs.

[7] For information on the status of Contracting Parties' ratification, acceptance of approval of the agreement, see https://www.consilium.europa.eu/en/documents-publications/treaties-agreements/agreement/?id=2019049&DocLanguage=en.

[8] European Commission, "Just and sustainable economy: Commission lays down rules for companies to respect human rights and environment in global value chains", 23 February 2022, https://ec.europa.eu/commission/presscorner/detail/en/ip_22_1145.

[9] ICSID, "ICSID Administrative Council Approves Amendment of ICSID Rules", 21 March 2022, https://icsid.worldbank.org/news-and-events/communiques/icsid-administrative-council-approves-amendment-icsid-rules.

[10] World Trade Organization, "Joint Statement on Investment Facilitation for Development", 10 December 2021, https://docs.wto.org/dol2fe/Pages/SS/directdoc.aspx?filename=q:/WT/L/1130.pdf&Open=True.

[11] For more information on the 10th UN Forum on Business and Human Rights, see https://www.ohchr.org/en/events/forums/2021/10th-un-forum-business-and-human-rights.

[12] Under Annex 14-C of the USMCA, the parties consent to the submission of so-called "legacy investment claims" under NAFTA until three years after its termination, i.e. on 1 July 2023.

[13] Studies and investor surveys have consistently found that incentives are second-order considerations in determining decisions on investment location, behind factors such as political stability and security, a stable and transparent legal and regulatory environment, and the quality of infrastructure and skills. They appear mostly effective in determining the final choice between similar options. See World Bank (2018) or Freund and Moran (2017).

[14] In a recent survey of 305 MNE affiliates operating in 34 developing countries, tax relief was cited among the most important areas of government support for businesses to address the challenges of the COVID-19 pandemic, and over half of the surveyed companies were receiving some form of tax relief (e.g. tax cuts, tax credits, deferred payments) as of the end of 2020. See Kronfol and Steenbergen (2020).

[15] For details on this classification, see UNCTAD (2000).

[16] The analysis carried out in this section is based on the data on the statutory CIT rate available at https://taxfoundation.org/publications/corporate-tax-rates-around-the-world/ for economies (sovereign States and other types of territorial units) included in the UNCTAD classifications of geographical groups and regional development status https://unctadstat.unctad.org/EN/Classifications.html. The list of economies included in the UNCTAD classifications may differ from the M49 standard of the Statistical Division of the United Nations Secretariat. The data set includes historic statutory CIT rates for 1980–2021.

[17] An analysis of a large pool of LDCs shows that unlike in developed countries, corporate rather than personal tax is the greater source of public finance for LDCs. It also highlights that although the corporate tax rate has been decreasing in LDCs, corporate tax revenues have been increasing as a share of total tax revenues and gross domestic product (Baker, 2017).

[18] For the purposes of this section, a measure is the enactment of an investment policy instrument (e.g. law, decree) that modifies either favourably or unfavourably the tax regime applicable to investment. Each measure may include the introduction of one or more new or revised incentives or their removal.

[19] A recent study of tax incentives for investment across 36 developing countries confirmed that tax exemptions were the CIT instrument they used most often (Celani et al., 2022).

[20] Most investment laws were adopted by developing countries (59 per cent), followed by LDCs (32 per cent) and developed countries (9 per cent).

[21] https://www.oecd.org/tax/treaties/multilateral-convention-to-implement-tax-treaty-related-measures-to-prevent-beps.htm

CHAPTER III

THE IMPACT OF A GLOBAL MINIMUM TAX ON FDI

INTRODUCTION

International investment and tax policies are inextricably linked. Tax influences the attractiveness of a location for international investors. Taxation, tax relief and other fiscal incentives are key policy tools to attract investors. Investors, once established, add to the economic activity and the tax base of host economies and make direct and indirect fiscal contributions. And international investors and multinational enterprises (MNEs), by the nature of their international operations, have opportunities for tax arbitrage between countries and for tax avoidance. This last issue has been the subject of intense debate over the past decade.

In 2013, the Organisation for Economic Co-operation and Development (OECD) and the G20 countries adopted the 15-point Action Plan on Base Erosion and Profit Shifting, commonly referred to as BEPS. Other organizations have also been active in promoting the reform of the international corporate tax system, including, most notably, the United Nations Committee of Experts on International Cooperation in Tax Matters (which has a particular focus on securing the interests of developing countries). The goal of the BEPS project was to curb the tax avoidance practices of MNEs and to make the international tax system fairer. Historically, policy coordination on international taxation has been rare, but the BEPS project is an exception. To date, 141 jurisdictions, including many developing countries, have joined the initiative through the OECD-led Inclusive Framework. In 2015 the BEPS project delivered a comprehensive package of 14 actions aimed at tackling tax avoidance, improving the coherence of international tax rules and ensuring a more transparent tax environment. That left one action to be completed: the taxation of the digital economy.

This has been the central focus of the BEPS project since then. Digitalization has caused a rapid increase in the share of intangibles in international trade and investment, with a corresponding increase in opportunities for MNEs to disconnect profits from real economic activities and to shift them to low-tax locations. To restore the nexus between where value added activities take place and where profits are taxed, BEPS participants reached agreement in 2020 to work on a two-pillar approach.

Pillar I aims to realign the reporting of MNE profits with value creation. It has three core elements. The first partly reallocates the right to tax the largest and most profitable MNEs towards "market" (or "destination") countries where they sell goods and services. The second simplifies the transfer pricing of distribution activities. The last element introduces mechanisms to tackle tax disputes.

Pillar II proposes a global minimum tax on the profits of MNEs. It applies to multinational groups with revenues of €750 million or more. Pillar II rules follow a "common approach", which means that the Inclusive Framework members adopt the rules on a voluntary basis. The OECD published model rules for Pillar II rules in March 2022, along with technical commentary and concrete examples of how to apply the Global Anti-Base Erosion (GloBE) model rules (OECD, 2022b). The goal is to start implementation in 2023.

The global minimum corporate income tax (CIT) is a major step in international tax regulation and coordination. Whereas the two-pillar proposal arose to address tax issues caused by digitalization, the scope of Pillar II is now much broader and involves fundamental changes to the international tax architecture. It not only aims to reduce profit shifting by MNEs, improve the fairness of tax systems and increase revenue collection. It also aims to reduce damaging tax competition between countries and to set a limit to the race to the bottom in CIT rates caused by countries competing to attract foreign direct investment (FDI).

From an investment perspective, the relevance of Pillars I and II differs substantially. Pillar I is designed to reduce profit shifting and lead to a fairer distribution of tax revenues, but it is not expected to affect real investment decisions to any significant degree. It will affect only the largest MNEs; these include many digital firms, which are asset-light in their international operations, and new tax liabilities will arise only above a defined profitability threshold. In contrast, because it introduces a global minimum tax, which could affect the locational choices of investors, Pillar II could have far-reaching consequences for FDI recipient countries and especially for those that compete to attract inward FDI through fiscal measures.

The OECD acknowledges the potential implications for investment, addressing them in a dedicated chapter of its Economic Impact Assessment (EIA). Yet, the EIA considers the overall effect of BEPS measures on investment to be small (box III.1). The EIA confirms the greater relevance of Pillar II, which generates all the impact, while Pillar I is substantially investment neutral. The focus of the economic and policy debate has thus been largely on the impact on tax revenues and on the overall tax bill for MNEs, with comparatively little attention paid to the effects on countries' ability to attract investment.

Box III.1. Assessments of the investment impact of Pillar II

The OECD Economic Impact Assessment (EIA) (OECD, 2020) extensively evaluates the reforms of Pillar I and Pillar II and quantifies their potential impact on international investment. The assessment brings together two sets of analyses. One, based on Hanappi and Gonzalez Cabral (2020), estimates the increase in tax rates from the reform; the other, based on Millot et al. (2020), links changes in tax rates to changes in investment.

In the first study, the authors follow the classic effective tax rate (ETR) framework of Devereux and Griffith (2003), described in more detail in the next section. They assume a stylized investment and work out the after-tax profits, deriving also the average and the marginal effective tax rate (AETR and METR) as well as the overall cost of investment, under different assumptions. The authors find that Pillar I and Pillar II do not substantially increase the AETR or METR in general, but they substantially increase them in offshore financial centres (OFCs). The overall expected impact on investment is limited. The second study performs a firm-level analysis based on ORBIS data, using 26,000 distinct MNE affiliates located in 17 mostly European countries. The analysis shows a negative relationship between METR and investment. The tax sensitivity of investment is higher in groups with low profitability.

Using the results from the two studies, the EIA finds that the reform will have only a small negative effect on global investment because the tax proposals target mainly large MNEs that are less sensitive to changes in tax levels. The average global change in the AETR is projected to be only about 0.5 percentage points, with a corresponding change in METRs of 1.85 percentage points. The total business investment rate (including by firms other than MNEs) would fall by 0.05 percentage points.

Beyond specific methodological choices, such as the use of forward-looking ETRs, two modelling assumptions in these analyses are worth specific mention. The most critical one is the focus on investment carried out in the country of the ultimate parent of the MNE group ("at home") rather than in any of the foreign locations where the MNE has operations. As highlighted by the OECD, this approach prioritizes a group-level perspective (what is the investment impact of BEPS for the MNE group?) rather than a project- or FDI-level perspective (what is the impact of BEPS on foreign investment by the MNE, i.e. on FDI?).

The second important assumption is that Pillar II, at least for the purpose of the investment impact assessment, is assumed not to change the profit-shifting behaviour of MNEs. All other things equal, this implies that increased costs for the MNE group due to an expected reduction in profit shifting as a result of Pillar II are not incorporated in the assessment of the investment impact. It is important to observe that both assumptions result in a smaller investment impact than otherwise.

The EIA further argues that the decline in investment following BEPS resulting from higher tax rates is likely to be offset by the positive effect from other less quantifiable but significant channels, such as increased tax certainty. It identifies six policy areas in which the response of individual governments to the changes in the international tax system could have important effects on investment: (i) greater fiscal space, (ii) lower compliance costs for firms given uniform rules, (iii) a reduction in tax competition, (iv) greater use of non-tax incentives by countries and policies encouraging innovation, (v) more efficient use of tax incentives and better allocation of capital, and (vi) more beneficial competition between firms, including a level playing field among MNEs and non-MNEs.

/...

Box III.1. Assessments of the investment impact of Pillar II (Concluded)

The EIA has the merit that it acknowledges the importance of incorporating the investment dimension in the overall assessment of the economic impact of BEPS, together with the revenue dimension. It is the only study to date to embark fully on the challenging task of modelling the investment impact of a global minimum tax. A few other studies have addressed specific aspects of the investment impact of Pillar II. Bares at al. (forthcoming) examine the effect for a subset of countries. Devereux et al. (2020) use a stylized two-country scenario to look at the effects on AETRs as a result of the interaction between the introduction of a global minimum tax and changes in profit-shifting patterns. Bauer (2020) raises the issue of the impact of Pillar II on investment in small, highly integrated economies.

Apart from the EIA and these three studies there has been no other attempt to systematically analyse the investment impact of BEPS measures. This follows a trend across all BEPS-related studies – even prior to the introduction of the two pillars – in which the analysis of the revenue impact has been largely dominant (see Cobham et al., 2022). The investment dimension has been much less explored, with the *World Investment Report 2015 (WIR15)* remaining the main reference on the interface between international investment and BEPS.

Source: UNCTAD; Casella and Souillard (2022).

The EIA's assessment of the implications of Pillar II for the overall tax bill of MNEs at the group level is helpful for gauging the impact on global investment flows – and the results have been reassuring. Nevertheless, where those taxes are due and what resulting tax rates are paid by foreign affiliates in individual countries (i.e. at the FDI level) are both likely to be highly significant for the ability of those countries to attract and retain investment. In addition, because tax rates and fiscal incentives are important investment promotion instruments, a minimum tax is bound to necessitate major adjustments to countries' investment policy toolkits.

In recognition of the important role of FDI for development, the role of tax as an FDI determinant and the extensive use of tax policies to attract FDI, this chapter aims to investigate more fully the impact of the introduction of a global minimum tax on investment and investment policies. It does so with a particular focus on developing countries, not only as tax collectors but also, and especially, as investment recipients.

The chapter is structured as follows:

- Section A explains the mechanics of the Pillar II proposals and provides a framework for the analysis of their effect on FDI.
- Section B provides a quantitative assessment of the impact on effective tax rates (ETRs) faced by foreign affiliates and of the possible changes in the volume and distribution of FDI.
- Section C discusses the implications of minimum taxation for tax incentives to attract foreign investment.
- Section D brings together the findings in a set of policy options for countries that depend on their current tax positioning and on their use of preferential schemes for investors.

The BEPS reforms represent a rare and remarkable achievement of economic multilateralism in recent years. The two pillars are a synthesis of almost a decade of efforts to tackle international tax avoidance and profit shifting – a key priority for most countries and for the international community. The objective of this chapter is not to question the proposed solutions but rather to analyse their impact on FDI and their implications for investment policy. The aim is to help investment policymakers, and especially those from developing countries, to identify the most effective investment policy responses.

A. HOW A MINIMUM TAX AFFECTS FDI – A THEORETICAL FRAMEWORK

This section reviews key elements of the theoretical foundations of the links between tax and investment, focusing on the level and location of investment, on the role of profit shifting and on tax competition. The theory is instrumental to understanding spillover channels and directional impacts of the Pillar II tax reform on FDI.

1. Tax-investment spillover channels

In a global economy characterized by internationally mobile capital, corporate tax policies can affect multiple aspects of the global investment landscape: where a given investment flows (location of investment), how much is invested (scale of investment), how much taxes are paid on the income generated by the investment and where they are paid (profit shifting), and how countries compete in designing their tax systems so as to attract investment (tax competition) (table III.1).

Table III.1. Tax-investment spillover channels

a. Location of investment	• Tax affects investor choices between different locations. If investments are equally profitable in different locations, investors will choose the location where taxes are lowest. • Even if the profitability of investments differs between locations, investors may still locate in the lower-profitability location if the tax rate differential is sufficiently high. This is the distortionary effect of tax on investment allocation. • A key concept in assessing the location effect of tax is the average effective tax rate (AETR), which is used in cross-country comparisons of the tax cost of investments, and hence a key factor in the analysis of the impact of Pillar II.
b. Scale of investment	• Taxing the income (return) on an investment affects how much an investor will commit. That is because tax will increase the amount of profit that the investment needs to generate in order to provide the minimum after-tax return that the investor requires. • An important concept in assessing the impact of tax on investment scale is the marginal effective tax rate (METR), which represents the amount by which, because of taxation, the pre-tax return on a project exceeds the investor's required after-tax return. • It is possible to devise tax rules to minimize the METR (and hence the size-impact of tax on investment decisions), while still raising revenues.
c. Profit shifting	• If profits generated by an investment in one location are declared for tax purposes in another (lower tax) location, the average tax rate for those profits becomes a weighted average of those in the countries involved; the overall AETR will thus be lower than the AETR in the country where the investment is located. • Because the possibility to shift profits generated by an additional investment to a lower-tax country reduces the tax payable on the additional earnings, it also reduces the METR, potentially increasing the scale of investment. • Profit shifting thus affects both the scale and location of investment. The goal for BEPS is therefore to tackle profit shifting while minimizing the potential negative effects on investment.
d. Tax competition	• A key objective of the global minimum tax is to set a limit on the downward tax competition between countries for the attraction of real investment and tax base. • Tax competition can take many forms. It is not only about the generally applicable tax regime, but also occurs through tax incentives such as reduced rates, allowances for investment or R&D spending, or special economic zones. Incentives have proliferated over the last few decades. • Because preferential tax schemes in one country can harm others, there is a strong rationale for collective action to limit tax competition.

Source: UNCTAD.

a. Location of investment

At the heart of tax effects on FDI are those affecting the location decision: in which country to invest. For an MNE that simply has to choose where to undertake an investment of some fixed scale, what matters is the proportion of the pre-tax profit it generates that each country will take in tax. This is known as the *average effective tax rate* (AETR). If the investment is equally profitable wherever it is located, then the MNE will locate it wherever the AETR is lowest. Even if the project is less profitable in one country than another – perhaps because it is harder to find the necessary labour skills there or because the public infrastructure is less supportive – it may nonetheless locate the project there if the AETR is sufficiently low.

The consequence is that cross-country differences in AETRs can distort location decisions, leading to investments being undertaken in places where their pre-tax profitability is actually lower. An efficient cross-country allocation thus calls for minimal differences in AETRs – especially for efficiency-seeking investments which are relatively mobile, in the sense that their pre-tax profitability does not inherently vary greatly across locations. (For location-bound market- and resource-seeking investments, the AETR matters less.)

In terms of practical measurement, the AETR depends not only on the statutory rate of tax but also on the nature of the tax base.[1] Additional investment will, for instance, generate additional depreciation or other tax allowances. The AETR can be calculated in two ways. One, the forward-looking approach, rests on calculating the tax due on a hypothetical project of some assumed pre-tax profitability. This has the advantage of being readily recalculated to assess the effects of tax changes, but it rests on untested assumptions and abstracts from many complications of the tax rules. The alternative, backward-looking approach rests instead on taxes actually paid. This is less well suited to mechanical simulation of tax changes but has the merit of being rooted in experience rather than simplification and hypotheticals. As discussed in detail in section B, it is the backward-looking approach that is adopted in the empirical work of this chapter.

b. Scale of investment

When considering a possible location, the investor must also decide on the scale of the investment. Taxation matters here too. To maximize earnings, investors will invest up to the point at which the additional profit, net of the additional tax that becomes due, just covers the return they require. If, for example, the net profit exceeds the required return, then the investor has an incentive to invest more, likely leading to a reduced pre-tax return – a process that continues until the post-tax return generates just enough to make the last investment worthwhile. Taxation thus affects the scale of investment by driving a wedge between the pre-tax return on an investment that just breaks even and the after-tax return received by the investor. That wedge is the *marginal effective tax rate* (METR).[2]

From a policy perspective, the neutrality criterion for good tax design – that the tax system insofar as possible does not distort private decisions but leave them as they would be in the absence of the tax (unless there is good reason to do otherwise, e.g. to limit pollution) – calls for an METR as close to zero as possible. It is important to balance average and marginal considerations in setting tax policies. It is possible to have a low and even a zero METR while still having a positive and possibly quite high AETR. This is because the METR reflects only the tax paid on the last dollar of investment that breaks even, whereas the AETR reflects the tax paid on all the profit generated by the totality of investment.

Take, for example, a "cash flow" form of CIT, under which all investment expenditure is immediately deductible. The government is then in effect a silent partner in all investments: it takes a fixed share in the returns as tax revenue, but it also bears the same fixed share of costs (as reduced tax revenue). The tax leaves investors worse off, but they will still find any investment that covers its costs to be worth undertaking, so the METR is zero.[3] But the AETR is positive because the government is sharing in the excess of earnings over costs. This is one instance of the more general point that a tax which bears only on "rents" – meaning earnings in excess of the minimum required – will have no impact on investment decisions. Intuitively, faced with giving up some fixed share of the pie, investors still want the pie to be as large as possible. And that remains so, however large is the government's share; however high, that is, is the rate at which rents are taxed. Indeed, since a tax on corporate rents does not distort private decisions – something that is not true of other standard tax instruments, such as personal income tax or value added tax – structuring the corporate tax to bear on rents has had considerable appeal for economists, with some impact on practical design of taxes.[4]

In practice, of course investors must choose both the location of their investments and their scale, so that both the AETR and the METR come into play. For the location choice, the comparison of AETRs is critical, whereas for the scale decision the local METR is key.[5] The ideal of tax policy, as just seen, is to combine a low METR with a high enough AETR to meet revenue needs. The primary (though not exclusive) focus of the BEPS project has been on how much tax MNEs pay and where (broadly corresponding to the pattern of ETRs) rather than on the impact on marginal incentives to invest (captured by an appropriate METR). It is thus the impact on the level and the cross-country dispersion of AETRs that is central to the empirical analysis in this chapter.

c. Profit shifting

By profit shifting is meant the use of artificial transactions and arrangements to shift tax base from higher- to lower-tax countries. MNEs have plenty of instruments they can use to this end: setting artificially high or low internal transfer prices, borrowing from related entities in low-tax countries, using treaty networks to repatriate earnings in tax-minimizing ways (treaty shopping) and many others (for an overview of these techniques, see IMF, 2014). A core focus of the BEPS project has been on making such avoidance harder.

Profit shifting has potentially significant effects on both the location and the scale of investments. For the location choice, profit shifting has the important implication that since the profit generated by an investment in one location may be shifted and declared for tax purposes in others, the total tax paid on those profits – and hence the overall average ETR – depends on where those profits are declared for tax purposes and how they are treated there. The overall AETR on an investment then becomes a weighted average of the AETRs across all countries in which some of the related profits are declared, the weights reflecting the amount of profit shifted. This is captured in the empirical work in this chapter by a new ETR metric, the *FDI-level [average] ETR* (this metric will be presented in detail in the empirical section B, box III.5). As the purpose of profit shifting is to reduce total taxes paid, this FDI-level ETR can be expected to be lower than the AETR for the country in which the investment is located. All else equal, investors will locate an investment in the country that offers the lowest FDI-level ETR. In assessing the effect of a minimum tax on the cost of locating investment in any country, it is the impact relative to the FDI-level ETR that is relevant.

As the ability to shift the profits generated by an additional investment in a high-tax country to a lower-tax country reduces the tax payable on those additional earnings, it also reduces the METR. Profit shifting can thus be expected to increase the scale of investment in such countries. To the extent, moreover, that substance tests and business realities make it easier to shift profits to low-tax countries if the MNE has some physical presence there, profit-shifting opportunities reduce the METR there, too.

There is extensive empirical evidence that profit shifting is indeed sizeable (for an overview, see Bradbury et al., 2018). Tørslov et al. (2021) estimate that MNEs shifted about 40 per cent of their profits to offshore financial centres (an estimate generally seen as on the high side). In terms of revenues, Clausing (2020) puts the loss for the United States alone in 2017 at about one third of corporate tax revenue. Importantly, there is some consensus that whereas the revenue lost by developing countries from profit shifting is likely to be smaller in dollar terms than it is for developed economies, relative to their gross domestic product and tax revenue it is likely to be greater (e.g. Crivelli et al., 2016; Johannesen et al., 2020). Particularly relevant to the discussion in this chapter is the connection between profit shifting by MNEs and FDI. The large share of FDI stock – between 30 and 40 per cent of the total – reported by few, relatively small, offshore financial centres (OFCs) attests to the important role of FDI in the tax optimization strategies of MNEs (*WIR15*; Bolwijn et al., 2018; Casella, 2019; Damgaard et al., 2019). UNCTAD (*WIR15*; Bolwijn et al., 2018) estimates the tax revenue losses for recipient countries from exposure to FDI through OFCs to be on the order of $200 billion globally, evenly distributed between developed and developing economies (see also Janský and Palanský, 2019; Guvenen et al., 2022).

d. Tax competition

A primary rationale for the minimum taxation that Pillar II will establish is to set a limit to the downward tax competition that arises from governments' efforts to attract (or retain) real investment and tax base by offering favourable tax treatment relative to that available elsewhere. Empirical evidence confirms a marked (but perhaps recently decelerating) downward trend – in all parts of the world – in statutory rates of corporation tax. Since cross-country differences in these headline rates are the primary driver of profit shifting, that would be consistent with governments acting to increase (or protect) their tax base by tilting those differences in their favour.

But tax competition, especially for real investment, is not only about the generally applicable business tax regime. Countries may, and in many cases do, offer preferentially favourable tax treatment for particular sectors, activities or regions. Such "tax incentives" may take the form, for instance, of a reduced tax rate (the extreme form being a tax holiday, which provides a zero rate for some specific period of time) and/or a narrowing of the tax base, such as accelerated depreciation for investment or enhanced deductions for R&D spending. Special economic zones (SEZs), which generally offer some kind of favourable tax treatment, are another prominent example. Incentives intended to lower effective tax rates have proliferated in the last decade (see chapter II, section C).[6] This is another strong indicator of intense tax competition at work.[7]

It is difficult to be precise about the intensity of international tax competition. It might in principle be that the trends in headline rates and incentives reflect not cross-border interactions in tax setting but, for example, common intellectual or political developments favourable to lower business taxes. And it might in principle also be that, as discussed further in section D, countries respond to lower taxation abroad, all else equal, not by reducing their own rates ("strategic complementarity") but by raising them ("strategic substitutability"). Economists have found it hard to identify these interactions in countries' tax-setting behaviour. For statutory rates, there are signs of the strategic complementarity that the trends mentioned suggest, with studies showing a 1 point cut in the corporate tax rate in all other countries inducing a cut in response of 0.25 to 0.67 points.[8]

The policy problem caused by tax competition, for which minimum taxation may serve as a partial remedy, is that in choosing the tax system best suited to a country's own interests, each country neglects the potential harm the choice does to others. A country may benefit from attracting inward profit shifting, for example, but this is damaging others, which are left with a reduced tax base. These kinds of interaction create scope for collective gain by coordinating tax policies in ways that limit the downward spiral that can result,[9] such as by setting a floor on how low taxes can go – as Pillar II aims to do. This is not to say that all countries stand to benefit from limiting tax competition. Some low-tax countries are likely to lose.

2. The mechanics of Pillar II

The two core objectives of Pillar II, reducing the scope for profit shifting (thereby aligning the payment of tax more closely with the location of productive activities) and limiting tax competition, are closely related but nonetheless distinct. Conceptually, at least, measures could be undertaken to inhibit profit shifting without limiting tax competition for real investment.[10] Views differ, moreover, as to the relative importance of these objectives, leading to a degree of compromise that is reflected in the structure of Pillar II.

A further objective sometimes referred to is reducing the importance of tax considerations in determining the location of investment. These considerations are likely to be greater the wider is the cross-country dispersion of AETRs, so that this objective translates to reducing that dispersion – with the relevant notion of AETR here being, for the reasons described in the previous section, the FDI-level ETR. Location, however, is only one aspect of efficiency in patterns of investment. Scale also matters, and therefore so too does the impact on METRs. The impact of the minimum tax on this dimension has received less attention in the design of Pillar II.

The structure of Pillar II is more complex than the headline feature of establishing a minimum effective rate of 15 per cent may sound. Broadly, the idea is to top up domestic taxes, if need be, to ensure that in each country the affiliates of large MNEs pay an amount of tax that is equal to at least 15 per cent, not of their profits but rather of those profits that exceed an amount – known as the *carve-out* – that is related to indicators of their real activities in the country. Reflecting differing views as to the purpose of Pillar II, the carve-out tempers the desire to limit tax competition by limiting the extent to which the minimum bears on real activity. The implication is that the total tax payable by an affiliate that is subject to the minimum will not be 15 per cent but lower, to an extent that depends on the amount carved out and the domestic taxes covered by the agreement (primarily corporation tax) payable before the top-up applies.

Implementing this minimum effective tax rate – under what is referred to more formally as the Global Anti-Base Erosion (GloBE) rules – requires four steps:[11]

(i) Establish whether a foreign affiliate is *in scope* for Pillar II, which requires that it be part of a multinational group with revenues of at least €750 million. This brings in only the largest MNEs, though these account for about two thirds of FDI projects worldwide. Moreover, it is widely expected that the threshold will fall over time.

(ii) For an in-scope entity, calculate its[12] *GloBE ETR* (or *GloBE ratio*), broadly defined as the ratio of *covered taxes* to accounting profit, these taxes being essentially any that are charged on income, most prominently the CIT. Potentially important for many developing countries is that resource rent taxes will be covered, but taxes related to turnover – such as royalties or the turnover-based minimum taxes that many levy – may well not be, nor are withholding taxes (WHT) on payments made by the entity.

(iii) If the ETR thus calculated is less than 15 per cent, apply a *top-up tax*, at a rate equal to the excess of 15 per cent over the ETR. The base to which that top-up tax will be applied is *excess profit*, calculated as the amount by which accounting profit exceeds a carve-out that is calculated as specified percentages (declining over time) of tangible assets (including natural resources) and payroll.[13] The carve-out is formally called the *Substance-Based Income Exclusion*.

From the perspective of the investor, total tax payable on an in-scope entity is the sum of covered taxes and any top-up calculated following these steps. The overall liability when the top-up applies, which emerges from the algebra of these arrangements (box III.2), is readily seen to be equivalent to the sum of (1) 15 per cent of excess profit (accounting profit less the carve-out), and (2) tax at the ETR on the amount carved out. One further implication of this will be helpful below. The lowest value that covered taxes can take is zero,[14] so that element (2) above is zero and only element (1) remains. There is thus generally no way in which the entity's tax liability can be reduced below 15 percent of excess profit: this can thus be thought of as an "absolute minimum" on its liability.

Box III.3 provides an example of these calculations. It also illustrates another important aspect of Pillar II: because of the operation of the carve-out (this amount being in effect taxed at the ETR rather than the higher minimum rate), the overall average tax rate – taking into account both the top-up and the covered taxes – is less than the 15 per cent minimum.

(iv) Having calculated the top-up, the question arises of which country will collect it: the host country in which the income arises, or the country in which the parent company is resident for tax purposes? *For investors, which government collects the top-up tax is immaterial (compliance issues aside), because the amount payable is the same.* For governments, however, it matters a good deal. The ultimate parent of a multinational group may levy the top-up under the *Income Inclusion Rule* (IIR).[15] If it does not, the source country may do so under an *undertaxed payment rule*.

Box III.2 The algebra of Pillar II

Denoting the total of covered domestic taxes by T and accounting profit by P, a top-up tax will be levied to the extent that the relevant effective tax rate (also referred to as the GloBE ratio) T/P is below the prescribed minimum rate, denoted by m (which is in practice 15 per cent). This top-up is applied only to financial profit in excess of carve-out C. The total tax payable, T^*, is then

$$T^* = \left(m - \frac{T}{P}\right)(P - C) + T$$

where the first term is the top-up and the second is covered tax payments. The impact of these arrangements becomes clearer on rewriting this equation as

$$T^* = m(P - C) + \frac{T}{P} * C$$

The effect is thus that total tax – domestic and top-up combined – is the sum of (1) tax at the minimum rate m on excess profit $P\text{-}C$ and (2) tax at the effective tax rate T/P on the amount carved out.

Expressed relative to accounting profit, total tax payable is thus

$$\frac{T^*}{P} = m - \left(m - \frac{T}{P}\right)\frac{C}{P}$$

Hence the average rate is lower than the minimum rate and is more so the lower are the covered tax payments and the higher is the carved-out amount as a share of financial profit. That average rate, nonetheless, is higher than it would be in the absence of Pillar II.

Source: UNCTAD.
Note: The notation here follows Devereux et al. (2022) and sets aside a number of complications that can arise in practice (for example, in the treatment of losses and accelerated depreciation, discussed in section C).

Box III.3. The GloBE rules of Pillar II: an example

An in-scope affiliate has accounting profit of 1,000 and pays covered taxes of 110. Its ETR is thus 11 per cent. Top-up tax is therefore due on excess profit at a rate of 4 (= 15 – 11) per cent.

The carve-out is calculated by applying (at 2023 rates) 10 per cent of the value of the affiliate's payroll (of 200, say) and 8 per cent of the value of its tangible assets (of 4,125, say), for a total carve-out of 350. Excess profit is thus 650 (= 1,000 – 350).

Applying the 4 per cent to the excess profit of 650 gives a top-up tax liability of 26.

In total, the entity is thus liable for taxes of 136: top-up of 26 plus covered taxes of 110. As shown in box III.2, this can alternatively be calculated as the sum of (a) a tax at 15 per cent on excess profit, 97.5 (= 0.15 × (1,000 – 350)) and (b) a tax at the ETR on the carve-out, 38.5 (= 0.11×350).

Overall, the average tax rate paid by the affiliate – top-up and covered taxes combined – is 13.6 per cent (= 136/1,000).

Source: UNCTAD.

In any case – and as a late addition to the development of Pillar II – the source country may charge a *qualified domestic minimum top-up tax* (QDMTT): this is a domestic tax that is structured to achieve exactly the same effect as an IIR, which will be fully creditable against any IIR. The effect, simply put, is that the QDMTT enables the host country to do the topping up.

Even this description, complex though it is, abstracts from a range of issues likely to be important in particular contexts.[16] These include, in particular, the prospective adoption by multilateral treaty of a *Subject to Tax Rule* (STTR), enabling WHT to be topped up to 9 per cent (in order to limit outward profit shifting).[17] There are also mechanisms related to specific forms of incentive. These additional features of the Pillar II arrangements will be addressed later (see section C).[18]

3. Pillar II and FDI

a. Primary targets: profit shifting and tax competition

A primary rationale for minimum taxation is to counter the artificial shifting of profits to low-tax countries. In practice, Pillar II is likely to mute profit shifting but not eliminate it: while it may no longer be possible to shift profits from a country in which the rate is 25 per cent to one in which it is 10 per cent, there is still a gain – smaller, but a gain nonetheless – from shifting to a 15 per cent one.

The possibility also remains of shifting profits between countries that are not directly constrained by the minimum. These options are unaffected by Pillar II but may become relatively more attractive as the route to a rate of less than 15 per cent is closed. With a generalized narrowing of rate differentials, the total amount of profit shifting from high-tax countries can nonetheless be expected to fall significantly – and so too will the overall benefit that multinationals derive from it. This effect is likely to be made more marked by the apparent tendency for profit shifting to increase at a rate greater than in proportion to such differentials (Dowd et al., 2017).

The setting of a floor on effective tax rates on excess profits inherently limits the downward potential for international tax competition. Higher-tax countries may also set tax rates higher than otherwise, a possibility examined further in section D. Moreover, raising the lowest AETRs is likely to ease distortions in the cross-border allocation of real investment, a further objective of Pillar II.

b. Spillover effects: investment location

In general, there is no location in which total tax payments are likely to fall as a consequence of Pillar II. They may be unaffected, if there is no impact of profit shifting under current arrangements and the GloBE ratio exceeds the minimum 15 per cent. In all other cases, tax liabilities can be expected to rise. In some cases, this may be an indirect effect of Pillar II, through a reduced ability to gain by shifting profits to third countries that are directly affected by the minimum. The largest effect, however, is to be expected in countries that are constrained by Pillar II: the average rate there will rise as a direct consequence of the application of the minimum.

The consequence is clearly to disfavour locating real investment in countries that will be directly affected by the minimum. With a general rise in AETRs, it is conceivable that there is no country in which a particular investment project under consideration can profitably be undertaken. More important, however, is the increased relative attractiveness of locations that are not constrained by the minimum. For example, if prior to Pillar II an MNE could undertake a project either in a country with a tax rate of 25 per cent on profits of 1,000, or in another country with the lower rate of 10 per cent but where profits are only 835, it would receive a net profit of 750 in either case and so would be indifferent as to the location of the project. But if the low tax rate were now raised to 15 per cent, locating in the country with the 25 per cent rate becomes the more attractive possibility. For any given level of investment, adoption of Pillar II may thus lead to reallocation of the investment towards higher-tax countries not directly constrained by the minimum.

c. Spillover effects: investment scale

With a particular location already decided on, the profit-maximizing scale of investment depends on the METR in that location. For countries that are not directly affected by the minimum, the impact is clear: the reduced opportunities for profit shifting increase not only the FDI-level AETR but also the METR, and through exactly the same mechanism. As shown in the next section, which focuses on the impact of Pillar II on FDI-level ETRs – the most directly impactful for decisions on the location of real investment – this means that the magnitude of changes in FDI-level ETRs also provides an indication of the magnitude of changes in the METR.

The situation is more complex for countries that are directly affected by Pillar II. METRs in those countries will rise to the extent that real investments were undertaken there simply to facilitate inward profit shifting. But there are other effects, arising for example from the role of the carve-out. It is even theoretically conceivable that METRs in those countries could actually fall.[19] To the extent, however, that the effects of the minimum are akin to an increase in the STR in these countries, the effect is most likely to be an increase in METR[20] – and one that is again likely to be larger the greater is the increase in the AETR.

B. ESTIMATING THE IMPACT OF PILLAR II ON FDI

The empirical analysis in this section aims to quantify the potential impact of Pillar II on FDI. The analytical exercise is performed in three steps:

(i) Section B.1 provides a comprehensive account of current ETRs paid by foreign affiliates and of the underlying profit-shifting dynamics. The two aspects – the host countries' ETRs and the exposure to profit shifting – are combined in a new synthetic indicator for tax rates, the FDI-level ETR.

(ii) This indicator is the key analytical input to the quantification in section B.2 of the increase in CIT paid by MNEs on their foreign investment.

(iii) The increase in FDI-level ETRs is the basis for the estimation in section B.3 of the expected impacts of Pillar II on the volume, distribution and route of global FDI.

1. Corporate income taxes on FDI

a. Statutory tax rates and effective tax rates

Over the two decades around the turn of the century, global STRs declined markedly but gradually, from almost 40 per cent in 1990 to just over 25 per cent in 2010 (figure III.1). A key factor, it is generally accepted, was competition between countries to attract and retain FDI – especially efficiency-seeking FDI – which put significant pressure on governments to decrease corporate tax rates and led to a "race to the bottom" in corporate taxation (Abbas et al., 2012).

Figure III.1. **Average statutory corporate income tax rates, 1990–2018**
(Per cent)

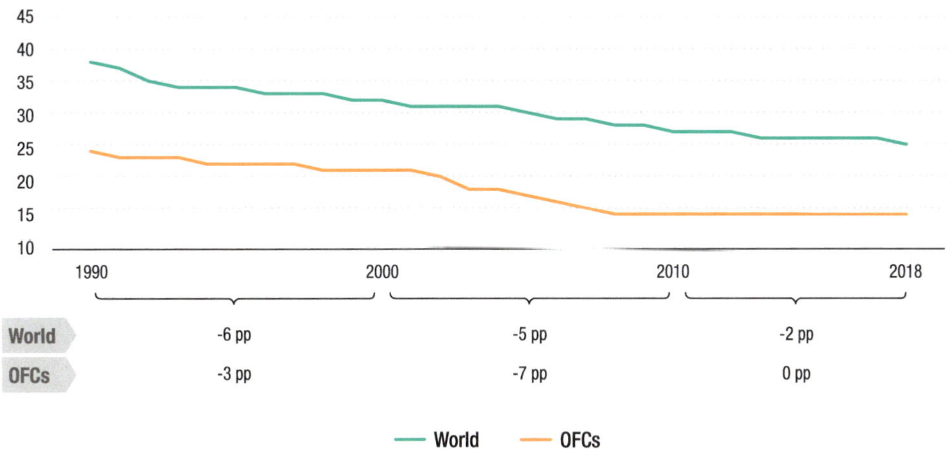

Source: UNCTAD; Tax Foundation.
Notes: Top statutory corporate income tax rates, simple averages across countries. OFCs = offshore financial centres. World does not include OFCs. The list of OFCs follows that of Tørsløv et al. (2021). Only countries for which statutory tax rates are available for all years between 1990 and 2018 are included.

The desire to protect against (or induce) profit shifting no doubt also played a role. In the decade since 2010, STRs have followed a flatter downward trend. This indicates that competition among countries, at least at the level of STRs, has cooled down. However, STR trends do not reflect cross-border competitive dynamics such as tax competition through tax incentives and profit shifting. Offshore financial centres display STRs some 10 percentage points below the global average.

Looking beyond STRs, countries offer fiscal incentives aimed at encouraging some type of investment by reducing corporate tax bills. Tax holidays, exemptions, deductions and credits are some examples (section C). ETRs – defined in the standard way as the ratio between CIT paid and reported profits[21] – enable accounting for the effects of tax incentives. ETRs from country-by-country reporting (CbCR)[22] employed in this chapter are first computed at the country level and then averaged across countries within various groups. The analysis covers 208 host countries, of which 53 are classified as developed and 155 as developing; 39 countries qualify as OFCs.[23] Notably, the perimeter of firms covered by CbCR – including only MNEs with more than €750 million annual revenues – matches the scope of Pillar II. CbCR data place the average ETR paid by foreign affiliates of large MNEs at 19 per cent globally, 6 points below the average STR (figure III.2).

The difference between ETRs and STRs is similar for both developed and developing economies. Generally, across all countries, differences in STRs remain an important factor explaining ETR variation. By contrast, firm nationality (foreign and domestic) and size (foreign affiliates of large MNEs or SMEs) do not appear to affect ETR levels substantially (box III.4).[24]

OFCs exhibit a remarkably low ETR, at 7 per cent on average, in part due to their lower-than-average STRs (18 per cent) but more importantly to greater resort to fiscal incentives and preferential tax treatments, as hinted at by the large difference between their ETRs and STRs of 11 percentage points.

Figure III.2. **Average statutory and effective tax rates of foreign affiliates of large MNEs, by economic grouping and region, 2017** (Per cent)

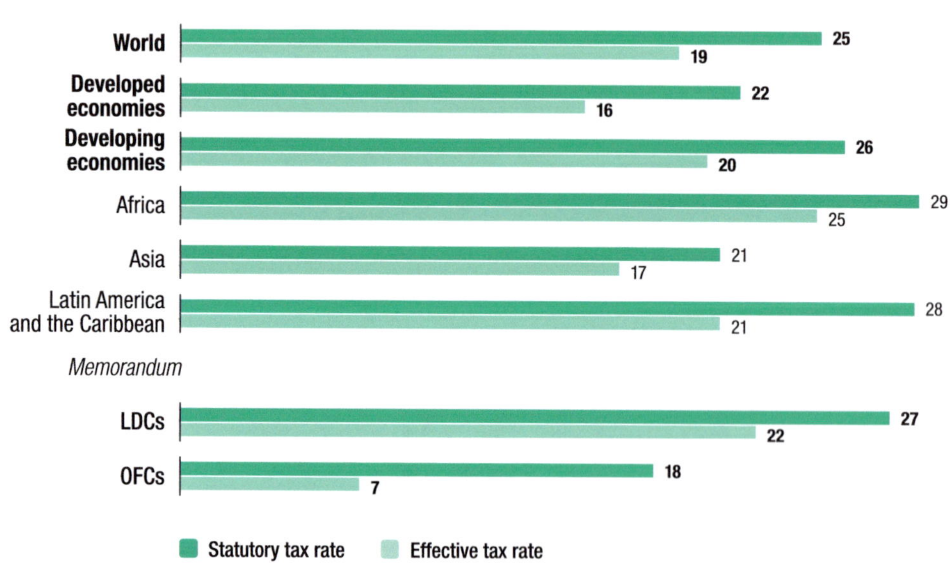

Source: UNCTAD; Tax Foundation for statutory tax rates and Garcia-Bernardo and Janský (2022) for CbCR-based effective tax rates.
Note: Simple averages across countries. CbCR = country-by-country reporting, LDCs = least developed countries, OFCs = offshore financial centres.

Box III.4. Metrics of corporate income tax rates

Statutory tax rates and [average] effective tax rates

It is critical to distinguish between STRs, established by law, and AETRs, reflecting the average rate at which reported profits are effectively taxed. Whether to use one or the other depends on the research question (Bradbury et al., 2018). The empirical analysis in this report is based entirely on AETRs, with the only exception being the historical trend in figure III.1, for which reliable and sufficiently long time series of AETRs are not available. For the purpose of this analysis, AETRs provide a more comprehensive picture of corporate taxation. Unlike STRs, they absorb deductions, exemptions and other tax breaks designed by governments to reduce the tax burden of companies. For BEPS-related analysis, in which aggressive tax practices by OFCs play a critical role, this point is even more relevant as the gap between STRs and AETRs in OFCs is considerable, two times larger than in other countries. Yet, STRs remain an important determinant of variations in ETRs across countries: i.e. countries with higher STRs tend also to have higher ETRs.

Forward-looking and backward-looking effective tax rates

"Forward-looking" and "backward-looking" ETRs both aim to measure effective corporate tax liability but, as touched on in section A, are conceptually and analytically quite different. Forward-looking ETRs are model based, consider a hypothetical investment project and include all corporate taxes due. They are particularly suited for simulating alternative tax regimes. Although abstract by nature and dependent on a number of assumptions (such as on interest rates, profitability and inflation), forward-looking (marginal and average) ETR analyses of corporate taxation and investment have a long-established theoretical tradition (Devereux and Griffith, 2002, 2003). Updated and comparable forward-looking ETRs are reported by the Centre for Business Taxation of Oxford University for 43 countries, limited to OECD and G20 countries (see also Bazel et al. (2018), which reports METRs for 2017 for a larger sample of 92 countries, but also excluding most developing economies).

Backward-looking ETRs do not require assumptions about future scenarios. They are based on the taxes actually paid in a given year relative to the (pre-tax) income generated in that year. They are data based, computed directly from reporting by countries or firms and calculated as the ratio of CIT paid over pre-tax profits. Recent major improvements in the availability and reliability of data on the international activity of multinational groups has given impulse and added credibility to the use of backward-looking ETRs in the analysis of international corporate taxation, particularly in the BEPS context (e.g. Garcia-Bernardo and Janský, 2022).

So far, the (few) analyses on the investment impact of Pillar II have employed both forward-looking ETRs (Hanappi and Gonzalez Cabral, 2020) and backward-looking ETRs (Devereux et al., 2020). The analysis in this report follows the latter approach for two main reasons. First, backward-looking ETRs are more directly comparable with the actual GloBE ratio – the main trigger of Pillar II – as they are based on reported taxes and profits from financial accounts. (They nonetheless differ, because, for instance, of timing differences in the calculation of the GloBE ratio; see section C). Second, forward-looking ETRs are largely not available for developing countries.

Backward-looking effective tax rates based on country-by-country reporting

The construction of an empirically consistent measure of backward-looking ETRs is challenging. Until the introduction of CbCR reporting, the main source for calculating backward-looking ETRs of foreign affiliates was the United States Bureau of Economic Analysis (BEA) database on outward activities of MNEs from that country. The database reports income taxes paid by, and net income accrued to, foreign affiliates of United States–headquartered MNEs in nearly 70 countries, including several developing economies. The ratio between the two variables provides in principle a consistent ETR measure, after some corrections for double counting of equity income (Blouin and Robinson, 2020). Yet, the focus on outward investment from only the United States is clearly problematic. As an alternative, Tørsløv et al. (2021) use national accounts, also available for many countries but encompassing all firms operating in a country, both domestic firms and MNEs. Data from both the BEA and Tørsløv et al. (2021) pool together profit- and loss-making firms, with the result of overestimating ETRs actually faced by firms. Firm-level data have also been used to derive ETRs (Marckle and Shackelford, 2012), but their application in developing economies – particularly in Africa and in Latin America and the Caribbean – is severely limited by poor data availability (Tørsløv et al., 2021).

In this context, the publication of CbCR data as part of BEPS Action 13 has been an information breakthrough. Large MNEs – those with annual revenues over €750 million – are required to prepare reports and give details about their activities in the countries where they operate. The information is then aggregated at the level of the headquarter-host country pair and made publicly available by the OECD. At the time of this analysis (December 2021), data were available for only 2016 and 2017. It is important to note that the reporting was not yet mandatory in 2016, but the data from 2017 used in this report capture all large MNEs from 38 countries that signed the multilateral agreement for the automatic exchange of country-by-country reports.

CbCR reporting is thus very recent and as CbCR practice consolidates, it is expected to improve. Yet, there is little doubt – and a general consensus among experts (Garcia-Bernardo et al., 2021) – that CbCR data are already both richer and more empirically consistent than alternative sources. They cover the largest investors worldwide (almost 40 countries, corresponding to 90 per cent of outward FDI stock globally) and almost all recipient countries (about 200, compared with nearly 50 in Tørsløv et al. (2021) and 70 in the BEA database).

/...

Box III.4. Metrics of corporate income tax rates (Concluded)

In addition, loss- and profit-making companies are separated, and national companies can be excluded to focus the calculation on foreign affiliates. Furthermore, in the context of the analysis of Pillar II, the CbCR perimeter exactly matches the scope of the tax reform, targeting foreign affiliates of large MNEs. Finally, in the version used in this report from Garcia-Bernardo and Janský (2022) – excluding stateless entities – CbCR data are less prone than BEA data to double counting (although some residual double counting is possible on intracompany dividends, especially for the United States and developed economies in general; see discussions in Clausing (2020), Garcia-Bernardo et al. (2021) and Garcia-Bernardo and Janský (2022)).

For the case of United States MNEs, for which there are reliable comparative data, recent studies (Garcia-Bernardo et al., 2021) provide extensive cross-validation of CbCR-based ETRs, adding significant transparency about their strengths and weaknesses. Box figure III.4.1 compares average backward-looking ETRs based on three different sources. Overall, despite differences in data sources and perimeters – CbCR covering foreign affiliates of large MNEs, BEA covering foreign affiliates of United States MNEs and national accounts covering all firms – results and patterns are aligned, most notably between CbCR and BEA data, as expected.

Box figure III.4.1. **Average effective tax rates, by economic grouping, different perimeters and sources, 2017** (Per cent)

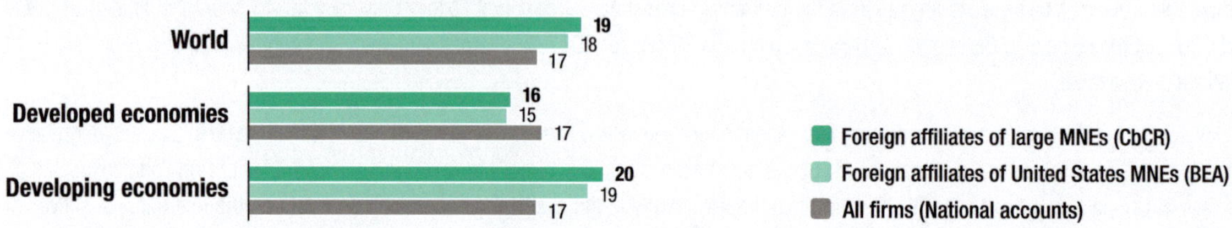

Source: UNCTAD; CbCR data based on Garcia-Bernardo and Janský (2022), USDIA BEA database, national accounts data based on Tørsløv et al. (2021).
Note: Simple averages across countries. World and economic groupings do not include OFCs. BEA = Bureau of Economic Analysis, CbCR = country-by-country reporting, ETR = effective tax rate.

Source: UNCTAD, based on Casella and Souillard (2022).

b. ETRs and the global minimum tax

The global average ETR stands at 19 per cent (excluding OFCs). Fewer than a third of developing economies report an average ETR below 15 per cent, with the share increasing to 50 per cent for developed economies. Thus foreign affiliates generally face higher ETRs than the minimum Pillar II rate of 15 per cent and tend to pay higher ETRs in developing economies than they do in developed economies (figure III.3). Among affiliates in developing economies, it is mainly those in small countries that report lower ETRs. As a result, weighting by the size of countries – captured by share of FDI stock – increases the average ETR in developing economies from 20 per cent to 23 per cent.

Developing economies with average ETRs below 15 per cent account for 6 per cent of total inward FDI stock to developing economies (figure III.4), suggesting that the large majority of FDI stock will not be directly affected by the minimum tax rate.[25] For comparison, the share of developing countries with an average ETR below 21 per cent – the alternative threshold originally discussed in the context of BEPS negotiations – would be about 55 per cent (double the proportion of those with ETRs below 15 per cent), and corresponding to a sizeable 35 per cent of the FDI stock of developing countries.

Notably, whereas the Pillar II threshold at 15 per cent appears conservative for the levels of taxation in most countries, it is high for OFCs, more than half of which face an average ETR of less than 5 per cent. This is a key consideration when incorporating profit-shifting dynamics into the analysis of ETRs and considering the impact on ETRs of the Pillar II global minimum tax.

Figure III.3. **Distribution of average effective tax rates of foreign affiliates of large MNEs across host countries, 2017** (Per cent)

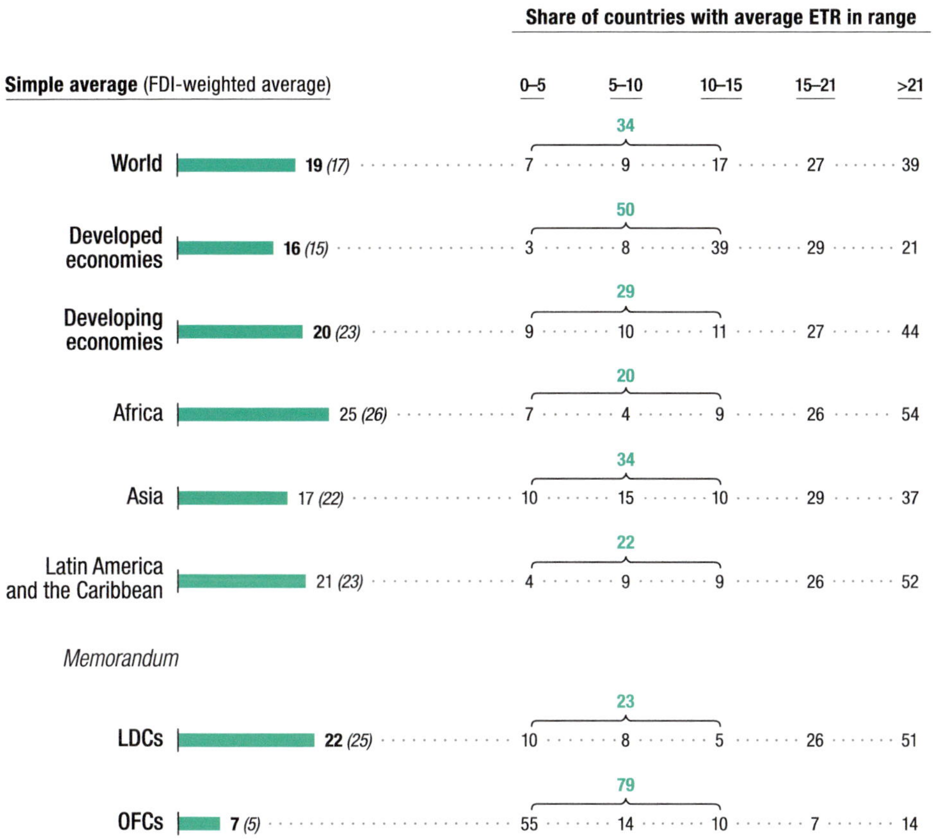

Source: UNCTAD; CbCR-based ETRs from Garcia-Bernardo and Janský (2022).
Note: World, economic groupings and regions do not include OFCs. CbCR = country-by-country reporting, ETR = effective tax rate, LDCs = least developed countries, OFCs = offshore financial centres.

Figure III.4. **Distribution of inward FDI stock by average effective tax rates of foreign affiliates of large MNEs in host countries, developing countries, 2017** (Per cent)

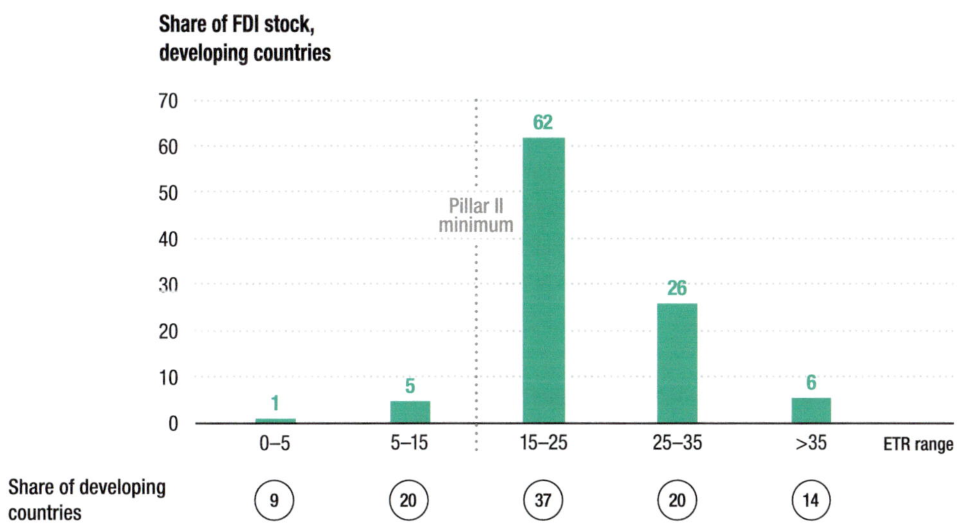

Source: UNCTAD; CbCR-based ETRs from Garcia-Bernardo and Janský (2022).
Note: Developing countries exclude OFCs. CbCR = country-by-country reporting, ETR = effective tax rate.

c. FDI-level ETRs

It is important to recognize that ETRs calculated as the ratio of taxes paid in some host country to the profits reported there do not fully reflect the actual tax rates paid on the income generated by the underlying investment. This is because of profit shifting: part of the FDI income created in host countries may well be shifted offshore and subjected to lower ETRs in OFCs.[26] ETRs reported in host countries are thus higher than the effective rates ultimately faced by MNEs on income generated by their investments there. A more comprehensive notion of ETR, encompassing all income generated by FDI – including shifted income – is defined here as *FDI-level average ETR*, or simply *FDI-level ETR* for convenience.[27]

The FDI dimension implies a shift in the analytical focus from the foreign affiliate's country of operations (host country) to the underlying, value-creating FDI project itself. More concretely, for a given host country C, the FDI-level ETR can be defined as the ratio between CIT on the income generated by the FDI stock in country C and the FDI income itself – recognizing, crucially, that those taxes may be paid and income reported in countries other than C itself (box III.5). In the absence of profit shifting, FDI-level ETRs are the same as standard ETRs. The difference between the two depends on the extent of profit shifting – i.e. the share of FDI income shifted to OFCs – and the difference between the ETR in host countries and in the OFCs. With profit shifting estimated to affect between 20 and 40 per cent of MNE profits (*WIR15*; Tørsløv et al., 2021; Garcia-Bernardo and Janský, 2022) and the difference in ETRs between OFCs and other countries larger than 10 percentage points, FDI-level ETRs are on average 2 to 3 percentage points lower than standard ETRs – from 17.3 to 15 per cent at the global level, after weighting by FDI stock (figure III.5, left-hand side).

For developing economies, the difference between standard ETRs and FDI-level ETRs is higher than in developed economies, at 3.4 percentage points (from 23 per cent to 19.6 per cent) against 1.9 points (from 15 per cent to 13.1 per cent). This is consistent with evidence that outward profit shifting is especially marked in developing countries. These differences correspond to a decrease in CIT paid on FDI income of about 15 per cent. This effect can be seen as the CIT "saving" made by MNEs on their foreign profits as a result of profit shifting – and, conversely, the collective revenue loss suffered by governments.

Incorporating profit-shifting dynamics – i.e. switching from the standard ETR view to the FDI-level view – not only decreases the average but also changes the distribution of ETRs (figure III.5, right-hand side). With the new metric, the share of developing countries with tax rates below 15 per cent increases to 48 per cent (from 29 per cent) and the corresponding share of FDI to 26 per cent (from 6 per cent). Given the high concentration of host-country ETRs in the range between 15 and 20 per cent, a shift of even a few percentage points in their distribution has a significant impact on the positioning of countries relative to the Pillar II minimum threshold. In other words, the Pillar II threshold of 15 per cent does not appear as low anymore when assessed from the perspective of FDI-level ETRs rather than that of the standard ETRs (though it is of course the latter to which the Pillar II rules directly apply). The Pillar II minimum rate of 15 per cent is thus more ambitious and far-reaching than it may seem. Investments in locations where ETR exceeds 15 per cent might appear to be unaffected by the minimum; but to the considerable extent that investors achieve a lower effective rate by shifting profits to countries with rates lower than 15 per cent, they will be. The next task is to assess quite how powerful this effect is likely to be.

Figure III.5. **Average FDI-level effective tax rates of large MNEs, by economic grouping and region, 2017** (Per cent)

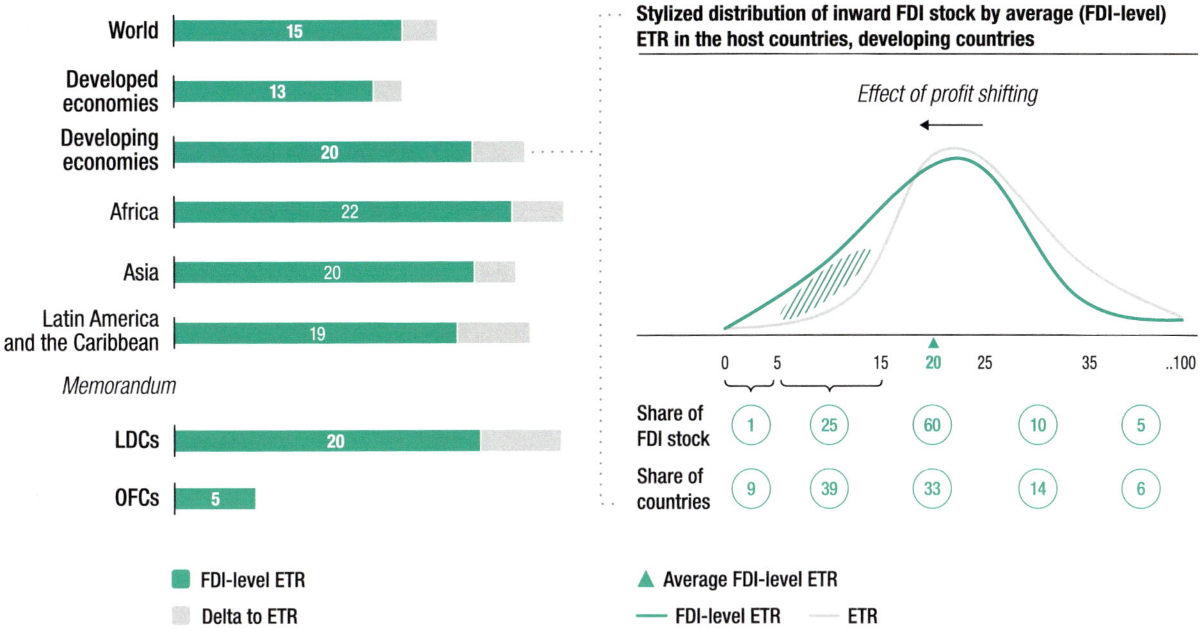

Source: UNCTAD estimates.
Note: FDI-weighted averages. World, economic groupings and regions do not include OFCs. ETR = effective tax rate, LDCs = least developed countries, OFCs = offshore financial centres.

Box III.5. A new ETR metric: the FDI-level ETR

As a result of profit shifting, taxes paid by MNEs on profits generated by FDI do not align with ETRs reported by foreign affiliates in host countries. Part of the FDI income is shifted offshore and subject to lower ETRs.

Thus, the ETR observed in host country C will be higher than the actual ETR faced by MNEs on income generated by FDI there. To account for this effect, an FDI-level ETR is then introduced:

$$ETR_C^{FDI} = \frac{CIT\ on\ income\ generated\ by\ FDI\ stock\ in\ host\ country\ C}{Income\ generated\ by\ FDI\ stock\ in\ host\ country\ C}$$

The standard host-country ETR, in contrast, is:

$$ETR_C = \frac{CIT\ paid\ by\ foreign\ affiliates\ in\ host\ country\ C}{Profits\ reported\ by\ foreign\ affiliates\ in\ host\ country\ C}$$

implying that $ETR_C^{FDI} \neq ETR_C$ if profit shifting takes place. The two ETRs are related as:

$$ETR_C^{FDI} = \sum_i \gamma_{C_i} * ETR_{H_i} + \left(1 - \sum_i \gamma_{C_i}\right) * ETR_C$$

where $H_1, H_2, ..., H_N$ are OFCs to which foreign affiliates operating in country C shift a share of their profits, respectively $\gamma_{C_1}, \gamma_{C_2}, ..., \gamma_{C_N}$. Bilateral profit-shifting shares can be calibrated using one of the available methodologies to estimate profit shifting. Casella and Souillard (2022) discusses and compares different approaches including the profit misalignment method (Garcia-Bernardo and Janský, 2022) – the baseline approach adopted in this report – as well as the method of comparison with domestic firms (Tørsløv et al., 2021) and the semi-elasticity method (Heckemeyer and Overesch, 2017).

Source: UNCTAD, based on Casella and Souillard (2022).

2. Pillar II and the taxation of FDI income

a. The increase of FDI-level ETRs

The increase in corporate taxation for MNEs caused by a minimum tax rate applied to foreign affiliates operates through two main channels: host countries' ETRs and profit shifting.

The first, and most obvious channel, is through the ETRs of the host countries whose GloBE ETRs are below the minimum of 15 per cent and so are subject to some top-up under Pillar II rules. How foreign affiliates in host countries distribute around the threshold determines the increase in the tax rates applied to their locally reported profits. In practice, for empirical purposes, given the prohibitive task of tracking within-country firm-level variations in ETRs, the analysis in this chapter uses countries' average ETRs as proxies for GloBE ETR distributions. In this context, the trigger of the ETR channel is the difference between the 15 per cent threshold and the host country's average ETR.

The second driver of change in corporate taxation paid by MNEs is the profit-shifting channel, which arises even when the standard ETR in a particular host country exceeds 15 per cent. Accounting for profit shifting substantially increases the estimated impact of Pillar II based on host countries' ETRs alone. The profit-shifting channel works through two related dynamics. On the one hand, higher taxation of income reported in OFCs leads the MNE to reduce the proportion of profit it shifts; on the other, the residual shifted profits are subject in those OFCs to higher ETRs – from an average of 7 per cent to the minimal rate of 15 per cent.

The calibration of the residual share of shifted profits after the introduction of the minimum is ultimately an empirical and modelling matter. The analysis that follows uses two scenarios to assess the impact on FDI-level ETRs: one that is likely to provide a conservative estimate of the induced increase in FDI-level ETRs ("baseline scenario"), and one that provides an upper bound on this increase ("upper bound scenario"). The baseline (conservative) scenario allows the share of shifted profits to decrease proportionally (linearly) to the reduction of the gap in the rate between host countries and OFCs.[28] The upper bound assumes that there is no longer any profit shifting after the introduction of the Pillar II minimum (a full reversal of profit shifting).[29] The actual effect is very likely to lie between the two, as confirmed by recent profit-shifting literature supporting significant non-linearity (namely, convexity in rate differentials) of profit shifting (Dowd et al., 2017; Garcia-Bernardo and Janský, 2022).

As a synthetic indicator combining both ETR levels and profit-shifting shares, the FDI-level ETR provides a flexible metric that allows account to be taken of both channels. From this perspective, it gives a more realistic picture of the increase in the CIT rate paid by MNEs on their foreign investment than do standard host-country ETRs alone, which cannot incorporate the effects on profit-shifting dynamics in the calculation of the ETR impact (box III.6).

Applying the FDI-level ETR framework described in box III.5 and box III.6 – and leaving aside for now the impact of the carve-out – this report estimates an increase of 2.4 percentage points in FDI-level ETRs faced by MNEs globally as a result of Pillar II, with an upper bound of 3 percentage points. This estimate is computed by averaging across host countries – accounting for *all* FDI (including by MNEs not in scope of Pillar II, i.e. with annual revenues below €750 million) – with host countries weighted by the size of their FDI inward stock (figure III.6, left-hand side, shaded quadrant). The assessment of the impact assumes that all countries covered by the analysis (more than 200) implement Pillar II.

Figure III.6. **Impact of Pillar II on average FDI-level effective tax rates without carve-out, by economic grouping and region** (Percentage points)

Increase in average FDI-level ETR, world

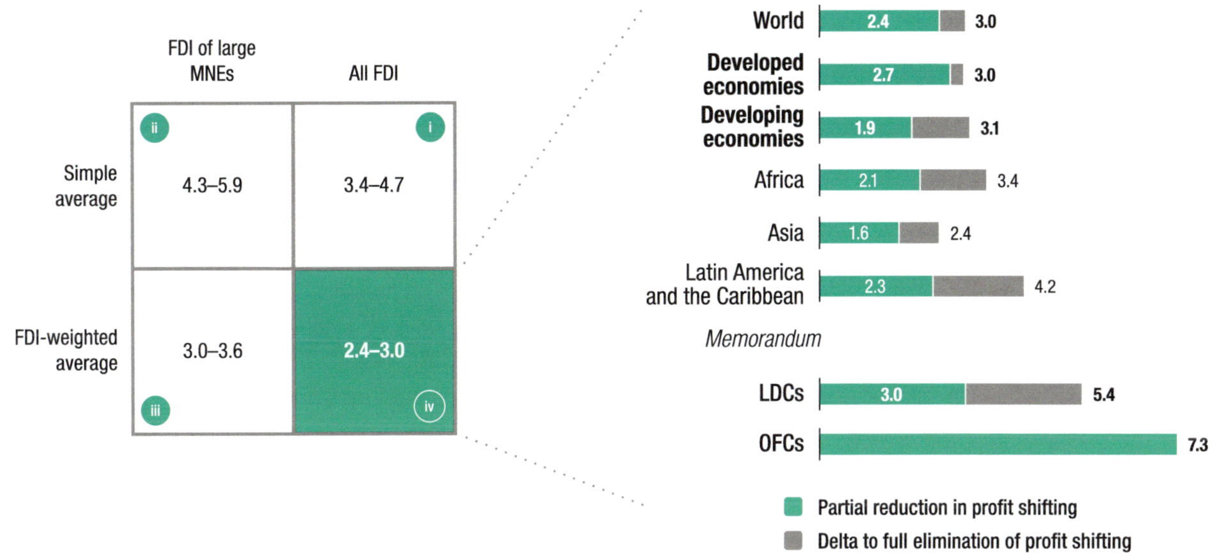

Source: UNCTAD estimates.
Note: World, economic groupings and regions do not include OFCs. ETR = effective tax rate, LDCs = least developed countries, OFCs = offshore financial centres.

Box III.6. How Pillar II changes FDI-level ETRs

The (average) FDI-level ETR in host country C defined in box III.5 can be written as:

$$ETR_C^{FDI} = \sum_i \gamma_{C_i} * ETR_{H_i} + \left(1 - \sum_i \gamma_{C_i}\right) * ETR_C = ETR_C - \sum_i \gamma_{C_i} * (ETR_C - ETR_{H_i})$$

where $H_1, H_2, ..., H_N$ denote OFCs to which foreign affiliates operating in country C shift a share of their profits, respectively $\gamma_{C_1}, \gamma_{C_2}, ..., \gamma_{C_N}$.

For foreign affiliates of large MNEs (in scope), the impact of the Pillar II minimum on the FDI-level ETR is given as follows:

$$\Delta ETR_{large,C}^{FDI} = (ETR'_C - ETR_C) + \left(\sum_i \gamma_{C_i} (ETR_C - ETR_{H_i}) - \sum_i \gamma'_{C_i} (ETR'_C - ETR'_{H_i})\right)$$

where ETR' is equal to the maximum between ETR and 15 per cent and γ' are the profit-shifting shares after implementation of Pillar II. Intuitively, the first term in the right-hand side represents the ETR channel, while the second and third capture the profit-shifting channel. The ETR channel depends simply on the level of the host country's ETR relative to the minimum, while the profit-shifting channel depends on the change in exposure to profit shifting, through adjustments to both the (shifted) tax base and to the tax rates (differentials). In a world without profit shifting, then $\gamma_{C_i} = \gamma'_{C_i} = 0$. Thus, the impact of Pillar II would be limited to the difference between the minimum and the host-country ETR if positive, or 0 if not positive.

With profit shifting, the impact depends on the assumptions about the change in profit-shifting behaviour as a result of Pillar II. This analysis considers two scenarios. The baseline conservative scenario allows profit shifting to decrease gradually after Pillar II, with $\gamma_{C_i} \geq \gamma'_{C_i} \geq 0$, where the latter shares are empirically calibrated at the bilateral level. The upper-bound scenario – maximizing the impact of the profit-shifting channel – assumes the elimination of profit shifting after Pillar II: $\gamma_{C_i} \geq 0$ and $\gamma'_{C_i} = 0$, for all i.

Finally, to obtain the impact of Pillar II at the host-country level – including all foreign affiliates, both in and outside the scope of Pillar II – the impact in the equation above is weighted by some (host country–specific) factor ω_C that reflects the share of income generated by foreign affiliates of large MNEs in the income generated by all foreign affiliates

Source: UNCTAD, based on Casella and Souillard (2022).

As small countries tend to report lower (pre-Pillar II) rates, unweighting increases the estimated impact of the reform, from 2.4 to 3.4 percentage points in the baseline scenario (from quadrant IV to quadrant I in figure III.6, left-hand side). FDI by large MNEs – falling within the scope of application of Pillar II – are subject to a stronger increase: in the baseline scenario, the increase in their FDI-level ETRs is 4.3 and 3.0 percentage points in the unweighted and weighted versions, respectively (quadrants II and III in figure III.6, left-hand side).

Comparing developing and developed countries, it is only in the upper-bound case (maximal response) that the impact on FDI-level ETRs is substantially the same, at about 3 percentage points (figure III.6, right-hand side). In the baseline scenario, where a part of profits continues to be shifted to OFCs, the increase in FDI-level ETRs in developing countries is two thirds of that in developed economies (1.9 percentage points against 2.7 percentage points). In this case, the growth in the tax rate faced by MNEs on their investment in developing economies is about half of that in developed economies. Among developing countries, those in Latin America and the Caribbean and in Africa see the largest increase in FDI-level ETRs (2.3 and 2.1 percentage points in the conservative scenario), while the impact in Asia is more moderate (1.6 percentage points). Excluding OFCs, LDCs are the most affected, with an increase in the average FDI-level ETR of 3 percentage points in the baseline scenario, with an upper-bound of 5.4 percentage points.

Different patterns of impact across regions in the two scenarios can be largely explained by exposure to the two channels, host-country ETRs and profit-shifting. Countries that have relatively lower ETRs and that are less prone to profit shifting tend to display a more limited gap between the baseline scenario and the upper bound, since the difference between scenarios depends on MNE profit shifting behaviour. This is fully exemplified by OFCs, which have very low ETRs and no outward profit shifting. To a lesser extent, this is also the case for developed economies. Developing countries, particularly in Africa and in Latin America and the Caribbean, are in the opposite situation, with relatively high ETRs and significant exposure to profit shifting, explaining a sizable difference between the baseline and the upper bound scenario for those countries.

These insights are further confirmed and qualified through an explicit decomposition of the impact, into the ETR channel and the profit-shifting channel (figure III.7). For ease of exposition, the decomposition is made under the assumption of full reversal of profit shifting (upper bound). All profits shifted pre-Pillar II are then simply reassigned to the host countries where they are generated.[30]

Globally, of the 3 percentage point increase in the FDI-level ETR, 2 percentage points can be attributed to the impact of the profit-shifting channel. By contrast, the increase in FDI-level ETR due to the (upward) realignment of host-country ETRs to the minimum (the ETR channel) drives a more modest increase.

Yet, the effects are very different between developed and developing economies. In developed economies, the contribution to the impact is evenly shared between the two channels. In developing economies, including LDCs, the profit-shifting channel is the more prominent, owing to the combination of greater exposure to profit shifting and their higher pre-Pillar II ETRs. As a result, the weight of the ETR channel is less than 10 per cent in developing economies, compared with almost 50 per cent in developed economies. Among developing economies, LDCs are somewhat different, with a stronger weight of the ETR channel. Conversely, in OFCs, the ETR channel drives all the difference, an increase of 7.3 percentage points.

Looking through the lens of the FDI-level ETR at the objectives of the tax reform – countering profit shifting on the one hand and limiting tax competition on the other – it appears that Pillar II acts mainly through the impact on profit shifting from applying the minimum rate to OFCs rather than through the application of the minimum elsewhere.

Figure III.7. Decomposition of the impact of Pillar II on FDI-level effective tax rates, by economic grouping and region (Percentage points and per cent)

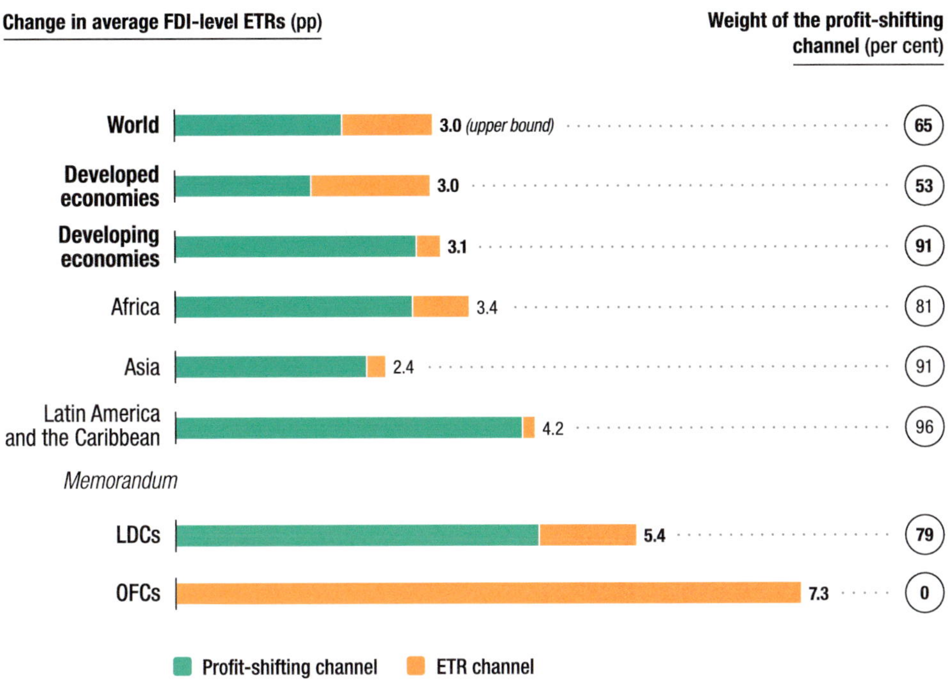

Source: UNCTAD estimates.
Notes: FDI-weighted averages. World, economic groupings and regions do not include OFCs. Upper-bound scenario assumes full elimination of profit shifting after Pillar II and no carve-out. ETRs = effective tax rates, LDCs = least developed countries, OFCs = offshore financial centres.

This is particularly true for developing countries. Put differently, in a world without profit shifting, the increase in corporate taxation on FDI income as a result of Pillar II would be very limited in developing economies. The empirical evidence of this limited impact demands two important caveats.

First, an FDI-weighted average understates the impact of the ETR channel across individual countries. Since smaller countries generally apply lower ETRs, a simple (unweighted) average across countries would result in a higher impact – a global 4.7 percentage point increase in the FDI-level ETR in the upper-bound estimate (compared with 3 percentage points in the weighted version), with most of the additional impact driven by the ETR channel.

Second, and more importantly, the calculation of the impact of the ETR channel assumes that all foreign affiliates are subject to the average ETR in the host country. This assumption captures de facto the impact on *average ETRs* rather than, more relevant for considering investment effects of Pillar II, the *average impact* on ETRs (box III.7). It can be proved that the impact on the average ETR is smaller than the average impact on ETRs. From this perspective, the baseline estimate in this study understates the actual impact.

A key feature of Pillar II is the application of a substance-based carve-out to reduce the tax base to which the Pillar II top-up tax rate applies (section A). This is intended to preserve the possibility for countries to compete for real and productive investment. As such, the share of profit that can be carved out – i.e. the share of a foreign affiliate's total profit that can be spared from the application of the minimum tax rate – is anchored to indicators of tangible assets and employment. The existence of this carve-out leaves an "open window" for countries to engage in a degree of tax competition through their domestic tax system, as highlighted in section D.

Box III.7. Accounting for ETR variance within countries

Tax incentives are one important reason why ETRs are generally lower than STRs. However, tax incentives are not granted uniformly to all foreign affiliates: the average ETR observed at the country level is the result of very different tax rates faced by individual foreign affiliates. As Pillar II applies to those individual foreign affiliates, impact assessments based solely on average ETRs have their limitations. However, for developing countries, data that can be used to infer the full distribution of ETRs are extremely scarce.

Assuming ETRs concentrated at the country level leads to a systematic underestimation of the impact of a minimum tax. In the case where the country-average ETR is higher than the minimum threshold – the most common situation in developing countries – the direction of the bias is obvious. The analysis records no impact (excluding, for the moment, profit-shifting considerations) whereas in practice Pillar II produces an increase of the ETR faced by a subset of foreign affiliates, and hence of the average ETR as well. However, underestimation of the impact of the minimum can be shown to hold also in the general case.

The degree of underestimation of the impact depends on the distribution of the ETRs, which varies by country and is not empirically observable for most countries. A rough indication can be provided by a simulation-based analysis, assuming for each host country a discrete distribution of ETRs with only two values, at zero and at the STR, and with the mean at the national average ETR. This loosely corresponds to the case where host countries provide exemptions (zero rate) as the only type of tax incentive; when exemptions do not apply, FDI income is taxed at the full STR. The impact on average (FDI-level) ETRs globally then becomes around twice the impact calculated in the scenario that disregards ETR variance (box figure III.7.1).

Box figure III.7.1. **Simulation of the additional impact of Pillar II in presence of variance of effective tax rates within countries** (Percentage points)

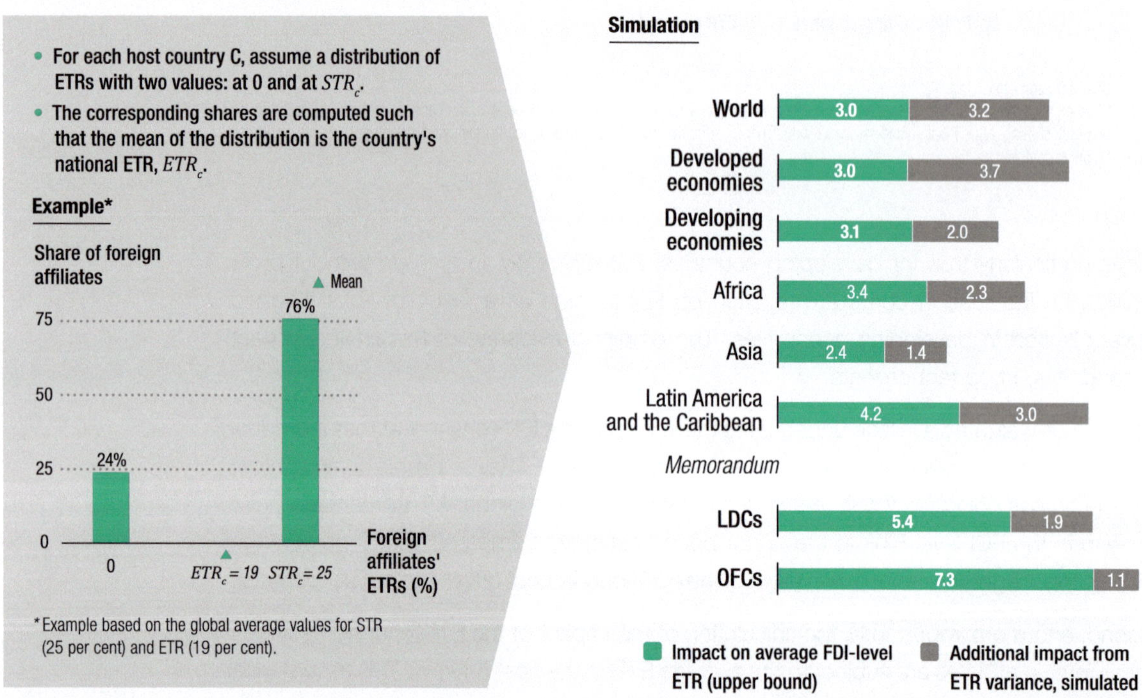

Source: UNCTAD estimates.
Notes: World, economic groupings and regions do not include OFCs. FDI-weighted averages. Upper-bound scenario assumes full elimination of profit shifting after Pillar II and no carve-out. The list of OFCs follows that of Tørsløv et al. (2021). ETR = effective tax rate, LDCs = least developed countries, OFCs = offshore financial centres.

Source: UNCTAD, based on Auclair and Casella (forthcoming).

The introduction of the carve-out mitigates the impact of the Pillar II minimum tax rate on FDI-level ETRs, to the extent that it reduces the tax base to which the top-up applies in host countries (hence affecting the ETR channel).[31] The magnitude of the reduction depends on the size of the carve-out. Proper calibration of the carve-out shares is empirically challenging.

Figure III.8. **Impact of Pillar II on average FDI-level effective tax rates with a carve-out, by economic grouping and region** (Percentage points and per cent)

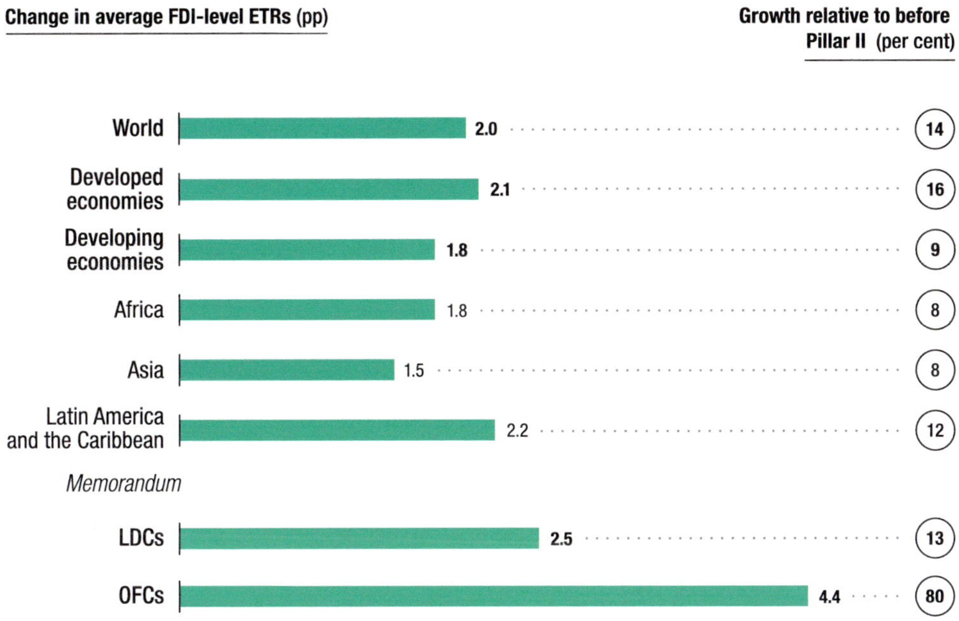

Source: UNCTAD estimates.
Notes: FDI-weighted averages. This baseline estimate refers to a conservative scenario with a partial (linear) reduction of profit shifting after Pillar II. World, economic groupings and regions do not include OFCs. ETR = effective tax rate, LDCs = least developed countries, OFCs = offshore financial centres.

Available data on reported payroll, intangible assets and profits from the OECD CbCR and the OECD Activity of Multinational Enterprises (AMNE) Database hint at an average carve-out share of about 40 per cent of reported profits across host countries. This share implies an increase in FDI-level ETRs at the global level of 2 percentage points in the baseline estimate, from a pre-Pillar II level of 15 per cent. This corresponds to a relative growth in tax liabilities faced by MNEs of 14 per cent (figure III.8).

Combining the results across different scenarios and assumptions on the carve-out (see figures III.6 and III.8), the increase in FDI-level ETR brought about by Pillar II is estimated to be between 2 and 3 percentage points globally. This implies a growth relative to the pre-Pillar II level between 14 per cent, in the baseline conservative scenario with a carve-out, and 20 per cent as an upper bound. This relative increase will be higher for FDI in developed economies (16 per cent in the baseline scenario) than in developing economies (9 per cent). The ETR impact on FDI by large MNEs alone (with annual revenues above €750 million) may be up to 17 per cent in the baseline. It should also be noted that the baseline estimate reflects the average increase faced by FDI (an FDI-weighted average); this is smaller than the simple average change in FDI-level ETR across countries, as high as 17 per cent too.

The baseline estimate of the ETR impact of Pillar II in this report is higher than that provided by the OECD in its EIA (OECD, 2020; Hanappi and Gonzalez Cabral, 2020; see also box III.1). Based on a smaller subset of 66 countries, the results in Hanappi and Gonzalez Cabral (2020) indicate that the average effective tax rate of MNEs would increase on average by 0.46 percentage point (with the estimated impact on the marginal effective tax rate significantly higher, at 1.85 percentage points). While also adopting different methodological approaches, a more fundamental difference between the estimates in this report and the OECD estimates is that they reflect different underlying perspectives on the investment impact of Pillar II. Whereas the objective of this chapter – focusing specifically on policy implications for developing (recipient) countries – is to analyse the impact of Pillar II on corporate income taxation of FDI, the analysis of the OECD looks at the impact on CIT associated with group-level investment. This fundamental difference is reflected analytically in the two different notions of ETR introduced to measure CIT impact – the FDI-level ETR introduced in this report (see box III.5) and the OECD's group-level ETR (OECD, 2020, section 4.4). Intuitively, impacts of Pillar II on group-level tax bills are lower than at the FDI level because MNEs have the opportunity to optimize investment decisions by choosing the best location within their geographic network, an obvious option being to invest in the home country, where the minimum does not apply. In fact, the OECD study investigates the effect of Pillar II on the group-level ETR associated with an investment conducted in the home country of the MNE.

b. Mitigation of tax rate differentials

By setting a floor to the race to the bottom in CIT, the introduction of a minimum tax rate mitigates tax rate differentials between countries by mechanically compressing standard ETRs into a smaller range. Without profit-shifting considerations, the reduction in tax rate differentials caused by the Pillar II minimum (at 15 per cent) is particularly sizeable. Assuming for simplicity that there is no carve-out, a third of developing countries – and about half of developed ones – will see their standard ETRs re-aligned (upward) to the minimum, reducing the gap between those countries and others that have ETRs above 15 per cent. The post-Pillar II distribution of the average ETR across countries appears "truncated" at the minimum tax rate, resulting in a 30 per cent lower standard deviation (figure III.9; compare first box plot in the left-hand side with right-hand side).[32]

Figure III.9. **Comparison between the distributions of effective tax rates and FDI-level effective tax rates across host countries, before and after Pillar II implementation** (Per cent)

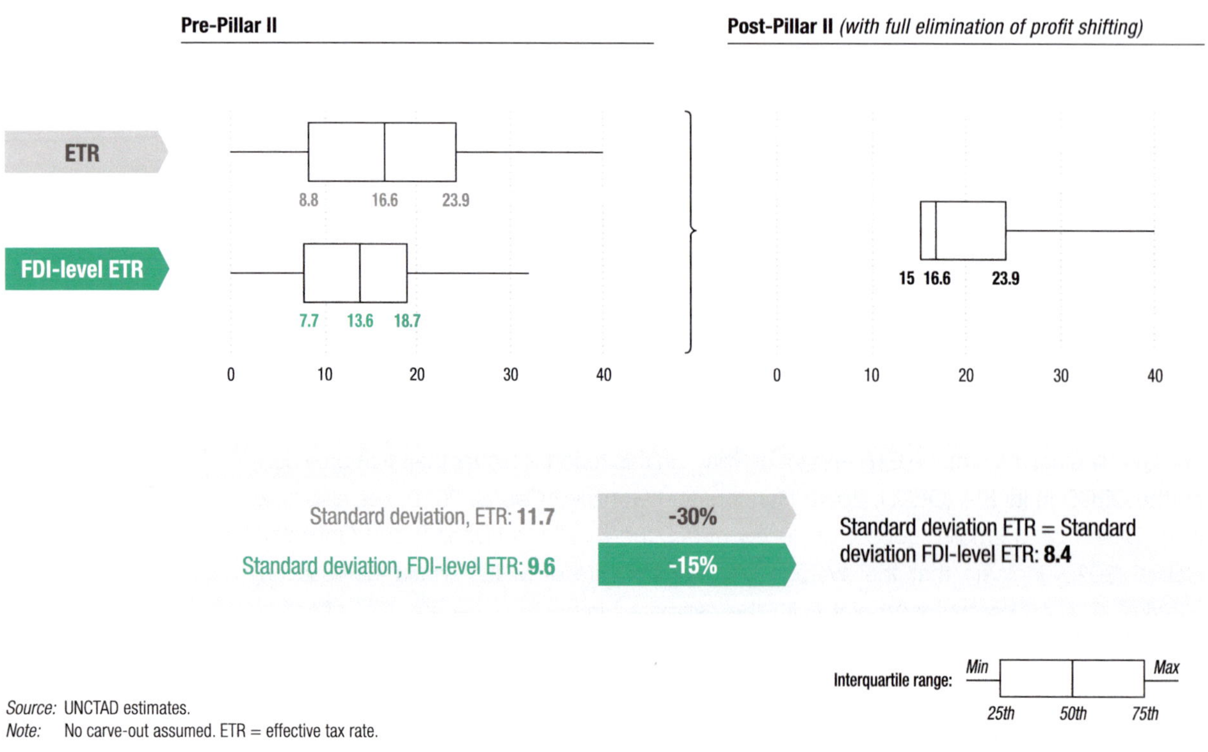

Source: UNCTAD estimates.
Note: No carve-out assumed. ETR = effective tax rate.

Accounting for profit shifting decreases the impact of the Pillar II minimum on ETR differentials. Generally, FDI-level ETRs are less dispersed than standard ETRs. That occurs because profit shifting mitigates tax rate differentials: widespread access to fiscal benefits provided by OFCs partially offsets differences in tax rates across host countries. This mitigating effect can be observed by comparing the dispersion of ETRs and FDI-level ETRs pre-Pillar II (compare first and second box plot in the left-hand side of figure III.9). As the minimum kicks in, however, some profit shifting does not take place anymore. The difference between the dispersion of ETRs and FDI-level ETRs will then narrow, as the distribution at the FDI level will become closer to that of ETRs. In the extreme case, assuming full reversal of profit shifting (upper bound), the distributions of ETRs and FDI-level ETRs after Pillar II coincide (right-hand side of figure III.9).

As a result, the effects of Pillar II on differentials of FDI-level ETRs are more limited than those on standard tax rate differentials. In the upper-bound case, the standard deviation of the distribution of the FDI-level ETRs decreases by a more moderate 15 per cent, i.e. half of the reduction observed with standard ETRs (compare right-hand side and left-hand side of the figure). The alternative scenario, with a partial reduction in profit shifting, shows a stronger decrease of tax rate differentials, but smaller than with standard ETRs. Thus, interestingly, on the one hand profit shifting adds to the direct impact of Pillar II on the *level* of host countries' ETRs; on the other, it partially mitigates its impact on their *differentials*.

c. Implications for revenue collection

The combined effect of the introduction of a minimum tax rate on host countries' ETRs and the reduction in profit shifting generates an increase in the government revenues collected by host countries on the income generated by FDI up to 20 per cent globally.[33] This result refers to the upper-bound case with full reversal of profit shifting and no carve-out (figure III.10; see World). Taking into consideration more conservative assumptions on profit shifting

Figure III.10. **Impact of Pillar II on tax revenues generated by FDI income, by economic grouping**
(Per cent)

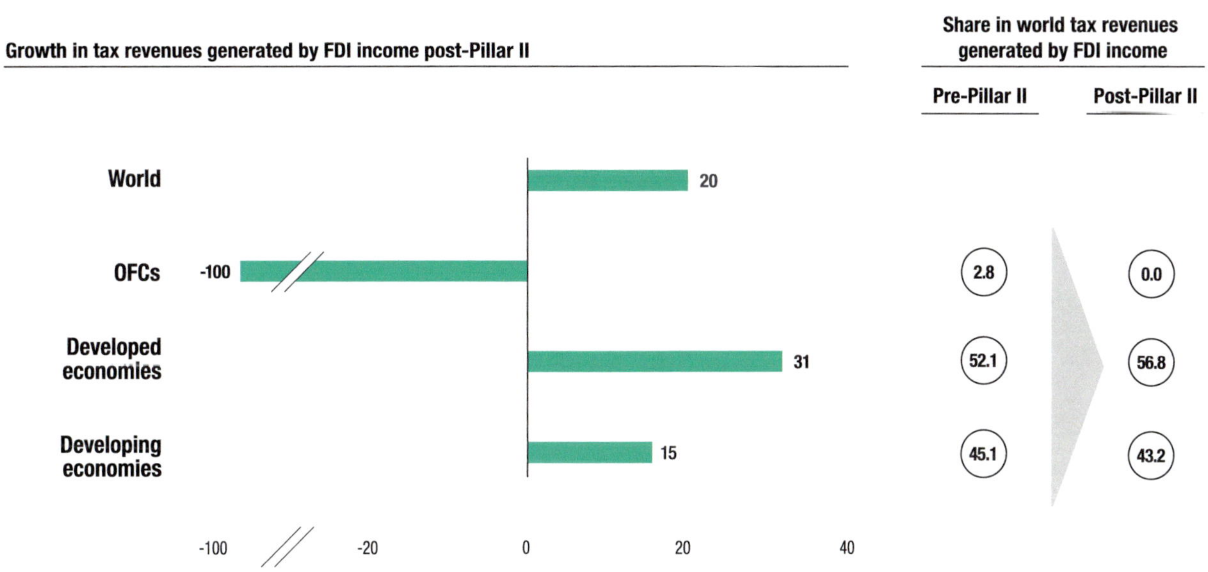

Source: UNCTAD estimates.
Notes: Three simplifying assumptions were used for this analysis: (a) full elimination of profit shifting without a carve-out, providing an upper bound for the impact; (b) application of a QDMTT by host countries; (c) all income in OFCs pre-Pillar II is shifted. The analysis excludes income generated in OFCs. Preliminary estimates indicate that the application of the IIR instead of the QDMTT in assumption (b) does not significantly modify the distributional effect. IIR = Income Inclusion Rule, OFCs = offshore financial centres, QDMTT= qualified domestic minimum top-up tax.

and assuming a carve-out share would lead to a growth in revenues in an approximate range between 15 per cent and 20 per cent. As expected, the increase in government revenues fully aligns with the increase in FDI-level ETR faced by MNEs (at some 3 percentage points or 20 per cent in the upper-bound case with no carve-out; see figure III.6).

Which government receives this additional tax revenue, while essentially immaterial to investors, is of considerable importance to the governments involved, and the allocation of this revenue has been a subject of great controversy. As discussed in section A, Pillar II envisages two possibilities. One is that the top-up is allocated to the home country of the entity involved, through the application of the IIR. The other is that it is allocated to the host country, through the application of a QDMTT. The latter has been widely welcomed as more favourable to low-income countries. Yet, even assuming that all host countries adopt a QDMTT regime, as is the case in the simulation of the revenue effects of Pillar II in figure III.10, developing countries will gain relatively less revenue from the tax reform than developed ones (a 15 per cent increase, compared with 31 per cent for developed countries). As a result, despite the gain in absolute terms, the share of developing countries in the allocation of total government revenues slightly declines, while that of developed countries increases by almost 5 percentage points.

It is likely, and consistent with the policy discussion in this chapter (section D), that host countries will adopt a QDMMT regime; in that case, the results from the simulation in figure III.10 represent a realistic picture of the revenue effects of the reform. Questions remain on what the distributional effects would be of the application of the IIR instead. Notwithstanding the same growth in global terms, the allocation of the government revenues under the IIR is expected to favor developed economies over developing ones. Quite surprisingly, however, preliminary insights from ongoing analysis suggest that the difference between the two possibilities in terms of the overall impact of Pillar II on tax revenues in developed and developing countries is quite small. In other words, the larger gain in government revenues of developed economies would not be due to the allocation of the top-up tax to the parent entity but rather to the relatively higher increase in taxes paid by MNE on FDI in developed economies compared with developing economies.[34] As a possible explanation, the expected redistribution of taxing rights from developing to developed economies as a consequence of the IIR is limited by the fact that the impact of the ETR channel in developing countries (i.e. the component triggering the distribution effect under the IIR regime) is small, with the profit-shifting channel accounting for the bulk of the increase in taxation.

Importantly, these considerations are based on highly aggregated weighted averages, thus providing only big-picture directional indications. For smaller developing countries – which generally apply lower ETRs – the allocation of the top-up tax can make a major difference in revenue collection. Similarly, accounting for ETR variance within countries would substantially increase the impact of the ETR channel and amplify the distributional effects of the top-up in developing countries.

3. The effect of higher taxes on global FDI

Pillar II is expected to affect all three dimensions of the global FDI network: volume, distribution and route (figure III.11):

- Volume: The previous section estimates an increase in tax liabilities faced by MNEs on their FDI of about 15 per cent, due to a reduction in profit shifting and to the realignment of host countries' ETRs to the Pillar II minimum. This will exert downward pressure on the total volume of productive investment; however, indirect effects may compensate. Less scope for tax competition could intensify competition for investment based on non-tax factors, such as an improved business climate.

Figure III.11. | **Framework for assessing the impact of Pillar II on FDI**

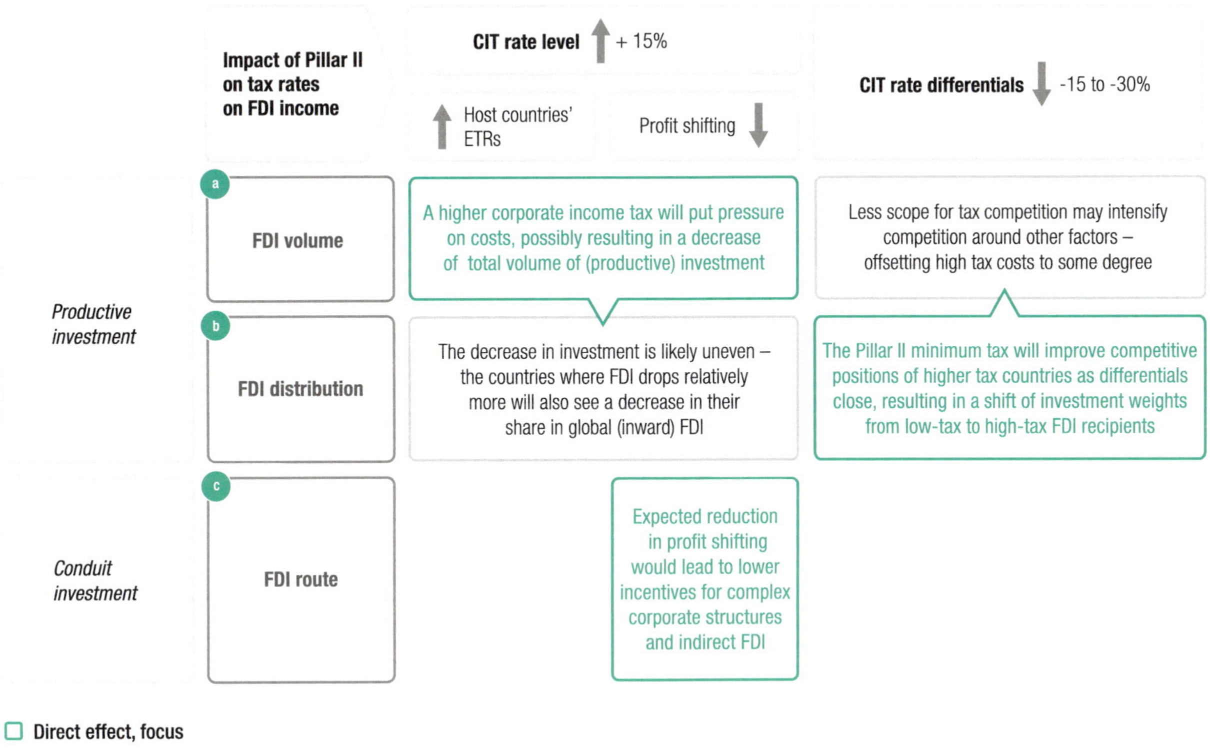

Source: UNCTAD.
Note: Impact figures rounded. CIT = corporate income tax.

- Distribution: The introduction of the Pillar II floor will reduce tax rate differentials between host countries – measured by the standard deviation of the distribution of FDI-level ETRs – by 15 to 30 per cent globally. As tax rate differentials narrow, low-tax countries will become less appealing investment destinations and MNEs will have stronger incentives to redirect investment to higher-tax locations. This may open opportunities for countries that are not OFCs and particularly for developing countries, which tend to have higher average ETRs.
- Route: Along with productive investment, the FDI perimeter includes a financial component. A sizeable share of FDI passes through *special purpose entities* (SPEs) – offshore vehicles often used in tax planning – thereby generating sizeable conduit investment. As Pillar II erodes incentives to shift profits, conduit FDI through these structures are expected to become less prevalent and investors to establish more direct connections with recipients. While this does not affect productive investment (but only the conduit component), changes in the financial component of FDI may be large.

The analysis in this section focuses on the quantification of the direct effects for each dimension. It draws on a large body of empirical research looking at the relationship between tax and FDI. However, there is a significant degree of uncertainty about how Pillar II will affect productive investment, because the reform is unprecedented in scale, scope and the extent to which it is coordinated across a large number of countries. Most empirical studies on tax and FDI (or MNE investment) capture uncoordinated tax rate changes by individual countries. This introduces several caveats into the analysis (discussed in box III.8).

Figure III.12. Pillar II volume effect: decrease in global FDI flows (Per cent)

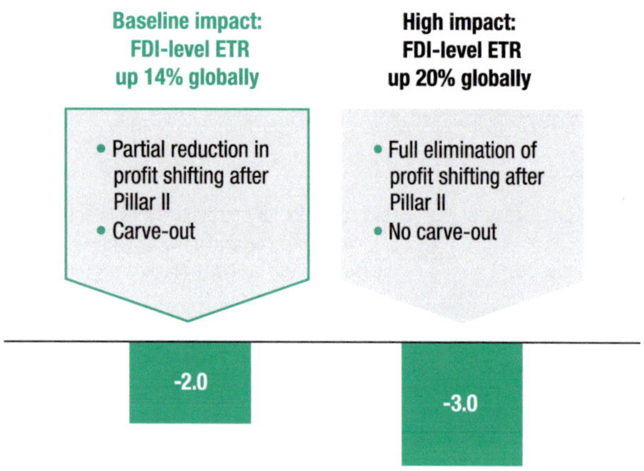

Source: UNCTAD estimates.
Note: The estimate of change in volume refers to productive investment and excludes conduit FDI. ETR = effective tax rate.

a. Impact on FDI volume

The baseline scenario places the potential downward effect of increased CIT on FDI global volume at about -2 per cent (figure III.12). This estimate refers to productive investment only, and thus it cannot be directly compared with historical trends in standard FDI flows, which are characterized by large variations caused by the financial component of FDI. Nevertheless, even removing the most volatile component – looking at the underlying FDI trend (*WIR19*) – the estimated decline remains moderate, although not negligible. This estimate rests on the assumption that some profit shifting continues after the BEPS reform is implemented (the baseline scenario in the ETR impact analysis) and that the carved-out share on (non-shifted) profits is 40 per cent. At the upper end, the full elimination of profit shifting and the absence of a carve-out result in a decline in global FDI flows of 3 per cent. Applying different assumptions about tax elasticity of investment produces a range of estimates of impact between -1 per cent and -4 per cent (box table III.8.2).

Box III.8. The tax (semi-)elasticity of investment

The estimates of the impact of Pillar II on the total volume of investment draw on a large body of empirical research attempting to measure the response of FDI to changes in tax rates. Yet, FDI can encompass stocks and flows at different levels (country, sector, industry or firm), on an aggregate or bilateral basis. Summary measures of tax effects used in the literature include STRs, AETRs and/or METRs and bilateral tax differentials between countries. Accordingly, estimates of the tax elasticity of investment vary with the data source, the type of data used and the estimation technique. The tax (semi-)elasticity of investment used in this analysis represents the percentage change in investment for a 1 percentage point increase in the tax rate. Estimates of the semi-elasticity of MNE investment from a number of prominent studies are reported in box table III.8.1.

Box table III.8.1. Studies focusing on the response of MNE investment to changes in tax rates

Study	Basis	Estimated semi-elasticity
Arnold et al. (2011)	User cost of capital	-0.69
Becker and Riedel (2012)	STR	-1.42
De Mooij and Ederveen (2008)	METR	-0.80
De Mooij and Liu (2020)	STR	-1.26
Feld and Heckemeyer (2011)	STR	-0.57
Vartia (2008)	User cost of capital	-0.60

Note: METR = marginal effective tax rate, STR = statutory tax rate.

The upper and lower bounds for the tax (semi-)elasticity of investment encompass a relatively confined range (-0.6 and -1.4), reflecting the range of notionally consistent estimates in the literature. The baseline of -1 used for this report is the middle value. The range includes elasticities reported by studies using METRs and STRs. Calculation of the investment impact is a straightforward multiplication of the tax (semi-)elasticity by the (percentage point) change in the relevant tax rate, which is taken here to be the increase in the FDI-level ETR.

In principle, for the reasons discussed in section A, the change in an appropriately defined METR might be preferable, but adequate information for a wide set of countries on pre- and post-Pillar II METRs is not available. Nevertheless, the AETR, METR and STR are generally positively correlated, with the AETR tending to lie (under some conditions) between the STR and the METR. The literature review reported by

/...

Box III.8. The tax (semi-)elasticity of investment (Concluded)

box table III.8.1, using different measures of ETRs, including not only METRs but also (most notably for this analysis) STRs, is reassuring: the range of values for the tax semi-elasticity remains relatively confined across different definitions of tax rates.

Different scenarios indicate a decline in global FDI flows between 1 and 4 per cent as a result of lower investment volume by MNE affiliates post-Pillar II (box table III.8.2), with the upper bound reflecting the full elimination of profit shifting, no carve-out and a high tax elasticity of investment (-1.4), and the lower bound reflecting continued profit shifting, a carve-out at 40 per cent of profits and a low tax semi-elasticity (-0.6). Overall, results are most sensitive to assumptions on the tax semi-elasticity followed by the assumptions on profit shifting, whereas the calibration carve-out is less important.

Box table III.8.2. Expected change in FDI flows post-Pillar II

	Semi-elasticity	Baseline scenario	Upper-bound scenario
Low response	-0.6	-1.2%	-1.8%
Baseline	-1.0	**-2.0%**	-3.0%
High response	-1.4	-2.8%	-4.0%

Note: Baseline scenario assumes partial elimination of profit shifting post-Pillar II and a carve-out. Upper-bound scenario assumes full elimination of profit shifting post-Pillar II and no carve-out.

Source: UNCTAD.

b. Impact on FDI distribution

Bilateral tax rate differentials are a determinant of efficiency-seeking FDI, and the change in the distribution of FDI-level ETRs post-Pillar II may reshape the competitive landscape for MNEs' foreign investment and divert some investment from (previously) low-tax to higher-tax countries (figure III.13; box III.9). As OFCs lose their tax advantage, developing countries are likely to gain investment from diversion. The largest gains are expected in Africa and Asia, where conservative estimates indicate a 2.4 per cent and 1.7 per cent increase in FDI inflows, respectively. Gains in Latin America and the Caribbean and in developed economies are likely more limited but still positive. Overall, this analysis shows that, in developing

Figure III.13. Pillar II diversion effect: change in FDI inflows by region (Per cent)

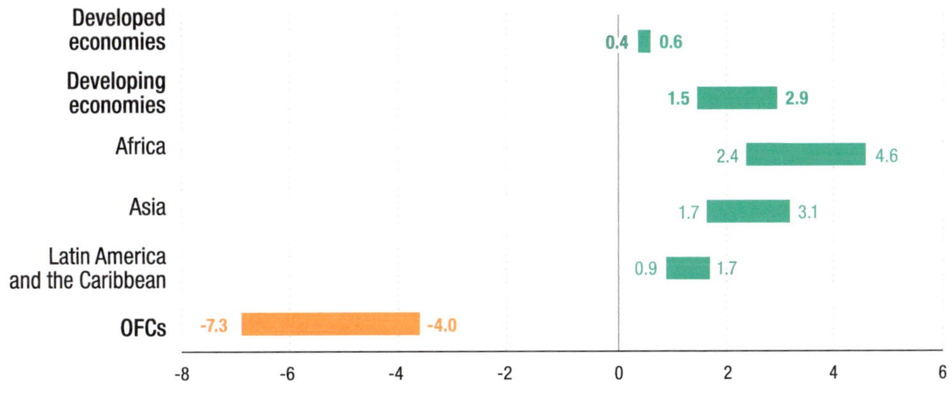

Source: UNCTAD estimates, based on Keen et al. (forthcoming).
Note: Economic groupings and regions do not include OFCs. Lower bound and upper bound reflect the 95 per cent confidence interval and the point estimates reported by Keen et al. (forthcoming), respectively. Baseline scenario and constant FDI volume assumed.

Box III.9. Estimating the FDI diversion effect post-Pillar II

In setting limits on international tax competition, Pillar II will diminish the competitive advantages of particularly low tax rates and of many tax incentives. Without their former advantage, low-tax countries risk attracting fewer projects, and higher-tax countries will become relatively more attractive for investment. Aside from effects on the global level of investment, there may thus be a reallocation of investment towards higher-tax countries.

Assessing the likely strength of this "diversion" effect is not straightforward. The approach here builds on the work of Keen et al. (forthcoming), who find that real investment in a potential host country *C* from MNEs with a parent in country *P* is significantly higher, the lower is the tax rate in C relative to the average tax rate that MNEs in country *P* face elsewhere. Applying their methodology to FDI-level ETRs, bilateral tax rate differentials, $\Delta\tau_{CP}$, are calculated. This measure is the difference between the tax rate in a host country and the weighted average of the tax rates in all the other potential investment destinations j that the parent might invest in, as given by:

$$\Delta\tau_{CP} = \frac{\sum_{j=1}^{N} T_j\theta_{jP} - T_C}{1 - T_C}, \text{ where: } \theta_{jP} = \frac{sales_{jP}}{sales_P}$$

For each country pair, the change in tax rate differentials induced by Pillar II is given by $\Delta\tau_{CP}$ *post-Pillar II* – $\Delta\tau_{CP}$ *pre-Pillar II*, with the countries' tax rates measured by the FDI-level ETRs. MNE bilateral sales' shares across countries are not always available however, so bilateral ultimate FDI stocks from Casella (2019) are used as a proxy. The data closely match sales by foreign MNEs as reported in OECD inward data on foreign affiliate trade in services (FATS) (a univariate regression gives a coefficient of 1.03 and a R^2 of about 0.87). The semi-elasticity of MNE investment reported by Keen et al. (forthcoming) of 3.04 – meaning that an improvement in the tax rate differential of a country by 1 percentage point will increase FDI by 3 per cent – is then applied to the change in differentials in FDI-level ETRs to find the expected change in the allocation of investment following the implementation of Pillar II. To isolate the reallocation effect, a constant level of global FDI pre- and post-Pillar II is assumed.

Source: UNCTAD, based on Keen et al. (forthcoming).

countries in particular, the diversion effect has the potential to counterbalance investment losses caused by the volume effect. Yet this potential will not be realized automatically. Developing countries will be able to fully leverage the competitive gains associated with a decrease in tax rate differentials if they push on other more critical investment determinants such as those associated with economic or institutional fundamentals.

c. Impact on FDI routes

UNCTAD estimates the share of FDI stock through OFCs at about 35 per cent of all inward FDI stock (*WIR15*).[35] This share corresponds to more than $10 trillion of FDI stock. This component does not reflect productive investment and is associated with conduit FDI and tax planning practices.[36] To the extent that Pillar II will reduce profit shifting, it can be expected that some FDI stock in OFCs will be dismantled. Ultimate investors will be more likely to establish direct links with recipients, reducing the share of conduit FDI. Assuming for illustrative purposes that the decrease in FDI stock in OFCs as a result of Pillar II is the same as the expected reduction in profit shifting, the effect on total FDI stock would range from -10 per cent (baseline case, with partial reduction of profit shifting) to -35 per cent (upper-bound case, with full elimination of profit shifting). The value of the FDI stock "at stake" in OFCs would be large, ranging from $4 trillion to $12 trillion. Major disinvestment of the FDI stock in OFCs would also weigh heavily on trends in FDI flows.[37]

C. IMPLICATIONS OF PILLAR II FOR TAX INCENTIVES

This section focuses on the implications of Pillar II for tax incentives, a key policy tool adopted by countries to attract FDI. There are both policy and analytical arguments calling for specific analysis of the effects of the reforms on tax incentives. The transformation of tax incentives will ultimately be determined by how the new tax environment affects each specific category of incentives, especially those most commonly used to attract FDI. The granular assessment here can serve as a guide for investment policymakers and investment promotion institutions as they assess and review their incentive systems in light of the innovations brought about by Pillar II.

1. Tax incentives and ETRs

Tax incentives are one of the main reasons for the observed gap at the country level between average STRs and average ETRs (see figure III.2). Although the cost-benefit ratio of such incentives is debated, the investment they attract can bring job creation and knowledge spillovers, help develop local industries and connect countries to global value chains (GVCs).

A few incentives are unaffected by Pillar II. Others – for example, tax holidays and blanket exemptions – may be largely negated. All countries will have to reconsider their incentive system, even those with an average ETR significantly above the minimum of 15 per cent, because incentives may well bring the ETR for individual investors below the minimum. It should be noted that, even though some incentives may appear small in absolute terms, they can be strategic for countries' economic and industrial development objectives.

In rethinking tax incentives, countries may shift to non-tax measures, such as subsidizing project infrastructure. As an alternative, countries can change their tax structures and lower other taxes, such as payroll or value added taxes. Pillar II leaves ample scope for such measures; critically, however, their own cost-benefit ratios will need close attention.

The diversity of tax incentive systems implies that the impact of the reform will fall unevenly across countries and firms. This uneven impact has analytical implications for the estimation of the fiscal effects of Pillar II. Assessments that rely on countries' average ETRs – such as those in the previous section and in other analyses of the investment impact of Pillar II so far – are based on summary statistics that reflect the average level of CIT faced by FDI in host countries. This is likely the best approximation, given the data available, to the ETRs of entities present in the country; however, distribution of (firm-level) ETRs across foreign affiliates are highly relevant for the impact of Pillar II. These distributions are largely determined by the structure of tax incentives and can vary significantly (figure III.14). Any realistic distribution curve that implies some variance of ETRs would lead to greater impact than the assumption of a uniform ("representative") country-level ETR. The effect of accounting for the variance of ETRs can be so large as to double the fiscal impact of Pillar II (see box III.7; Auclair and Casella, forthcoming).

Figure III.14. **Illustrative distribution of effective tax rates of foreign affiliates in a host country**

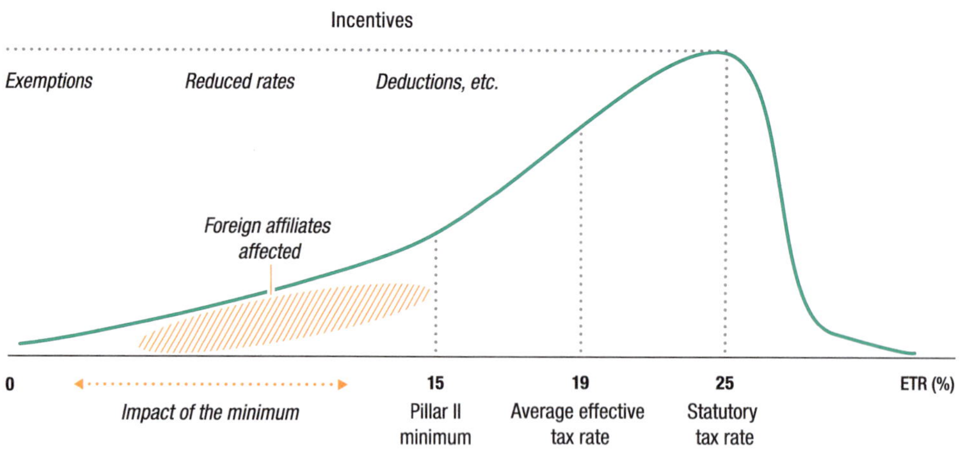

Source: UNCTAD.
Notes: Illustrative shape of an ETRs' distribution for a generic host country (with STR and ETR equal to the global averages). In this example, a large group of foreign affiliates pays the full statutory rate (resulting in a "peak" at the STR). Host countries provide a variety of incentives to specific subsets of foreign affiliates; these firms face ETRs lower than the STR. Incentives can range from deductions to reduced rates to exemptions, for which the tax reduction is maximized. The example shows that the country's average effective tax rate (19 per cent) is not a fully representative indicator for the impact of Pillar II. Simply based on the average ETR, the host country would not be affected by a minimum at 15 per cent; however, a subset of foreign affiliates is. As they align their ETR to the minimum, the country's overall average increases above 19 per cent.

2. Pillar II and tax incentives: an empirical assessment

As a general rule, the GloBE model rules will have an impact only when an MNE is within its scope of application, an incentive brings the ETR below 15 per cent and accounting profit exceeds the carve-out. This means that any incentive will remain intact if these conditions are not met – e.g. when it brings the ETR to, say, 16 per cent; when an MNE has global turnover of less than €750 million; or when the industry to which the incentive applies runs on tight profit margins and is intensive in labour and tangible assets, thereby causing the substance carve-out to produce a negative result for GloBE net tax. Envisaged as acting parallel to existing corporate tax systems, the GloBE rules hence do not affect any incentive in all circumstances. Even when a given incentive is rendered economically ineffective up to the minimum rate of 15 per cent it is never legally prohibited by Pillar II, as the latter aims to ensure a minimum level of taxation of excess profits without interfering directly with the domestic system of corporate taxation. Moreover, some tax measures – such as accelerated depreciation, loss carry-forward or participation exemption regimes – do not reduce the ETR calculation for GloBE purposes, thus minimizing the impact of Pillar II on such domestic regimes.

As not all incentives are affected and not all are affected to the same extent, to establish the implications of Pillar II on tax incentives, it is important to discriminate between them: that is, to determine how large is the set of tax incentives affected by the reform and, within this group, what is the share of the categories that are most affected. A precise quantitative assessment would require an empirical mapping of tax incentives through the lens of Pillar II, which is not possible given current data availability. Nonetheless, the new Government Tax Expenditure Database (GTED), published for the first time in the fall of 2021, reports tax expenditure provisions published by countries worldwide from 1990 onwards and allows some empirically informed high-level sizing.[38] As a main feature, each provision in the database is classified according to four key dimensions: beneficiary, tax base, policy purpose and type of reduction. Each of these dimensions provides useful information on the possible relevance of Pillar II for the current structure of overall tax incentive systems.[39]

As a first approximation, the scope of Pillar II can be delimited by tax expenditures addressed to *business beneficiaries*, and within that subset, those targeting *income-related taxes* – mainly CITs but also other income-based taxes such as taxes on capital gains. This perimeter includes (but is not limited to) incentives affected by Pillar II.[40] Yet, it is notable that the vast majority of tax expenditures lies outside this perimeter, targeting non-corporate beneficiaries and/or taxes other than income-based ones.

Only one fifth of global tax expenditure provisions reported by countries in the last 30 years are targeting corporate income (figure III.15). More specifically, of about 17,000 tax expenditures reported by the GTED database, 41 per cent have a business beneficiary. Within this group, about half target income-based taxation – the focus of Pillar II – with the other half covering other tax categories such as taxes on goods and services or on payroll. The relative share of tax expenditures targeting corporate income in the total number of tax expenditures does not differ substantially between developed and developing economies; however, LDCs are a notable exception, with income-related tax expenditures amounting to less than 10 per cent of the total number of tax expenditures reported by these economies. The (forgone) revenue pool associated with provisions targeting corporate income equals some 5 per cent of total tax revenues of the reporting countries, a limited but non-negligible value. As a share of GDP, forgone revenues associated with income-related expenditures amount to about 1 per cent, for both developed and developing countries.

Importantly, the share of income-related tax expenditures in the total number of tax expenditures with business beneficiaries increases from 50 per cent to 75 per cent when focusing on expenditures aimed at attracting FDI. This suggests that the coverage of Pillar II is higher for those incentives that are more directly targeted by the scope of the reform.

The focus on income-related incentives is only the first and most obvious filter that can be used to size the relevance of Pillar II for tax incentives. Zooming in on the dimension of policy purpose allows some additional refinement. More affected will be incentives whose main purpose is to attract foreign investment and/or target investment from large MNEs and/or those that have a heavier intangible component (owing to the lesser tax reduction

Figure III.15. | Tax expenditure provisions targeting business beneficiaries, 1990–2020 (Per cent)

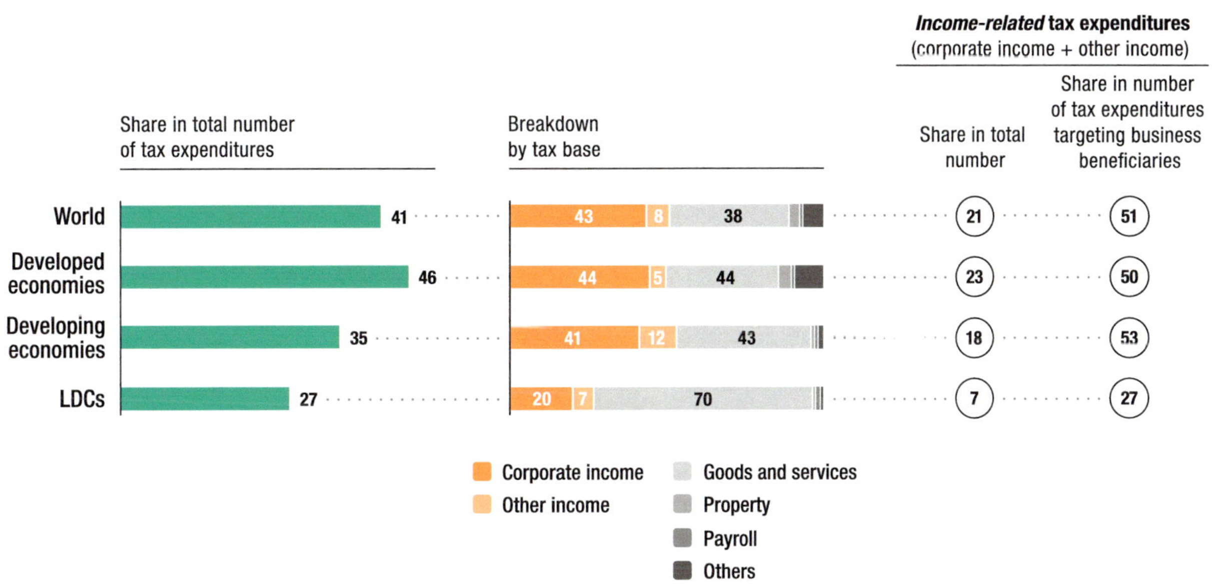

Source: UNCTAD, based on the Government Tax Expenditure Database.
Note: Number of tax expenditure provisions reported = 16,900. LDCs = least developed countries.

in that case from the substance-based carve-out). How large these categories are within the group of income-related incentives is difficult to assess from the provisions reported in the GTED database.[41]

Nevertheless, it is reasonable to exclude from the relevant group up to a third of tax provisions with reported objectives that focus on domestic and/or small business (figure III.16, left-hand side). It is indicative that among the most frequently cited policy objectives in the group of income-related tax expenditures reported by the GTED database are "develop the agricultural sector" – an industry that typically has low FDI intensity – and "promote SMEs", which are likely outside the scope of Pillar II. For about 40 per cent of tax provisions the allocation is not straightforward, as they have objectives that cut across the scope of Pillar II. Finally, one quarter report policy objectives that generally place them in the domain of application of Pillar II. These include a minority of provisions that explicitly state as their objective to "attract FDI" as well as provisions aimed at promoting activities at high degrees of internationalization such as knowledge-intensive activities or exports, or at developing sectors that have high FDI intensity. Although necessarily high-level, this analysis shows that, even within the perimeter of Pillar II (income-related incentives), countries still retain an unaffected policy space on a large range of tax incentives, aimed at promoting policy objectives that do not interfere with the scope and objectives of Pillar II.

The fourth dimension in the GTED database, "type of reduction", allows further discrimination between incentives in terms of their design and expected interaction with GloBE rules (figure III.16, right-hand side). In the set of incentives with broad focus on foreign investment and/or large MNEs, two main categories emerge: those reducing the CIT rate, including exemptions, tax holidays and reduced rates (42 per cent of the total),

Figure III.16. **Income-related tax expenditures, by policy objective and type of reduction, 1990–2020** (Per cent)

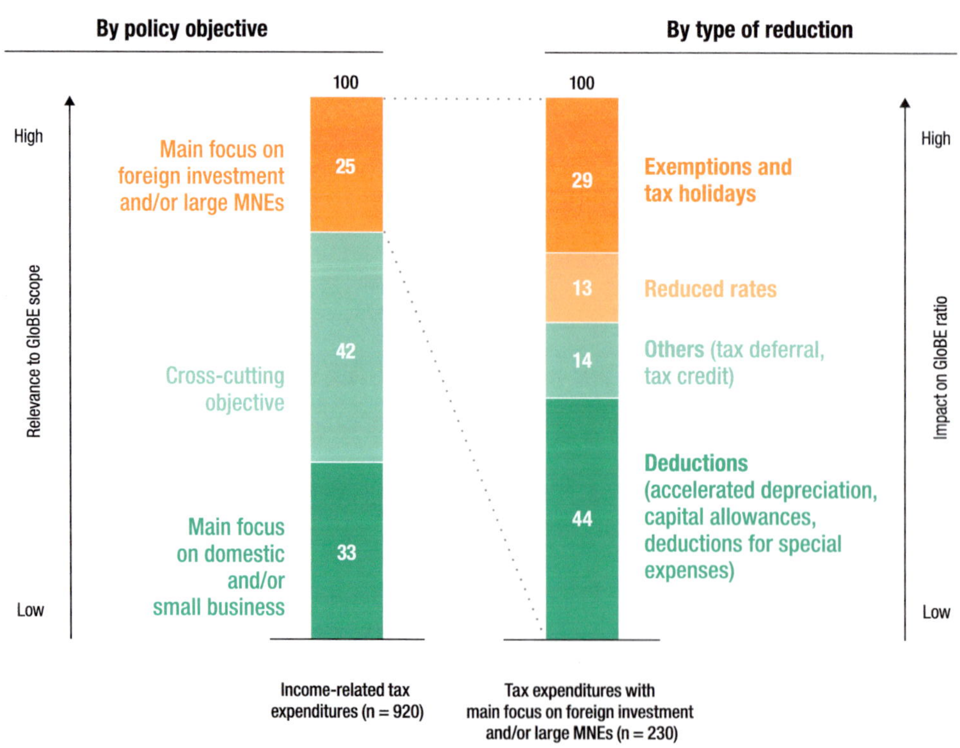

Source: UNCTAD, based on the Government Tax Expenditure Database.

and those reducing the tax base (44 per cent), including deductions, accelerated depreciation and capital allowances. Generally speaking, the former group will be much more heavily affected by Pillar II. The remaining categories (14 per cent), including for example tax credits, will also be only moderately affected by Pillar II.

Despite some important limitations – particularly related to the incomplete reporting of tax expenditures across countries – this high-level analysis helps put the impact of Pillar II on tax incentives in some perspective. Although Pillar II has certainly significant and direct effects on tax incentives to attract FDI, countries still retain ample policy space on a large range of tax incentives: those falling outside the perimeter of Pillar II; those aimed at promoting policy objectives that do not interfere with the scope and objectives of Pillar II; and those covered by Pillar II in principle, but ultimately not significantly affected by the GloBE rules. The next section focuses on this latter analytical dimension, providing a detailed assessment of the impact of the GloBE rules for the most common incentives used by countries to attract FDI.

3. Impact of the GloBE rules on tax incentives

A detailed assessment of the implications of GloBE rules on specific incentives to attract FDI involves understanding the impact of each category of incentives on the GloBE ratio, defined by the GloBE rules as the ratio between covered taxes and GloBE income. This GloBE ratio (or GloBE ETR) is the trigger for the application of the Pillar II top-up.

The key rationale for granting an income-based tax incentive is to stimulate certain responses from a corporate entity by reducing its ETR (relative to the standard treatment). In this respect all tax incentives operating through the corporate tax and other covered taxes potentially produce some kind of reduction in the ETR faced by the beneficiary, and hence in the resulting GloBE ratio. However, the nexus is not so straightforward, and an assessment of the Pillar II impact on specific categories of incentives demands a number of considerations and steps (figure III.17). In exploring them, this analysis focuses on the implications, through the GloBE ratio, for any top-up tax. Yet, it is important to bear in mind that the total liability of the MNE is the sum of that top-up tax plus the usual domestic liability. So, incentives also affect investors through the latter route, just as they do at present. The net effect is that topping up may reduce the impact of an incentive but does not in general eliminate it.

i. Is the tax incentive in scope?

Among income-related tax incentives, the GloBE rules establish some important exceptions. These exceptions include incentives that target out-of-scope entities (SMEs and excluded entities) and specific portions of the income tax base (excluded income).

SMEs. In general, the application of the top-up tax is limited to MNE groups with annual consolidated revenues of at least €750 million.[42]

Excluded entities. Some entities are not subject to the GloBE rules because they are excluded from the definition of constituent entities. These include government bodies, international organizations, non-profit organizations, pension funds and investment funds, and real estate investment vehicles that are the ultimate parent of an MNE group.

Excluded income. Income derived from international shipping is excluded from the computation of the GloBE income. This means that such income will not be included in the GloBE tax base in the ETR calculation and, thus, tax benefits granted to such income may not be affected by the GloBE rules, as they will not reduce the ETR for a country.[43]

Figure III.17. Framework to assess the impact of Pillar II on (income-related) tax incentives

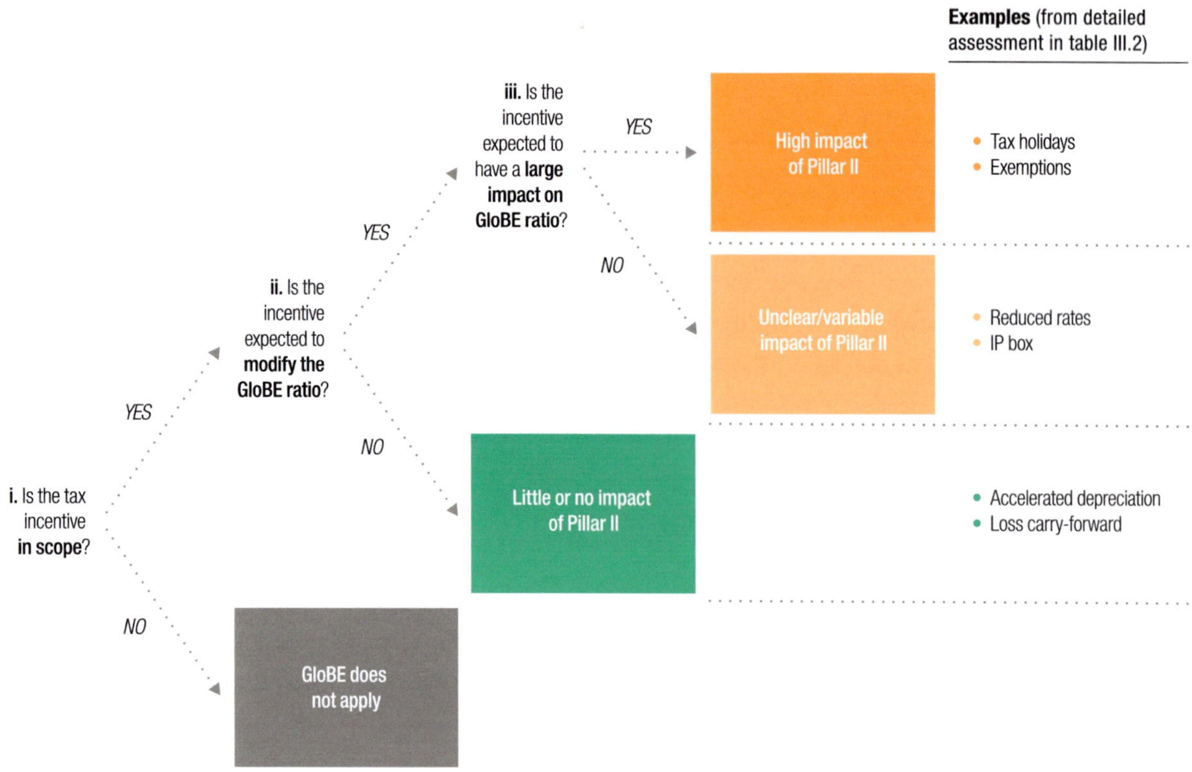

Source: UNCTAD.

ii. Does the tax incentive modify the GloBE ratio?

A decrease in the standard ETR generated by a tax incentive does not necessarily translate into a corresponding decrease in the GloBE ratio. It does so unless the GloBE model rules, recognizing the distinctive nature of some categories of incentives, prescribe specific adjustments to the GloBE ratio. These adjustments are generally aimed at offsetting the downward pressure exerted by the incentive on the standard ETR.

This offset usually happens either through a deduction of some relevant part of the tax base from the GloBE income in the denominator of the GloBE ratio or through the inclusion of some additional tax items in the taxes covered in the numerator. One of the most important cases arises in the GloBE treatment of timing differences, where the model rules prescribe an approach based on deferred tax accounting, seeking to match taxes to the period when the income or expenses is recognized for tax purposes. This in general implies that covered taxes in the numerator of the GloBE ratio are adjusted to align with the GloBE income in the denominator, resulting in small or no impact of GloBE rules on the underlying incentive. This general treatment of timing differences involves several types of tax incentives, including for example accelerated depreciation and loss carry-forward (see the detailed assessment in table III.2).

These adjustments have the effect of preserving a higher GloBE ratio. In the end, it is the GloBE ratio, not the standard ETR, that triggers the top-up. Thus, in these cases the intended benefits of the incentive are not limited or affected by Pillar II (i.e. the incentive brings down the standard ETR, resulting in a benefit for the investor, but not the GloBE ratio, which determines the top-up tax). The impact of the GloBE rules on the tax incentive is therefore expected to be small or null.

iii. Does the tax incentive have a significant impact on the GloBE ratio?

In general, if the incentive is in scope and not regulated by the model rules – and thus has no specific adjustment prescribed – the GloBE ratio is expected to decrease consistently with the standard ETR. In this general case, to the extent that a specific incentive brings the GloBE ETR faced by an entity below the minimum, its intended benefits will be partially or totally offset by the Pillar II top-up (notwithstanding the mitigating effect of the carve-out). The tax incentive is then assessed to be generally affected by Pillar II.

The magnitude of the impact depends on the gap between the fiscal benefits of the incentive prior to the application of the top-up and the benefits that remain after. This assessment is difficult a priori for broad categories of incentives, as it is country-, entity-, and incentive-specific. However, some categories of incentives, because of their design, are expected to have a greater impact on the GloBE ratio; these are thus prone to being highly affected by Pillar II. For other categories, the impact remains unclear and case-specific.

Two key factors underpin this assessment. The first concerns the magnitude of the fiscal benefit. A total CIT exemption that brings the tax rate down to 0 per cent has greater impact than a reduced rate. In addition, impact is clearly not linear in the decrease of the GloBE ratio but instead starts "biting" only when the ratio falls below 15 per cent. The second factor is the relevance of the tax base to which the incentive applies in total GloBE income of the entity concerned. Even generous incentives on a relatively limited portion of income, say on income from capital gains or intellectual property, will generally produce a smaller effect on GloBE income than broad-based discounts applied to total income.

4. Detailed assessment of impact on in-scope incentives

Table III.2 summarizes an overall assessment of the impact of Pillar II on the main categories of tax incentives typically adopted to attract FDI, focusing on in-scope incentives. The table is followed by a brief explanation of the assessment. More detailed elaboration and discussion is provided by Lazarov et al. (2022).

a. Reduced rates

Zero rated and less than 15 per cent: *high impact*

Governments may set a lower CIT rate as an exception to the general tax regime in order to attract FDI into specific sectors or regions. If the statutory corporate tax rate is less than 15 per cent, it is likely that the ETR under the GloBE rules will also be less than 15 per cent. It is important to note that "covered taxes" for the purpose of calculating the GloBE ETR do not rely only on the CIT rate. The ETR calculation also depends on other taxes on corporate income, such as taxes on resource rents and taxes on capital gains. Where the GloBE ETR is less than 15 per cent, it would trigger the top-up tax and to that extent eliminate the effect of the low CIT rate up to the minimum.

Rates above 15 per cent: *little/no impact*

In general, a tax incentive that decreases the CIT rate to a level that remains above 15 per cent should not trigger any impact of Pillar II, though it may do so if the base is sufficiently narrow relative to accounting profit (in the denominator of the ETR). As many countries have an STR of 30 per cent this (unaffected) reduction could be as large as half of the CIT due. Yet, it is important to consider that the standard ETR does not necessarily coincide with the relevant ratio according to the GloBE rules, which provide their own formulas that are separate from similar calculations under CIT systems.

/...

Table III.2. Summary assessment of the impact of Pillar II on incentives to attract FDI

Incentive type	Pillar II impact	Overview
a. Reduced rates		
Zero-rated	High impact	Reduced rates below 15 per cent, or even down to zero, will generally result in a GloBE ratio below the minimum, triggering the activation of the Pillar II top-up. Magnitude of impact depends on the size of the reduction.
Below 15 per cent	High impact	
Above 15 per cent	Little/no impact	Generally, reduced rates to a level above 15 per cent would not be affected. Yet, countries would need to calculate the effective rate under GloBE rules as this may still lead to a result below the minimum threshold.
b. Deductions		
Accelerated depreciation and immediate expensing	Little/no impact	Impact on accelerated depreciation and immediate expensing will be limited as deferred tax adjustments are taken into account when calculating covered taxes in the GloBE ratio.
Loss carry-forward	Little/no impact	Impact on loss carry-forwards will be limited as deferred tax adjustments are taken into account when calculating covered taxes in the GloBE ratio.
Deductible qualified expenses	Variable/unclear impact	Special tax exclusions, deductions or tax accounting conventions that are common among Inclusive Framework members are deductible from GloBE income for purposes of calculating the GloBE tax base; those that are less common may not be deductible.
c. Exemptions		
Tax holidays	High impact	Tax holiday regimes are not expressly addressed under the GloBE rules and are likely to bring the GloBE ratio below 15 per cent.
Specific exemptions: location, sector, entity	Variable/unclear impact	Exemptions granted to specific sectors, entities or locations (other than out-of-scope situations) are likely to be affected as they may bring the GloBE ratio below 15 per cent. However, exemptions applying to out-of-scope situations such as SMEs, excluded entities or excluded income are not affected.
Participation exemptions	Little/no impact	Dividends received under participation regimes are excluded from the tax base for the computation of the GloBE ratio, resulting in little or no impact.
d. Other incentives on income-related taxes		
Incentives on withholding taxes	Little/no impact	Taxation of outbound passive income by the source country is not included in the computation of the GloBE ratio, resulting in little or no impact in the source country.
IP box	Variable/unclear impact	Not directly addressed by the GloBE rules, may bring GloBE ratio below 15 per cent by reducing covered taxes, depending on the regime.
Tax credits	Variable/unclear impact	Lead either to inclusion in the income of the MNE (if credit is refundable within four years) or to a reduction in covered tax expenses (if not). Both may bring the GloBE ratio below 15 per cent.
Incentives on capital gains taxes	Variable/unclear impact	Not directly addressed by the GloBE rule, may bring the GloBE ratio below 15 per cent by reducing covered taxes, depending on the regime.

Source: UNCTAD, based on Lazarov et al. (2022).
Note: ETR = effective tax rate.

Little/no impact | High impact | Variable/unclear impact

b. Deductions

Accelerated depreciation and immediate expensing: *little/no impact*

Accelerated depreciation rules permit a taxpayer to expense the cost of an asset faster than its expected economic depreciation. Immediate expensing permits the deduction of the entire cost of the asset in the year it was purchased. Both incentives lower taxable profits for the years when they are applied and give rise to timing differences when compared with financial accounts.

Since the GloBE rules rely on consolidated financial accounts to calculate the tax base, they do not take into account domestic tax treatment of depreciations that is more beneficial than under the accounting rules, including the timing benefits of immediate expensing and accelerated depreciation. To prevent this reversal, the model rules rely on the deferred tax accounting method used by the constituent entity with respect to assets eligible for these incentives for tax purposes. The GloBE rules permit the inclusion of accelerated depreciation and immediate expensing as deferred taxes when computing the adjusted covered taxes. This treatment arises from the recognition in the Inclusive Framework that these are the most common tax incentives offered by countries and that their elimination could cause challenges for capital-intensive businesses, in particular. This adjustment therefore prevents the GloBE ETR from falling below the minimum solely as a result of accelerated depreciation.

Loss carry-forward: *little/no impact*

A tax loss may occur when allowable expenses exceed taxable income. This loss may be carried forward to future years as long as national tax rules permit or until the loss has been completely offset against future tax liability, returning the company to a payable position. The GloBE rules permit adjustments for carry-forward of losses. Since loss carry-forwards create timing differences in a similar way as does accelerated depreciation, the GloBE model rules also provide for entities to use the deferred tax accounting approach to neutralize the effect on the ETR. As a result, loss carry-forwards are permitted as deferred tax adjustments that will be taken into account in computing the covered taxes.

Deductible qualified expenses: *variable/unclear impact*

Deductions for qualified expenses refer to the allowable expenses that businesses are permitted to deduct for tax purposes. Tax-allowable expenses sometimes differ from those permitted by accounting rules. For GloBE computation purposes, this means that even if the actual costs of doing business have been taken into account under the accounting rules, the local tax rules might disallow certain deductions for tax purposes. Moreover, the reverse is also possible where a certain expense might be treated more beneficially for tax purposes as compared to the accounting expensing: e.g. super-deductions (150 per cent allowance for manufacturing equipment). The GloBE model rules recognize that it is not possible or desirable to develop a comprehensive set of adjustments that will bring the GloBE tax base fully into line with the tax base calculation rules of all Inclusive Framework members. Instead, the rules establish a list of the most common expenses that may be allowed in order to calculate the GloBE tax base. Special tax expenses that fall outside of this list or are not common may not be deductible from the GloBE income base.

c. Exemptions

Tax holidays and other specific exemptions: *high impact*

Tax holiday schemes are government incentive programmes that offer a temporary reduction or elimination (full exemption) of corporate income taxes. Alternatively, specific exemption regimes may apply, such as those exempting certain sectors of the economy, types of entities or locations from taxation. These categories are likely to be affected by the application of the rules because the GloBE documents do not explicitly exclude untaxed income from the GloBE tax base, which may bring the ETR for a relevant group of entities below 15 per cent. Therefore, unless exemptions are granted to out-of-scope situations, they will be affected by the application of the GloBE rules and the levy of the top-up tax.

Participation exemptions: *little/no impact*

To prevent economic double taxation, many countries exclude dividends from the taxable income of a corporate shareholder, usually through a mechanism referred to as participation exemption. To tax these dividends under the GloBE rules would give rise to the risk of overtaxation; thus the model rules ensure that participation exemption regimes will not be affected by the application of those rules.

As dividends received under participation exemption regimes are excluded from the GloBE tax base, they will not reduce the GloBE ETR. These excluded dividends refer to any distributions paid on shares or other equity interests where the MNE group holds 10 per cent or more of the ownership interests in the issuer, or the full economic ownership of the ownership interest has been held for a period of at least 12 months. An exception is made for dividends received from short-term portfolio shareholdings, which are not excluded from the GloBE tax base and will likely be affected by the application of the GloBE rules.

d. Other incentives on income-related taxes

Incentives on withholding taxes: *little/no impact*

Some countries provide foreign investors with favourable treatment of WHT by eliminating or greatly reducing their domestic WHT on outbound passive payments such as on dividends (or liquidation payments), interest or royalties.

The GloBE rules calculate the minimum level of taxation in each State where an MNE group has subsidiaries or permanent establishments. For this reason, Pillar II does not affect directly the WHT treatment of passive income streams that this group receives because WHT is a tax imposed by the source State on a foreign resident that has no subsidiary or permanent establishment on its territory to which the passive income is attributable.

Nevertheless, if the GloBE rules lead to topping-up of the taxation on passive income in the hands of the recipient, the fiscal benefits of WHT incentives may be partially or totally offset.[44] For this reason, countries may wish to revisit their WHT incentive policy, granting such incentives only as long as no neutralization takes place in the State of residence.

Thus, WHT incentives might be still granted on dividend payments when the residence State operates a participation exemption regime, which is recognized and endorsed by the GloBE rules. For interest and royalties, the applicability of the GloBE rules would depend on whether the ETR in the residence State is below 15 per cent and, if that is the case, whether the GloBE net tax result is positive. In such circumstances, the source State may wish to consider introducing WHT that equals the difference between the actual ETR and 15 per cent: e.g. if the ETR in the residence State is 10 per cent, the source State may wish to levy 5 per cent WHT so that the WHT incentive is not collected by another country.

In addition, the Pillar II rules introduce a Subject to Tax Rule (STTR), mentioned briefly in section A. This will have an impact on WHT incentives. The STTR applies to the WHT arising with respect to payments between connected persons. It will be a rule in tax treaties and will be triggered when a payment is subject to a nominal tax rate in the payee country that is below the minimum nominal rate of 9 per cent. It covers interest, royalties and other payments for mobile factors such as capital, assets or risks owned or assumed by the person entitled to the payment; it is not yet clear if management and technical fees will be covered. The STTR can be applied even where the IIR or the Undertaxed Payments Rule have been implemented. Where it applies, its adoption would risk diminishing the incentive effect of reduced WHT rates; the possible advantage is in discouraging outward profit shifting.

IP box: *variable/unclear impact*

The intellectual property (IP) box regime is a tax incentive related to favourable tax treatment of income derived from IP rights. As the GloBE rules do not explicitly regulate the treatment of such regimes, to the extent that they lead to an ETR below 15 per cent for an MNE in a given country, the effects of the incentive are limited or neutralized in computing the GloBE ratio. The specific effects of IP box regimes depend on the exact activities that an MNE group performs in the country that offers the regime. If the IP income is diluted in other income, it is possible that even if the ETR on the IP income is less than 15 per cent, the ETR on the overall income (which is what matters for the GloBE calculation) is more than 15 per cent. Moreover, in terms of the impact on the total tax faced by the investor, IP box regimes compatible with BEPS Action 5 – i.e. regimes in which the IP rights were developed by substantive activities in the country in question – might be positively affected by the substance carve-out under the GloBE rules since non-harmful IP box regimes presuppose that there is substantive development activity.

Tax credits: *variable/unclear impact*

Refundable tax credits are instances of negative tax liability, providing a business with a refund when the taxes it owes are lower than its entitlement to a tax credit. They seem to be rarely used at present, but the GloBE rules may give them heightened importance.

Those rules divide refundable tax credits into two main groups – qualified (refundable within four years) and non-qualified (refundable for more than four years). Under the GloBE rules, qualified credits are treated as income for the company, while non-qualified credits reduce tax expenses. Both of these measures have the potential of reducing the GloBE ETR below the 15 per cent mark: the qualified credits by increasing GloBE income, and the non-qualified by reducing covered tax expenses. As discussed further in section D, refundable tax credits can even reduce total tax payable below what would otherwise be the absolute minimum of 15 per cent of excess profit.

Incentives on capital gains taxes: *variable/unclear impact*

The capital gains incentive relates to differentiating the treatment of capital gains from the general treatment of income – e.g. in a country that maintains a CIT regime, any income realized from capital gains is treated more beneficially. Save for some exceptions, the GloBE rules treat (realized) capital gains as part of GloBE income. Therefore, if a country treats capital gains income preferentially and this preferential treatment leads to an ETR below 15 per cent, the GloBE rules may affect the incentive, up to the minimum tax rate of 15 per cent. However, just as with IP box regimes, the eventual outcome depends on the activities that the MNE performs in the given country and whether the beneficial capital gains treatment can be compensated by other items of income that are taxed above 15 per cent, leading in this way to an overall ETR above 15 per cent.

* * *

This overview of the impact of Pillar II on different categories of tax incentives can help countries reconsider existing incentives schemes, potentially with a view to restructuring categories that are highly affected, and prioritize unaffected categories as well as considering whether non-tax measures might be more effective in encouraging inward investment.

D. RESHAPING INVESTMENT POLICY FOR A GLOBAL MINIMUM TAX ENVIRONMENT

This section explores options available to countries, particularly developing countries, to optimize their investment policy response to the Pillar II reforms. It looks first at the practical implications of the global minimum tax for the investment policy toolkit, including fiscal and other instruments. It then discusses the broader implications for investment policy in the context of sustainable development strategies.

1. Fiscal investment policy responses

MNE investment decisions depend on much more than taxation. Determinants such as the availability of a suitable workforce, infrastructure quality and political stability are at the top of the list of investor concerns.[45] Nonetheless, countries continue to deploy tax measures as one of their primary tools to attract (or retain) inward investment, through both the generally applicable tax rules and incentives. As discussed in previous sections, widespread adoption of Pillar II will fundamentally alter the framework within which these policies are set. Policymakers will face new challenges in their efforts to achieve an appropriate balance between the desire to attract inward investment and the need – now heightened in many countries by the pandemic – for tax revenues.

There is little experience for countries to build on in adapting to the new global environment for tax and FDI. The idea of minimum corporate taxation is not new, but implementation has been rare and limited in scope. Only two trading blocs in sub-Saharan Africa, CEMAC (Economic and Monetary Community of Central Africa) and WAEMU (West African Economic and Monetary Union), have adopted minima, and these differ substantially from Pillar II in structure and in breadth of application. It has only been in the course of designing Pillar II that real thought has been given to how the concept of how a minimum effective corporate tax rate can be turned into practice. This, as seen in section A, has turned out to require a more complex set of rules than the headline idea of a global minimum tax might suggest. Countries are entering into unnavigated territory in both business tax policies and – the ultimate concern in this chapter – investment strategies.

No country can afford to ignore the implementation of Pillar II (table III.3). The most obviously affected, of course, will be those that endorse the prospective Inclusive Framework agreement and find that some of the MNE affiliates they host will be subject to the application of the minimum. But the changes that such countries will be obliged to make will have cross-border effects on countries that are not directly affected, whether because they have endorsed the agreement but set sufficiently high ETRs so that the minimum does not bite, or because they are outside the Inclusive Framework and have not endorsed the agreement. The effects on such countries are indirect, but – as the empirical results have made clear – such indirect effects, notably through the impact on profit shifting, can be powerful.

Table III.3. Adjusting the fiscal investment policy toolkit: key insights

a. Outside the Inclusive Framework	• Investment strategies need rethinking even in countries not endorsing Pillar II
b. Direct effects of Pillar II (lower-tax regimes, preferential rates for investors)	• Applying the Qualified Domestic Minimum Top-Up Tax protects revenue without affecting investment • The effectiveness of traditional tax incentives will be diminished • Some scope remains for domestic tax measures to reduce ETRs on investment
c. Indirect effects of Pillar II (higher-tax regimes)	• Higher-tax countries will also need to respond strategically to the changing tax-investment landscape
d. Implications for regional cooperation	• Regional tax cooperation still has a role in facilitating investment and economic integration
e. Implementation issues	• Complexities related to implementation should be timely addressed to ensure investor certainty
f. Effects on tax competition	• Tax competition is blunted, but not ended – and will likely take new forms

Source: UNCTAD.
Note: ETRs = effective tax rates.

Once the effects of layering Pillar II on top of current tax policies are understood, the question arises as to how countries – including those not directly affected – can best configure their own tax and investment policies.

a. Outside the Inclusive Framework

Investment strategies need rethinking, even in countries not endorsing Pillar II.

About 140 jurisdictions have indicated acceptance of Pillar II in principle. That is a very large number and covers about 95 per cent of global FDI stock. But many developing countries, including small island States, in particular, remain outside the agreement.

It might seem that countries that adhere to the minimum are placing themselves at a disadvantage relative to low-tax countries that remain outside the agreement – and that there is consequently a gain to not participating in the agreement. But this is far from clear, so long as the countries where the ultimate parents of in-scope MNEs are based do participate. This is because these residence countries will apply the top-up tax under the IIR to countries that have not accepted the agreement in exactly the same way as they will to countries that have. The key point is that topping up to the minimum can be achieved unilaterally by the residence country. Measures of this kind – bringing the income of foreign affiliates immediately into tax in their parent country and so topping up the tax paid in the host country to a higher level – have operated for decades through foreign tax credits and controlled foreign corporation rules. Pillar II is to a large degree the global extension of the idea of residence-enforced minimum taxation brought to the fore by the GILTI (global intangible low-taxed income) provisions of the 2017 United States tax reforms.[46]

What lends Pillar II its force is thus not the acceptance of minimum taxation by low-tax countries, but the willingness of higher-tax parent countries to enforce it. In that sense, the effective global minimum tax envisaged in Pillar II does not require global agreement and, moreover, is hard for host countries to escape.

Thus, for the most part participating countries need not fear being undercut by countries that have not signed on to the Pillar II agreement. Their policy calculus can proceed as if all other countries had signed on to it. By the same token, there may be little for countries to gain by not signing on. Indeed, the possibility of applying the QDMTT to capture revenue that would otherwise accrue to others, with no impact on the overall tax liability of investors, suggests a positive gain from participation.

It is, of course, the sovereign right of any country to remain outside the Inclusive Framework. Prudence may perhaps warrant a wait-and-see approach of postponing a decision on participation until the timing, breadth and detail of the application of Pillar II are fully clear. This decision also needs to be taken in light of the full consequences of membership, including in relation to Pillar I (see for example Eden, 2020). In relation to Pillar II, however, adoption by the major capital importers will make it difficult for low tax countries to escape increased tax liabilities on inward investment in line with the global minimum.[47] Participation allows this to be pre-empted by a QDMTT. In terms of Pillar II, as currently envisaged, if a critical mass of investor home countries signs up, the case for determined non-participation appears to be weak.

b. Direct effects of Pillar II

The number of countries directly affected by the minimum tax may appear relatively limited. In terms of national average ETRs, it comprises primarily investment hubs (with limited real investment), and only about a third of the other countries, as shown in the empirical analysis in section B. Nevertheless, as also discussed in section B, the national average effective rate is made up of a range of rates applicable to individual investors, some of which may well fall below the minimum rate. Therefore, even countries with average rates above the minimum may be affected to some degree. Moreover, the impact of Pillar II on directly affected countries (whether or not they are formally within the agreement) and how they respond is important not only for them but as the trigger that sets off indirect effects on others.

Applying the qualified domestic minimum top-up tax protects revenue without affecting investment.

The essence of the minimum tax is the application of a top-up tax to ensure that a rate of at least 15 per cent applies to the "excess profit" – profit, that is, in excess of the substance-based carve-out – of all affiliates of MNEs large enough to be in scope of the new rules. Critically, as noted in previous sections, it is immaterial to investors whether this top-up is levied by the country that hosts the investment or that in which the affiliate's parent resides: their tax liability is the same whichever collects the tax. There may be differences in the practicalities of compliance but none, in principle, in actual liability. *Which country collects the revenue from the top-up tax therefore does not affect investment decisions.*

From the perspective of tax policy, however – and hence for governments seeking to balance investment promotion against revenue concerns – it clearly does matter who collects the top-up revenue. The "rule order" issue of which government this should be, host country or home country, was a heated aspect of the debate in developing Pillar II. The final model rules provide a clear route for the host country to assert a first right to collect this revenue by applying the QDMTT.

There is a very strong case for countries that are affected by Pillar II to apply the QDMTT: failure to do so potentially cedes tax revenue to the parent country while conveying no tax benefit to investors. One concern might be that application of a QDMTT could create dissimilarities in the treatment of out-of-scope domestic enterprises and affiliates of large multinational groups; but the difference would favour the former and so, politically at least, appears unlikely to be problematic. Not applying the QDMTT might also be seen as sending a signal of a country's business-friendly inclinations: but that is an inclination upon which, in terms of the minimum tax, it cannot deliver. Preliminary results on the effects of the reform on national revenues suggest that, in the broad comparison between developed and developing economies, it makes surprisingly little difference to the final impact which rule order is adopted (likely, because the impact of the profit-shifting channel on revenues – the same whichever rule is adopted – is particularly large in developing economies). For specific countries, however, the difference can be substantial. For developing countries in particular, adoption of a QDMTT can do little harm and may do much good.[48]

The effectiveness of traditional tax incentives will be diminished by Pillar II.

The model rules of Pillar II make no reference to the tax holidays or other types of fiscal incentives that many countries provide as a central element of their national investment strategies.[49] They are not grandfathered and they are not removed from application of the GloBE rules. The minimum tax rules are simply laid on top of existing regimes and will directly reduce the attractiveness of any incentives that investors might enjoy.

Yet, application of Pillar II does not mean that pre-existing incentives become wholly ineffective, as discussed in section C. Their attractiveness does not change for entities that are not part of MNE groups large enough to fall within the new rules. And even for those that are, there are some ways – discussed here – to mitigate the effect. Nonetheless, Pillar II dampens the effectiveness of incentives, and this will become increasingly the case if, as expected, the threshold of MNE size for application of the minimum tax is reduced over time.

This prospect raises challenges for countries that deploy tax incentives as a core element of their investment policy toolkit. Views on the efficiency and effectiveness of tax incentives differ. Many experts believe that tax incentives have generally not delivered effects on investment commensurate with the revenue forgone, and that tax incentives feed mutually disadvantageous tax competition between countries.[50] From their perspective, one of the attractions of a global minimum tax is to discourage the proliferation of tax incentives and encourage greater reliance on other ways to create a business-friendly environment. Opinions will continue to differ (not least within countries, between sceptical ministries of finance and activist line ministries). The aim here is not to pronounce on the merits of tax incentives as tools to promote investment but simply to assess how they are affected by the global minimum tax.

The key fact in considering the implications of Pillar II for tax incentives is thus that such incentives are not excluded from its application. There are some respects in which they will retain an impact, and – as will be seen next – some ways in which domestic tax measures can still reduce the tax liability even of entities directly affected by the global minimum tax. Nonetheless, the change in the landscape in which tax incentives have operated so far is fundamental. The adoption of Pillar II will require countries to review not only their design but also their role in national investment strategies.

Some scope will remain for domestic tax measures to reduce effective tax rates on investment.

Once a sufficient number of investor home countries adopt Pillar II rules, there is (almost) no escaping the absolute minimum of a 15 per cent tax on profit in excess of the carve-out implied by Pillar II. There are, however, three notable ways in which domestic tax policy can be used to bring effective tax rates closer to – and in one case even below – that minimum.[51]

Reducing domestic covered taxes amplifies the benefit to investors of the substance-based carve-out.

The effectiveness of reducing corporate taxes in order to attract investment is substantially diminished by Pillar II. Leaving aside (potentially important) complications regarding tax credits taken up later, a foreign affiliate's total tax liability when it is subject to the minimum is the sum of (1) a tax of 15 per cent on profits in excess of the carve-out, and (2) a tax on the carve-out itself at the effective rate of domestic taxation, this being the GloBE ratio of covered taxes (including corporate income tax in particular) to accounting profit. With the amounts of both the carve-out (mechanically related to tangible assets and payroll) and accounting profit (essentially determined by business realities), tax design can have no effect on amount (1). As such, it represents an absolute minimum on the entity's tax liability. Only amount (2) can be directly affected by domestic tax design, through the total liability of covered taxes. Reducing these will still convey some benefit to investors, but the effect is reduced: if the carve-out is 40 per cent of accounting profits, for instance – which it was suggested in section B is broadly plausible – then cutting covered taxes by $1 benefits the investor by only 40 cents.[52] At a lower carve-out (e.g. 5 per cent) the effect is correspondingly less (2 cents).

Through this route incentives continue to benefit the investor despite the topping up under Pillar II. However, there are downsides and risks in considering a reduction in covered taxes. The benefits to investors will fall as the carve-outs are gradually reduced over the coming decade. More fundamentally, simply reducing corporate taxation will have implications for the taxation of the many firms, including domestic firms, that are out of the scope of Pillar II. In principle, this could be limited by restricting access to reduced corporate taxation to firms that are directly affected by Pillar II (including, to avoid non-discrimination issues, domestic ones) – perhaps by tying it to taxation under the QDMTT. Beyond the legal issues this might raise, it would be politically difficult: observers are likely to notice the corporate tax break being given to large MNEs more than they will the top-up that leads MNEs to pay more.

While bearing in mind those downsides, it is important to note that some traditional tax incentives will serve to reduce covered taxes and so will continue to have some effect. In the example above, the $1 reduction in corporate tax might come, for instance, from application of a preferentially reduced rate. That will still benefit the investor – but by only 40 (or 5) cents, not, as at present, by the full $1.

Covered tax payments – primarily, domestic corporate tax – can be reduced by either lowering the applicable statutory rate or narrowing the tax base. For the impact on the affiliate's total tax liability, it is immaterial which path is taken. It is only the amount of covered taxes that enters the calculation, not how they are computed. In terms of the marginal effective rate, however, both rate and base matter – but essentially just as they do now in the absence of the global minimum tax (with an investment-based case for corporate tax structures that imply low METR, as set out in section A).

Accelerated depreciation, however – a common form of incentive – is treated differently (section C.4). The attraction of accelerated depreciation for investors is that, without changing the total value of depreciation allowances over the lifetime of the investment it brings them forward in time, and so increases their present value. Under Pillar II, an adjustment for deferred taxes negates the effect this would otherwise have on the calculation of covered taxes (and the same is true for other incentives that operate through similar timing effects). While the impact on the top-up tax is thus undone, accelerating depreciation still conveys a benefit to investors, to the extent of the carve-out, in terms of their domestic tax liability.

Worth noting too is that in one case traditional tax incentives will continue to have their full effect – though its practical importance may well be limited. This is the case in which other members of the same MNE operating in the same country pay a sufficient amount of covered taxes for the ETR of all within-country entities to exceed 15 per cent. There appears, in principle, to be some incentive for MNEs to structure themselves to exploit this feature.

Refundable tax credits can also be used to benefit investors.

The model rules do include one mechanism by which total tax liability can be reduced below the otherwise-absolute minimum of 15 per cent on profit in excess of the carve-out. This is by offering tax credits (provisions that reduce liability dollar for dollar)[53] that are refundable, meaning that, if the credit exceeds the tax liability, the investor receives a payment from the government. Refundable tax credits do not reduce covered taxes in the way just described,[54] but instead are taken to increase accounting profit. That reduces the ETR used to determine the amount of the top-up, while also increasing the base to which that top-up applies. The net effect, taking account of the credit itself, can be to reduce total tax payable below the otherwise-absolute minimum.[55] In effect, refundable tax credits are treated like cash grants, i.e. as an increase in the firm's income.

It is not yet fully clear how much scope refundable tax credits might provide for incentivizing investment. The refundability provision is critical: a government seeking to encourage investment in this way would need to recognize that, should the credit exceed tax liability, it will need to make a payment to investors.[56] Outright grants may be the more transparent route to achieving the same effect.

Reducing non-covered taxes remains an option – but not all taxes bear on investment.

With the application of Pillar II increasing the average effective rate paid by affected affiliates, the impact on investors of taxes that are not covered by the agreement may become more prominent. From the perspective of investment promotion this calls for consideration of non-covered taxes too. One possibility is to cut them; however, the danger in doing so – beyond the loss of tax revenue – is of reducing taxes that convey little real benefit to investors because they do not bear the real burden they impose.[57] An additional possibility is to restructure non-covered taxes into covered taxes, thereby reducing the top-up while having little effect on total domestic liability.

Precisely which of the non-covered taxes are most important in this context will be country- and sector-specific. In some cases, it may be customs duties; in the extractive industries it may be royalties, with pressure to rebalance towards income-type taxes that would be covered. In many developing economies, thought may also need to be given to the minimum taxes that are often levied on turnover, perhaps converting these too to income-type taxes.[58]

c. Indirect effects of Pillar II

Higher-tax countries will also need to strategically respond to the changing tax-investment landscape.

Higher-tax countries will clearly be relatively less exposed to the impact of Pillar II, but they will still be affected as a result of two dynamics. The first is the reduction in outward profit shifting, leading to an increase in the FDI-level ETRs on the income generated by inward FDI. The second is the possible presence in such countries of a subset of foreign affiliates that do face an ETR below the minimum, even if the national average ETR is above the minimum. Both factors – a key insight of the empirical analysis in section B – can significantly increase the corporate taxes paid by MNEs on FDI taking place in higher-tax countries. Most notably, in developing countries, the role of reduced profit shifting in the increase of the average FDI-level ETR caused by Pillar II is dominant.

This means that higher-tax countries are not spared from the potential downside effects on investment caused by the introduction of the Pillar II minimum. The empirical analysis shows that, as a consequence of the increase in FDI-level ETRs associated with Pillar II

(14 per cent globally in the baseline estimate), the overall amount of investment may decrease by 2 per cent, or up to 3 per cent under more pessimistic assumptions. Thus, when evaluating the potential impact of and response to Pillar II, high-tax countries should consider all relevant aspects beyond the headline average national tax rates. In a generalized context of increasing taxation on FDI, specific measures may be needed to support investment and shift the focus from fiscal measures to other investment facilitation tools. This is true for low-tax countries and high-tax countries alike.

In relative terms, though, even if they do not change their own tax policies, higher-tax countries are likely to become *relatively* more attractive locations for real investment. This is because their FDI-level ETRs, while they may increase, will generally fall relative to those in countries that are substantially affected by the minimum. The effect will no doubt be more marked for some countries than for others, but the general direction is clear. In revenue terms too, these higher-tax countries, especially if they are home to large MNEs, are also likely to gain through the profit-shifting channel: even if the topping-up is done by host countries under a QDMTT, higher tax countries become less vulnerable to outward profit shifting.

These countries may be able to do even better by changing their tax policies. The key question here is whether they will find it in their interests to raise their tax rates in a post-Pillar II world (or reduce them less than they otherwise would) or, to the contrary, to reduce them. The latter possibility – that the floor set by the minimum will also prove to be a ceiling – has troubled some observers who see current corporate tax rates as generically too low. The answer to this question also matters for low-tax countries that are directly affected by the minimum. To the extent that higher-tax countries respond to the minimum by raising their rates, that will convey an indirect benefit to low-tax countries, mitigating the effect of their own need to raise rates. Indeed, for countries that are initially only modestly below the minimum, it is possible that this effect, arising from the strategic response of countries that are not affected directly by Pillar II, will mean that they too benefit from adoption of the minimum tax.[59]

The likely direction of response by higher-tax countries remains one of the imponderable aspects of implementing Pillar II. On the one hand, higher-tax countries have less to fear from paper profits and real investment being shifted to lower-tax countries, reducing pressures on them to keep their tax rates low; higher taxes abroad may thus lead to higher taxes at home (the case of "strategic complementarity"). On the other hand, the increased tax revenue that these countries are likely to experience at their initial tax rates creates some fiscal space to cut those rates in order to compete for investment more aggressively: higher taxes abroad then lead to lower taxes at home ("strategic substitutability").[60]

Existing empirical evidence provides little guidance as to which of these forces is most likely to dominate. There is some sign of strategic complementarity in headline rates of corporation tax. But the adoption of a generalized minimum has no precedent, so that experience is an inherently unreliable guide. Different countries may react differently, depending on the relative weight they attach to revenue and investment promotion objectives. Yet, the need to enhance revenue collection has been a primary motive for the development of Pillar II, and the deceleration of reductions in statutory corporate tax rates suggests a diminished appetite for corporate tax cuts. In the current fiscal climate, few governments are expected to react to a revenue increase induced by actions elsewhere by cutting rates and effectively transferring that additional revenue in large part to the domestic private sector; some have indicated an intention to increase statutory rates. This reduces the risk of the floor becoming a ceiling, at least in the short term.[61]

d. Implications for regional cooperation

Regional tax cooperation still has a role in facilitating investment and economic integration.

Regional economic integration efforts often lead to calls for coordination in corporate taxation in order to facilitate cross-border investment within the bloc while limiting potentially mutually damaging tax competition between members. In Europe, such proposals date back to the 1960s; however, only in Africa, in CEMAC and WAEMU, have measures of this kind been adopted. And they have had only mixed success. In WAEMU, for example, the statutory rate is restricted to between 25 and 30 per cent, and there are provisions for a common base. Any intent to limit downward tax competition has been undermined by the exclusion from the restriction of incentives provided for in investment codes or other laws. As a consequence, tax holidays, for example, have continued.[62]

This difficulty in implementing a minimum tax at the regional level reflects an inherent limitation of agreements to restrict tax competition among only a subset of countries: the problem posed by outsiders. While countries participating in such an agreement may benefit, by worsening their position relative to non-participants they convey even greater benefits to those remaining outside of the agreements.[63]

The global nature of Pillar II, implied by participation of the largest capital exporters, means that it faces no outsider problem. Yet, there will remain a potential role for regional cooperation, to establish and implement within-bloc minimum levels of taxation that are consistent with investment promotion.[64]

One reason is that Pillar II applies only to the affiliates of the largest MNEs. The significance of in-scope affiliates varies across regional blocs and across countries but, in all, many firms will remain out of scope. The case for coordination therefore does not disappear. In fact, the lesser ability to compete to attract entities of the largest MNEs may make competition for these out-of-scope firms more aggressive, reinforcing the case for coordination towards an effective minimum applicable to them. Just as Pillar II naturally provides an opportunity to review policy towards tax incentives, so it may also usefully prompt a parallel review of regional coordination agreements.

In addition, implementation of Pillar II may be facilitated by regional cooperation on a range of practical issues, supporting investment and economic integration within a bloc by easing MNE compliance costs and enhancing certainty in their tax treatment. This might involve, for instance, developing common templates for national QDMTTs, refundable tax credits or accounting standards. Regional cooperation can also be useful in fostering a common understanding of the new tax environment and in presenting a common position – not only within the Inclusive Framework but in other influential fora, such as the United Nations Committee of Experts on International Cooperation in Tax Matters – on technical issues that remain to be resolved.

e. Implementation issues

Complexities related to implementation should be timely addressed to ensure investor certainty.

The two-pillar agreement is not a simplification. Significant changes to tax and investment policies will be needed. A period of adjustment and some uncertainty is inevitable. Several tax administrations of developed economies have already indicated that the 2023 target for implementation is very ambitious, and this is surely even more true for weaker-capacity countries. Moreover, significant political hurdles to final adoption of Pillar II remain. This may create a natural inclination for countries to "wait and see", but the potential impact is so great that they would be well advised not to delay in reviewing the proposals (and providing input into any final changes), evaluating their policy options and preparing their responses. Such preparedness will also help in dealing with MNEs, which also face increased uncertainty, and so help alleviate the tax uncertainty that can act as a bar to investment. Not least, in this period of adjustment, it is important for policymakers to avoid missteps (such as, for example, extending long-lasting legal commitments to provide tax incentives) and reassure investors that they are aware of and sensitive to the concerns that they too will naturally have.

Moreover, although the tax rules have been agreed in principle, there may be further changes ahead. The model rules already embody a lengthy transition to the final carve-out rates, and the general expectation is that the minimum tax will come to affect an increasingly large set of MNEs. Many fine but important details of the arrangements also remain to be addressed. More fundamentally, while it is a remarkable achievement in multilateralism and consensus-building, the two-pillar agreement is nonetheless a compromise between several quite different approaches to international business taxation, including in Pillar I elements of arms-length pricing, taxation in the destination country and some use of formulaic methods as well as the minimum tax in Pillar II itself. It is possible that the tensions this compromise creates will eventually lead to further reform of international tax arrangements. The minimum tax element, however, is to a large degree separable from the rest. Once adopted, it seems likely to become a permanent and increasingly significant element of the international tax framework and, hence, for investment strategies.

Looking ahead, it will then be key for developing countries to strengthen mutual support and cooperation as well as technical capacities to increase their influence in the negotiation of the next steps and the follow-ups of Pillar II within the context of the Inclusive Framework (Christensen et al., 2022).

f. Effects on tax competition

Tax competition is blunted, but not ended – and will likely take new forms.

As laid out earlier, Pillar II sets an (almost) absolute minimum tax liability for in-scope affiliates. It substantially reduces, though it does not necessarily wholly eliminate, the opportunities for shifting profits to low-tax countries; hence it also reduces the motivation for reducing tax rates in order to benefit from (or prevent) profit shifting. SEZs, tax holidays and other forms of tax incentives, where they are affected, will convey much lower tax benefits to investors. The floor may even enable some countries to raise their tax rates, as they become less constrained by the downward pressures they felt in the absence of the minimum. In these respects, Pillar II thus will reduce international tax competition.

But tax competition is not eliminated. Scope remains for reshaping domestic tax regimes to encourage investment, particularly real investment. Tax competition is thus set to continue, particularly for real investment. Reducing covered taxes – primarily the CIT – can bring effective rates closer to the absolute minimum. And reducing non-covered taxes, or converting them to covered ones, can also dull the impact on affected affiliates.

Domestic measures can also still be crafted to benefit the many investors not directly affected by the global minimum tax. In those cases, traditional tax incentives retain their full force. In fact, with a reduced ability to use tax measures to compete for investment by the largest MNEs, pressures to compete for the smaller ones may intensify.[65]

Measures beyond tax policy also seem likely to receive heightened attention. There may be more focus on tax administration processes and practices that reduce compliance costs for firms and increase certainty about their tax treatment, addressing what survey evidence shows are significant concerns for many investors, including in developing countries.

Finally, a lessened ability to lure investment by large MNEs through tax incentives may lead countries to use spending measures instead, whether tailored to particular investments (providing easy road access, for instance) or improving general infrastructure (reliability of energy supply, for example). Experience shows that spending measures can be used very aggressively to compete for large investments. Tax competition may thus shift towards competition in public spending. This can be beneficial: spending measures are generally seen as more transparent than tax incentives, and social returns from infrastructure investments are high in many countries. But there are risks too. Public spending may become distorted by investment objectives (e.g. too many airports and not enough health spending), [66] and governance issues arise in relation to spending just as they do in relation to tax incentives. Ultimately, mutually damaging international competition may re-emerge in a different form – and Pillar II may result in even greater importance of measures to control and monitor public spending.[67]

2. Challenges for investment policymakers and institutions

The adjustments to fiscal investment policy discussed above have major implications for national investment policymakers and institutions dealing with investment promotion, and for international investment policymakers and treaty negotiators.

Investment promotion agencies (IPAs) will see important changes in their standard toolkit. Worryingly, the current awareness of the reforms among IPAs and SEZs is still very low. UNCTAD's annual IPA survey, carried out in the first quarter of 2022, revealed that more than one third of respondents were not yet aware of the reforms, and only about a quarter had begun an assessment of the implications. Given the planned start of the implementation of Pillar II in 2023, investment policymakers and institutions will need to act quickly. At a minimum, they should review their current use of incentives, evaluate the implications for their portfolio of existing investors and identify the best approach for both investment retention and promotion (box III.10). This review should go hand in hand with strengthening the overall governance of incentives, in any form (fiscal, financial or other). In particular, incentives should be granted on the basis of a set of pre-determined, objective, clear and transparent criteria. Their long-term costs and benefits should be carefully assessed prior to implementation, and they should be periodically reviewed to ensure continued effectiveness in achieving the desired objectives. Finally, their administration should be the responsibility of an independent entity or ministry that does not have conflicting objectives or performance targets for investment attraction (UNCTAD, 2015). SEZ authorities and management companies, which rely on very much the same toolkit, will have to follow suit.

The implications of Pillar II are not limited to national investment policies. Negotiators of international investment agreements (IIAs) may come to play a significant role in enabling the necessary national policy adjustments. Where countries have committed, contractually or in practice, to providing preferential tax treatment to investors, removing such benefits to apply top-up taxes or rescinding fiscal incentives could potentially lead to investor–State dispute settlement cases. Changes to preferential tax regimes have been challenged by investors in international arbitration under IIAs in the past (e.g. *Micula v. Romania*; *Charanne v. Spain*; *Eiser v. Spain*; *Antaris Solar v. the Czech Republic*). There is no clear jurisprudential trend in investor–State dispute case law concerning changes in tax regimes, which increases unpredictability for States that wish to make changes to their tax regimes.

Contrary to stabilization clauses in State contracts, which protect investors against perceived adverse legislative change, IIAs do not include explicit obligations that guarantee the stability of the regulatory regime, and they rarely include obligations relating specifically to taxation. However, most IIAs include the fair and equitable treatment (FET) standard, and many also contain umbrella clauses. The FET standard can be interpreted as including elements of legal stability. Changes in laws perceived as arbitrary, sudden or radical can be challenged by investors as breaching FET. Umbrella clauses oblige States to honour commitments they have undertaken with regard to the investment. This obligation generally relates to contractual obligations; in a limited number of cases, umbrella clauses have been interpreted as extending to the stability of the general legislative framework.

States can minimize potential challenges in various ways. First, they may incorporate references to and clarifications of the relationship between IIAs, State contracts and the QDMTT in a multilateral treaty instrument, to ensure that the tax implementation is not considered as breaching these commitments. Such a multilateral instrument could be envisaged as part of the OECD/G20 Inclusive Framework on BEPS, although that would benefit only Inclusive Framework participants. Second, they may clarify the relationship between IIAs and the QDMTT bilaterally. This can be done through either IIA amendments

Box III.10. How should IPA and SEZ managers respond to the global minimum tax?

The global minimum tax is due to take effect from 2023, so the need for action is now. As essential first steps:

- The changes envisaged are profound and highly technical. Obtain expert tax advice and seek collaboration with institutions such as UNCTAD.
- The changes raise fundamental issues of tax policy and administration. Seek views and advice from the ministries of finance and tax administration.
- Investors will be wondering how their tax treatment will change, and how to react. Engage with relevant stakeholders, including MNEs, to convey the message that serious evaluation is under way and that law and regulations will be adjusted in a transparent and participatory way.

Drawing on this support and dialogue, assess the likely impact of the global minimum tax:

- Advocate for a comprehensive mapping of all tax incentives currently offered and the entities making use of them, including the extent of their activities and the revenue directly forgone as a result of the incentives.
- Identify all cases in which taxes paid are likely to be less than 15 per cent of an entity's accounting profits, as adjusted under the GloBE rules.
- Assess, where the rate is less than 15 per cent, whether the increase in total tax payments implied by the global minimum is likely to be material for the investor.
- Identify all cases in which legal commitments have been made to provide incentives for some period of time, and obtain legal advice as needed (because, from the perspective of government revenue, their effect may be undesirable).

To develop the most effective tax framework for investment promotion in the changed global environment:

- Review the effectiveness of incentives in attracting investment relative to the revenue loss they imply. Independent expert advice is the most credible way to do this.
- Recognize that Pillar II will fundamentally and substantially reduce the benefit of tax incentives to investors. The rules of the investment promotion game will be fundamentally changed.
- Strengthen the overall governance of tax incentives. Make sure incentives are granted on the basis of a set of pre-determined, objective, clear and transparent criteria.
- Consider, and discuss with the finance ministry, possible tax policy changes to support investment promotion: reviewing corporation tax, reviewing other taxes not covered by the agreement (but only if there is evidence that doing so will affect investor costs) or restructuring taxes to be covered.
- Recognize that it may be inappropriate to restrict these changes to affected entities and too costly in revenue to extend them to all firms.
- Examine how the tax administration can provide greater certainty and predictability to investors.

Perhaps most important, explore the potential for non-tax measures to promote investment, including the following:

- Investment facilitation measures, including information provision, transparency on rules and regulations, and streamlined administrative procedures for investors
- Spending on local infrastructure (such as energy supply and transport facilities) and development of local human capital
- Advocacy and support for improved tax services, such as the speed with which value added tax refunds are paid and tax disputes resolved

Source: UNCTAD.

or joint interpretative notes related to IIAs. Third, in case of a dispute arising under an IIA, they can argue that the QDMTT represents a global consensus on corporate taxation, embraced by States and international organizations worldwide.

Due to the risk of costly challenges to top-up applications arising from potential tax-related ISDS cases, policymakers would do well to take potential conflicts into account as part of the IIA reform process and under the Inclusive Framework.

3. Strategic investment policy implications

The strategic implications of the reforms for investment promotion are important. The global minimum tax will apply only to MNEs with consolidated revenues over €750 million. This threshold may seem high, but it captures more than two thirds of new investment projects carried out over the past five years, with even higher shares in developing regions (figure III.18). Moreover, even if initially many firms will remain out of scope, the fact that more and more FDI is carried out by the largest MNEs (overseas investment by SMEs is in decline; see chapter I), combined with the likely gradual reduction of the threshold, could mean that over time almost all FDI will be subject to the minimum.

Attracting international investment in productive assets, especially in GVC-intensive manufacturing sectors, will become harder. Already in recent years, global investment in such activities has seen a backlash against production offshoring and increased barriers to cross-border trade and investment. The removal of fiscal arbitrage opportunities for efficiency-seeking firms, for which investment decisions are often driven by small margins, could mean that developing economies looking to attract investment to build productive capacity and to increase participation in GVCs will be competing for a shrinking pool of such investment.

That observation is critical for industrial policies. The "transformation of international production" (see *WIR20*) that was already under way – characterized by reshoring, regionalization and resilience-driven restructuring – could be reinforced and accelerated by the tax reforms. Industrial policies can no longer rely exclusively or predominantly on attracting efficiency-seeking investment by large-scale industrials and in GVC-intensive sectors.

Figure III.18. **Share of greenfield investment projects by MNEs with annual revenues of more than €750 million, 2015–2021** (Per cent)

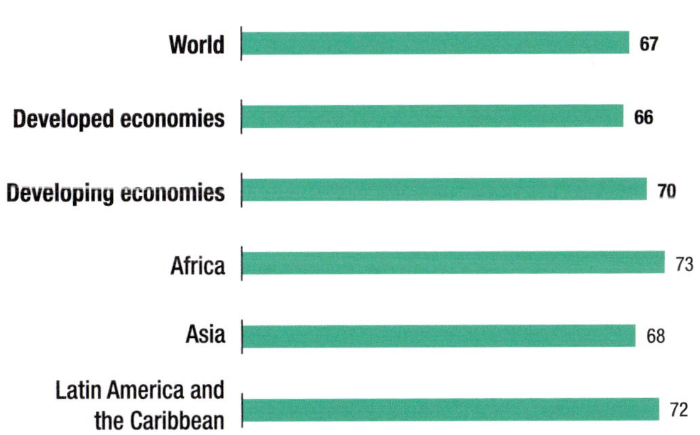

Source: UNCTAD, based on information from the Financial Times Ltd., fDI Markets (www.fDImarkets.com).

In the meantime, domestic and regional market-seeking investment, smaller-scale, asset-light digital investment, and investment in green and blue economies, as well as investment in domestic services and infrastructure, may provide more opportunities for promotion and targeting. All of these are less affected by the tax reforms, at least initially.

While, on the one hand, the partial depletion of the investment promotion toolbox will make attracting investment more difficult for some countries, on the other, competition from low-tax locations will be much reduced. That could benefit developing economies which, on average, have higher ETRs. Nevertheless, as competition shifts from tax levers to alternative investment determinants, and from fiscal incentives to financial incentives, many could still find themselves at a disadvantage because they are unable to afford the substantial upfront financial commitments associated with infrastructure provision or subsidies. Levers such as easing administrative procedures for tax payment and reducing tax uncertainty, as well as improving regulatory transparency and streamlining in general, will become more important. More attention will thus be paid to investment facilitation, also driven by the prospective agreement on investment facilitation for development under discussion among more than 110 members of the World Trade Organization.[68]

The need to review the portfolio of incentives on offer to foreign investors provides an opportunity to rethink them wholesale. In recent years, UNCTAD has urged countries to engage in such an evaluation, with a view to shifting incentives towards the promotion of investments with better performance in terms of sustainable development – specifically linking incentives to the Sustainable Development Goals (SDGs). The shift from reduced-rate incentives and exemptions towards incentives linked to real capital expenditures – which are affected less by Pillar II – fits well with this objective, because investment in SDG sectors is often capital intensive and relatively low margin. It should be noted that the degree to which SDG-relevant investment will be affected by Pillar II – the extent to which relevant investments and investors are in scope – is not yet fully clear, because a significant part of such investment is carried out through international project finance and split between multiple investors, including financial institutions.

The SDG financing imperative raises further important strategic considerations. It highlights the trade-off that could emerge – under specific circumstances and particularly in low-income countries – between the need to boost domestic resource mobilization for the SDGs and the need to promote investment in SDG-relevant projects. Investments in some sectors important for the SDGs or for climate change mitigation and adaptation can yield social returns in excess of private and thus call for incentives or subsidies, or they may have risk-return profiles that require public support to make them viable. In LDCs, the upfront financial cost of subsidies are usually unaffordable, and fiscal advantages may be the only available lever. In such cases, careful consideration of the flexibilities that exist under the Inclusive Framework and the Pillar II rules is warranted.

What flexibilities exist has been briefly discussed in the earlier section on fiscal investment policy responses. The strategic options for countries appear to be (i) joining or not joining the Inclusive Framework and signing up to Pillar II, and (ii) applying or not applying top-up taxes. In reality, the mechanics of Pillar II are such that the options for individual countries are very much constrained by the fact that the actions of investor's home countries can undo any advantage for investors that host countries might provide through preferential tax rates.

The flexibilities and mitigating factors within the Pillar II framework are important to bear in mind for the promotion of investment in sustainable development. A few forms of fiscal incentives, such as accelerated depreciation, will still be effective, although the most common forms of investment incentives – tax holidays and exemptions – will be severely affected.

The carve-out related to investment in physical assets will be an important mitigating factor for SDG investment. By definition, investments in SDG or climate change sectors such as renewable energy, water management or other forms of adaptation will be highly capital intensive and hence have a high carve-out (i.e. the expected increase in ETRs will be lower).

Still, in moving forward with implementation, the need to promote investment in the SDGs and in climate change mitigation and adaptation should be front of mind for policymakers, at the same level as domestic resource mobilization.

* * *

This chapter has shown that the introduction of a global minimum tax in BEPS Pillar II will have significant implications for FDI and for investment policy. The chapter has provided a guide through the complex reforms and indications as to possible fiscal investment policy responses. It has categorized investment incentives, describing the impact of Pillar II for each category. The concluding section highlighted the potential implications for industrial policy, for the promotion of sustainable investment, and for investment promotion institutions and international investment agreement negotiators.

The BEPS reforms are a major achievement of multilateral policymaking on a critical issue that is a priority for the international community. The reforms have the potential to bring substantial benefits, including to developing economies, in terms of increased government revenues and reduced distortions to international business.

Three final considerations for tax and investment policymakers and for the international community engaged in the reform process are worth highlighting:

1. As observed in this chapter, developing economies have obtained an important instrument in the Pillar II rules allowing them, in principle, to apply top-up taxes first, before investor home countries can do so. Yet, some developing countries that have weaker tax collection capabilities or that are more constrained by old-generation IIAs may be unable to exercise this benefit, at least for a foreseeable initial implementation period. Where this is the case, developed home countries may wish to consider pooling any revenues raised through the IIR and converting them to development assistance.
2. As discussions are ongoing in the Inclusive framework, due attention should be given to the constraints to implementation that may be posed by IIAs. A multilateral solution would be the most effective option to avoid disputes arising from host countries removing or reducing preferential tax treatment for investors. The IIA regime itself is also undergoing a process of reform. The urgency brought on by the implementation of Pillar II may provide further impetus to this process.
3. In developing countries, many institutions will struggle not only with the evaluation of policy options and the implementation of the – highly technical – tax reforms but also with the implementation of investment policy responses. International support and technical assistance in both areas, including from organizations such as UNCTAD, will be crucial to ensure that the potential benefits from the reforms are realized, while negative effects on international private investment for sustainable development are minimized.

NOTES

[1] A further complication that arises in the cross-border setting is the potential application of taxes by both the host and the home country (or – language differs – the "source" and the "residence" jurisdiction). Note that this chapter will generally prioritize investment-driven terminology over tax-driven terminology; i.e. the notion of "country" or "economy" over that of "jurisdiction" and the notion of "home" and "host" over those of "residence" and "source". For the purpose of this chapter, however, these concepts can generally be used interchangeably, but when this is not the case, the precise qualification will be applied.

[2] Suppose, for instance, that the investor requires a 5 per cent rate of return. In the absence of tax, the investor would invest up to the point at which the pre-tax return is also 5 per cent. Imagine, though, that taxation leads the investor to invest less, only to the point at which the pre-tax return is 7 per cent. Then the METR, expressed in absolute terms, is 2 percentage points; expressed relative to the required return, it is 40 per cent. By contrast, the AETR reflects tax paid on the totality of profits, not just on the last dollar, and will typically be higher.

[3] For elaboration on this point, see chapter 1 of Devereux et al. (2021).

[4] Elements of cash-flow taxation appear in, for example, the United States tax reform of 2017, which provided for immediate expensing while limiting – though not eliminating – interest deductibility. Another form of rent tax is the Allowance for Corporate Equity (which gives a tax deduction for a notional required return on equity), experience which is assessed in IMF (2016). Explicit rent taxes are also quite widely used in the extractive industries.

[5] The scale decision in any country is independent of the METR in others (unless the MNE is constrained in the total amount of investment it undertakes). Cross-country comparisons of METRs are thus less relevant to understanding cross-border investment than are such comparisons of AETRs. There is one however respect in which the METR affecting FDI may differ from that affecting a purely domestic investment. Expanding the scale of an MNE's investment in one country – the exercise underlying the METR – may affect its tax liability in others (expanding operations in one affiliate, for example, may require diverting scarce managerial expertise from others); see Keen et al. (forthcoming).

[6] Also from James (2014), cited in figure 1 of Platform for Collaboration on Tax (2016a) and table 2 of Keen and Mansour (2010): about 85–90 per cent of low-income countries offered tax holidays in 2015 as compared with 75 per cent in 2005.

[7] To the extent that countries are able to use tax incentives to compete aggressively for especially mobile capital, this may result in less aggressive competition for less mobile capital. See Keen and Konrad (2013), which, more generally, provides a review of the theory of tax competition and responses to it.

[8] The evidence on interactions in tax-setting is reviewed in Leibrecht and Hocgatterer (2012) and OECD (2020). The numbers cited are from Devereux et al. (2008), who find, for a sample of developed countries, a response of 0.34–0.67 points to a 1-point increase in the average statutory rate abroad; in a sample that includes developing countries, Crivelli et al. (2016) find a response of 0.25–0.3 points. IMF (2022, online annex 2.2) reaches broadly similar conclusions.

[9] Some (notably Brennan and Buchanan, 1980) have argued that downward tax competition can be socially beneficial because it limits the ability of governments to finance wasteful spending. Yet, given governments' pressing revenue needs, now amplified by the pandemic, and the increased use of fiscal rules to control aggregate tax and spending, this argument is now rarely heard. There may also be circumstances – for example, when domestic firms are held largely by foreigners – in which international considerations lead countries to set taxes not lower but higher than would otherwise be the case (a possibility highlighted by Mintz, 2022b).

[10] Indeed, this was arguably the objective of the BEPS project prior to the Pillar II proposal.

[11] As set out in the model rules and commentary issued by the OECD (2021, 2022a).

[12] More precisely, the calculation is across all entities within a particular country that belong to the same multinational group.

[13] These are initially at rates of 10 per cent for payroll and 8 per cent for tangible assets, transitioning gradually to 5 per cent on each in 2033.

[14] Leaving aside here tax refunds of various kinds.

[15] This is similar to (and likely inspired by) the GILTI (Global Intangible Low-Taxed Income) provisions of the 2017 United States tax reform, with the difference that those provisions apply the minimum with blending across affiliates in different countries (rather than, as in Pillar I, country by country). Controlled foreign corporation rules – which bring an affiliate's earnings immediately into taxation in the parent country – have a similar effect.

[16] These issues relate, for instance, to the treatment of deferred taxes (ones that are reasonably expected to be payable in the future) and – an issue that has as yet received little attention – the differences between the various accounting standards that multinationals may apply.

[17] At the time of writing, draft rules for the STTR had not yet been issued.

[18] Relating, for instance, to the treatment of "deferred" taxes (ones that are reasonably expected to be payable in the future) and the differences between the various accounting standards that multinationals may apply (an issue that is receiving increased attention).

[19] This will be the case, for instance, if all taxes are initially zero and the carve-out more than covers the investors' required return: the investor is then in effect able to deduct more than the full costs of investment – in effect, a subsidy from the government that makes the METR negative.

[20] In general, if the tax base is such that the initial METR is positive, an increase in the statutory rate of tax increases the METR. Simulations by Bares et al. (forthcoming) and Mintz (2022a) find an increase in the METRs for countries directly affected by Pillar II.

[21] ETRs based on the common ratio between taxes paid and reported profits are sometimes referred to in this chapter as "standard ETRs" to emphasize their difference from related, but nonetheless different, tax rates such as the FDI-level ETR or the GloBE ETR.

[22] CbCR was introduced in the context of the BEPS project (Action 13). The data set contains information about the activities of large MNEs (i.e. with annual revenues over €750 million) at the bilateral parent-host country level.

[23] The sample includes the 193 host countries directly covered by CbCR data from 2017; a few additional ones were imputed using available STR data. The list of the 39 OFCs is from Tørsløv et al. (2021), largely consistent with other OFC lists, including that adopted in *WIR15*.

[24] Evidence reported in chapter II (section II.C) confirms that tax incentives are usually not granted to foreign firms only; even when their main objective is to attract foreign investment, their perimeter tends to cover both foreign and domestic firms.

[25] In each host country, however, average ETRs disguise significant heterogeneity across ETRs paid by individual foreign affiliates. Some foreign affiliates will face an ETR below 15 per cent even when the country average is above that level – a compositional effect not captured by country-level analysis. The treatment and interpretation of within-country variance in the analysis of ETRs is one key methodological and empirical issue in this analysis (see discussion in box III.7 and Auclair and Casella (forthcoming)).

[26] In theory, profit shifting does not occur only through the use of OFCs. However, the bulk of it is coordinated by a limited set of countries that qualify as OFCs (*WIR15*).

[27] As the impact analysis is entirely based on FDI-level ETRs, the text may refer only to "ETR" or "ETR impact", omitting the qualification "FDI-level" when the context is clear. By contrast, the wording "standard ETR" is used to refer to the common ETR ratio (between average taxes paid and profits reported), if the context requires emphasizing the difference with the FDI-level ETR.

[28] The OECD EIA adopts an even more conservative assumption of no change in shares of profit shifting (OECD, 2020; Hanappi and Gonzalez Cabral, 2020). This scenario can be useful to set a theoretical lower bound. In practice, it is unlikely, and its occurrence would imply that Pillar II would be ineffective in tackling profit shifting, an outcome that is neither realistic nor desirable. In all circumstances, the gap in terms of the estimated impact of Pillar II on FDI-level ETRs between the most extreme cases – "full reversal of profit shifting" and "no impact on profit shifting" – is relatively limited, at less than 1 percentage point on average (see Casella and Souillard, 2022).

[29] The empirical evidence on profit shifting – largely caused by a limited set of countries with very low ETRs – lends some credibility to this scenario. In addition, the reputation and transaction costs associated with profit shifting are high for MNEs and expected to grow further as a consequence of the BEPS process.

[30] In the upper-bound scenario, it is more intuitive to neatly separate the impact of the profit-shifting channel and the ETR channel. First, profits are "brought back" from OFCs to the host countries where they are generated; the corresponding increase in ETR is due to the application of host countries' (higher) ETRs to the entire FDI income base (profit-shifting channel). Second, the host countries' ETRs are adjusted upward, if need be, to align with the minimum tax rate, given the entire FDI income as the tax base (ETR channel).

[31] To exemplify, consider the case of an investment for which part of the income is reported in the host country and part is shifted to an OFC. On shifted profits, the carve-out must be close to zero, as the underlying substance is expected to be small or negligible. Hence the minimum top-up fully applies (without the carve-out exclusion). In this context, the introduction of the carve-out does not change the motivation to reduce profit shifting, relative to the case without a carve-out. If anything, it further strengthens it because the OFC (which does not benefit from the carve-out) becomes relatively more expensive. In the upper-bound case, profit shifting will still be fully eliminated so that the profit-shifting channel will continue to exert its full impact (2 percentage points). Instead, the ETR channel will be affected, as the post-Pillar II average ETR in the host country may be reduced by the carve-out. In the extreme case of a 100 per cent carve-out, no top-up applies and thus the impact of the ETR channel is zero. The overall impact then remains confined to the profit-shifting channel, at 2 percentage points, a floor bounded away from zero. More generally, depending on the share of the carve-out in the host country, the overall impact ranges from 2 percentage points (100 per cent carve-out) to 3 percentage points (no carve-out). Similar considerations apply to the alternative, more conservative, scenario of a partial reduction of profit shifting.

[32] Bares et al. (forthcoming), adjusting the AETR for profit shifting in a different way from that here, find that dispersion may actually increase at modest levels of the minimum (because those in higher tax countries are affected by the reduced opportunities to shift profits outward).

[33] This simulation of the revenue impact is done by applying for each host country (non-OFC) the estimated increase in FDI-level ETRs to the (FDI-)income base reported by CbCR data (2017).

[34] Recalling figure III.8, under the baseline scenario, the growth in the average FDI-level ETR caused by Pillar II is 16 per cent in developed economies against 9 per cent in developing ones.

[35] Similar estimates have been produced by Damgaard et al. (2019) and Turban et al. (2020).

[36] The analysis in *WIR15* observes a negative relationship between direct investment from OFCs and the reported rate of return on this investment in host countries, which is indicative of FDI-enabled profit shifting (see also Bolwijn et al., 2018; Janský and Palanský, 2019).

[37] UNCTAD FDI statistics (stock and flows) will be mostly unaffected as they already remove FDI in and by SPEs (as reported by countries) and Caribbean financial centres.

[38] The GTED database is the first of its kind, collecting all publicly available data on tax expenditure provisions published by national governments worldwide from 1990 onwards, including many developing countries (as long as they report tax expenditures) (Redonda et al., 2022). One appealing feature of the database is that it reports all and only the information reported by countries in their tax expenditure reporting, limiting as much as possible the degree of discretion while ensuring significant coverage. As a major downside, the results are affected by heterogeneity in the quality of reporting across countries, particularly between developed and developing countries. Importantly, the GTED database also provides information on the forgone revenues associated with each tax expenditure, whenever reported. While the primary approach adopted in this analysis is based on a simple "counting", the main findings do not change substantially when results are "weighted" by forgone revenues.

[39] The notion of tax expenditure is different from that of tax incentive, although the two are strongly linked. While the objective here is to map and size the relevant categories of tax incentives, the empirical analysis uses tax expenditure data as proxies – mainly the number of provisions but also the corresponding forgone revenues, as reported by the GTED database.

[40] For example, it does not discriminate between foreign and domestic firms or between foreign affiliates of large MNEs and others. Throughout this section, incentives targeting taxes on corporate income – the broad perimeter of Pillar II – will be identified for convenience as "income-related incentives", where the qualification "corporate" may be omitted when implied by the context.

[41] The GTED database provides information on the main policy purpose of the tax expenditures, as stated by publishing countries. This information is available for about half of (corporate) income-related tax expenditure provisions. The list of objectives includes "attract FDI". This category of objectives – only 2 per cent of the relevant sample – is expected to heavily underestimate the share of incentives aimed at attracting foreign investment, as a major part of them falls under other categories of policy objectives, such as "promote priority activities" or "promote priority industries".

[42] In addition, a de minimis exclusion may apply: the filing constituent entity may elect to deem the top-up tax as zero if, for that country, its average revenue is less than €10 million and the average of GloBE income or loss is less than €1 million in the current and the two preceding fiscal years.

[43] This exclusion exists because the industry is generally subject to special tax rules in a number of countries, which have introduced alternative or supplementary tax regimes for them outside the scope of CIT.

[44] Suppose that an MNE based in country X (ultimate parent country) has a foreign subsidiary in country Y. The subsidiary in country Y provides an interest-bearing loan to an entity in country Z. Country Z levies no WHT on outbound interest payments. The subsidiary in country Y realizes only interest income and is

subject to 10 per cent ETR under the GloBE rules. If we assume that country Y levies a QDMTT or that country X levies an IIR as the country of the ultimate parent, the lack of WHT in the ultimate source country Z would be offset by the minimum rate of 15 per cent in another country (country Y in an QDMTT scenario or country X in an IIR scenario).

[45] See *WIR99* on determinants of FDI and UNCTAD (2000) on importance of tax incentives to attract FDI.

[46] For details on the United States tax reforms and their impact on investment, see UNCTAD's Global Investment Trends Monitor Special Edition on Tax Reform in the United States (UNCTAD, 2018a), and *WIR18* (box I.2, page 17).

[47] The only way to escape topping up, in the absence of a QDMTT recognized by others, would be to ensure a domestic GloBE ratio of 15 per cent. This, however, would actually imply a higher average tax rate than does the top-up tax (because of the carve out available under the latter).

[48] Though not addressed here, attention will also need to be given to the possible adoption of the STTR, balancing the additional protection from outward profit shifting that this may provide against the discouragement of inward investment; see Perry (forthcoming).

[49] Except for a few sectoral exceptions.

[50] This is the established view, for instance, of the IMF, the OECD and the World Bank. Their arguments are set out in Platform for Collaboration on Tax (2016a, b).

[51] There are others too: the focus here is on those that are most evidently inherent in the structure of the envisaged arrangements.

[52] If a QDMTT applies, it also costs the host country only 40 cents in forgone revenue, because the reduction in the covered tax ratio increases the amount of the top-up that the QDMTT enables the host country to collect. In the absence of QDMTT, the revenue cost to the host country would be the full $1.

[53] A 60 per cent R&D tax credit, for example, reduces tax due by 60 per cent of the firm's expenditure on R&D.

[54] This is in contrast to non-refundable credits, or refundable credits that do not meet the qualifying conditions, which simply reduce covered taxes.

[55] An example may help. Suppose that the carve-out is zero, so that total tax is at its otherwise-absolute minimum of 15 per cent of accounting profit. Then, a $1 tax credit conveys a direct benefit to the investor of $1 while (by the addition to accounting profit) increasing the investor's liability by only 15 cents: a net gain of 85 cents.

[56] In order to qualify for the treatment just described, for instance, credits in excess of tax liability must be refundable within four years of their arising.

[57] The role of MNEs in "collecting" rather than "paying" taxes is touched on briefly in the *WIR15* discussion on the contribution of MNEs to government fiscal revenues (p. 182).

[58] See for instance Perry (forthcoming).

[59] The reason is that in this case the low-tax country is only negligibly affected by the induced increase in its own rate, since it has already chosen the rate that best serves its interests, given the tax rates set by others; however, tax increases elsewhere convey a non-negligible benefit (see Hebous and Keen, 2022). Other aspects of the welfare impact of minimum corporate taxation are addressed in Hines (2022), Janeba and Schjelderup (2022) and Johannesen (2022).

[60] See for instance Vrijborg and De Mooij (2016).

[61] The effects of such strategic reactions might be considerable: IMF (2022a) finds that the addition to global revenues arising from strategic reactions by high-tax countries can be larger – given the strength of strategic complementarity suggested by the literature – than the gain assuming no change in their policies.

[62] See Mansour and Rota-Graziosi (2013).

[63] See for instance Konrad and Schwedler (1999).

[64] It may also be that some regions come to find the rate of 15 per cent on in-scope affiliates to be too low. If so, in addressing this they will face the same problem of outsiders, but mitigated because the gap in effective rates created by more ambitious regional minima will likely be lower than it was when there was no minimum in force.

[65] In aggregate, it is even theoretically possible that the damaging consequences of tax competition will be exacerbated by adoption of a minimum tax applying only to a subset of investments. See for instance the discussion in Keen and Konrad (2013).

[66] Keen and Marchand (1997).

[67] This might mean for example, wider adoption of State aid rules similar to those of the European Union.

[68] WTO, "Investment faciliation for development", Informal Discussions, https://www.wto.org/english/tratop_e/invfac_public_e/invfac_e.htm.

CHAPTER IV

CAPITAL MARKETS AND SUSTAINABLE FINANCE

INTRODUCTION

During the pandemic, and partly as a result of pandemic recovery plans, sustainable finance saw strong growth across equities, fixed income products and alternative assets, and in both public and private markets *(WIR20, WIR21)*. This is related to several factors. The accelerating and cascading impacts of climate change are rapidly revealing the physical and transition risks of non-sustainable investments. More recently, the war in Ukraine has also provoked reflection on the energy transition and its consequences for investors. Inflationary pressures and supply chain resilience, for example in energy, are adding further impetus to sustainability concerns. At the same time, the regulatory response to environmental and other sustainability-related issues, including climate change commitments, has accelerated and will support moves towards more sustainable financial markets in both developed and developing countries.

In 2021, the sustainable finance market continued to grow, in terms of both the number and the value of sustainable products. UNCTAD estimates the total value of sustainable financial products at $5.2 trillion, up by 63 per cent from 2020. They were made up of sustainable funds, whose assets grew by 53 per cent to $2.7 trillion, and sustainable bonds (including green, social and mixed-sustainability bonds), whose assets grew by 72 per cent to $2.5 trillion. However, UNCTAD analysis shows that not all of this investment is truly sustainable and that alignment with the SDGs remains limited.

The growing importance of sustainable finance is not just a question of market growth and expanding interest in related investment opportunities. It has also been supported by the increasing number of actions being taken by investors and asset owners to support more sustainable investments and to mitigate sustainability-related risks. This chapter shows that institutional investors, such as pension and sovereign wealth funds, are becoming more active in their assessment of sustainability risks and the responsiveness of their investment strategies to these risks. However, many investors still do not disclose or report on sustainability-related risks and are not moving quickly enough to reorient portfolios, especially with regard to climate-related action.

Stock exchanges and other market operators continue to integrate environmental, social and governance (ESG) factors into public market infrastructure. The number of exchanges with written guidance on ESG disclosure for issuers, for example, continues to grow rapidly, from just 13 in 2015 to 63 at the end of 2021. Likewise, the number of exchanges providing training on ESG topics to issuers and investors continues to increase, with more than half of exchanges offering annual training in this area. Mandatory ESG reporting has also been on the rise in recent years, supported by both exchanges and securities market regulators. The number of exchanges covered by mandatory rules on ESG disclosure, currently 30, has more than doubled in the past five years.

Overcoming fragmentation through the harmonization and comparability of frameworks and standards for corporate sustainability accounting and reporting is important to the achievement of SDG 12.6, sustainability reporting, and the further development of sustainable finance. Member States, working through UNCTAD's Intergovernmental Working Group of Experts on International Standards of Accounting and Reporting (ISAR), are playing an active role in this area. Since ISAR's publication of guidance in this area (UNCTAD, 2019), UNCTAD has been implementing capacity-building projects to assist member States in addressing regulatory, institutional and training needs.

The International Organization of Securities Commissions (IOSCO) continues to develop its work in this area to provide guidance to securities regulators, and development of international standards for ESG disclosure is accelerating. Between 2021 and 2022, the International Financial Reporting Standards (IFRS) Foundation formally launched its International Sustainability Standards Board (ISSB) (which is now recognized by the G7 and the G20) and signed a new agreement with the Global Reporting Initiative (GRI): combined, these developments aim to create a new global baseline for corporate sustainability reporting that is now recognized by the G7 and the G20. The consolidation of standards will further accelerate the integration of ESG into market infrastructure.

At the national level, the regulatory response to both sustainability-related risks and the growth of the sustainable finance market has been gathering pace. This chapter presents findings from a new UNCTAD project on national sustainable finance regulations. The findings are based on data from 35 economies, accounting for about 93 per cent of the world's gross domestic product (GDP), and show the accelerating efforts of major economies to introduce regulatory frameworks as well as standards and other policies in support of sustainable finance. The proliferation of regulations and standards by national governments (and regional groupings) relates both to country commitments, for example on climate change, and to the need to regulate financial markets in this space and mitigate problems such as greenwashing.

While it is a truism that investors face uncertainty and risk in many guises, one risk is foreseen and even financially quantifiable: climate change. As the world tries to move on from the pandemic while dealing with inflation, supply chain disruptions and the impact of war, investors, governments and international organizations should remain focused on the physical and transition risks of climate change. Towards this end, UNCTAD is mandated to support international efforts to finance climate change adaptation and other sustainability issues, as well as monitor the sustainable finance market and efforts to enhance its impact and contribution to sustainable development.[1] Through its programmes on sustainable finance, in particular its Global Sustainable Finance Observatory, UNCTAD will continue to provide analysis, advocacy and networking arrangements for governments, investors, regulators and other stakeholders to improve the sustainability of capital markets.

A. SUSTAINABILITY-THEMED CAPITAL MARKET PRODUCTS

UNCTAD estimates that the value of sustainability-themed financial products amounted to $5.2 trillion in 2021, up 63 per cent from 2020. These capital market investments consist mainly of sustainable funds (over $2.7 trillion) and sustainable bonds (including green, social and mixed-sustainability bonds) ($2.5 trillion). Most of these products are domiciled in developed countries and targeted at assets in developed markets. Most are self-labelled. Although these products tend to outperform their peers in the overall capital market in terms of sustainability, preliminary analysis reveals that the low-performing ones may not fulfil their sustainability credentials.

1. Sustainable funds

a. Market trends

The global market for sustainable funds experienced another year of exceptional growth in 2021, mainly driven by developed markets. According to Morningstar data, the number of sustainable funds reached 5,932 by the end of 2021, up 61 per cent from 2020. The total assets under management (AUM) of these funds reached a record $2.7 trillion, an increase of 53 per cent from the previous year (figure IV.1).

Investment inflows to sustainable funds also accelerated. Net investment in 2021 reached $557 billion, up 58 per cent from 2020 and more than 200 per cent from 2019 (figure IV.2). This trend reflects robust demand for mixed-sustainability products. Institutional investors are increasingly integrating sustainability in their portfolios to mitigate long-term climate and other environmental and social risks while tapping into opportunities offered by the energy transition. European funds attracted net investment inflows of $472 billion, or 85 per cent of the world's total.

Much of the growth of sustainable funds remained concentrated in developed markets. Europe dominates the market with an 81 per cent share of all such assets (figure IV.3). In 2021, assets in sustainable funds in Europe were boosted by record inflows (up 63 per cent), strong product development and rising equity prices. Sustainable funds accounted for 18 per cent of the assets of the European fund market, reflecting the relative maturity of the market and the catalytic impact of sustainable finance regulation in Europe.

The United States is the second largest market; however, in terms of assets, sustainable funds represent roughly 1 per cent of the total United States fund market. Changes to regulations implemented by the Labor Department to make it easier for retirement plans to invest in sustainable funds[2] and new regulations adopted by the Securities Exchange Commission on disclosure of climate risk may speed up development of the sustainable fund market in the United States.

Figure IV.1. **Sustainable funds and assets under management, 2010–2021**
(Billions of dollars and number)

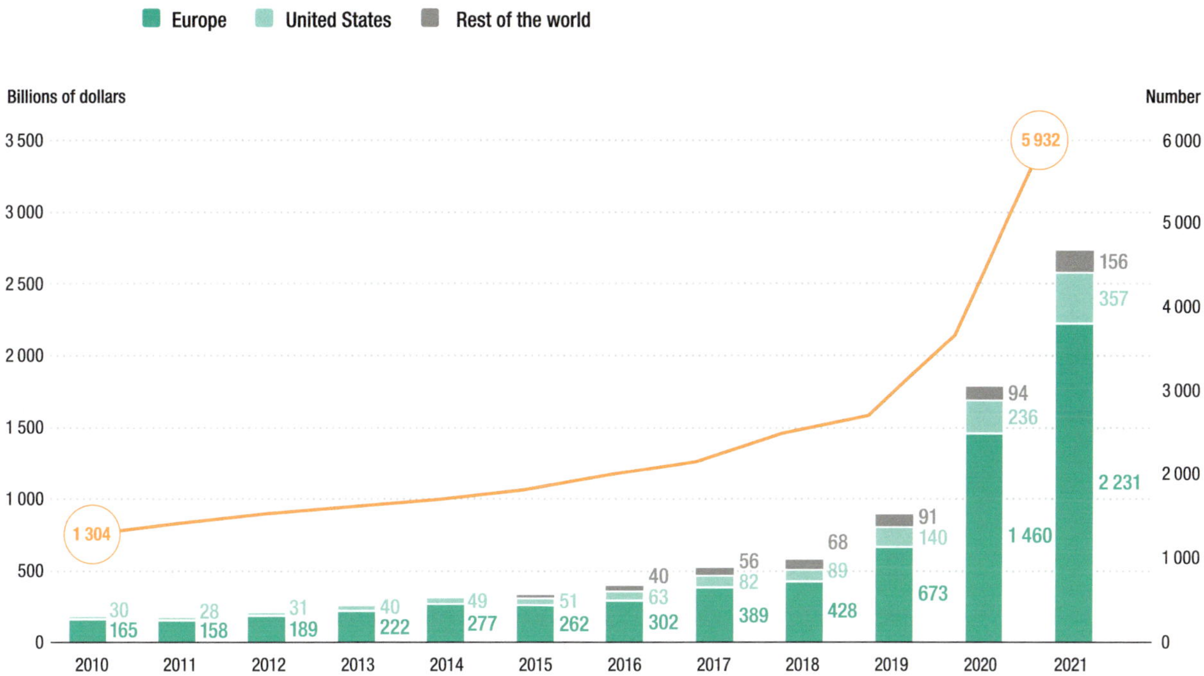

Source: UNCTAD, based on Morningstar data.
Note: The numbers for 2020 were updated based on the latest data.

Figure IV.2. **Net flows to sustainable funds, 2010–2021** (Billions of dollars)

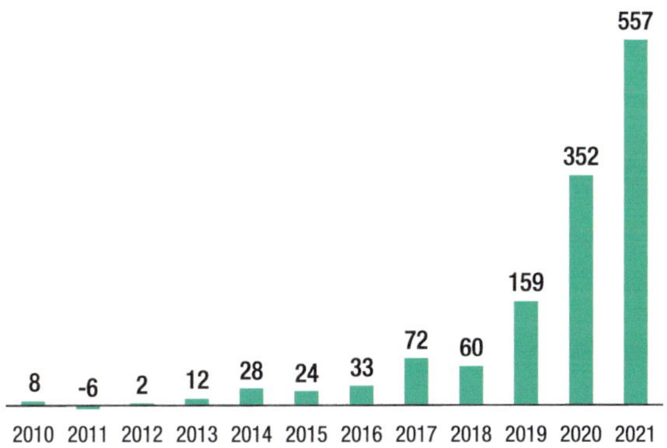

Source: UNCTAD, based on Morningstar data.

Figure IV.3. **The global sustainable fund market, by region, 2021** (Per cent)

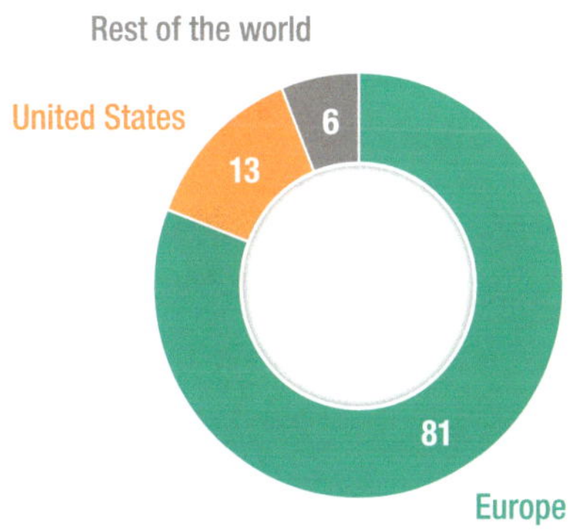

Source: UNCTAD, based on Morningstar data.

Sustainable funds in other developed markets also expanded rapidly in 2021, albeit from a relatively low level. The total assets of sustainable funds in Australia and New Zealand (combined), Canada and Japan reached $30.6 billion, $27.3 and $35.2 billion respectively.

In Asia (excluding Japan), sustainable fund assets grew to $63 billion, up 70 per cent from 2020. In total, 118 sustainable funds were launched in the region in 2021, more than double the number launched in 2020 (55). This growth was mainly driven by China (49 funds) and the Republic of Korea (36). China remains the dominant player in the region and the third largest sustainable fund market worldwide, with AUM of nearly $50 billion. Asset managers in major emerging economies in other regions, such as Brazil and South Africa, also launched sustainable funds in recent years, but their market size remains small.

The growth momentum of sustainable funds is expected to continue. Demand remains strong and governments in both developed and emerging economies have stepped up their efforts to support the growth of sustainable investment. A large number of countries are putting in place necessary frameworks, industry standards and regulations (see section D), which will bring more transparency and credibility to the market and help build a viable ecosystem for its further growth.

However, a number of challenges need to be addressed in order to fully tap into the potential of the sustainable fund market. Despite the surge in recent years, sustainable funds account for only about 4 per cent of the global fund market in terms of assets. Most of these funds are self-labelled, and the lack of consistent standards and high-quality data to assess their sustainability credentials and impact has given rise to greenwashing concerns and credibility issues. While regulation efforts at national level can help address these issues, international cooperation is needed to enhance interoperability and harmonization of regulations and standards across countries to facilitate international investment.

Another structural issue that needs to be addressed is the absence of most developing economies in the sustainable fund market. Despite positive developments in recent years in a few leading emerging markets such as Brazil, China, India, South Africa and some economies in the Association of Southeast Asian Nations, sustainable funds remain largely a developed-market phenomenon. Most developing economies, in particular the least developed ones, face tremendous barriers to developing their own sustainable fund market or benefiting from the international sustainable fund market, owing to their limited market size and the perception of relatively high risks in their capital markets.

The relative scarceness of company-level sustainability data in developing economies does not work to their advantage either. In this regard, UNCTAD and the ISAR facilitated the creation of regional partnerships in Latin America and in Africa to promote a communication channel among peers in the region and to support the development of national strategies and policies. The partnerships aim to (i) establish and/or strengthen the national infrastructure to prepare high-quality sustainability reports by companies; (ii) implement the new global sustainability reporting standards; (iii) measure the contribution of the private sector to the implementation of the SDGs; and (iv) promote sustainable enterprise development.

To support the growth of the sustainable fund market, developing economies need to address these issues. Small developing economies may also consider developing a regional market for sustainable investment, one in which high-quality companies, including small and medium-size enterprises (SMEs) and social enterprises that meet necessary sustainability and reporting standards, can be listed and traded, and sustainable financial instruments can be developed to meet the needs and requirements of international investors.

b. Sustainability performance

The rapid rise of sustainable funds shows the huge potential of this emerging financial instrument in financing sustainable development. However, the risk of ESG- or sustainability-washing constitutes a severe challenge to the future growth of the sustainable fund market. So far, sustainable funds have been self-labelled. Although several economies, such as the European Union (EU) and Hong Kong (China), have introduced regulations on sustainability disclosure by issuers at the product level, there are no industry standards for qualifying sustainable funds at the national or international level. Meanwhile, the lack of high-quality sustainability data and the inconsistent company sustainability ratings available in the market make it challenging to evaluate the sustainability performance of these funds. All these issues have led to legitimate concerns about the credibility of the sustainable fund market and its potential damage to investor confidence, which could hold back further growth of the market.

To shed more light on the sustainability profile of these funds, UNCTAD, with the support of its data partner Conser, has been monitoring more than 800 sustainability-themed equity mutual funds since 2020. This research builds on ESG data based on the average of leading ratings available in the market and in this sense reflects the "consensus" of the market (UNCTAD, 2021). This section provides the preliminary results of the monitoring assessment.

(i) Overall sustainability

Sustainable funds are highly heterogeneous in their approaches to integrating sustainability. For analytical purposes, the sustainable integration strategies of these funds are grouped into three categories: (i) sustainability engagement, a strategy of mainly engaging with portfolio companies, for example through voting or other specific actions, to push for positive changes in terms of sustainability integration; (ii) general incorporation, a strategy that incorporates ESG or other material sustainability factors into investment selection processes to mitigate risks or enhance returns, including by using positive or negative screening or by applying responsible investment principles; and (iii) sustainability thematic strategy, which focuses on one concrete sustainability theme (for example low carbon or gender equality) for asset allocation. A sustainable fund can use one or a combination of these strategies.

Overall, the sustainable funds covered by the monitoring exhibit a better sustainability profile than their conventional peers. As a group, these funds have a mean sustainability score of 7.2 (out of 10) in the assessment,[3] significantly higher than the 4.0 average sustainability rating of the MSCI global equity index (the MSCI ACWI).[4] This shows that, on average, sustainable equity funds tend to outperform the mainstream equity markets on sustainability ratings, regardless of their choices of sustainability integration strategies.

However, the sustainability ratings of the funds, as a whole and by strategy, are distributed over a wide range, and the low-performing funds in each group may not fulfil their self-claimed sustainability credentials (table IV.1). Most notably, the quartile of funds with the lowest scores, in each strategy category and overall, have an average sustainability rating below 6, owing to significant exposure to ESG or climate-related risks or sensitive sectors (such as fossil fuels, tobacco and alcohol, and weapons). This raises legitimate concerns about their sustainability claims. Their sustainability integration practices and performance therefore require careful examination, and external auditing may be warranted.

Table IV.1. Distribution of sustainability score by fund strategy, 2021
(Average sustainability rating)

	Percentile			
Strategy	**0–25**	**25–50**	**50–75**	**75–100**
Overall	4.6	6.6	8.1	9.5
Sustainability engagement	4.6	6.5	8.1	9.5
Sustainability incorporation	4.7	6.7	8.3	9.5
Thematic funds	5.3	7.9	9.2	10

Source: UNCTAD, based on Conser data.
Note: The distribution of fund sustainability ratings by strategy is broken into four quartiles; e.g. percentile 0–25 represents the bottom quartile of funds that have the lowest sustainability ratings.

Figure IV.4. **Exposure of sustainable funds to climate-positive and -negative assets, 2021** (Per cent)

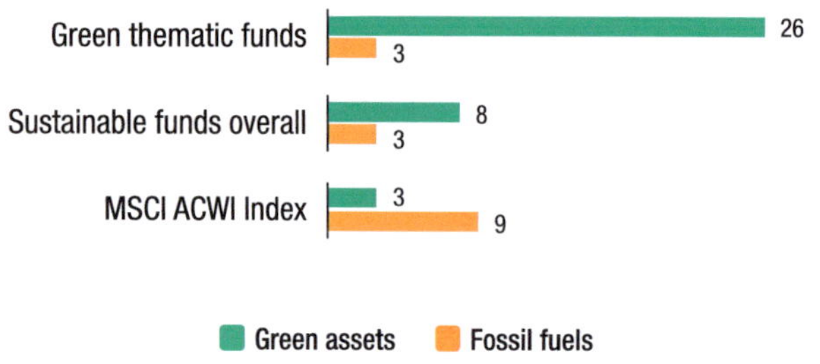

Source: UNCTAD, based on Conser data.

(ii) Climate impact

With respect to the funds' impact on climate sustainability, the analysis shows that both thematic funds with a green investment focus and the sustainable fund universe in general tend to perform better than the overall fund market. On average, low-carbon thematic funds have a net exposure of 23 per cent of their portfolio to climate-positive assets (low-carbon assets minus fossil fuels), compared with a net exposure of -6 per cent for the MSCI ACWI index. It should be noted that, although some sustainable funds are fossil-fuel-free by prospectus, most are not. About 25 per cent of self-declared green funds have an exposure of more than 5 per cent to fossil fuels, and some cases nearly 20 per cent, which calls into question the "greenness" of these funds (figure IV.4).

Morningstar data also show that sustainable funds are improving their low-carbon performance. At the end of 2021, 63 per cent of United States sustainable funds had a Morningstar low-carbon risk rating, up from less than 50 per cent in 2019. The share is significantly higher than the 48 per cent of the United States fund universe that has a low-carbon risk rating (Morningstar, 2021).

This trend reflects a steady rise of climate funds in the sustainable fund market, driven by opportunities offered by renewable energy, electric vehicles, energy efficiency and storage, and other cleantech industries. Meanwhile, more fund managers have committed to greening their portfolios. According to the Net Zero Asset Managers initiative, 236 asset managers, with $57.5 trillion in AUM, have signed up to the initiative with a commitment to support the goal of net zero greenhouse gas (GHG) emissions by 2050 or sooner. However, these commitments need to be substantiated by an accurate evaluation of, and reporting on, the greenness of asset managers' portfolios, in particular in light of the unsatisfying ratings of some low-performing products in the market. A solid evaluation and disclosure of their carbon footprint and related risks is not only necessary but, thanks to the growing availability of carbon emissions data, also feasible. For example, an increasing number of banks and asset owners have started to assess their exposure to climate risk through systematic stress tests (UNCTAD, forthcoming); however, there is limited disclosure at the product level, and fund issuers need to do more in this respect.

(iii) SDG alignment

As sustainable investment products, sustainable funds can play an important role in filling the Sustainable Development Goals (SDGs) financing gap, in both developed and developing economies. Leading fund providers, such as BlackRock, Amundi and Robecco, have launched funds dedicated to the SDGs, and some funds have used the SDGs as a framework to evaluate the impact of their portfolio. However, the lack of a taxonomy to define what counts as SDG investment as well as the poor quality of existing SDG ratings for individual companies make it challenging to measure or assess the SDG alignment of investment funds and determine how much of their portfolio is invested in assets that contribute to delivery of the SDGs.

UNCTAD has identified several key SDG sectors (encompassing all 17 SDGs), which are critical for achieving the SDGs and represent the largest investment needs and opportunities in terms of SDG financing (*WIR14*). Accordingly, UNCTAD has been monitoring private sector investment in these sectors (*WIR21*).

Examining the holdings of the more than 800 sustainable equity funds in the sample, the analysis identified assets of these funds across eight of the key SDG sectors: transport infrastructure, telecommunication infrastructure, water and sanitation, food and agriculture, climate change mitigation (renewable energy and cleantech), health, education and ecosystem diversity (figure IV.5). This investment totalled $156 billion, or 26 per cent of their total AUM at the end of 2021. Four sectors – health, renewable energy, food and agriculture, and water and sanitation – account for almost 95 per cent of the assets committed to these SDG sectors. The health sector, which covers health infrastructure, medical services, pharmaceuticals and medical devices, is the most common and single largest SDG sector for fund investments, followed by climate change mitigation. Compared with 2020, the funds' investment in the health sector declined by 1.7 per cent, while their investment in climate change mitigation rose by 1.5 per cent, pointing to increased interest in green assets.

Figure IV.5. **Allocated assets by sustainable funds across eight SDG sectors, 2021**
(Per cent)

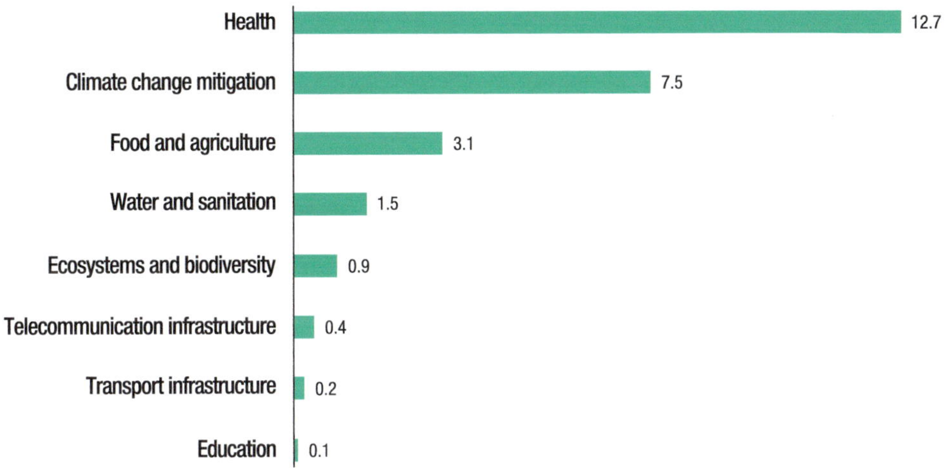

Source: UNCTAD.

2. Sustainable bond markets

The sustainable debt market is primarily composed of use-of-proceeds bonds. They include any type of debt instrument from which the net proceeds are used exclusively to finance, in part or in full, eligible green or social projects. There are three main subcategories:

(i) Green bonds: Instruments that raise funds for projects that have environmental benefits including renewable energy, green buildings and sustainable agriculture

(ii) Social bonds: Instruments that raise funds for projects that address or mitigate a specific social issue and/or seek to achieve positive social outcomes, such as improving food security and access to education, health care and financing, especially but not exclusively for target populations

(iii) Mixed-sustainability bonds: Instruments that raise funds for projects that have both environmental and social benefits

In addition to use-of-proceeds bonds, sustainability-linked bonds (SLBs) are a new and rapidly growing product class within the sustainable bond market that can be useful for corporations funding their sustainability transitions (box IV.1).

Global issuance of sustainable bonds surpassed $1 trillion in 2021, and industry estimates project that it will exceed $1.5 trillion in 2022 (figure IV.6). The green bond market exceeded $517.4 billion in 2021, with a five-year growth rate of 70 per cent. Social and mixed-sustainability bonds repeated the strong growth trend observed in 2020 and totalled $395 billion in 2021. The EU and the corporate sector are set to be key players in 2022 and continue to push social and mixed-sustainability bond issuance to new heights as the market is driven by projects that support the SDGs and the 2030 Agenda.

Sustainable bond issuance has been increasing, especially in emerging markets, where it almost tripled in 2021 (figure IV.7), with China accounting for 60 per cent of the emerging-markets total and estimated to surpass $100 billion in 2022 (figure IV.8).

Box IV.1. Sustainability-linked bonds

Unlike established green and social bonds, sustainability-linked bonds (SLBs) come with no constraints on how the proceeds can be used. Instead, they are based on predefined sustainability or ESG objectives set by the issuer, which links this guarantee directly to the coupon paid to investors. For example, Italian utility group Enel issued a sustainability-linked $1.5 billion five-year bond in September 2019, which had a 2.65 per cent annual coupon if the company reached a target of 55 per cent renewable energy installed capacity by 2021. If that target was not achieved, a step-up mechanism would be applied, increasing the rate by 25 basis points until the bond matures in September 2024. A third-party expert report confirmed that by December 31, 2021, Enel's renewable installed capacity has reached 57 per cent. This flexibility in customizing objectives is particularly relevant for enterprises transforming their business to more sustainable modalities. Thus, SLBs are a forward-looking, performance-based instrument and the issuer's objectives should be measured through predefined key performance indicators (KPIs) and assessed against predefined sustainability performance targets.

While the market for SLBs is still small, these instruments were a highlight of 2021, growing by more than tenfold to reach $92 billion. To date, 70 per cent of all KPIs have centred on reduction of scope 1 and 2[a] GHG emissions. This is mainly due to the availability of data on scope 1 and 2 emissions performance. However, some diversification is becoming evident. It appears that KPIs linked to scope 3 emissions reduction are gaining market acceptance, with only 22 issuers reporting in 2021 compared with only one in 2020. It is also important to note the growing importance of KPIs linked to gender diversity, which goes in line with the trend observed in social bonds where gender will be a key theme in 2022.

Source: UNCTAD, based on information from Environmental Finance.

[a] Scope 1 emissions are direct emissions from the reporting entity. Scope 2 are emissions derived from the production of electricity consumed by the reporting entity. Scope 3 are emissions derived from the production of goods and services consumed by the reporting entity. For more details on the GHG Reporting Protocol, see https://ghgprotocol.org.

Figure IV.6. Global sustainable bond issuance by bond category, sector and region, 2021

(Billions of dollars and per cent year-on-year growth)

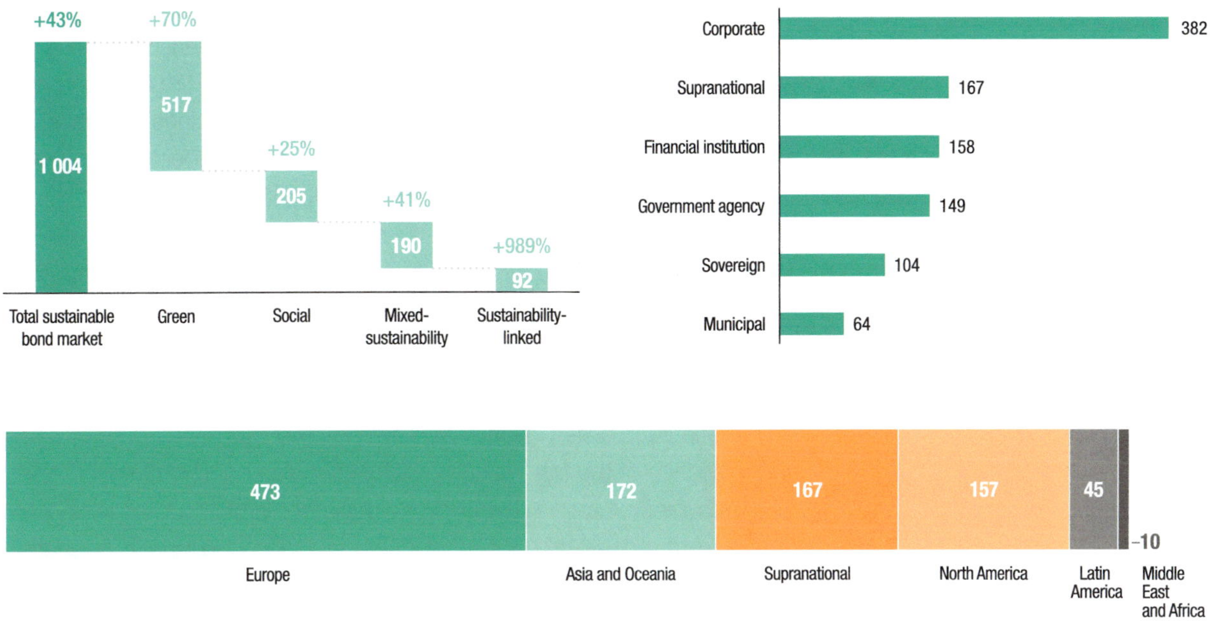

Source: UNCTAD, based on information from the Climate Bonds Initiative and Environmental Finance.
Note: Total market value can vary slightly by data source and provisional value calculations.

Figure IV.7. Annual sustainable bond issuance in emerging-market economies, 2019–2021 (Billions of dollars and per cent)

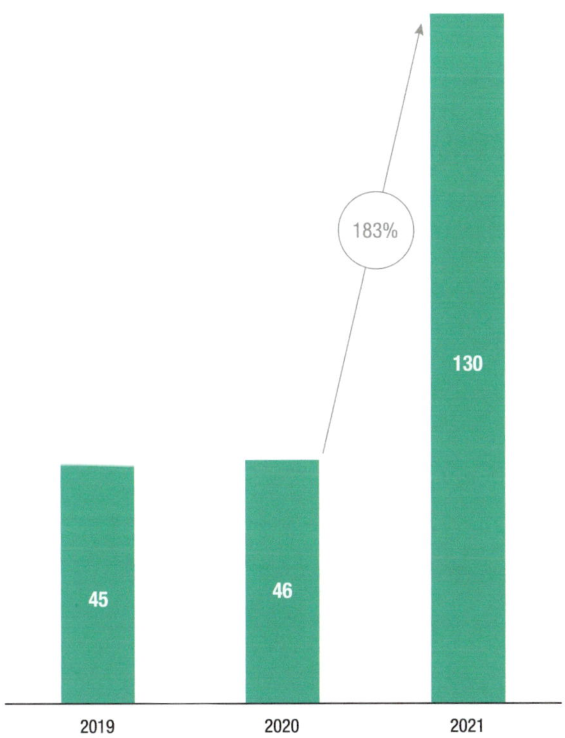

Source: UNCTAD, based on information from Environmental Finance.

Figure IV.8. China: green bond issuance, 2016–2021 (Billions of dollars)

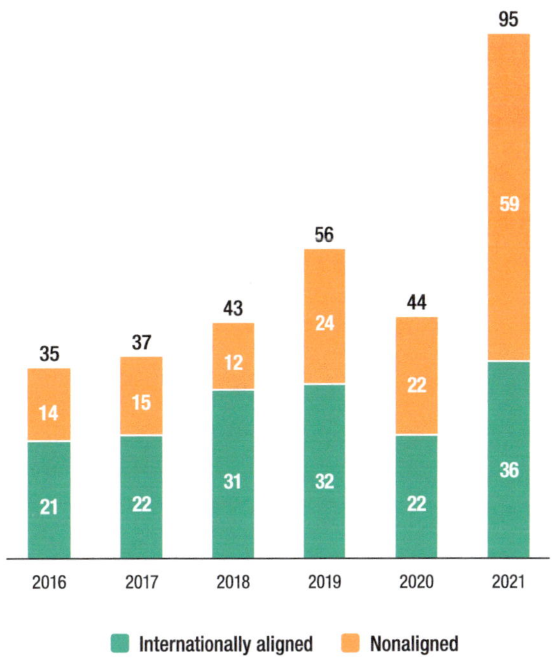

Source: UNCTAD, based on information from Environmental Finance.
Note: Volume includes bonds aligned with international standards and bonds aligned with only local standards. Internationally aligned green bonds are limited to those where at least 95 per cent of proceeds are designated for green projects aligned with the Climate Bonds Taxonomy, produced by the Climate Bonds Initiative.

a. Green bonds

Green bonds are meant to promote investment in environmentally based SDGs such as climate action (SDG 13), affordable and clean energy (SDG 7), and sustainable cities and communities (SDG 11). The industries receiving the largest investment through green bonds all fund key elements of basic infrastructure: energy, buildings, transport and water (figure IV.9). Initially the energy industry received most of the funds invested through green bonds (50 per cent of the total market in 2014). In recent years, the buildings and transport sectors have caught up, making up 30 per cent and 18 per cent, respectively, in 2021. Although the renewable energy sector still has the largest share of green investment across categories, with 35 per cent of the market, the share invested in low-carbon buildings has grown by 33 per cent since 2014. This shows increasing effort to achieve the Paris Agreement goals since GHG emissions of cities are significant: up to 70 per cent of a large city's emissions relate to its buildings.

Europe remains a clear leader in the green bond market. After adopting the independently evaluated NextGenerationEU Green Bond framework, the European Commission proceeded with the issuance of the first NextGenerationEU green bond in October 2021. The 15-year bond was more than 11 times oversubscribed, and the proceeds went on to finance the share of climate-relevant expenditure in the Recovery and Resilience Facility (non-repayable financial support and loans to member States to support public investments and reforms). Also in 2021, the United Kingdom (£10 billion), Italy (€8.5 billion) and Spain (€5 billion) issued their first sovereign green bonds, which attracted record investor demand. These successful entries will pave the way for new sovereign green bonds from other countries in 2022.

In 2021, issuance of green bonds by the corporate sector saw a yearly increase of 49 per cent (figure IV.10). The rapid growth in corporate green bonds will likely continue, given global campaigns such as Race to Zero (see section E).

Figure IV.9. **Green bond market size by industries financed, 2014–2021**
(Billions of dollars)

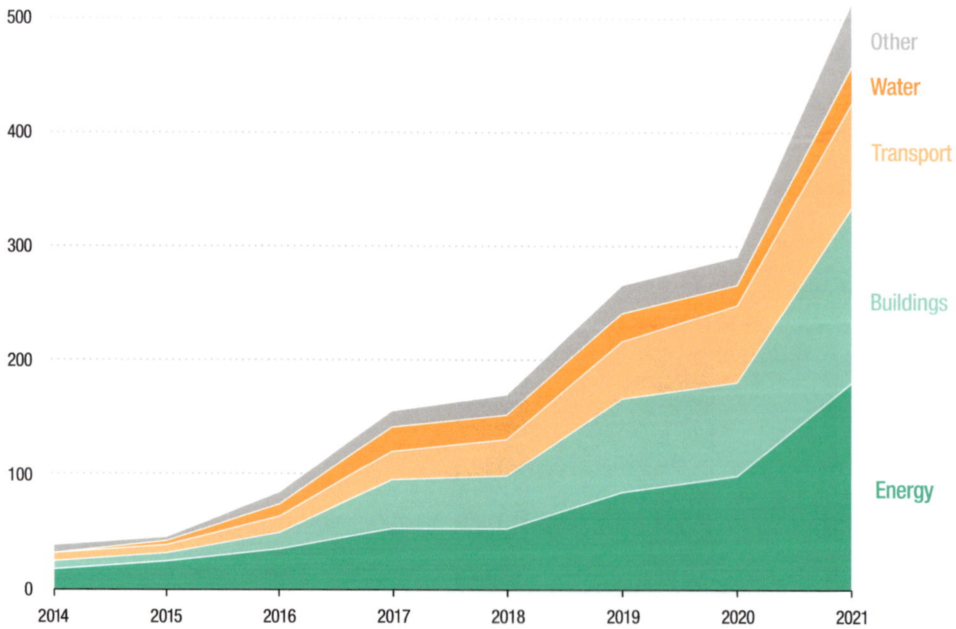

Source: UNCTAD, based on information from Climate Bonds Initiative.

Figure IV.10. | **Annual green bond issuance by sector** (Billions of dollars)

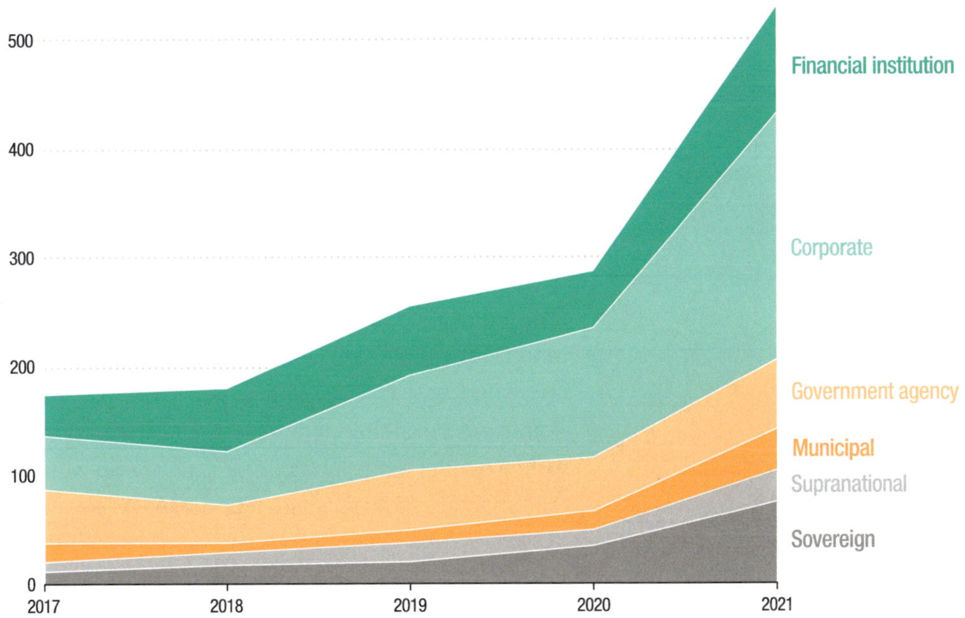

Source: UNCTAD, based on information from Environmental Finance.

b. Social and mixed-sustainability bonds

In 2021, the pandemic continued to push issuance of social and mixed-sustainability bonds to new heights, with year-on-year growth of 25 per cent and 41 per cent, respectively (figure IV.11). The total social bond issuance of about $205 billion represents an increase of more than 10 times over the level in 2019; the same holds for mixed-sustainability bonds, which totalled $190 billion, a 77 per cent increase over 2019.

Figure IV.11. | **Social and mixed-sustainability bond issuance, 2017–2021** (Billions of dollars and per cent)

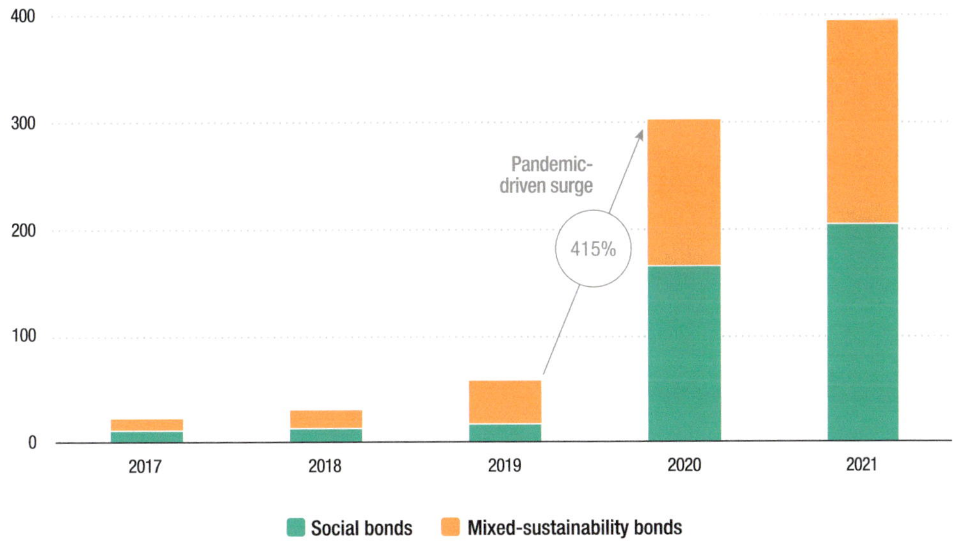

Source: UNCTAD, based on information from Environmental Finance.

Figure IV.12. **Social bond issuance by issuer type, 2021** (Per cent)

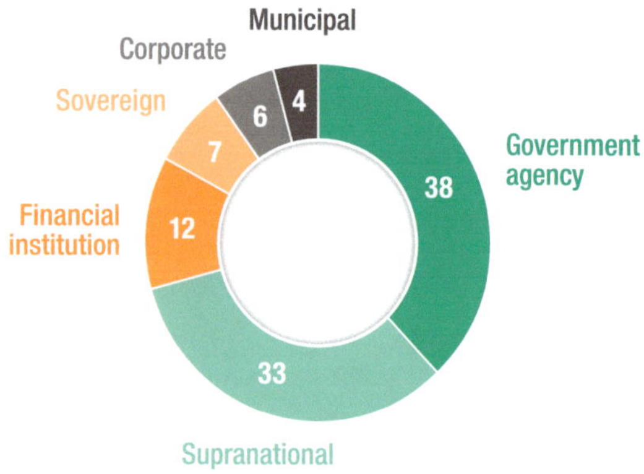

Source: UNCTAD, based on information from Environmental Finance.

Social bonds will likely continue to have a prominent share of the sustainable bond market even as the immediate effects of the pandemic subside. Government and supranational agencies will lead the way to new types of social issuance (figure IV.12).

However, the impacts of the global pandemic and the growing focus on the SDGs and the 2030 Agenda have been driving investor demand to socially minded investments. In this scenario, it is probable that financial institutions will take the opportunity to launch innovative financing schemes and drive private sector social bond issuance. It is expected that in 2022 the areas to receive more focus will be SMEs, affordable housing and credits with a gender focus, particularly to empower women entrepreneurs (UN Women, IFC, ICMA, 2021).

B. INSTITUTIONAL INVESTORS

Institutional investors can exert significant influence over their investees and the sustainable investment market through both the size of their holdings and the active nature of their ownership. UNCTAD research shows that institutional investors that have a long-term investment horizon, such as pension and sovereign wealth funds, are taking action on risks associated with sustainability, especially climate change. Nevertheless, more than half of the world's 100 largest public pension and sovereign wealth funds do not disclose or report on sustainability issues, and institutional investors as a group have a long way to go in mainstreaming sustainability.

Pension and sovereign wealth funds, as asset owners and investors at the very upstream end of the investment chain, are in a strong position to drive sustainability integration in capital markets, especially in view of the size of their total assets and the often large stakes they hold in publicly listed companies. In 2021, the AUM of the global pension industry grew to $56.6 trillion, up from $52 trillion the year before (Thinking Ahead Institute, 2022). Public pension funds (PPFs) account for $22.3 trillion, or roughly 39 per cent, of global pension assets.[5] The AUM of sovereign wealth funds (SWFs) in 2021 grew to $10.9 trillion, up from $9.2 trillion the year before.[6] UNCTAD has been monitoring sustainable investment-related practices of the world's largest public pension funds and SWFs. This section examines the latest developments in sustainability integration by these institutional investors in their operations.

In recent years, the real risks to investments of a rapidly heating planet, as well as the transition risks stemming from regulatory and other responses related to CO2 emissions, have been recognized and acted on by an increasing number of investors (*WIR21*). Indeed, for a small number of front-runner funds, the need to address sustainability concerns or ESG integration, including climate action, is so obvious that it is no longer seen as even a priority focus area for boards.[7] There is now a clear recognition that institutional investors with a longer-term investment horizon, such as pension and sovereign wealth funds, which own a growing share of equity markets, need to pivot rapidly to a more sustainable investment portfolio that can help contribute to sustainable financing through, for example, investment in renewable energy or clean technologies.

There are many ESG-related issues of material concern to investors, but, in the past year, net zero has come to dominate attention. The latest instalment of the sixth assessment report of the Intergovernmental Panel on Climate Change (IPCC) makes clear that global CO2 emissions have to peak before 2025 if the world is to remain on track to achieve net zero along a 1.5-degree Celsius warming pathway by 2050 (IPCC, 2022). The report notes that, while investors may understand and report on climate risks (through, for example, the Financial Stability Board's Task Force on Climate-related Financial Disclosures (TCFD), they in fact have a long way to go on taking action on fossil fuels:[8] the report states that "despite [regulatory and voluntary] initiatives, climate-related financial risks remain greatly underestimated by financial institutions and markets, limiting the capital reallocation needed for the low-carbon transition" (IPCC, 2022).

UNCTAD has analysed the sustainability integration practices of the world's top 100 PPFs and SWFs. They included the top 70 PPFs, accounting for $13.1 trillion of AUM – or almost 60 per cent of total AUM of PPFs – and the top 30 SWFs, accounting for $9 trillion of AUM –

or 83 per cent of total AUM of SWFs (UNCTAD, forthcoming). Of the top 100 funds, 47 published meaningful reporting on sustainability and ESG integration in their investment decisions (38 PPFs and 9 SWFs). Although this number is slightly up from 2020, when 40 per cent of funds reported (UNCTAD, 2020), the results appear to reflect the point made by the IPCC – that many investors are underestimating climate-related risks and they need to do more to address the climate challenge.

Of the 100 funds in the sample, 53 still do not report on ESG integration. They include 21 SWFs, accounting for 70 per cent of the SWFs in the sample, and 32 PPFs, accounting for 43 per cent of the PPFs. As discussed in the 2020 UNCTAD report, SWFs remain relatively less transparent and have further to go in terms of sustainability performance disclosure. Geographically, the non-reporting funds are based mainly in Asia and North America. Funds in China, Japan, Saudi Arabia and the United Arab Emirates are typically non-reporting, and a large share of funds in the United States also do not report on ESG. The non-reporting funds rarely include any information regarding ESG and sustainability on their websites and only occasionally in their annual reports, if at all. The size of the fund does not have a significant influence on non-reporting: all non-reporting funds had an average of $229 billion in AUM, as compared with reporting funds which had average AUM of $227 billion. Geographical location and governance seem to have the largest influence on whether a fund publishes an ESG report, and both are likely influenced by the strength of regulations within the national framework. This highlights the importance of national or regional regulatory frameworks and the need for technical assistance in some cases.

Nevertheless, among the 47 per cent of front-runner funds that do publish information on sustainability integration, there is serious acknowledgement of the material risks posed by ESG issues, and funds have changed their investment strategies and policies accordingly. The great majority of reporting funds have made efforts to elaborate a clear vision for their sustainable investments and have introduced internal policies and guidelines to support the integration of an ESG or SDG perspective in their investment strategy, often anticipating transition risks.[9] While an ESG perspective is often integrated into existing investment teams, two thirds of funds have put in place a dedicated team to coordinate ESG-related investments. Despite many funds now targeting net zero by 2050 in their asset allocation, less than half of reporting funds set an overall target or goal for sustainable investment or asset allocation in their portfolios (figure IV.13).

Figure IV.13. **Relevant sustainability-related policies of funds, 2022**
(Per cent of reporting funds)

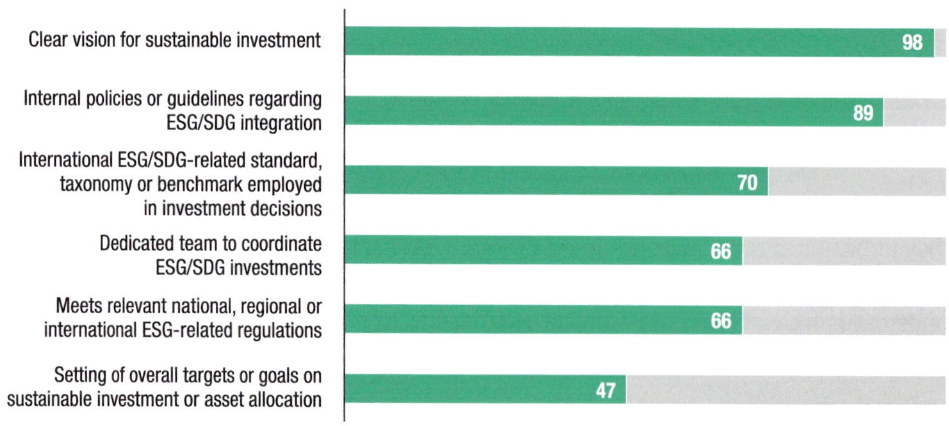

Source: UNCTAD, based on fund annual reports or sustainability reports, n = 47.

Most reporting funds are using at least one international standard or benchmark in their investment decision-making and reporting. In particular, they are increasingly using a couple of international sustainability disclosure standards. The most common reporting framework is that of the TCFD; many funds also use the Principles of Responsible Investment (PRI) Scorecard and Transparency Report to evaluate and improve their sustainability performance (figure IV.14). More than two out of three funds now need to meet relevant national, regional or international regulations, such as the EU's Sustainable Finance Disclosure Regulation, in the case of European funds, and more disclosure and reporting is expected to accompany compliance with these regulatory changes.

Figure IV.14. **Relevant sustainability-related reporting standards used by funds, 2022** (Number of reporting funds)

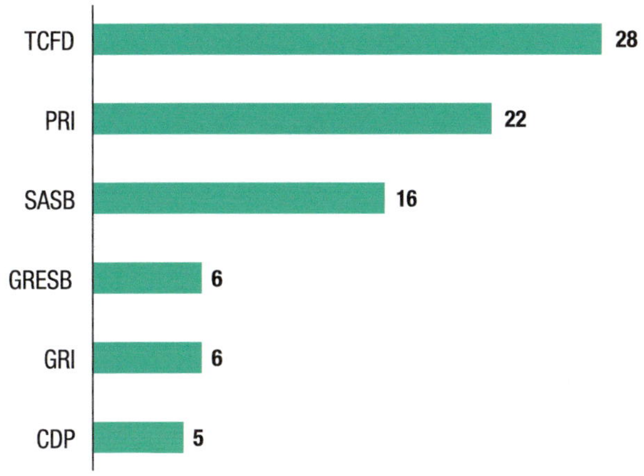

Source: UNCTAD, based on fund annual reports or sustainability reports, n = 47.
Note: The funds use a total of 66 standards, initiatives and partnerships. CDP = Carbon Disclosure Project, GRESB = Global Real Estate Sustainability Benchmark, GRI = Global Reporting Initiative, PRI = Principles for Responsible Investing, SASB = Sustainability Accounting Standards Board, TCFD = Task Force on Climate-Related Financial Disclosures.

With regard to how funds implement sustainability concerns in their investment strategies, both PPFs and SWFs employ a combination of strategies that are not mutually exclusive. The majority integrate a sustainability perspective across their investment activities, including equities, fixed income, alternative assets, and public and private markets, which may also employ a negative screening of certain assets (in particular, tobacco, weapons and thermal coal). Nearly three out of four reporting funds now have an impact investment strategy. This strategy either targets thematic sectors, such as renewables, or uses a specific ESG-related instrument, such as green bonds, and sometimes targets emerging-market-based climate-solutions companies (Cheema-Fox, Serafeim and Wang, 2022). The SDGs are themselves becoming a benchmark for sustainability performance, and almost half of funds explicitly consider one or more SDGs in their investment decision-making process or have made attempts to align their holdings with the SDGs. However, this sometimes equates to mapping holdings against the 17 goals and is more of a reporting exercise than an investment strategy. Over a third of reporting funds use a positive or best-in-class screening strategy (figure IV.15).

Figure IV.15. **Sustainability investment strategy of funds, 2022** (Per cent of reporting funds)

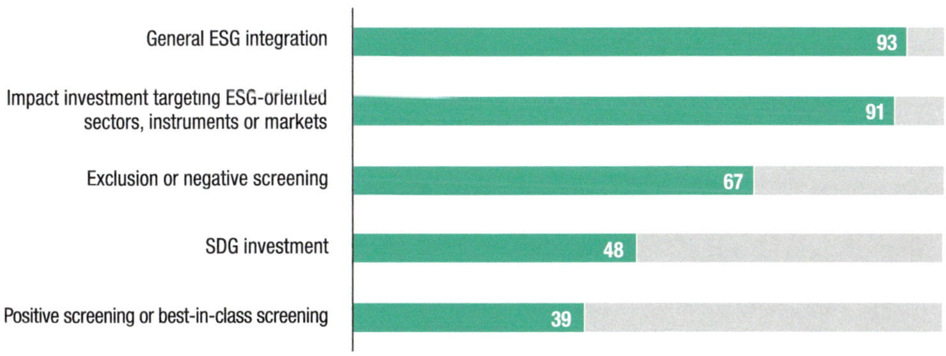

Source: UNCTAD, based on fund annual reports or sustainability reports, n = 47.

The results of UNCTAD's study on the sustainability practices and investment strategies of the largest PPFs and SWFs provide a mixed picture. While there is good practice to be applauded, there is also room for improvement, especially on disclosure and reporting where there is a great variance among even reporting funds in terms of what and how to report. Meanwhile, the use of key performance indicators is still rare, making sustainability disclosure highly subjective in some cases. In this respect, the regulatory environment is critical, and some regions are more advanced than others. What is needed is greater harmonization of standards and regulations to promote more widespread action on sustainability integration and performance.

C. STOCK EXCHANGES AND MARKET INFRASTRUCTURE

The number of stock exchanges with written guidance on ESG disclosure for issuers (SDG 12.6) continues to grow rapidly, from 13 in 2015 to 63 at the end of 2021. Likewise, the number of exchanges providing training on ESG topics to issuers and investors continues to increase, with more than half offering at least one training course or workshop per year. Mandatory ESG reporting has also been on the rise in recent years, supported by both exchanges and security market regulators. The num ber of exchanges covered by mandatory rules on ESG disclosure more than doubled in the past five years, to 30.

1. Stock exchanges and derivatives exchanges

The sustainability activities of stock exchanges – those related to ESG factors – have increased exponentially since the beginning of the century (figure IV.16). Collectively these trend lines show a sharp uptick in sustainability activities among the world's exchanges. The number of exchanges with ESG bond segments continues to grow rapidly, from 5 exchanges in 2015 to at least 44 at the end of 2021 (Key instruments and developments supporting these trends are discussed in more detail in section C.) Likewise, the number of stock exchanges providing training on ESG topics to issuers and/or investors continues to rise rapidly, from fewer than 10 in 2013 to more than 60 by the end of 2021.

Figure IV.16 | Stock exchange sustainability trends, 2000–2021 (Number of exchanges)

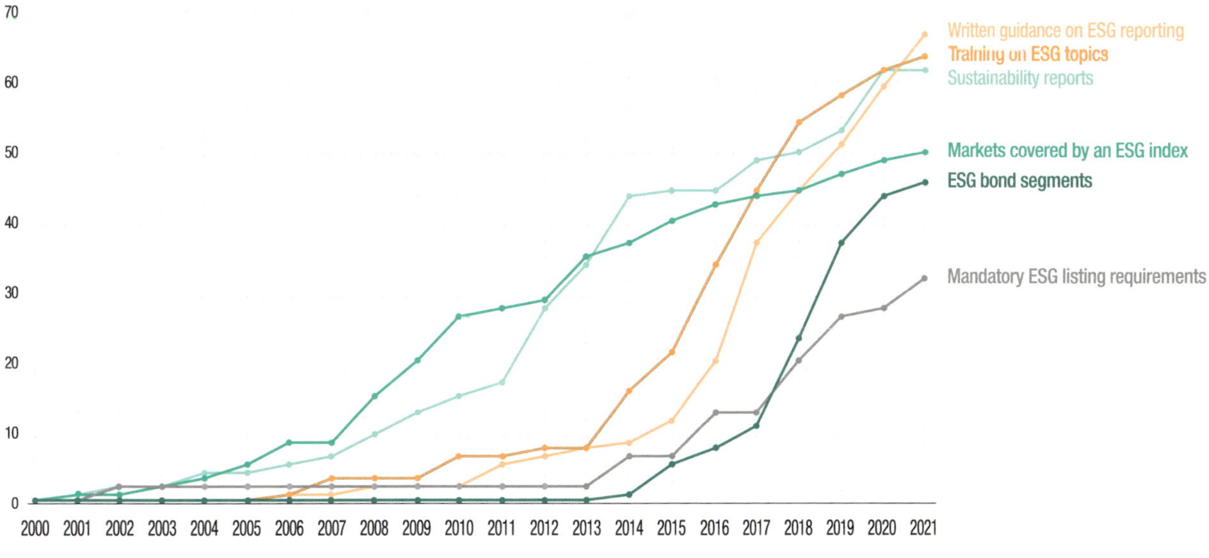

Source: UNCTAD, SSE database.
Note: ESG = environmental, social and governance.

Figure IV.17. **SSE initiative members, 2012–Q1 2022** (Number of exchanges)

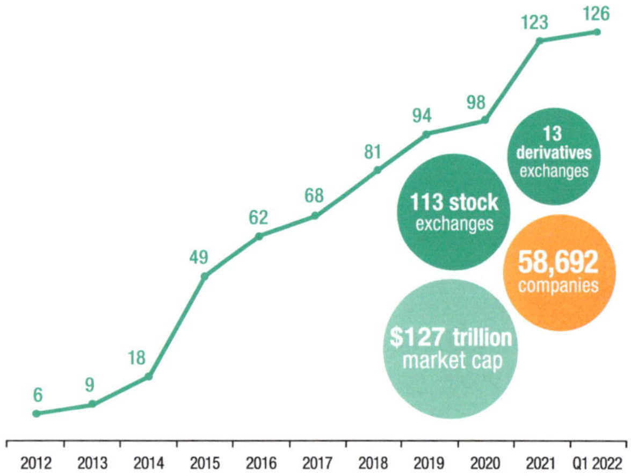

Source: UNCTAD, SSE database.

a. Sustainable Stock Exchanges initiative

Since its launch in 2009, the United Nations Sustainable Stock Exchanges (SSE) initiative has grown to include most of the exchanges in the world: as of Q1 2022, the initiative had 113 stock exchange members, collectively listing more than 58,000 companies with a combined market capitalization of more than $127 trillion (figure IV. 17). The growth of this United Nations partnership programme illustrates the demand for ESG guidance and peer learning in the exchange industry. The SSE has emerged as the premier platform for collaboration and learning for stock exchanges, together with capital market regulators, investors, issuers and financial service providers, to meet global sustainability goals.

In 2021, derivatives market operators joined the SSE for the first time, as members of the SSE derivatives network, which was launched with 12 founding members from across the world.[10] The establishment of this network recognizes the next step in the market's evolution towards aligning market signals with sustainable development imperatives across all markets.

b. ESG disclosure: stock exchange guidance, listing requirements and standards

Stock exchanges continue to play an important role in helping markets navigate emerging ESG disclosure and management demands. By the end of 2021 the number of exchanges providing formal guidance to issuers on reporting ESG information had reached 63 (figure IV.18). Only 13 did so in 2015, when the UN SSE launched its global campaign and model guidance to encourage exchanges to provide guidance on sustainability reporting.

Figure IV.18. **Global trends in ESG disclosure rules and guidance** (Number of exchanges)

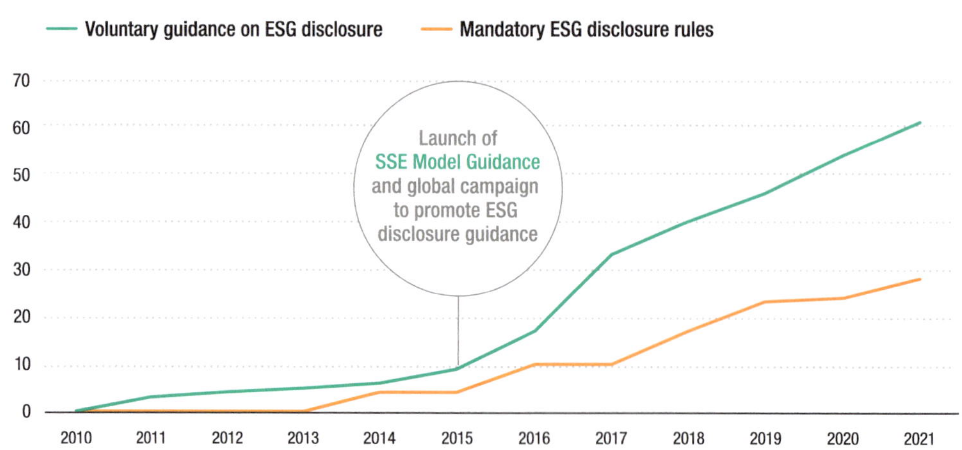

Source: UNCTAD, SSE database.

There has also been a steady increase in mandatory ESG disclosure rules, with a five-year growth rate of 60 per cent. This trend suggests that SDG 12.6 on sustainability reporting should be achieved by 2030.

UNCTAD and UN Environment, as co-custodians of SDG indicator 12.6.1, "number of companies publishing sustainability reports", have developed a measurement methodology for the indicator and are overseeing data collection and the reporting process to the global SDGs database used to assess progress up to 2030. This promotes harmonization of SDG reporting by companies and facilitates countries reporting on the contribution of the private sector to the implementation of the SDGs.

The spectrum of approaches to reporting ESG data incorporates a few key reporting instruments (figure IV.19). An overwhelming majority of guidance documents reference the instruments of the GRI, followed by those of the Sustainability Accounting Standards Board (SASB) and the International Integrated Reporting Council (IIRC), which are each referenced in about three quarters of guidance documents. Climate-specific reporting instruments such as the recommendations of the Financial Stability Board's TCFD and the Carbon Disclosure Project (CDP) are referenced by over half of the guidance, and about a third reference the work of the Carbon Disclosure Standards Board (CDSB). Developments in the global ESG reporting landscape may see reviews of guidance as necessary (see section 2.b).

Exchanges are also starting to provide focused guidance on climate disclosure since the growing demand for decision-useful, climate-related financial information in annual reports and financial filings has led to an increased need for issuers to update their knowledge on climate-related risks and reporting frameworks. Following the UN SSE initiative launch of the Action Plan to Make Markets Climate Resilient and a Model Guidance on Climate Disclosure in 2021, the Johannesburg Stock Exchange launched for comment its Sustainability and Climate Change Disclosure Guidance, specifically tailored to the South African context. It is expected that more exchanges will start providing guidance on climate disclosure as global financial markets take steps towards better integrating climate risks and opportunities into pricing mechanisms (see section E).

Figure IV.19. **ESG reporting instruments referenced in stock exchange guidance, as of Q1 2022** (Per cent of guidance documents referencing the instrument)

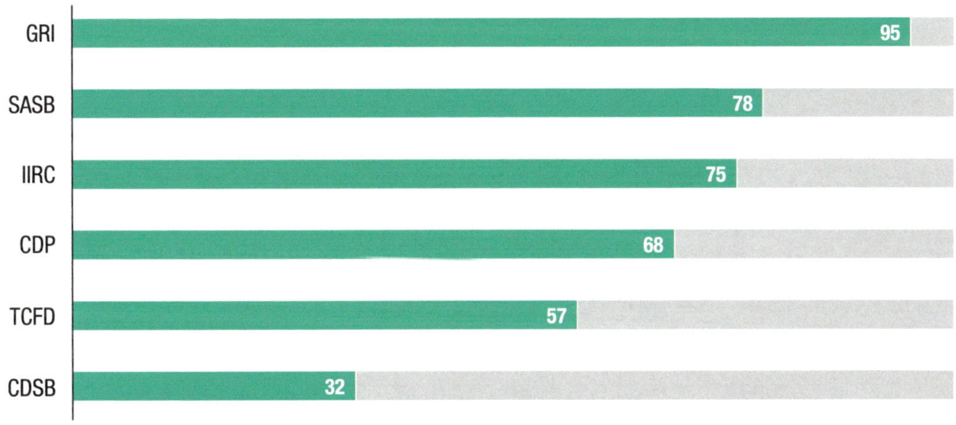

Source: UNCTAD, SSE database.
Note: CDP = Carbon Disclosure Project, CDSB = Climate Disclosure Standards Board, GRI = Global Reporting Initiative, IIRC = International Integrated Reporting Council, SASB = Sustainability Accounting Standards Board, TCFD = Task Force on Climate-Related Financial Disclosures.

c. Derivatives exchanges

While the incorporation of ESG into products traded on the derivatives market is considered nascent compared with the growth seen in equity and bond markets, the pace of change continues to intensify in this sphere of the financial sector, spurred by factors such as demand in the physical market, regulatory changes and commitments by market players (including exchanges) to play a role in the transition to more sustainable economies and capital markets. It seems inevitable that this market will also experience exponential advancement on ESG issues in the coming years, with industry experts noting that a marketplace previously considered niche has "a key role to play in the advancement of ESG objectives in the financial markets and the global transition to a green economy".[11]

Already exchanges have seen significant growth in the ESG index-based derivatives segment, with futures and options tracking equity indices that incorporate ESG weightings and ratings.[12] More conventional "ESG-linked" derivatives (which involve such environment-linked underlying commodities as carbon credits, sustainability prescriptions in contract requirements of the underlying asset and hedging products that focus on the use of proceeds for ESG purposes) have also become increasingly commonplace. More recently derivatives markets are seeing mounting interest in sustainability-linked derivatives (SLDs), which link ESG components to traditional derivatives. The first SLD was traded in August 2019. Similar to sustainability-linked bonds, sustainability-linked derivatives (SLDs) provide flexibility by not prescribing the use of proceeds. Although SLDs are still mostly bespoke products, it remains a challenge to ensure that the intended ESG objectives are achieved; hence, to enable measurement and monitoring, KPIs must be agreed and incorporated into the contractual documents. To support the safe and efficient progression of the SLD market, to attract new market participants and to grow liquidity, in 2021 the International Swaps and Derivatives Association (ISDA) published guidelines and regulatory considerations.

In addition to exchanges, industry a ssociations and regulators in the derivatives market are keenly following developments and conducting their own research to keep track of progress while ensuring that they are positioned to respond as needed or to take the lead on new initiatives. The newly established derivatives network of the SSE aims to provide a platform for exchanges and other market participants to gain learning by sharing information and experiences in this regard. During 2022, the SSE will also engage and collaborate with key industry players such as the Futures Industry Association to examine developments in the market and provide insights into the role of derivatives and exchanges in supporting the SDGs.

2. Advancing gender equality

Gender equality is a human right and a critical component of the SDGs. It is also a driver of economic growth and enterprise development: progress towards gender equality is a core contributor to more economically prosperous and socially cohesive societies. Exchanges play a central role in the economies in which they operate, and as such they have the direct and indirect ability to influence listed companies' actions on gender equality.

The number of exchanges supporting greater gender equality in businesses has soared over the past decade. For example, seven years ago, seven exchanges started to raise awareness about the Women's Empowerment Principles and the importance of gender parity to businesses, by jointly ringing the bell for gender equality. Organized by UN SSE, UN Women, UN Global Compact, WFE and Women in ETFs, this event developed into an annual activity and by 2022, more than 100 exchanges around the world participated and organized events.

Apart from awareness-raising, further exchange action on gender equality falls into three broad categories, as detailed in the joint UN SSE–IFC gender equality action plan for exchanges (figure IV.20), included in the report *How Exchanges Can Promote Gender Equality* (UN SSE and IFC, 2022). Two of these categories are market-focused, and one is focused on what exchanges can do internally. Exchanges can lead by example when they increase internal efforts for gender equality, but it is their market-focused actions that have the potential to initiate large-scale changes. These actions include mobilizing finance and improving women's access to financial markets by providing products and services as well as strengthening market performance on gender equality by improving transparency.

Figure IV.20. | Gender equality action plan for exchanges

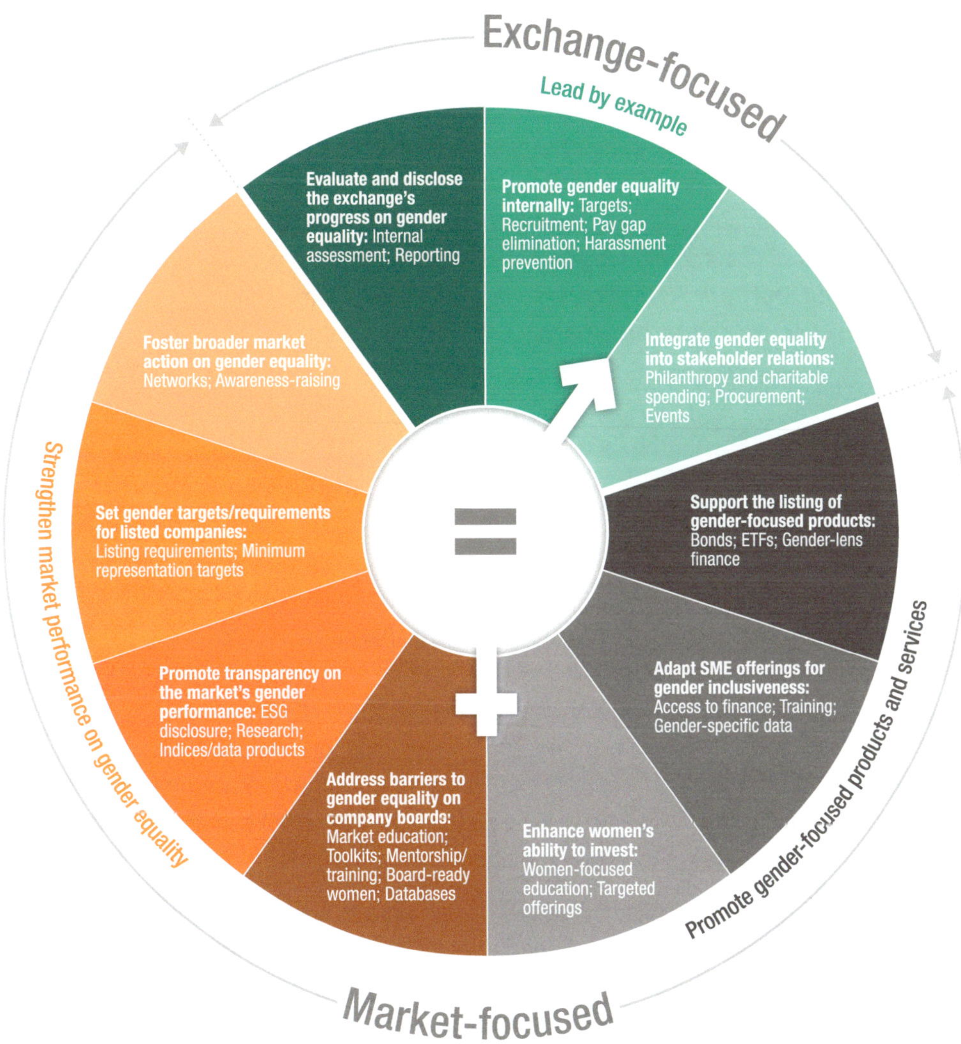

Source: SSE, IFC (2022).

D. POLICIES, REGULATIONS AND STANDARDS

With the rise of sustainability-themed financial products, governments around the world are stepping up their efforts to develop regulatory frameworks for sustainable finance. Thirty-five leading developed and developing economies and country groupings had 316 sustainable finance-dedicated policy measures and regulations in force by the end of 2021. Sustainability disclosure and sector-specific measures account for the majority of these measures; policy and regulation developments concentrate in emerging policy areas such as taxonomies, product standards and carbon pricing. Although sustainable finance policies and regulations need to take a nation's specific development context into consideration, international collaboration is also needed to ensure necessary coherence with international standards. At the international level, more work is being done within IOSCO to standardize the approach of securities regulators on sustainable finance, including efforts to strengthen product and corporate ESG disclosure. The second half of 2021 and first half of 2022 also saw a historic consolidation in ESG corporate reporting standards with the merger of several instruments into the new ISSB of the IFRS Foundation and the agreement between the latter and the GRI, which now sets a clear global baseline for corporate sustainability reporting.

1. National sustainable finance policies and regulations

a. An overview

The rise of sustainability-dedicated financial products that can also help finance sustainable development has been accompanied by a proliferation of principles and standards. These have been primarily driven by the private sector and international initiatives, as exemplified by a large number of voluntary standards on products, disclosure and sustainability integration. More recently, governments in both developed and developing economies are stepping up their efforts to support the growth of sustainable finance by putting in place the necessary policies and regulatory frameworks.

UNCTAD has been monitoring the latest developments in sustainable finance measures and regulations in 35 economies and country groupings. These include the G20 member states and Switzerland, as well as 13 developing economies (Bangladesh, Chile, Colombia, Egypt, Hong Kong (China), Kenya, Malaysia, Nigeria, the Philippines, Singapore, Thailand, the United Arab Emirates and Viet Nam) and ASEAN, which together account for about 93 per cent of the world's GDP. According to the UNCTAD sustainable finance regulation database, by the end of 2021 these economies had 316 sustainable finance-dedicated policy measures and regulations in force (figure IV.21). Over 40 per cent of these measures were introduced in the last five years, and 41 new measures were adopted in 2021 alone. At least 45 more measures are under development. These trends illustrate the accelerating pace of growth in sustainable finance policymaking.

This large pool of policy measures and regulations covers seven key policy areas (table IV.2). Almost half of policies are dedicated to sustainability disclosure. Sector-specific regulations with respect to asset management, sustainable banking and sustainable insurance are the

Table IV.2. Key sustainable finance policy areas covered by major developed and developing economies, 2022

Group	Economy	National strategy	National framework and guidelines	Taxonomy	Product standards	Sustainability disclosure	Sector-specific regulations	Carbon pricing
G20	Argentina	No measures	In use	No measures	In use	In use	In use	In use
	Australia	No measures	No measures	In development	No measures	In use	In use	In use
	Brazil	In use	No measures	In development	No measures	In use	In use	In development
	Canada	In use	No measures	In development	In development	In use	In use	In use
	China	In use	In use	In use	In use	In use	In use	In use
	European Union	In use	In use	In use	In use	In use	In use	In use
	France	In use	In use	No measures at the national level but EU measures apply	No measures at the national level but EU measures apply	In use	In use	No measures at the national level but EU measures apply
	Germany	In use	In use	No measures at the national level but EU measures apply	No measures at the national level but EU measures apply	In use	In use	No measures at the national level but EU measures apply
	India	No measures	In use	In development	No measures	In use	In use	No measures
	Indonesia	No measures	In use	In development	In use	In use	In use	In development
	Italy	No measures at the national level but EU measures apply	In use	No measures at the national level but EU measures apply	No measures at the national level but EU measures apply	In use	In use	No measures at the national level but EU measures apply
	Japan	No measures	In use	In use	In use	In use	In use	In use
	Mexico	No measures	In use	No measures	No measures	In use	In use	In use
	Republic of Korea	No measures	In use	In development	No measures	In use	In use	In use
	Russian Federation	No measures	In use	In development	In use	In use	No measures	In development
	Saudi Arabia	No measures	No measures	No measures	No measures	In use	No measures	No measures
	South Africa	In use	In development	In development	No measures	In use	In use	In use
	Turkey	No measures	No measures	No measures	No measures	In use	In use	In development
	United Kingdom	In use	In use	In development	No measures	In use	In use	In use
	United States	No measures	No measures	No measures	No measures	In use	In use	In use
Other developed economies	Switzerland	No measures	In use	No measures	No measures	In use	In use	In use
Other developing economies and groupings	Bangladesh	No measures	In use	In use	No measures	In use	In use	No measures
	Chile	In use	No measures	In development	In use	In use	No measures	In use
	Colombia	No measures	No measures	In development	No measures	In use	In use	In use
	Egypt	No measures	No measures	No measures	No measures	In use	No measures	No measures
	Hong Kong (China)	In use	In use	No measures	No measures	In use	In use	No measures
	Kenya	No measures	No measures	No measures	In use	In use	In use	No measures
	Malaysia	No measures	In use	In use	In use	In use	In use	In development
	Nigeria	No measures	In use	No measures	No measures	In use	In use	No measures
	Philippines	No measures	In use	In development	No measures	In use	No measures	No measures
	Thailand	No measures	No measures	In development	No measures	In use	In use	In development
	United Arab Emirates	No measures	In use	No measures	No measures	In use	No measures	No measures
	Viet Nam	No measures	No measures	In development	No measures	In use	No measures	In development
	Singapore	In use	In use	In development	No measures	In use	In use	In use
	ASEAN	No measures	No measures	In use	In use	No measures	No measures	No measures

In use In development No measures No measures at the national level but EU measures apply

Source: UNCTAD sustainable finance regulation database.

Figure IV.21. **Sustainable finance policy measures and regulations in selected developed and developing economies, 2010–2021** (Number)

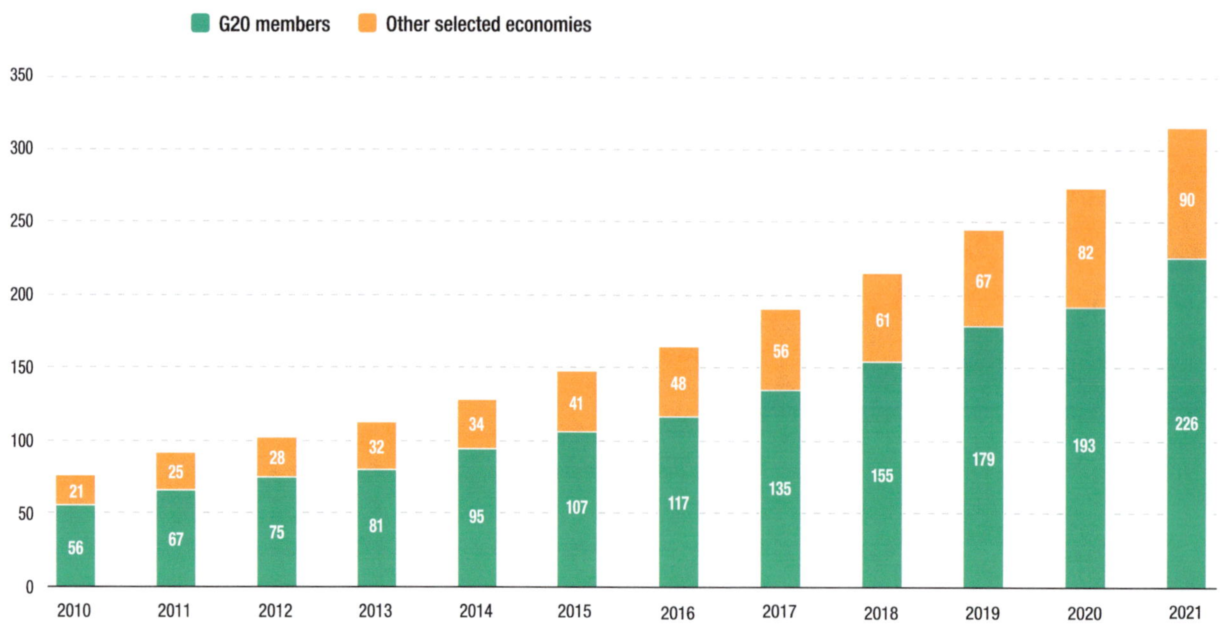

Source: UNCTAD.

Note: Other selected economies include Switzerland, as well as 13 developing economies (Bangladesh, Chile, Colombia, Egypt, Hong Kong (China), Kenya, Malaysia, Nigeria, the Philippines, Singapore, Thailand, the United Arab Emirates and Viet Nam), and ASEAN. Relevant measures of the EU are included in the number for the G20.

second biggest policy area, representing about 20 per cent of all measures. The majority of the 35 economies already have in place either a national sustainable finance strategy or framework, or guidelines on sustainable finance. Policy and regulatory gaps are more visible in three relatively new policy areas: taxonomies, product standards and carbon pricing. Most measures under development concentrate in these areas, and the situation may change in the coming years.

G20 members account for 226 of the 316 measures identified by the database. The EU (and its member states) and China take the lead, with policies developed in all seven areas. Significant progress has been made by non-G20 economies covered by the UNCTAD sustainable finance regulation database. These economies have been proactively pushing ahead with their sustainable finance agenda and have played an important role in shaping the global sustainable finance policy landscape.

b. Latest developments in key policy areas

(i) National strategies and frameworks

A well-developed national strategy, framework or action plan is imperative in setting national goals and galvanizing efforts to support the growth of sustainable finance. In response to the 2030 development agenda and the pandemic, many governments in developing and emerging economies have recognized the need to focus on economic resilience and have started including climate mitigation and adaptation measures and green investment targets in their national recovery plans (Zhan and Santos-Paulino, 2021). In this context, several countries launched national strategies, frameworks and action plans to support the development of sustainable finance in 2021.

After announcing its intention to achieve peak carbon by 2030 and carbon neutrality by 2060, China adopted a national action plan to achieve the goal in October 2021. As another milestone in achieving the European Green Deal, in July 2021 the EU published the renewed EU Sustainable Finance Strategy, which sets a clear policy agenda to finance the sustainable transition to 2024. Indonesia launched the Sustainable Finance Roadmap, Phase II (2021–2025) to accelerate the transition of the financial sector to sustainability through the establishment of a sustainable finance ecosystem. In Japan, the Ministry of Economy, Trade and Industry launched a Green Growth Strategy to enable industry alignment with 2050 carbon neutrality. The Japanese Government also established a task force on transition finance and published the Basic Guidelines on Climate Transition Finance for sustainable bonds and loans. Singapore adopted the Singapore Green Plan to advance its national agenda on sustainable development, including through the implementation of its Green Finance Action Plan. The National Treasury of South Africa published an updated version of "Financing a Sustainable Economy" to encourage long-term investments in sustainable economic assets, activities and projects. The United Kingdom launched Greening Finance: A Roadmap to Sustainable Investing, setting out the long-term ambition for a green financial system. Phase one of the road map will focus on "ensuring decision-useful information on sustainability is available to financial market decision-makers". By the end of 2021, most of the 35 economies in the database had in place a national sustainable finance strategy, framework or guidelines.

(ii) Taxonomies and product standards

As a fundamental building block of the sustainable finance ecosystem, taxonomies help clarify what economic activities are considered environmentally or socially sustainable for investment purposes. As such, they help bring more clarity, credibility and transparency to the sustainable investment market. Taxonomies have become a very active policy area in recent years.

In 2021, ASEAN, China, Japan and Malaysia launched or revised their sustainable finance taxonomies on sustainable finance. Together with Bangladesh and the EU, six of the 35 economies in the UNCTAD sustainable finance regulation database have developed a taxonomy. Meanwhile, 16 other economies (Australia, Bangladesh, Brazil, Canada, Chile, Colombia, India, Indonesia, the Philippines, the Republic of Korea, the Russian Federation, Singapore, South Africa, Thailand, the United Kingdom and Viet Nam) are in the process of developing one.

Most of the taxonomies in use, and under development, are dedicated to climate transition and environmental protection. However, a few countries have started to incorporate social development into their taxonomies. After the launch of its green taxonomy, the EU is working on a comprehensive taxonomy for social sustainability. The Bangladesh taxonomy pursues both climate and social development objectives, and covers cottage, micro and SME development and socially responsible investment. South Africa also included social resilience activities, such as education, skills development and knowledge management in its draft taxonomy, and it plans to further strengthen the social dimension in the future. Given the acute need to mobilize more investment for social development in less developed countries, inclusion of the social aspect in their sustainable finance taxonomies is necessary.

The expanding taxonomy universe varies significantly in objectives, scope, technical criteria, verification and disclosure requirements, and countries use different approaches to define sustainable activities (IPSF, 2021a). This inconsistency hinders interoperability of standards and can raise transaction costs and discourage sustainable investment flows across economies (Ehlers, Gao and Packer, 2021). A certain level of international coordination and cooperation is necessary.

As an instrument for identifying sustainability-compatible investment activities, taxonomies can serve as a useful framework for sustainable financial product labelling and for standards setting. Following the adoption of the EU Taxonomy, the EU Commission presented the European Green Bond Standard in 2021, with the aim of improving the effectiveness, transparency and credibility of the market and encouraging market participants to issue and invest in green bonds. Also in 2021, the Japan Bank for International Cooperation launched a Green Bond Framework to guide the issuance of green bonds.

With the proliferation of taxonomies, the number of labelling standards for sustainable investment products at the national level is expected to increase. However, most of the existing standards are dedicated to green bonds. More work needs to be done on the development of standards of other sustainable investment products, including social bonds, SDG bonds and sustainable funds.

(iii) Sustainability disclosure

Sustainability disclosure is a dynamically evolving field that accounts for almost half of all sustainable finance policy measures and regulations in the 35 economies analysed. Most of these measures target companies, with 75 per cent applying to large corporations, in particular listed companies, and 28 per cent to financial institutions.

Sustainability integration and related requirements are the main focus of disclosure (36 per cent), followed by corporate governance (32 per cent) and environmental and climate issues (26 per cent). Most climate disclosure measures were introduced in the last five years and their number is growing rapidly. Yet the use of KPIs remains rare, including in environmental and climate disclosure. To help improve the comparability and credibility of disclosures, the introduction of more KPIs, aligned with international standards such as the Paris Agreement or the SDGs, is necessary.

Another trend in corporate sustainability disclosure is the rise of mandatory measures, although voluntary measures remain more common (figure IV.18). Almost all economies in the database have at least one mandatory sustainable disclosure measure in place, and new mandatory measures are planned by many economies, including Brazil, Canada, Chile, China, the EU, Hong Kong (China), India, Japan, Singapore, Switzerland, the United Kingdom and the United States.

Disclosure measures at the product level are rare, and much work needs to be done in this area. The EU, China and Hong Kong (China) have introduced disclosure measures that apply to sustainable bonds or funds and other financial products. The United Kingdom and Singapore are working on similar measures. The absence of product-level sustainability disclosure regulations makes it difficult to address the lack of sustainability data for financial products and the associated greenwashing concerns.

Leading international corporate reporting standards, such as the TCFD, the SASB and the GRI, have started to make their way into national regulations. For example, the Financial Conduct Authority of the United Kingdom is planning to introduce product- or portfolio-specific disclosure guidelines connected to the TCFD. The EU's Corporate Sustainability Reporting Directive integrated all the key concepts of the TCFD recommendations. The Japanese Government has also launched initiatives to support TCFD-aligned disclosure by large companies (IPSF, 2021b). The formation of the ISSB could accelerate the consolidation of international disclosure standards (see the following section) and thus lead to improved harmonization of sustainability reporting at the national level.

Although SMEs represent a significant part of the economy, they are largely exempted from corporate sustainability disclosure regulations, especially when it comes to mandatory measures. This can help reduce the burden of disclosure for SMEs but also makes it harder for them to benefit from sustainable finance. One solution is to implement adapted frameworks and requirements that are more suitable for SMEs, such as UNCTAD's Core SDG Indicators for Entity Reporting.

(iv) Sector-specific policies

Climate, other environmental and social issues are increasingly recognized as systemic risks to the financial sector, precipitating increased policymaking and the introduction of regulations on sustainability incorporation for financial institutions. This has encouraged financial sector supervisors and central banks to include climate transition and environmental protection into their mandates (WWF, 2021). Among the 35 economies in the database, 27 have put in place sector-specific measures designed to promote the integration of climate, environmental or social considerations in the governance, strategy, risk management, investment decision-making and disclosure practices of asset managers, banks or insurance companies. About 75 per cent of these measures target asset management, focusing on climate change and environmental issues, with the rest being shared between sustainable banking and insurance roughly equally.

An important development in investment management regulation is that advanced economies are taking action to modernize fiduciary duty rules, focusing on specifying institutional investors' obligations and duties in relation to sustainability integration. In 2021, the EU Commission published six amendments to delegated acts on fiduciary duties and investment and insurance advice, which require financial firms (e.g. asset managers, advisers and insurers) to include sustainability factors in their procedures (PRI, 2021). In the United States, the Labor Department enacted changes to the fiduciary duties of retirement plans to make it easier for them to invest in sustainability-themed financial funds. The Pension Schemes Act 2021 of the United Kingdom strengthened the obligations of trustees of occupational pension schemes on governance and reporting with respect to climate and environmental issues.

Emerging economies are also putting in place sector-specific measures to leverage the potential of financial institutions to finance sustainable development. Bangladesh, China, Colombia, Nigeria and Turkey have developed guidelines for sustainable banking with the aim of directing more investment into key sustainable development areas, including SME development, job creation, social infrastructure and agriculture.

(v) Carbon pricing

Carbon-pricing measures, including carbon taxes and emission trading schemes, have been gaining further momentum in recent years as a policy tool to internalize negative externalities and reduce carbon emissions. Among the 35 economies covered by the database, carbon-pricing measures have been implemented by 18 economies and are under development in a 7 others. Most notably, all the new development activities are happening in emerging economies, which include Brazil, Indonesia, Malaysia, the Russian Federation, Thailand, Turkey and Viet Nam. Emission trading schemes have become more popular in recent years and account for a majority of carbon-pricing measures in use and under development.

The multiplication of net-zero commitments not only by governments but also by companies is driving growth in the carbon market. Meanwhile, climate-related disclosure policies, such as those aligned with the TCFD, are also pushing companies to internalize carbon prices (World Bank Group, 2021a).

One challenge associated with carbon-pricing measures, in particular for developing economies, is to determine an appropriate price or tax level for carbon and GHG emissions. Such a price or tax needs to be high enough to achieve meaningful emissions reductions aligned with a country's climate change commitments while not imposing an excessive fiscal burden on business. In order to avoid any unexpected macroeconomic impacts, in particular in developing economies, it is important to assess countries' readiness to deploy carbon-trading schemes or participate in international carbon markets (World Bank Group, 2021b).

2. International regulations and standard setting

a. Securities regulation and sustainability

Securities regulators are now actively considering their role in supporting the transition to more sustainable capital markets. IOSCO intends to professionalize all aspects of sustainable finance and work intensively in 2022 to deliver acro ss a range of focus areas.[13]

(i) Corporate reporting: pathway towards endorsement of ISSB standards

The work to consider whether the IOSCO Board will endorse the ISSB standards began in earnest with the publication of the ISSB exposure drafts on 31 March 2022 (see section 2.b). IOSCO will base its analysis of the drafts on a set of criteria published in June 2021 (IOSCO, 2021a). Overarching considerations include whether the proposed requirements can serve as an effective global baseline of investor-focused standards; whether they are fit for purpose in helping financial markets accurately assess sustainability risks and opportunities; and whether they can form the basis for the development of a robust audit and assurance framework.

(ii) Sustainability assurance

IOSCO's work stream on sustainability assurance began in February 2022 with an international round table of 140 participants, including such key stakeholders as the International Federation of Accountants, the International Auditing and Assurance Standards Board and the International Ethics Standards Board for Accountants. The round table showed strong support for IOSCO in coordinating and promoting global consistency for sustainability assurance standards, similar to what IOSCO has done with sustainability reporting and its support for the establishment of the ISSB. Building upon the round table, IOSCO will publish its vision for sustainability assurance, including the following aspects: (i) issuer readiness, (ii) investor needs and practices, (iii) auditors' current practices and future needs, and (iv) the state of play with regard to assurance standards and any future considerations required.

(iii) Promoting good industry practices and supervisory approaches

IOSCO issued two reports in November 2021, one covering asset managers and one covering ESG ratings and data providers (IOSCO, 2021b and 2021c). Both contained recommendations and good practices that are expected to be implemented by both regulators and industry. IOSCO will engage with market participants and regulators to promote these good practices. With regard to industry, IOSCO will collaborate with voluntary standard-setting bodies and industry associations and other relevant stakeholders to ensure that market participants begin implementing the IOSCO recommendations. This will also enable stakeholders to comply with national rules and regulations, which aim to be consistent with the IOSCO recommendations. With regard to supervisors, IOSCO will also act as a forum where members can exchange their experiences on implementation and supervision, with a view to ultimately achieving consistent implementation of the IOSCO recommendations.

(iv) Carbon markets

IOSCO's carbon markets work aims to promote the understanding and sound functioning of carbon markets – of both the compliance and the voluntary kinds, while being mindful that cross-border trading of carbon credits may expand. The underlying objective is to better understand the set-up and potential vulnerabilities of these markets, with a view to identifying essential attributes that foster market integrity. IOSCO plans to publish a report by COP27, setting out recommendations on the good functioning of compliance markets and identifying key facets and risks for further consideration in voluntary markets.

(v) Capacity-building

IOSCO's capacity-building efforts will encompass a comprehensive programme to assist its members in assessing their readiness and achieving implementation of ISSB standards and asset management obligations. This is particularly important for emerging markets, as they need to develop appropriate resources to be able to conduct this analysis in their efforts to implement the ISSB standards.

b. Consolidation of global ESG disclosure standards

During the second half of 2021 and the first half of 2022, the world witnessed a major shift towards consolidation of ESG disclosure standards, frameworks and tools. In June 2021, the IIRC and the SASB merged to form the Value Reporting Foundation. At the COP26 climate summit in November 2021, IFRS Foundation trustees announced the establishment of the ISSB) as well as consolidation of the Value Reporting Foundation and the CDSB into the IFRS Foundation.

The ISSB's formation responds to strong demand from public authorities and market participants for a high-quality, consistent global baseline of sustainability disclosures that enable investors to evaluate sustainability-related risks and opportunities when making investment decisions and assessing enterprise value. The concept has been welcomed by the G7,[14] the G20,[15] IOSCO, Financial Stability Board and by companies and investors from around the world.

The IFRS Foundation expects the consolidations to be completed during 2022. Meanwhile, the relevant instruments remain in place (i.e. the CDSB Framework, the SASB Standards and the International Integrated Reporting Framework). The ISSB is developing sustainability standards; in March 2022 it published for public comment its first two proposed standards – a draft climate standard and a general requirements standard, complete with industry-based requirements.[16] Its goal is to issue final requirements by the end of 2022, depending on the feedback received. The ISSB's future agenda and priorities will be determined on the basis of further public consultations commencing in Q3 2022, but it has also announced a working group to enhance compatibility between the global baseline and jurisdictional initiatives.

In another significant move affecting the broader spectrum of ESG disclosure, in March 2022, the IFRS Foundation signed a memorandum of understanding with the GRI, which provides global best practices for multi-stakeholder sustainability reporting. Under the collaboration, the sustainability standard-setting boards of the IFRS Foundation (the ISSB) and GRI (the GSSB) will seek to coordinate their work programmes and standard-setting activities and join each other's consultative bodies related to sustainability reporting activities.[17] In the interests of all stakeholders, together they aim to reinforce a corporate reporting system based on two pillars: one for reporting information on economic value creation at the level of the reporting entity for benefit of investors, and one for reporting information on the impact of the reporting entity on the economy, environment and people. The two pillars will have a core set of common disclosures and be on equal footing.

The GRI is also working with the European Financial Reporting Advisory Group on the development of the European Sustainability Reporting Standards, following an agreed statement of cooperation in July 2021. The effort is complementary to that of the IFRS and ISSB.

The developments described here are an unprecedented shift to reduce the existing fragmentation and prevent further fragmentation of sustainability disclosure instruments. The efforts build directly upon and protect the heritage of the leading sustainability disclosure instruments, with widespread adoption and use likely to reduce market confusion and costs for data preparers while improving usability of the information for a range of data users. Implementation of this global baseline will require action by others, including public authorities, stock exchanges and market participants, to contribute towards developing the baseline and to require or encourage its widespread use.When the new standards come into effect, exchanges and regulators will need to review their ESG disclosure requirements and/or guidance to ensure that they adhere to the new standards.

3. Lessons learned

Overall, sustainable finance regulations have flourished in recent years, both resulting from and reinforcing the mainstreaming of sustainable finance. An increasing number of economies across the globe are developing regulatory frameworks for sustainable finance. Both the number and the scope of policy measures and regulations are expanding rapidly. New policy tools, such as taxonomies, sustainable financial product standards, climate disclosure and carbon pricing, are being developed in a push for a green transition.

Yet, sustainable finance policies and regulations cannot work in silos. Countries need to take a holistic approach, by integrating sustainable finance regulations into their overall sustainable development strategy and ensuring coherence between sustainable finance and fiscal, technology, industry and other policies. For this purpose, it may be necessary to review all the policies that could have implications for sustainable finance regulation and policy consolidations may be needed. A well-developed national sustainable finance strategy or framework could serve as a useful tool to provide overall guidance for policy review and could thus be a good starting point for the exercise.

Meanwhile, government policies and regulations need to be complemented by market-driven standards and guidelines on disclosure, governance and other issues ("soft regulations"). It is important to engage all stakeholders to create a viable ecosystem that embeds sustainability along the entire investment chain. Given the early stage of development of sustainable finance and the quickly evolving market, policies and regulations need to be adapted in response to changes in specific market situations and in the overall development environment within which the investment system functions.

While sustainable finance policies and regulations need to take into consideration a nation's specific development context, international collaboration is important to ensure necessary coherence with international standards. This can help facilitate and attract cross-border investments, since consistence with international standards may be required by international investors (as is the case for green bonds issued in developing markets).

E. CLIMATE ACTION

Capital market participants along the whole investment chain are making progress to decarbonize and to embed climate conscious decision-making into their activities. To promote transition to a net zero economy, stock exchanges are tracking the carbon emissions of listed companies. An indicator of the momentum and demand for capacity-building on climate-related disclosures is the number of exchanges now hosting training on TCFD-aligned disclosure. In the last quarter of 2021 and the first half of 2022, more than 20 stock exchanges hosted training sessions on climate-related disclosure for more than 6,000 companies around the world. Several initiatives have been created to assist public markets and investors in navigating regulations and reporting standards, including the SSE Model Guidance on Climate Disclosure. Despite the many institutional investors that do not publish information on climate action, UNCTAD's continuous monitoring reveals that an increasing number of institutional investors have been taking action on climate risk with regard to their investment strategies and their active ownership of assets.

The global efforts to rapidly decarbonize the world's economies has important implications for business and the investment community. Increasingly, physical risks from climate change such as droughts, sea-level rise and flooding pose financial risks to listed companies and investors. For example, between 2017 and 2019 natural catastrophe losses intensified by climate change exceeded $600 billion (TCFD, 2021). Simultaneously, transition risks (such as technological and energy-mix changes, policy and legal implications, and changes in market trends) have financial impacts on an organization's financial performance and financial position. The total value of manageable assets at risk as a result of climate change by 2100 is estimated to exceed $40 trillion (The EIU, 2015). In addition to the risks posed by climate change, new opportunities are emerging that both investors and issuers can capitalize on. Many of the world's largest companies have identified and quantified financial impact from climate change, estimating a potential impact nearing $1 trillion ($970 billion). The same companies have also identified $2.1 trillion in climate-related opportunities (CDP, 2019). Capital markets have witnessed intensified actions on climate challenges and related investment opportunities along the investment chain.

1. Carbon emissions in public markets

In 2021, world leaders met in Glasgow, Scotland, for the 26th United Nations Climate Change Conference (COP26) to emphasize the urgent need to address the climate crisis. Moving towards a net zero emissions world is a key action point on the international agenda to ensure that the average global temperature rises no more than 1.5°C above pre-industrial levels. Tracking the carbon emissions of listed companies provides a useful benchmark for exchanges and other key stakeholders to assess progress in promoting transition to net zero emissions among listed companies (figure IV.22).

Research into the scope 1 GHG emissions of the top 100 issuers by market capitalization on G20 stock exchanges shows that the top companies listed on the Shenzhen exchange in China and on the Nasdaq exchange in the United States have the lowest scope 1 emissions among G20 exchanges. Together the top 100 companies on each of these exchanges combined represent only 0.6 per cent of emissions from the top 100 companies listed on the remaining G20 exchanges. By contrast, over half of the scope 1 emissions from the companies analysed in the G20 are emitted by companies listed on just five exchanges.

Figure IV.22. **G20 stock exchanges by scope 1 carbon emissions of top 100 issuers** (Million metric tonnes CO2 equivalent)

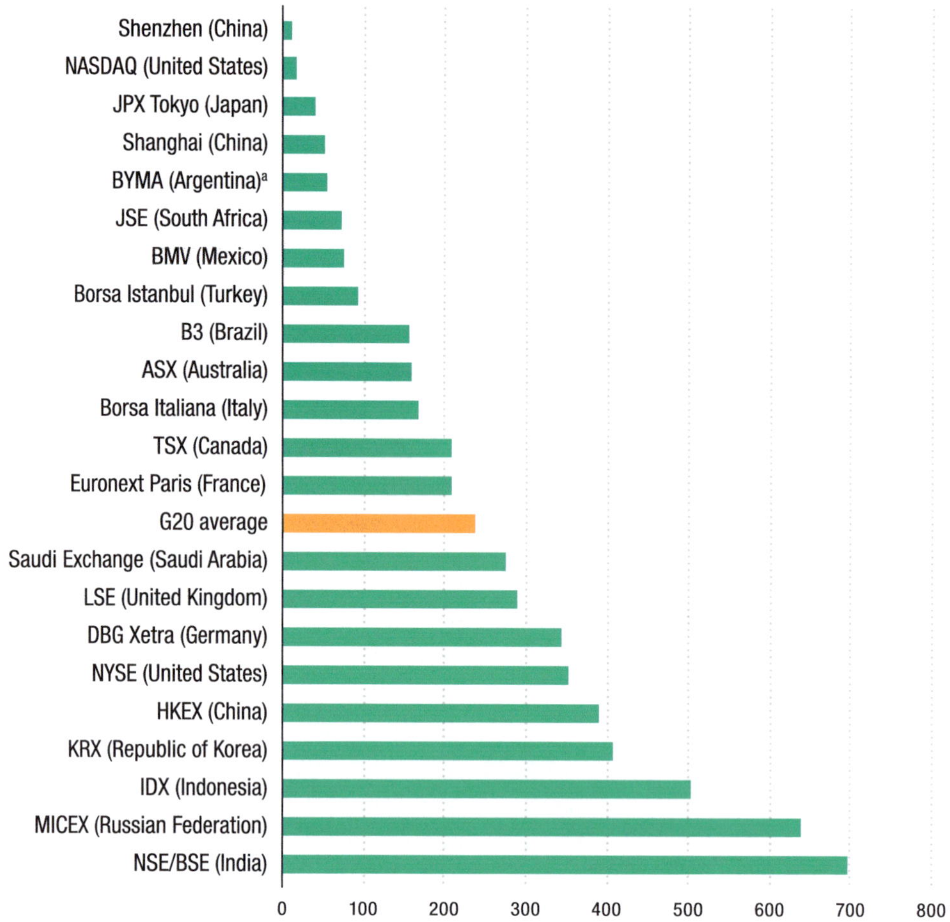

Source: UN SSE (2021).
[a] For the exchange in Argentina, which has fewer than 100 issuers, all the issuers were included in the analysis.

Significant differences can also be observed between individual exchanges; for example, the market with the highest-emitting top 100 issuers produces 50 times the level of scope 1 emissions as the market with the lowest-emitting issuers. Even within the same jurisdiction, exchanges' markets can vary significantly, highlighting the difference in industry and sector composition of the companies listed on those markets, which may be used by the exchanges to estimate their markets' risk of being affected by forthcoming regulations on carbon emissions.

2. The Net Zero movement

GHGs are the key driver behind global warming and climate change. Over the past decade, global GHG emissions have risen steadily, contrary to the goals set by the 2015 Paris Agreement, which defined the goal to limit global temperature rise to 1.5°C. In order to remain within the parameters set out in Paris, global emissions need to be halved by 2030 and have to be "net zero" by 2050 at the latest. In contrast to the absolute reduction of emissions, the concept of "net zero" allows the removal of unavoidable emissions through technical innovations or natural means (e.g. plants that remove carbon dioxide from the atmosphere).

To assist private and public sector organizations in reducing their overall emissions and moving towards net zero emissions, the United Nations Framework Convention on Climate Change created the global campaign "Race to Zero" (figure IV.23). With 1,049 cities, 67 regions, 5,235 businesses, 441 of the biggest investors, 1,039 higher education institutions and 120 countries, Race to Zero has become the largest alliance committed to achieving net zero carbon emissions by 2050. Collectively, actors involved in the initiative cover nearly 25 per cent of global CO2 emissions and over 50 per cent of global GDP.[18]

To coordinate efforts of the financial sector, United Nations Special Envoy on Climate Action and Finance Mark Carney created the Glasgow Financial Alliance for Net Zero (GFANZ). As part of the Race to Zero, GFANZ is a global coalition of leading financial institutions committed to accelerating the decarbonization of the economy (SSE, 2021b). Financial institutions join sector-specific alliances that establish science-based commitments and targets for each individual industry to fulfil. There are currently seven sector alliances active within GFANZ, catering to asset owners and asset managers, insurers, investors, banks and investment consultants. Each alliance is supported by a secretariat, which in some cases is led by the United Nations. Together, the actors involved publish guidance and targets to achieve within the next 12 months and the coming years. Exchanges are included in the Net Zero Financial Service Providers Alliance (NZFSPA).

The NZFSPA is a diverse group of 23 financial service provider organizations, including 6 exchanges. Members are committed to elevating the urgency of net zero alignment and integrating net zero efforts into their operations, services and products. The UN SSE acts as an accelerator for the growth of the alliance and offers secretariat services to exchanges within the alliance to guide, support and speed up their net zero efforts. Due to the diversity of members, the commitment and the action points developed by the NZFSPA must be interpreted within each individual subgroup, to ensure they align with each sector's operations and abilities.

Figure IV.23. | Structure of the Race to Zero movement in the finance industry

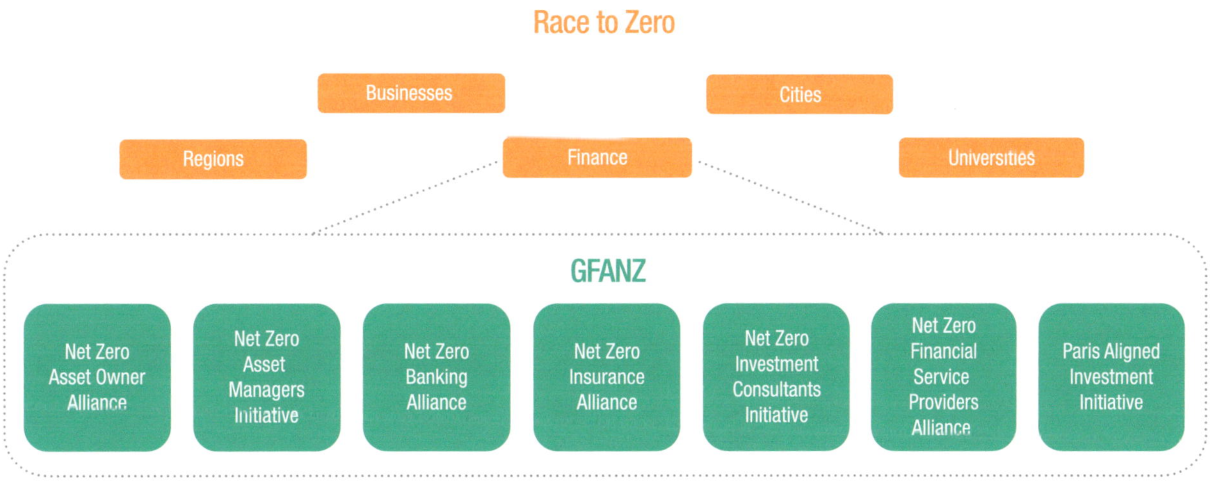

Source: UNCTAD, adapted from GFANZ/NZFSPA presentation.

3. Climate action by public pension and sovereign wealth funds

Climate and environmental concerns are the dominating subjects of sustainability action taken by PPFs and SWFs, with a focus on the identification and mitigation of the impact of climate change on future returns. Climate action by funds focuses principally on five areas:

1. Risk identification and mitigation related to transitional and physical risks
2. The application of metrics and reporting or disclosure of climate-related risks
3. The use of targets and benchmarks to reorient portfolio holdings and investment strategies in response to climate-related risk
4. The institutional response to climate-related risks – and ESG integration more broadly – through resource mobilization and organizational change
5. Increasingly active ownership on climate risk, through engagement, voting and exclusion or divestment

Their climate action usually starts with the identification of both physical and transitional risks. For example, climate change is considered the primary portfolio risk for many funds, such as AP Fonden (Sweden), and several funds, such as HOOPP (Canada), have developed in-house climate models to identify at-risk investments. The focus on climate is partly related to the scale of the risks involved and their impact on future financial returns and partly related to reporting and other initiatives that facilitate disclosure on carbon emissions.

Most reporting funds now elaborate a specific strategy on climate or CO2 emissions (figure IV.24). This is often linked to a specific goal, which for the majority of funds means net zero carbon emissions in their portfolios by 2050, if not before. A majority of reporting funds use an international reporting framework for reporting on climate action and have signed up to an international climate response initiative, one of the most popular being Climate Action 100+, signalling their commitments on climate action to shareholders and beneficiaries and to policymakers. Over two thirds of reporting funds now publish specific information on climate risk, sometimes in a report separate from either their annual or sustainability report.

Information on the size of investments in climate-related assets is not comprehensive, but anecdotal evidence from fund reports suggests that they are making rapid changes to portfolios and that the actual or potential impact of regulatory changes will accelerate

Figure IV.24. **Climate-specific action by funds, 2022**
(Per cent of reporting funds)

Source: UNCTAD, based on fund annual reports or sustainability reports, n = 47.

investment decisions in this area. For example, funds such as ABP (Netherlands) have developed specific investment instruments for investing in the energy transition. Meanwhile, two Californian pension funds, CalPERS and CalSTRS (United States), are facing a proposed state law requiring them to divest all their fossil fuel assets – about $9 billion – by 2027.[19]

Despite calls for divestment from beneficiaries and the likely impact of regulatory changes, funds often choose to engage with investees rather than exclude them. The rationale for engagement, from the fund's perspective, is the understanding that the fund has a huge degree of influence and leverage through engagement and voting that it would not otherwise have if it divested. For this reason, funds privilege engagement in the expectation that investees will be encouraged to implement their own transition strategy to net zero. Most reporting funds exercise their voting rights, either directly or through a proxy, and actively engage with their investees. Nearly two thirds of funds provide guidance on ESG integration to asset managers or investees (figure IV.25).

UNCTAD's continuous monitoring reveals that an increasing number of institutional investors have been taking action on sustainability and climate risk, in line with their long-term outlook and fiduciary responsibilities. This goes beyond reporting to implementing meaningful actions with regard to fund investment strategies and their active ownership of assets. Yet, a majority of the world's largest funds, either by number or AUM, still do not publish information on ESG integration or climate action. The first step towards reallocating capital towards sustainable outcomes and mobilizing more finance to support climate change mitigation and adaptation is to recognize and quantify risk through disclosure and reporting. Such reporting needs to improve and become mandatory in financial markets and among institutional investors as it already is in several countries and regions, such as in the EU and in the Republic of Korea.

With the IPCC clear that further rises in emissions after 2025 puts a 1.5°C warming scenario out of reach, and facing the cascading risk impacts related to hydrocarbons and energy security arising from geopolitical crises, such as the war in Ukraine, investors should be taking more urgent action to decarbonize their portfolios through reorienting assets or engaging investees. UNCTAD, through its Global Sustainable Finance Observatory and its Sustainable Institutional Investment programme, is contributing towards accelerating the reorientation of investments and in channeling more finance to sustainable outcomes, including the energy transition.

Figure IV.25. **Active ownership by funds, 2022**
(Per cent of reporting funds)

Source: UNCTAD, based on fund annual reports or sustainability reports, n = 47.
Note: ESG = environmental, social and governance, SDG = Sustainable Development Goal.

4. Stock exchange strategies for climate action

Stock exchanges are playing an important role in helping their markets navigate the low-carbon transition. An indicator of the momentum and demand for capacity-building on climate-related disclosures is the number of exchanges now hosting training on TCFD-aligned disclosure. In the last quarter of 2021 and the first half of 2022, more than 20 stock exchanges have hosted training sessions on climate-related disclosure for more than 6,000 participants around the world, working with UN SSE, IFC and other partners. Key areas of concern that participants highlight in these sessions are how to identify the financial impact of climate-related risks and opportunities and how to integrate this information into mainstream financial reports.

The TCFD has identified climate-related risks and opportunities that are more likely to have a financial impact on a company's financial position or financial performance. Companies can use these risks and opportunities as a starting point by incorporating them into their risk management processes and identifying their strategic relevance to the organization. By conducting a materiality analysis or identifying how risks and opportunities may affect the organization's financial position and performance, companies can integrate this information into their mainstreaming reports. The risks and opportunities deemed to have a financial impact should be a part of their strategic planning and risk management processes in order to mitigate risks and capitalize on opportunities pertaining to climate.

To help exchanges lead a transition to more climate-resilient markets, the UN SSE, in collaboration with the UN Special Envoy on Climate Action and Finance, launched a voluntary practical Action Plan (SSE, 2021c) together with a set of tools for guiding markets on climate-related disclosures (SSE, 2021d). The Action Plan highlights two streams of activities which focus either on changing the internal operations, disclosure and governance within a stock exchange, or on influencing the external market's operations, disclosure and governance practices. The SSE provides exchanges with a template, the *SSE Model Guidance on Climate Disclosure*, that can be used to create bespoke guidance for each unique market, and a TCFD checklist to conduct a gap analysis of current reporting practices. Building on the tools and guidance developed specifically for stock exchanges, the SSE, together with the World Bank Group's International Finance Corporation and the CDP, developed a three-part training programme on aligning disclosure practices with the recommendations of the TCFD recommendations.

* * *

With the rapid proliferation of sustainability-themed financial products, the growth of the sustainable finance market has reached a tipping point. Its growth is expected to further accelerate in the coming years, with more institutional investors mainstreaming sustainability in their investment decisions and more governments, stock exchanges and industry associations making systematic efforts to create a viable policy and regulatory ecosystem for sustainable investment.

Much remains to be done to fully leverage the potential of the capital market for sustainable finance. The current focus is on strengthening the integrity of sustainability-themed products and corporate ESG disclosure. The biggest challenge that needs to be addressed is the sustainability-washing concern and the credibility of sustainable financial products associated with it. UNCTAD analysis shows that huge variance remains in the sustainability profiles in self-labelled sustainable funds and that the low-performing ones may not fulfil their sustainability credentials. Meanwhile, although an increasing number of asset owners and asset managers have announced their commitment to carbon neutrality, more than half of the world's 100 largest PPFs and SWFs are not disclosing or reporting on sustainability issues. This situation needs to change, and the most effective way to address the credibility issue is to further strengthen sustainability reporting, at both the entity and the product levels, covering both companies and financial institutions. Regulators and stock exchanges can drive the change by making more disclosure and external auditing requirements mandatory, especially for sustainability-oriented products traded in securities markets. Taxonomies and product standards can also bring more clarity and credibility to the market and have been multiplying in recent years. However, the lack of standards for sustainable funds and other emerging sustainable financial products at national and international levels needs to be addressed, and better alignment of existing standards for sustainable bonds across countries is necessary to enhance transparency.

To make sustainability a norm of investment, a holistic approach is necessary. National strategies and policies aimed at supporting sustainable finance and the growth of the market need to be embedded in the national development strategy, and fiscal, financial, industry, technology and other relevant policies may need to be reoriented to work together to facilitate sustainable investment. Meanwhile, in order to build a viable ecosystem for sustainable finance to flourish, the entire investment value chain needs to be involved, including asset owners and asset managers, exchanges, issuers and regulators.

A coherent market with better geographical balance will not be achieved without more international cooperation and support. Already, regional approaches have helped harmonize standards and policies across markets and, ultimately, harmonization at the international level would be beneficial, perhaps on existing standards and policies. For countries with less developed markets and infrastructure, particularly with regard to regulation and standard setting, technical assistance would be helpful to support market development and beneficial outcomes.

Through the work of its Global Sustainable Finance Observatory (box IV.2) and other sustainable investment-related programmes, such as the SSE, the Sustainable Institutional Investment and the International Standards of Accounting and Reporting programmes, UNCTAD is committed to working together with key stakeholders from both the public and the private sector to make the financial market ecosystem more sustainable and better contribute to sustainable outcomes, including the SDGs, as mandated by the UN General Assembly.[20]

Box IV.2. UNCTAD Global Sustainable Finance Observatory

The Global Sustainable Finance Observatory was launched by UNCTAD in the 2021 World Investment Forum with a vision to build a future global financial ecosystem in which sustainable development, as defined by the SDGs, is fully embedded into the business model and investment culture and to bring more credibility, transparency and consistency to the market.

The Observatory is committed to addressing the challenges of fragmentation in standards, proliferation in benchmarking, complexity in disclosure and sustainability-washing. It works in tandem with the standard-setting processes of the financial industry and regulatory bodies to promote the full and effective integration of sustainable development into all aspects of the global financial ecosystem.

In particular, the Observatory

- Promotes the integration of SDGs into the sustainability assessment ecosystem in a coherent and synergistic manner, including through the Guidance on *Core Indicators for Entity Reporting on Contribution towards Implementation of the SDGs* published by the ISAR.
- Manages a global database of sustainable investment funds and other products to improve the open-source availability of sustainability data for key stakeholders and the public.

/...

Box IV.2. UNCTAD Global Sustainable Finance Observatory (Concluded)

- Conducts sustainability assessments of "self-labelled" sustainable products on global capital markets, and awards best performers.
- Establishes a pool of sustainability ratings on capital markets to encourage better reporting methodologies in different industries.
- Maintains a global inventory of good regulatory and policy practices for sustainability integration and to facilitate peer learning.
- Provides a capacity-building platform for assisting developing countries on policies, regulatory measures, product development, industry standards, reporting and other related issues to ensure they benefit from sustainable finance.

The Observatory leverages UNCTAD's partnership with leading sustainable finance-related initiatives, such as the UN Global Compact, the PRI, the UNEP Finance Initiative, IOSCO and the World Federation of Exchanges, in the area of sustainable investment.

Source: UNCTAD.

NOTES

[1] United Nations General Assembly resolution on "Promoting investments for sustainable investment" (A/RES/74.199) and (A/RES/75/207).

[2] Tergesen, A., "ESG funds easier for 401(k)s to buy under Labor Department plan", *The Wall Street Journal*, 13 October 2021, https://wsj.com/articles/esg-funds-for-401-k-s-easier-to-buy-under-labor-department-plan-11634160291.

[3] The score is based on the relative rating, with 10 for the highest-rated funds and 1 for the lowest-rated ones.

[4] The MSCI ACWI covers about 3,000 holdings from 23 developed and 27 emerging markets and approximately 85 per cent of the free float-adjusted market capitalization in these markets. The index is the benchmark against which the relative sustainability performance of sustainable funds is evaluated in this section.

[5] According to data from the Global SWF data platform, 2022, https://globalswf.com.

[6] According to data from the Global SWF data platform, 2022, https://globalswf.com.

[7] Cybersecurity was seen as the biggest risk warranting focus from boards (a bigger risk focus than ESG). KPMG (2022).

[8] About 30 per cent of oil, 50 per cent of gas and 80 per cent of coal reserves will remain unburnable if warming is limited to 2°C (IPCC, 2022).

[9] For example, Temasek (Singapore) has introduced an internal carbon-pricing policy in response to its assessment that carbon pricing may need to surpass $100 per tonne of carbon dioxide equivalent (tCO2e) by 2030 to drive effective decarbonization and deliver on the Paris Agreement. The fund has set an initial internal carbon price of $42 per tCO2e to inform its investment decisions. The fund will further refine its carbon-pricing strategies as it gets further clarity on the economic and policy levers of change (https://temasekreview.com.sg/.

[10] The 12 founding members of the SSE Derivatives Network are the Australian Securities Exchange (ASX) (Australia), Borsa Istanbul (Turkey), Bursa Malaysia (Malaysia), CBOE Global Markets (United States), CME Group (United States), Deutsche Börse AG/Eurex (Germany), Matba Rofex (Argentina), MexDer (BMV Group) (Mexico), NZX Limited (New Zealand), Singapore Exchange (Singapore), The Intercontinental Exchange (ICE) (United States) and TMX Group/Montreal Exchange (Canada).

[11] *MayerBrown Perspectives*, "ESG derivatives: a sustainable trend", 21 October 2021.

[12] *BDO Insights*, "ESG Derivatives: a new way to promote sustainability", 22 October 2021.

[13] *Investment News* "IOSCO targets greenwashers", 15 March 2022.

[14] G7 Finance Ministers and Central Bank Governors Communiqué, 5 June 2021.

[15] G20 Third Finance Ministers and Central Bank Governors meeting, Communiqué, 9–10 July 2021.

[16] IFRS, "ISSB delivers proposals that create comprehensive global baseline of sustainability disclosures", 31 March 2022.

[17] GRI, "IFRS Foundation and GRI to align capital market and multi-stakeholder standards, 24 March 2022.

[18] UN Climate Change, "Race to Zero Campaign", https://unfccc.int/climate-action/race-to-zero-campaign.

[19] "Proposed bill would require CalPERS, CalSTRS to divest fossil fuels", *Chief Information Officer*, 15 March 2022, https://ai-cio.com.

[20] United Nations General Assembly resolution on "Promoting investments for sustainable development" (A/RES/74.199) and (A/RES/75/207).

REFERENCES

Abbas, S. M., S. Bedi, J. Park and A. D. Klemm (2012). "A partial race to the bottom: Corporate tax developments in emerging and developing economies". *IMF Working Paper*, No. 12/28. Washington, DC: International Monetary Fund.

AfDB (African Development Bank), ADB (Asian Development Bank), AIIB (Asian Infrastructure Investment Bank), EBRD (European Bank for Reconstruction and Development), EIB (European Investment Bank), IDBG (Inter-American Development Bank Group), IsDB (Islamic Development Bank) and WBG (World Bank Group) (2021). *2020 Joint Report on the Multilateral Development Banks' Climate Finance.* London: European Bank for Reconstruction and Development. http://www.ebrd.com/2020-joint-report-on-mdbs-climate-finance.

Arnold, J. M., B. Brys, C. Heady, A. Johansson, C. Schwellnus and L. Vartia (2011). "Tax policy for economic recovery and growth". *The Economic Journal*, 121 (550): F59–F80.

Auclair, G., and B. Casella (forthcoming). "The elephant in the room? The role of tax incentives in the measurement of the fiscal impact of the global minimum tax rate".

Baker, P. (2018). "An analysis of the corporate income tax policy of less developed countries". *Scandinavian Journal of Economics*, 120 (2): 400–427.

Barclay, E. J., and P. M. Valeer (2021). "State ownership and project financing". In Wright, M., G. Wood, A. Cuervo-Cazurra, P. Sun, I. Okhmatovskiy and A. Grosman (Eds). *Oxford Handbook on State Capitalism and the Firm*, Oxford, UK: Oxford University Press.

Bares, F., M. Devereux and I. Güçeri (forthcoming). "Business location decisions with a minimum tax rate". Oxford, UK: Oxford University Centre for Business Taxation.

Bauer, M. (2020). "Unintended and undesired consequences: The impact of OECD Pillar I and II proposals on small open economies". *ECIPE Occasional Paper*, No. 04/2020.

Bazel, P., J. Mintz and A. Thompson (2018). "2017 Tax Competitiveness Report: The calm before the storm". *The School of Public Policy Publications*, 11 (7).

Becker, J., and N. Riedel (2012). "Cross-border tax effects on affiliate investment – evidence from European multinationals". *European Economic Review*, 56 (3): 436–450.

Blouin, J., and L. A. Robinson (2020). "Double counting accounting: How much profit of multinational enterprises is really in tax havens?" *SSRN Working Paper*, No. 3491451.

Bolwijn, R., B. Casella and D. Rigo (2018). "An FDI-driven approach to measuring the scale and economic impact of BEPS". *Transnational Corporations*, 25 (2): 107–143. United Nations publication.

Bradbury, D., T. Hanappi and A. Moore (2018). "Estimating the fiscal effects of base erosion and profit shifting: Data availability and analytical issues". *Transnational Corporations*, 25 (2): 91–106. United Nations publication.

Brennan, G., and J. Buchanan (1980). *The Power to Tax: Analytical Foundations of a Fiscal Constitution.* Cambridge, UK: Cambridge University Press.

Casella, B. (2019). "Looking through conduit FDI in search of ultimate investors – a probabilistic approach". *Transnational Corporations*, 26 (1): 109–146. United Nations publication.

Casella, B., and B. Souillard (2022). "A new framework to assess the fiscal impact of a global minimum tax on FDI". *Transnational Corporations*, 29 (2): 1–34. United Nations publication.

Casella, B., and L. Formenti (2018). "FDI in the digital economy: a shift to asset-light international footprints". *Transnational Corporations*, 25 (1):101–130. United Nations publication.

Celani, A., L. Dressler and M. Wermelinger (2022). "Building an Investment Tax Incentives database: Methodology and initial findings for 36 developing countries". *OECD Working Papers on International Investment*, No. 2022/01. Paris: OECD.

Cheema-Fox, A., G. Serafeim and H. Wang (2022). "Climate solutions investments". *Working Paper* No. 22-054. Cambridge, MA: Harvard Business School.

Christensen R. C.M. Hearson and T. Randriamanalina (2022). "Developing influence: the power of 'the rest' in global tax governance". *Review of International Political Economy*, DOI: 10.1080/09692290.2022.2039264.

Clausing, K. A. (2020). "How big is profit shifting?". Unpublished, Reed College.

Cobham, A., T. Faccio, J. Garcia-Bernardo, P. Janský, J. Kadet and S. Picciotto (2022). "A practical proposal to end corporate tax abuse: METR, a minimum effective tax rate for multinationals". *Global Policy*, 13 (1): 18–33.

CPI (Climate Policy Initiative) (2021). *Global Landscape of Climate Finance 2021*.

Crivelli, E., R. De Mooij and M. Keen (2016). "Base erosion, profit shifting and developing countries". *FinanzArchiv/Public Finance Analysis*, 268–301.

Damgaard, J., E. Elkjaer and N. Johannesen (2019). "The rise of phantom investments". *Finance & Development (IMF)*, 56 (3).

De Mooij, R. A., and M. L. Liu (2020). "At a cost: the real effects of transfer pricing regulations". *IMF Economic Review*, 68 (1): 268–306.

De Mooij, R. A., and S. Ederveen (2008). "Corporate tax elasticities: a reader's guide to empirical findings". *Oxford Review of Economic Policy*, 24 (4): 680–697.

Devereux, M. P., and R. Griffith (2002). "The impact of corporate taxation on the location of capital: a review". *Swedish Economic Policy Review*, 9 (1): 79–106.

_____ (2003). "Evaluating tax policy for location decisions". *International Tax and Public Finance*, 10 (2): 107–126.

Devereux, M. P., B. Lockwood and M. Redoano (2008). "Do countries compete over corporate tax rates?" *Journal of Public Economics*, 92 (5-6): 1210–1235.

Devereux, M. P., F. Bares, S. Clifford, J. Freedman, İ. Güçeri, M. McCarthy and J. Vella (2020). "The OECD Global Anti-Base Erosion Proposal". PwC report. Oxford, UK: Oxford University Centre for Business Taxation, January.

Devereux, M. P., M. Keen, A. J. Auerbach, P. Oosterhuis, J. Vella and W. Schön (2021). *Taxing Profit in a Global Economy*. Oxford, UK: Oxford University Press.

Devereux, M.P., J. Vella and H. Wardell-Burrus (2022). "Will Pillar 2 achieve its objectives?" Oxford, UK: Oxford University Centre for Business Taxation.

Dowd, T., P. Landefeld and A. Moore (2017). "Profit shifting of US multinationals". *Journal of Public Economics*, 148: 1–13.

Eden, L. (2020). "Winners and losers: the OECD's Economic Impact Assessment of Pillar One". *Tax Management International Journal*, 49 (12): 597–609.

Ehlers, T., D. Gao and F. Packer (2021). "A taxonomy of sustainable finance taxonomies". *BIS Papers*, No. 118. Basel: Bank for International Settlements.

European Commission (2021). "Communication on a strategy for financing the transition to a sustainable economy". Communication from the Commission to the European Parliament, the Council, the European Economic and Social Committee and the Committee of the Regions. COM/2021/390 final. Strasbourg.

Feld, L. P., and J. H. Heckemeyer (2011). "FDI and taxation: a meta-study". *Journal of Economic Surveys*, 25 (2): 233–272.

Freund, C., and T. H. Moran (2017). "Multinational investors as export superstars: how emerging-market governments can reshape comparative advantage". *Working Paper*, No. 17-1. Washington, DC: Peterson Institute for International Economics.

Garcia-Bernardo, J., and P. Janský (2022). "Profit shifting of multinational corporations worldwide". *ArXiv Working Paper*, No. 08444.

Garcia-Bernardo, J., P. Janský and T. Tørsløv (2021). "Multinational corporations and tax havens: evidence from country-by-country reporting". *International Tax and Public Finance*, 28: 1519–1561.

Gaukrodger, D. (2021). "The future of investment treaties – possible directions". *OECD Working Papers on International Investment*, No. 2021/03. Paris: OECD.

Guvenen Jr., F., R. J. Mataloni, D. G. Rassier and K.J. Ruhl (2022). "Offshore profit shifting and aggregate measurement: Balance of payments, foreign investment, productivity, and the labor share". *NBER Working Paper*, No. 23324.

Hanappi, T., and A. C. Gonzalez Cabral (2020). "The impact of the Pillar One and Pillar Two proposals on MNE's investment costs: An analysis using forward-looking effective tax rates". *OECD Taxation Working Papers*, No. 50. Paris: OECD.

Hebous, S., and M. Keen (2022). "Pareto-improving minimum corporate taxation". *CESifo Working Paper*, No. 9633.

Heckemeyer, J. H., and M. Overesch (2017). "Multinationals' profit response to tax differentials: Effect size and shifting channels". *Canadian Journal of Economics*, 50 (4): 965–994.

Hines Jr, J. R. (2022). "Evaluating tax harmonization". Unpublished, University of Michigan.

Hines Jr, J. R., and E. M. Rice (1994). "Fiscal paradise: Foreign tax havens and American business". *The Quarterly Journal of Economics*, 109 (1): 149–182.

IMF (International Monetary Fund) (2014). "Spillovers in international corporate taxation". *IMF Policy Paper*, No. 71. Washington, DC: International Monetary Fund.

_____ (2016). "Tax policy, leverage and macroeconomic stability". *IMF Policy Paper*, No. 151. Washington, DC: International Monetary Fund.

_____ (2022a). *Fiscal Monitor: Fiscal Policy from Pandemic to War.* Washington, DC: International Monetary Fund.

_____ (2022b). *World Economic Outlook, April 2022: War Sets Back the Global Recovery.* Washington, DC: International Monetary Fund.

IPCC (Intergovernmental Panel on Climate Change) (2022). *Sixth Assessment Report: Mitigation of Climate Change.* New York and Geneva: United Nations.

IPSF (International Platform on Sustainable Finance) (2021a). "Common ground taxonomy – climate change mitigation".

_____ (2021b). *State and Trends of ESG Disclosure Policy Measures across IPSF Jurisdictions, Brazil, and the US.*

James, S. (2014). "Tax and non-tax incentives and investments: evidence and policy implications". Investment Climate Advisory Services. Washington, DC: World Bank Group, June.

Janeba, E., and G. Schjelderup (2022). "The global minimum tax raises more revenues than you think, or much less". *CESifo Working Paper*, No. 9623.

Janský, P., and M. Palanský (2019). "Estimating the scale of profit shifting and tax revenue losses related to foreign direct investment". *International Tax and Public Finance*, 26 (5): 1048–1103.

Johannesen, N. (2022). "The global minimum tax". *CESifoWorking Paper*, No. 9527.

Johannesen, N., T. Tørsløv and L. Wier (2020). "Are less developed countries more exposed to multinational tax avoidance? Method and evidence from micro-data". *World Bank Economic Review*, 34: 790–809.

Keen, M., and K. A. Konrad (2013). "The theory of international tax competition and coordination". *Handbook of Public Economics*, 5: 257–328.

Keen, M., and M. Mansour (2010). "Revenue mobilisation in Sub-Saharan Africa: challenges from globalisation I – Trade reform". *Development Policy Review*, 28 (5): 553–571.

Keen, M., and M. Marchand (1997). "Fiscal competition and the pattern of public spending". *Journal of Public Economics*, 66: 33–53.

Keen, M., L. Liu and H. Pallan (forthcoming). "Tax spillovers in cross-border real investment: evidence from a new dataset on multinationals".

Konrad, Kai A., and G. Schjelderup (1999). "Fortress building in global tax competition". *Journal of Urban Economics*, 46: 156–167.

Kotha, A. P. (2017). "The Mauritius route: the Indian response". *Saint Louis University Law Journal*, 62: 203–218.

Kronfol, H., and V. Steenbergen (2020). "Evaluating the costs and benefits of corporate tax incentives: methodological approaches and policy considerations". *Finance, Competitiveness and Innovation in Focus.* Washington, DC: World Bank.

Lazarov, I., B. Liotti, J. Ndubai, J. Owens and M. Ruth (2022). "The treatment of tax incentives under Pillar Two". *WU GTPC Working Paper, SSRN Working Paper.*

Leibrecht, M., and C. Hocgatterer (2012). "Tax competition as a cause of falling corporate income tax rates: a survey of empirical literature". *Journal of Economic Surveys*, 26: 616–648.

Mansour, M., and G. Rota Graziosi (2013). "Tax coordination, tax competition, and revenue mobilization in the West African Economic and Monetary Union". *IMF Working Paper*, No. 13/163. Washington, DC: International Monetary Fund.

Markle, K. S., and D. A. Shackelford (2012). "Cross-country comparisons of corporate income taxes". *National Tax Journal*, 65 (3): 493–527.

Millot, V., Å. Johansson, S. Sorbe and S. Turban (2020). "Corporate taxation and investment of multinational firms: evidence from firm-level data". *OECD Taxation Working Papers*, No. 51. Paris: OECD.

Mintz, J. (2022a). "A proposal for a 'big bang' corporate tax reform". *The School of Public Policy Publications*, 15 (7).

Mintz, J. (2022b). "The global corporate minimum tax: a cure or not?" Unpublished, University of Calgary.

Morningstar (2022). "Global sustainable fund flows: Q4 2021 in review". https://www.morningstar.com/lp/global-esg-flows.

OECD (Organisation for Economic Co-operation and Development) (2020a). *Investment Impacts of Pillar One and Pillar Two, in Tax Challenges Arising from Digitalisation – Economic Impact Assessment: Inclusive Framework on BEPS*. Paris: OECD.

_____ (2020b). *Tax Challenges Arising from Digitalisation* – Report on Pillar Two Blueprint – Inclusive Framework on BEPS. OECD/G20 Base Erosion and Profit Shifting Project. Paris: OECD.

_____ (2021). *Tax Challenges arising from the Digitalisation of the Economy – Global Anti-base Erosion Model Rules (Pillar Two)*. Paris: OECD.

_____(2022a). *Tax Challenges arising from the Digitalisation of the Economy – Commentary to the Global Anti-base Erosion Model Rules (Pillar Two)*. Paris: OECD.

_____ (2022b). "Tax challenges arising from the digitalisation of the economy – Global Anti-Base Erosion Model Rules (Pillar Two) examples". Paris: OECD.

Owens, J. ,and J. Zhan (2018). "Trade, investment and taxation: policy linkages". *Transnational Corporations Special Issue on Investment and International Taxation*, Part 1, 25 (2): 1–8. United Nations publication.

Perry, V. (forthcoming). "Pillar 2 and low income Sub-Saharan African countries". Oxford, UK: Oxford University Centre for Business Taxation.

Petkova, K., A. Stasio, and M. Zagler (2018). "On the relevance of double tax treaties". *WU International Taxation Research Paper Series*, No. 2018-05.

Platform for Collaboration on Tax (2016a). "Options for low income countries' effective and efficient use of tax incentives for investment". *A Report to the G-20 Development Working Group by the IMF, OECD, UN and World Bank*. United Nations and World Bank.

_____ (2016b). "Options for low income countries' effective and efficient use of tax incentives for investment". *A Background Paper to the G-20 Development Working Group by the IMF, OECD, UN and World Bank*. United Nations and World Bank.

PRI (Principles for Responsible Investment) (2021). "PRI statement on clarification of fiduciary duties and consideration of sustainability preferences in the EU".

Redonda, A., C. von Haldenwang and F. Aliu (2022). "Global Tax Expenditures Database [data set], Version 1.1.3", *GTED*, DOI: 10.5281/zenodo.6334212.

Smyth, J. (2022). "Pharma dealmaking hit by greater scrutiny of prices and competition". *Financial Times*, 28 February 2022.

Tørsløv, T. R., L. S. Wier and G. Zucman (2021). "The missing profits of nations". *NBER Working Paper*, No. 24701.

Trentini, C., J. de Camargo Mainente and A. U. Santos-Paulino (2022). "The evolution of digital MNEs: an empirical note". *Transnational Corporations*, 29 (1): 163–187. United Nations publication.

Turban, S., S. Sorbe, V. Millot and Å. Johansson (2020). "A set of matrices to map the location of profit and economic activity of multinational enterprises". *OECD Taxation Working Papers*, No. 52. Paris: OECD.

UNCITRAL (2022). *Report of Working Group III (Investor–State Dispute Settlement Reform) on the work of its forty-second session*. No. A/CN.9/1092. New York, 14–18 February. United Nations publication.

UNCTAD (1993). *Small and Medium-sized Transnational Corporations: Role, Impact and Policy Implications*. New York and Geneva: United Nations. United Nations publication.

______ (1998). *Handbook on Foreign Direct Investment by Small and Medium-sized Enterprises: Lessons from Asia.* New York and Geneva: United Nations. United Nations publication.

______ (2000). "Tax Incentives and Foreign Direct Investment – A Global Survey". *ASIT Advisory Studies*, No. 16. New York and Geneva: United Nations. United Nations publication.

______ (2015). *Investment Policy Framework for Sustainable Development.* New York and Geneva: United Nations. United Nations publication.

______ (2018a). *Global Investment Trends Monitor. Special Edition. Tax reforms in the United States: implications for international investment.* New York and Geneva: United Nations. United Nations publication.

______ (2018b). *UNCTAD's Reform Package for the International Investment Regime.* New York and Geneva: United Nations. United Nations publication.

______ (2019). *Guidance on Core Indicators for Entity Reporting on Contribution Towards Implementation of the Sustainable Development Goals.* New York and Geneva: United Nations. United Nations publication.

______ (2020a). *How Public Pension and Sovereign Wealth Funds Mainstream Sustainability: Practices of the Frontrunners and a Proposed Integration Framework.* New York and Geneva: United Nations. United Nations publication.

______ (2020b). *International Investment Agreements Reform Accelerator.* New York and Geneva: United Nations. United Nations publication.

______ (2021a). *Economic Development in Africa Report 2021: Reaping the Potential Benefits of the African Continental Free Trade Area for Inclusive Growth.* New York and Geneva: United Nations. United Nations publication.

______ (2021b). *International Investment Agreements and Their Implications for Tax Measures: What Tax Policymakers Need to Know.* New York and Geneva: United Nations. United Nations publication.

______ (2021c). "The rise of the sustainable fund market and its role in financing sustainable development". New York and Geneva: United Nations. United Nations publication.

______ (2022) *Global Investment Trends Monitor.* No. 41, April. New York and Geneva: United Nations. United Nations publication.

______ (forthcoming). *Public Pension and Sovereign Wealth Fund Report 2022: ESG integration and climate action of leading funds.* United Nations: New York and Geneva. United Nations publication.

United Nations (2021). "Report of the Working Group on the issue of human rights and transnational corporations and other business enterprises". No. A/76/238. New York and Geneva: United Nations.

UN SSE (Sustainable Stock Exchanges) (2021a). *Action Plan to Make Markets Climate Resilient: How stock exchanges can integrate the TCFD recommendations.* https://sseinitiative.org. United Nations publication.

______ (2021b). "Carbon emissions in public markets". Policy Brief. https://sseinitiative.org. United Nations publication.

______ (2021c). "The Net Zero Movement". Policy Brief. https://sseinitiative.org. United Nations publication.

UN SSE and IFC (Sustainable Stock Exchanges and International Finance Corporation) (2022). *How Exchanges Can Advance Gender Equality – Updated Guidance and Best Practices.*

Vartia, L. (2008). "How do taxes affect investment and productivity? An industry-level analysis of OECD countries". *OECD Economics Department Working Papers*, No. 656. Paris: OECD.

Vrijburg, H., and R. De Mooij (2016). "Tax rates as strategic substitutes". *International Tax and Public Finance*, 23: 2–24.

WIR99. UNCTAD (1999). *World Investment Report 1999: Foreign Direct Investment and the Challenge of Development.* New York and Geneva: United Nations. United Nations publication.

WIR14. UNCTAD (2014). *World Investment Report 2014: Investing in the SDGs: An Action Plan.* New York and Geneva: United Nations. United Nations publication.

WIR15. UNCTAD (2015). *World Investment Report 2015: Reforming International Investment Governance.* New York and Geneva: United Nations. United Nations publication.

WIR17. UNCTAD (2017). *World Investment Report 2017: Investment and the Digital Economy.* New York and Geneva: United Nations. United Nations publication.

WIR18. UNCTAD (2018). *World Investment Report 2018: Investment and New Industrial Policies*. New York and Geneva: United Nations. United Nations publication.

WIR19. UNCTAD (2019). *World Investment Report 2019: Special Economic Zones*. New York and Geneva: United Nations. United Nations publication.

WIR20. UNCTAD (2020). *World Investment Report 2020: International Production Beyond the Pandemic*. New York and Geneva: United Nations. United Nations publication.

WIR21. UNCTAD (2021). *World Investment Report 2021: Investing in Sustainable Recovery*. New York and Geneva: United Nations. United Nations publication.

World Bank (2018). *Global Investment Competitiveness Report 2017/2018: Foreign Investor Perspectives and Policy Implications*. Washington, DC: World Bank.

_____ (2021a). *State and Trends of Carbon Pricing 2021*. Washington, DC: World Bank.

_____ (2021b). *Enhancing Carbon Pricing & International Carbon Market Readiness through the Mitigation Action Assessment Protocol*. Washington, DC: World Bank.

WWF (World Wildlife Fund) (2021). *2021 SUSREG Annual Report: A Baseline Assessment of Sustainable Financial Regulations and Central Bank Activities*.

Zhan, J., and A. U. Santos-Paulino (2021). "Investing in the sustainable development goals: mobilization, channelling and impact". *Journal of International Business Policy*, 4: 166–183.

ANNEX TABLES

List of annex tables available on the UNCTAD website, www.unctad.org/wir

Annex table 1. FDI flows, by region and economy, 2016–2021 (Millions of dollars)

Region/economy	FDI inflows 2016	2017	2018	2019	2020	2021	FDI outflows 2016	2017	2018	2019	2020	2021
World[a]	2 045 424	1 632 639	1 448 276	1 480 626	963 139	1 582 310	1 596 716	1 610 113	941 293	1 123 894	780 480	1 707 594
Developed economies	1 384 814	937 683	753 320	764 456	319 190	745 739	1 210 679	1 162 247	565 200	736 840	408 195	1 269 212
Europe	794 426	513 250	398 049	404 756	80 786	219 033	653 726	544 012	467 785	342 648	-20 572	551 598
European Union	342 615	274 904	366 347	401 677	209 509	137 541	495 406	347 293	293 339	368 335	66 412	397 637
Austria	-8 508	14 953	5 390	3 035	-15 044	5 823	-2 033	10 251	5 612	12 509	-2 400	10 781
Belgium	59 243	-708	35 713	1 752	11 913	25 577	36 374	29 698	40 882	-3 371	10 588	45 624
Bulgaria	1 040	1 814	1 143	1 835	3 423	1 496	405	331	249	449	242	150
Croatia	273	539	1 203	397	136	569	-1 938	-725	201	-116	35	122
Cyprus	10 928	9 438	-413	34 362	4 669	463[c]	8 690	8 932	-6 941	34 454	255	-3 329[c]
Czechia	9 815	9 522	11 010	10 108	9 411	5 806	2 182	7 560	8 663	4 128	2 990	5 583
Denmark	235	3 749	1 715	7 073	3 210	5 541	10 110	10 023	-75	16 843	10 899	22 399
Estonia	1 059	1 951	1 517	3 184	3 395	989	487	890	45	1 966	220	1 547
Finland	8 582	2 864	-2 172	13 456	-1 427	9 393	24 277	-574	11 455	4 865	5 863	4 092
France	23 077	24 833	41 833	28 363	4 870	14 193	64 848	35 985	102 042	33 818	46 010	-2 839
Germany	15 633	48 641	72 098	52 665	64 589	31 267	63 661	86 518	97 233	137 293	60 624	151 690
Greece	2 765	3 485	3 973	5 019	3 213	5 732	-1 667	168	477	642	549	926
Hungary	-5 439	3 515	6 460	4 328	6 800	5 459	-8 272	1 220	3 364	3 211	4 222	2 882
Ireland	39 414	52 835	-12 017	149 433	80 871	15 702	30 086	-2 048	5 154	32 083	-44 997	61 979
Italy	28 469	24 047	37 682	18 146	-23 622	8 487	16 181	24 531	31 542	19 787	-1 856	11 759
Latvia	255	711	964	901	1 013	5 325	161	141	207	-103	266	3 361
Lithuania	303	1 021	977	3 022	3 492	2 053	43	80	704	1 747	2 874	663
Luxembourg	17 581	-27 370	-26 045	12 801	102 269	-9 054	-1 241	15 019	-25 478	-2 576	102 624	25 398
Malta	4 248	3 407	4 024	3 778	3 944	4 005	5 409	7 237	7 442	6 960	7 122	7 247
Netherlands	55 124	13 925	87 633	-14 141	-105 394	-81 056	186 139	25 660	-47 484	16 313	-191 397	28 861
Poland	15 690	9 172	15 996	13 510	13 831	24 816	11 600	2 169	891	1 854	1 295	178
Portugal	5 066	7 752	7 115	12 361	7 756	8 020	872	-749	799	3 638	2 333	-1 441
Romania	5 000	5 419	6 219	5 791	3 432	8 610	5	-97	379	363	53	-31
Slovakia	806	4 017	1 675	2 511	-1 931	59	96	1 325	322	43	235	389
Slovenia	1 246	898	1 384	1 463	206	1 517	290	338	281	610	509	922
Spain	31 569	41 966	57 463	17 417	5 678	9 777	43 945	56 045	37 546	24 827	23 567	-1 625
Sweden	19 141	12 509	3 806	9 108	18 803	26 973	4 699	27 363	17 829	16 100	23 687	20 347
Other Europe	451 811	238 346	31 702	3 079	-128 723	81 491	158 321	196 719	174 447	-25 688	-86 984	153 961
Albania	1 101	1 149	1 290	1 288	1 108	1 234	64	26	83	128	88	63
Belarus	1 238	1 279	1 421	1 293	1 397	1 233	114	70	50	16	82	-85
Bosnia and Herzegovina	350	492	581	342	395	519	39	79	2	31	57	38
Iceland	-427	-41	-381	-225	-933	174	-1 147	-208	76	479	-391	19
Moldova	83	152	297	508	150	264	9	13	38	40	-2	25
Montenegro	226	559	490	416	529	664	-185	11	109	75	-5	11
North Macedonia	375	205	725	446	230	606	24	2	12	40	53	91
Norway	-3 900	-5 849	226	16 715	-1 326	-1 628	3 092	-2 220	11 408	12 524	7 669	1 382
Russian Federation	37 176	25 954	13 228	32 076	10 410	38 240	26 951	34 153	35 820	22 024	6 778	63 602
Serbia	2 352	2 878	4 091	4 270	3 469	4 563	250	147	363	294	112	275
Switzerland	150 241	111 201	-83 155	-105 807	-162 704	1 016	166 569	21 944	43 599	-56 174	-36 152	-19 120
Ukraine	4 055	3 727	4 732	6 017	-36	6 549	100	281	-127	842	22	-198
United Kingdom	258 699	96 354	87 837	45 454	18 194	27 561	-37 606	142 373	82 961	-6 081	-65 363	107 741
North America	495 475	331 723	240 896	275 257	174 004	427 052	353 976	403 968	-99 357	107 985	281 446	492 975
Canada	36 056	22 767	37 662	50 149	23 176	59 676	69 507	76 188	58 049	79 389	46 527	89 874
United States	459 419	308 956	203 234	225 108	150 828	367 376	284 469	327 780	-157 406	28 596	234 919	403 101
Other developed economies	94 913	92 710	114 375	84 442	64 400	99 655	202 977	214 267	196 772	286 207	147 321	224 638
Australia	48 401	46 114	68 322	39 406	16 726	25 085	2 304	7 800	7 141	9 858	9 935	9 224
Bermuda	82	-288	95	5	112	1	72	-42	-35	-38	-11	-25
Israel	11 988	16 893	21 515	17 363	24 283	29 615	14 579	7 624	6 087	8 690	6 375	9 713
Japan	19 359	9 356	9 963	13 755	10 703	24 652	155 937	164 588	144 982	232 627	95 666	146 782
Korea, Republic of	12 104[b]	17 913	12 183	9 634	8 765	16 820	29 890[b]	34 069	38 220	35 239	34 832	60 820
New Zealand	2 979	2 723	2 298	4 279	3 810	3 482	196	227	377	-169	523	-1 876
Developing economies[a]	660 609	694 955	694 956	716 170	643 949	836 571	386 037	447 866	376 093	387 054	372 284	438 382
Africa	46 250	40 176	45 384	45 678	38 952	82 991	8 425	11 813	8 189	4 914	-622	2 653
North Africa	13 841	13 275	15 407	13 550	9 800	9 335	1 514	1 370	2 269	1 727	356	813
Algeria	1 636	1 232	1 475	1 382	1 143	870	46	-18	854	31	15	-52
Egypt	8 107	7 409	8 141	9 010	5 852	5 122	207	199	324	405	327	367
Libya	-	-	-	-	-	-	440	110	276	377	-487	-55[c]
Morocco	2 157	2 686	3 559	1 720	1 419	2 153	580	1 021	782	893	458	506
South Sudan	-8[c]	1[c]	60[c]	-232[c]	18[c]	68[c]	..	..	..	..	..	..
Sudan	1 064	1 065	1 136	825	717	462	..	..	..	..	..	..

/...

Annex table 1. FDI flows, by region and economy, 2016–2021 (Continued)

Region/economy	FDI inflows 2016	2017	2018	2019	2020	2021	FDI outflows 2016	2017	2018	2019	2020	2021
Tunisia	885	881	1 036	845	652	660	242	57	34	22	43	47
Other Africa	32 409	26 901	29 978	32 128	29 152	73 655	6 911	10 443	5 920	3 187	-978	1 840
West Africa	11 726	10 112	8 102	10 863	9 340	13 849	1 246	1 222	1 098	1 280	297	2 593
Benin	132	201	194	218	174	242	17	32	10	27	22	28
Burkina Faso	391	3	268	163	-102	137	51	10	68	16	-7	26
Cabo Verde	126	111	112	103	74	118	-8	16	-20	-9	-11	-7
Côte d'Ivoire	578	975	620	936	713	1 382	29	676	145	120	1	490
Gambia	-28	18	52	71	190	252	-1	2	0.5	-2	-3	-3
Ghana	3 485	3 255	2 989	2 827	1 876	2 614	15	16	81	588	542	192
Guinea	1 618	578	353	44	176	173[c]	21	1	-0.3	1	2	-4[c]
Guinea-Bissau	24	16	21	72	21	24	0.5	0.3	-0.4	0.4	0.3	0.2
Liberia	453	248	129	87	87	46[c]	168	54	84	102	80	91[c]
Mali	356	563	467	721	537	660	97	15	0.3	1	1	40
Mauritania	271	587	773	887	928	22[c]	1	10	4	5	6	5[c]
Niger	301	339	466	717	361	755	40	29	39	32	15	58
Nigeria	3 453	2 413	775	2 305	2 385	4 844[c]	335	311	566	285	-338	1 237[c]
Senegal	472	588	848	1 065	1 846	2 232	224	82	53	71	99	217
Sierra Leone	138	129	218	301	135	218[c]	..	..	..	..	..	..
Togo	-46	89	-183	346	-59	130	257	-33	70	43	-112	225
Central Africa	5 403	8 946	9 353	8 858	9 506	9 409	338	291	290	257	263	323
Burundi	0.1	0.3	-	1	8	8	-	-	-	1	2	1
Cameroon	664	814	762	1 027	675	850[c]	-39	22	110	127	84	105[c]
Central African Republic	7	7	18	26	35	30[c]	..	..	..	..	..	..
Chad	245	363	461	567	558	562[c]	..	..	..	..	..	..
Congo	1 612	4 417	4 315	3 366[c]	4 016[c]	3 691[c]	10	45	14[c]	23[c]	27[c]	25[c]
Congo, Democratic Republic of the	1 205	1 340	1 617	1 488	1 647	1 870	272	292	209	134	149	192
Equatorial Guinea	54	305	396	452	530	491[c]	..	..	..	..	..	..
Gabon	1 244	1 314	1 379	1 553	1 717	1 635[c]	45[c]	-84[c]	-63[c]	-34[c]	-	-
Rwanda	342	356	382	354	274	212	48	16	18	5	-	-
Sao Tome and Principe	31	29	23	24	47	60[c]	1	0.3	2	1	1	-0.1[c]
East Africa	8 302	8 784	8 054	7 893	6 062	8 179	140	215	233	168	139	164
Comoros	4	4	6	4	4	4[c]	..	..	..	..	..	..
Djibouti	160	165	170	175	158	167	..	..	..	..	..	..
Eritrea	52[c]	55[c]	61[c]	67[c]	74[c]	70[c]	..	..	..	..	..	..
Ethiopia	4 143	4 017	3 310	2 549	2 381	4 259	..	..	..	..	..	..
Kenya	1 139	1 404	1 139	1 098	717	448[c]	11	14	11	11	-7	-35[c]
Madagascar	451	358	353	474	358	300[c]	90	106	118	102	119	115[c]
Mauritius	379	480	461	444	225	253	28	89	98	58	16	86
Seychelles	155	192	120	144	122	157	10	6	5	-2	10	-3
Somalia	330[c]	369[c]	408[c]	447[c]	464[c]	456[c]	..	..	..	..	..	..
Uganda	626	803	1 055	1 274	874	1 142	0.1	0.3	0.3	0.3	0.3	0.3
United Republic of Tanzania	864	938	972	1 217	685	922[c]	..	..	..	..	..	..
Southern Africa	6 978	-941	4 469	4 514	4 244	42 219	5 188	8 715	4 299	1 481	-1 677	-1 241
Angola	-180	-7 397	-6 456	-4 098	-1 866	-4 150	273	1 352	6	-2 349	91	-1 057
Botswana	143	261	286	94	32	55	170	-1	82	-20	-68	-53
Eswatini	21[b]	-56[b]	36[b]	130[b]	41[b]	126[b]	-7[b]	65[b]	-11[b]	22[b]	-14[b]	59[b]
Lesotho	159	123	129	36	30	27	..	..	..	..	..	..
Malawi	116	90	959	55	45	50[c]	42	-3	1	-23	-19	-21[c]
Mozambique	3 093	2 293	2 703	2 212	3 035	5 102	35	26	-25	-31	153	194
Namibia	356	280	209	-179	-156	412	-5	-66	98	9	52	17
South Africa	2 235[b]	2 008[b]	5 450[b]	5 125[b]	3 062[b]	40 889[b]	4 474[b]	7 371[b]	4 076[b]	3 147[b]	-1 951[b]	19[b]
Zambia	663	1 108	408	860	-173	-457	177	-72	45	696	35	-453
Zimbabwe	372	349	745	280	194	166	29	42	27	31	44	55
Asia	478 148	501 382	496 898	511 632	518 893	618 983	366 619	400 135	360 653	336 213	378 382	394 118
East and South-East Asia	371 987	407 841	403 110	407 316	406 836	504 232	322 376	345 990	301 021	282 388	330 067	320 227
East Asia	258 665	253 391	254 334	232 339	284 726	328 918	272 810	257 442	243 474	202 886	267 680	244 389
China	133 711	136 315	138 305	141 225	149 342	180 957	196 149	158 288	143 037	136 905	153 710	145 190
Hong Kong, China	117 387	110 685	104 246	73 714	134 710	140 696[d]	59 703	86 704	82 201	53 202	100 715	87 450[d]
Korea, Democratic People's Republic of	89[c]	-13[c]	2[c]	30[c]	6[c]	18[c]	..	..	..	..	..	..
Macao, China	1 942	1 509	2 494	6 687	-7 104	-298[c]	-1 002	864	141	869	1 728	1 528[c]

/...

Annex table 1. FDI flows, by region and economy, 2016–2021 (Continued)

Region/economy	FDI inflows 2016	2017	2018	2019	2020	2021	FDI outflows 2016	2017	2018	2019	2020	2021
Mongolia	-4 156	1 494	2 174	2 443	1 719	2 140	14	49	37	127	26	113
Taiwan Province of China	9 692[b]	3 401[b]	7 114[b]	8 240[b]	6 053[b]	5 405[b]	17 946[b]	11 537[b]	18 058[b]	11 783[b]	11 500[b]	10 108[b]
South-East Asia	113 322	154 450	148 776	174 976	122 110	175 314	49 565	88 548	57 546	79 502	62 387	75 838
Brunei Darussalam	-150	460	517	375	577	205	..	..	..	..	..	..
Cambodia	2 476	2 786	3 208	3 662	3 625	3 484	79	115	124	102	127	92
Indonesia	3 921	20 579	20 563	23 883	18 591	20 081	-12 215	2 077	8 053	3 352	4 448	3 596
Lao People's Democratic Republic	935	1 686	1 358	756	968	1 072	15	10	-	-	-	-
Malaysia	11 336	9 399	7 618	7 813	3 160	11 620	8 011	5 638	5 114	6 231	2 419	4 750
Myanmar	2 930	4 409	2 892	2 509	1 907	2 067	..	..	..	..	..	..
Philippines	8 280[b]	10 256[b]	9 949[b]	8 671[b]	6 822[b]	10 518[b]	2 397[b]	3 305[b]	4 116[b]	3 351[b]	3 562[b]	2 402[b]
Singapore	67 502	82 483	73 932	106 323	75 437	99 099	36 872[b]	62 706[b]	22 169[b]	55 607[b]	31 758[b]	47 395[b]
Thailand	3 486	8 285	13 191	4 790	-4 849	11 423	13 393	14 217	17 373	10 395	18 999	17 303
Timor-Leste	5	7	48	75	72	85[c]	13	-	-	-	694	-[c]
Viet Nam	12 600	14 100	15 500	16 120[b]	15 800[b]	15 660[b]	1 000	480	598	465[b]	380[b]	300[b]
South Asia	54 281	51 640	52 262	59 086	70 957	52 417	5 520	11 493	11 630	13 275	11 206	15 986
Afghanistan	94[b]	52[b]	119[b]	23	13[b]	21[c]	14[b]	11[b]	39[b]	26	37[b]	31[c]
Bangladesh	2 333	2 152	3 613	2 874	2 564	2 896	41	142	23	28	12	92
Bhutan	-34	-10	7	3	1	2	..	..	..	..	..	..
India	44 481	39 904	42 156	50 558	64 072	44 735	5 072	11 141	11 447	13 144	11 109	15 522
Iran, Islamic Republic of	3 372	5 019	2 373	1 508	1 342	1 425[c]	104	76	75[c]	85[c]	78[c]	82[c]
Maldives	457[b]	458[b]	576[b]	956[b]	348[b]	443[b]	..	..	..	..	..	..
Nepal	106	198	67	185	126	196	..	..	..	..	..	..
Pakistan	2 576	2 496	1 737	2 234	2 057	2 102	52	52	-21	-85	-45	242
Sri Lanka	897[b]	1 373[b]	1 614[b]	743[b]	434[b]	598[b]	237[b]	72[b]	68[b]	77[b]	15[b]	17[b]
West Asia	38 499	33 103	34 502	36 732	34 824	55 334	43 917	41 599	49 009	43 139	39 191	56 383
Armenia	334	253	267	101	47	379	71	29	7	-133	-27	25
Azerbaijan	4 500	2 867	1 403	1 504	507	-1 708	2 574	2 564	1 761	2 432	825	77
Bahrain	243	1 426	1 654	1 501	1 021	1 766	-880	229	111	-197	-205	64
Georgia	1 654	1 981	1 317	1 336	572	1 153	407	269	340	282	23	322
Iraq	-6 256	-5 032	-4 885	-3 508	-2 859	-2 613	304	78	188	194	147	135
Jordan	1 553	2 030	955	730	760	622	3	7	-8	43	26	16
Kuwait	419	348	204	351	-142	198[c]	4 528	9 013	3 715	-2 696	7 988	3 631[c]
Lebanon	2 568	2 522	2 658	1 361	1 306	273[c]	1 005	1 317	631	338	10	66[c]
Oman	2 265	2 918	5 940	4 377	2 861	3 619[c]	356	2 424	715	627	536	581[c]
Qatar	774	986	-2 186	-2 813	-2 434	-1 093	7 902	1 695	3 523	4 450	2 730	160
Saudi Arabia	7 453	1 419	4 247	4 563	5 399	19 286	8 936	7 280	19 252	13 547	4 911	23 860
State of Palestine	297	188	252	132	80	256	45	3	31	56	59	-78
Syrian Arab Republic	-	-	-	-	-	-	..	..	..	..	..	..
Turkey	13 651	11 113	12 573	9 594	7 821	12 530	2 954	2 626	3 658	2 966	3 229	4 979
United Arab Emirates	9 605	10 354	10 385	17 875	19 884	20 667	15 711	14 060	15 079	21 226	18 937	22 546
Yemen	-561	-270[c]	-282[c]	-371[c]	-	-	1[c]	6[c]	4[c]	3[c]	-	-
Central Asia	13 381	8 797	7 023	8 499	6 276	7 000	-5 194	1 052	-1 006	-2 589	-2 082	1 522
Kazakhstan	8 514	4 714	3 898	3 284	3 675	3 172	-5 235	913	-1 095	-2 620	-2 156	1 468
Kyrgyzstan	616	-107	144	404	-402	248	-	-29	5	5	2	4
Tajikistan	345[b]	307[b]	360[b]	364[b]	107[b]	84[b]	35[b]	159[b]	82[b]	23[b]	70[b]	48[b]
Turkmenistan	2 243[c]	2 086[c]	1 997[c]	2 129[c]	1 169[c]	1 453[c]	..	..	..	..	..	..
Uzbekistan	1 663[b]	1 797[b]	625[b]	2 316[b]	1 726[b]	2 044	6[b]	9[b]	2[b]	3[b]	2[b]	3
Latin America and the Caribbeana	136 221	153 536	151 978	158 744	86 172	134 458	10 887	35 815	7 515	46 766	-4 664	41 770
South America	90 989	103 727	103 943	110 805	50 671	88 149	9 929	31 111	-1 370	35 061	-7 706	41 411
Argentina	3 260	11 517	11 717	6 663	4 019	6 534	1 787	1 156	1 726	1 539	1 294	1 363
Bolivia, Plurinational State of	335	712	302	-217	-1 129	594	89	80	-84	48	-111	104
Brazil	53 700	66 585	59 802	65 386	28 318	50 367	-5 901	19 040	-16 336	19 031	-12 935	23 083
Chile	12 503	4 064	10 348	15 231	9 637	12 719	7 188	2 927	6 798	9 879	2 329	12 220
Colombia	13 858	13 701	11 299	13 989	7 459	9 402	4 517	3 690	5 126	3 153	1 656	3 362
Ecuador	764	630	1 389	975	1 104	621	..	..	..	..	..	..
Guyana	58	212	1 231	1 695	1 834	1 162[c]	26	-	-	17	14	-[c]
Paraguay	505	336	156	225	120	122	..	..	..	..	..	..
Peru	6 459	6 530	6 761	6 179	-871	5 908	1 180	538	98	983	29	188
Suriname	300	98	119	-8	0.3	-164	-	-	-	-	-	-

/...

Annex table 1. FDI flows, by region and economy, 2016–2021 (Concluded)

Region/economy	FDI inflows						FDI outflows					
	2016	2017	2018	2019	2020	2021	2016	2017	2018	2019	2020	2021
Uruguay	-1 821	-590	-67	1 965	635	1 646	2	1 447	641	568	-339	310
Venezuela, Bolivarian Republic of	1 068	-68	886	-1 278	-456	-761[c]	1 041	2 234	661	-159	358	781[c]
Central America	41 817	45 446	45 321	43 994	32 756	42 495	597	4 654	8 598	11 337	3 031	112
Belize	44	24	118	94	76	128	2	0.3	1	2	4	2
Costa Rica	2 204	2 778	2 487	2 812	1 763	3 196	77	126	53	117	118	86
El Salvador	347	889	826	636	280	314	-0.4	0.2	-	0.4	-1	1
Guatemala	1 174	1 130	981	976	932	3 472	209	196	201	180	149	161
Honduras	1 139	1 176	961	498	419	700	239	141	66	3	49	358
Mexico	31 173	34 131	34 090	34 411	27 934	31 621	193	3 988	8 365	10 640	2 710	-717
Nicaragua	989	1 035	838	503	747	1 220	65	65	75	59	40	14
Panama	4 745	4 282	5 019	4 063	607	1 844	-188	138	-163	337	-39	209
Caribbean[a]	3 416	4 364	2 715	3 945	2 745	3 814	361	49	287	368	11	247
Anguilla	115[b]	97[b]	210[b]	140[b]	61[b]	81[b]	5[b]	-12[b]	31[b]	19[b]	8[b]	-5[b]
Antigua and Barbuda	97[b]	151[b]	205[b]	128[b]	74[b]	104[b]	38[b]	12[b]	-1[b]	-1[b]	-8[b]	-9[b]
Aruba	28	88	110	-136	137	134	-0.4	9	5	-1	1	-2
Bahamas	1 260	901	947	611	897	360	359	151	117	148	157	279
Barbados	269	206	242	215	262	239[c]	-194	-28	9	28	8	18[c]
British Virgin Islands	49 023[c]	39 610[c]	34 390[c]	39 103[c]	39 620[c]	39 361[c]	30 168[c]	50 904[c]	41 587[c]	44 154[c]	42 280[c]	43 217[c]
Cayman Islands	58 816[c]	15 173[c]	20 681[c]	28 165[c]	23 621[c]	25 893[c]	16 604[c]	4 079[c]	8 261[c]	31 630[c]	10 835[c]	21 232[c]
Curaçao	133	173	127	56[c]	158	154[c]	39	-145	30	11	9	6[c]
Dominica	42[b]	23[b]	78[b]	63[b]	22[b]	44[b]	1[b]	-1[b]	0.1[b]	0.1[b]	-0.4[b]	-[b]
Dominican Republic	2 407	3 571	2 535	3 021	2 560	3 102	116[c]	27	209	-192	-99	153
Grenada	110[b]	156[b]	184[b]	199[b]	149[b]	144[b]	17[b]	4[b]	18[b]	21[b]	-0.5[b]	-6[b]
Haiti	105	375	105	75	23	50	-	-	-	-	-	-
Jamaica	928	889	775	665	265	321	270	34	13	446	7	56
Montserrat	4[b]	3[b]	3[b]	2[b]	3[b]	1[b]	..	..	..	..	..	..
Saint Kitts and Nevis	121[b]	48[b]	40[b]	48[b]	14[b]	40[b]	-3[b]	6[b]	29[b]	12[b]	4[b]	-3[b]
Saint Lucia	162[b]	90[b]	46[b]	73[b]	35[b]	47[b]	12[b]	-6[b]	-9[b]	41[b]	-39[b]	26[b]
Saint Vincent and the Grenadines	80[b]	163[b]	42[b]	74[b]	31[b]	65[b]	-9[b]	21[b]	7[b]	5[b]	3[b]	4[b]
Sint Maarten	55	64	-197	55	27	31[c]	3	2	4	1	2	6[c]
Trinidad and Tobago	-24	-471	-700	184	-103	342[c]	-25	-12	65	114	104	37[c]
Oceania	-9	-138	695	116	-68	139	107	102	-265	-839	-811	-160
Cook Islands	10[b]	2[b]	12[b]	8[c]	7[c]	8[c]	0.3[b]	0.3[b]	0.3[b]	0.3[c]	0.3[c]	0.3[c]
Fiji	390	386	471	321	241	401	-16	-2	-4	-36	14	35
French Polynesia	-37	-75	32	14	17	21[c]	24	15	-28	4[c]	-2[c]	1[c]
Kiribati	2	1	-1	-1	3	1[c]	0.1	0.1	0.1	0.1	0.1	0.1[c]
Marshall Islands	-3	6	10	4	7	5[c]	..	..	..	..	..	..
New Caledonia	-462	-410	-249	-655	-520	-494[c]	80	79	96	83	86	84[c]
Palau	36	27	22	22	24	23[c]	-	-	1	-	-	-
Papua New Guinea	-40[b]	-180[b]	306[b]	335[b]	112[b]	87[c]	-[b]	-[b]	-341[b]	-901[b]	-916[b]	-272[c]
Samoa	3	9	17	-2	4	9	15	0.1	-	4	2	1
Solomon Islands	39	43	25	33	9	50[c]	1	7	9	4	3	-11[c]
Tonga	9	14	15	2	4	2[c]	1	1	1	1	1	0.2[c]
Tuvalu	0.3	0.3	0.3	0.3	0.1[c]	0.2[c]	..	..	..	..	..	..
Vanuatu	44	38	37	35	25	26[c]	1	1	1	0.2	2	2[c]
Memorandum												
Least developed countries (LDCs)[e]	25 880	20 873	22 539	22 839	22 975	25 978	1 976	2 211	900	-1 004	1 508	-142
Landlocked developing countries (LLDCs)[f]	24 335	25 070	22 951	22 070	14 139	18 486	-1 738	3 911	1 072	753	-1 291	1 699
Small island developing States (SIDS)[g]	4 721	3 962	3 798	4 425	2 854	3 342	513	300	342	836	964	504

Source: UNCTAD, FDI/MNE database (www.unctad.org/fdistatistics).

[a] Excluding the financial centers in the Caribbean (Anguilla, Antigua and Barbuda, Aruba, the Bahamas, Barbados, the British Virgin Islands, the Cayman Islands, Curaçao, Dominica, Grenada, Montserrat, Saint Kitts and Nevis, Saint Lucia, Saint Vincent and the Grenadines, Sint Maarten and the Turks and Caicos Islands).

[b] Asset/liability basis.

[c] Estimates.

[d] Directional basis calculated from asset/liability basis.

[e] Least developed countries include Afghanistan, Angola, Bangladesh, Benin, Bhutan, Burkina Faso, Burundi, Cambodia, the Central African Republic, Chad, the Comoros, the Democratic Republic of the Congo, Djibouti, Eritrea, Ethiopia, the Gambia, Guinea, Guinea-Bissau, Haiti, Kiribati, the Lao People's Democratic Republic, Lesotho, Liberia, Madagascar, Malawi, Mali, Mauritania, Mozambique, Myanmar, Nepal, the Niger, Rwanda, Sao Tome and Principe, Senegal, Sierra Leone, Solomon Islands, Somalia, South Sudan, the Sudan, Timor-Leste, Togo, Tuvalu, Uganda, the United Republic of Tanzania, Yemen and Zambia.

[f] Landlocked developing countries include Afghanistan, Armenia, Azerbaijan, Bhutan, the Plurinational State of Bolivia, Botswana, Burkina Faso, Burundi, the Central African Republic, Chad, Eswatini, Ethiopia, Kazakhstan, Kyrgyzstan, the Lao People's Democratic Republic, Lesotho, North Macedonia, Malawi, Mali, the Republic of Moldova, Mongolia, Nepal, the Niger, Paraguay, Rwanda, South Sudan, Tajikistan, Turkmenistan, Uganda, Uzbekistan, Zambia and Zimbabwe.

[g] Small island developing States include Antigua and Barbuda, the Bahamas, Barbados, Cabo Verde, the Comoros, Dominica, Fiji, Grenada, Jamaica, Kiribati, Maldives, the Marshall Islands, Mauritius, the Federated States of Micronesia, Nauru, Palau, Saint Kitts and Nevis, Saint Lucia, Saint Vincent and the Grenadines, Samoa, Sao Tome and Príncipe, Seychelles, Solomon Islands, Timor-Leste, Tonga, Trinidad and Tobago, Tuvalu and Vanuatu.

Annex table 2. FDI stock, by region and economy, 2000, 2010 and 2021 (Millions of dollars)

Region/economy	FDI inward stock			FDI outward stock		
	2000	2010	2021	2000	2010	2021
World[a]	7 377 201	19 907 143	45 448 812	7 408 902	20 471 257	41 798 485
Developed economies	5 860 038	13 846 108	33 119 269	6 740 421	17 568 316	33 008 670
Europe	2 491 244	8 439 157	16 441 775	3 193 644	10 264 456	17 619 059
European Union	1 882 785	5 960 396	11 590 104	1 967 112	6 988 784	13 263 759
Austria	31 165	160 615	198 359	24 821	181 638	244 472
Belgium	..	473 358	604 647	..	431 613	691 297
Bulgaria	2 704	44 970	57 651	67	2 583	3 277
Croatia	2 785	32 215	38 898	952	4 914	6 052
Cyprus	2 846	260 132	406 435	557	242 556	413 294
Czechia	21 644	128 504	200 587	738	14 923	53 607
Denmark	73 574	96 136	154 189[c]	73 100	163 133	270 811[c]
Estonia	2 645	15 551	34 865	259	5 545	12 883
Finland	24 273	86 698	98 527	52 109	137 663	139 933
France	184 215	630 710	977 990[c]	365 871	1 172 994	1 544 964[c]
Germany	470 938	955 881	1 139 106[c]	483 946	1 364 565	2 141 269[c]
Greece	14 113	35 026	45 803	6 094	42 623	14 045
Hungary	22 870	91 015	101 698	1 280	23 612	38 705
Ireland	127 089	285 575	1 362 510[c]	27 925	340 114	1 273 778[c]
Italy	122 533	328 058	454 910	169 957	491 208	553 321
Latvia	1 691	10 869	23 744	19	931	5 928
Lithuania	2 334	15 455	29 396	29	2 647	10 828
Luxembourg	..	172 257	1 013 915	..	187 027	1 272 822
Malta	2 263	129 770	231 446	193	60 596	66 219
Netherlands	243 733	588 077	2 576 225	305 461	968 105	3 356 858
Poland	33 477	187 602	269 225	268	16 407	27 562
Portugal	34 224	121 239	175 531	19 417	71 676	57 051
Romania	6 953	68 699	108 743	136	2 327	2 666
Slovakia	6 970	50 328	59 367	555	3 457	5 418
Slovenia	2 389	10 667	20 043	772	8 147	8 390
Spain	156 348	628 341	819 725	129 194	653 236	600 808
Sweden	93 791	352 646	386 569	123 618	394 547	447 500
Other Europe	608 459	2 478 760	4 851 671	1 226 532	3 275 672	4 355 300
Albania	247	3 255	10 074	-	154	830
Belarus	1 306	9 904	15 165	24	205	1 358
Bosnia and Herzegovina	450	6 709	9 474	-	211	679
Iceland	497	11 784	7 714	663	11 466	5 139
Moldova	449	2 897	4 780	23	90	322
Montenegro	-	4 231	6 361[c]	-	-	106[c]
North Macedonia	540	4 351	7 248	16	100	202
Norway	30 265	177 318	150 246	34 026	188 996	198 181
Russian Federation	29 738	464 228	521 876	19 211	336 355	399 313
Serbia	-	22 299	52 775	-	1 960	4 537
Switzerland	101 635	648 092	1 369 626	232 202	1 043 199	1 578 515
Ukraine	3 875	52 872	62 131	170	6 548	-295
United Kingdom	439 458	1 068 187	2 634 202	940 197	1 686 260	2 166 414
North America	3 108 255	4 406 182	15 056 860	3 136 637	5 793 476	12 098 870
Canada	325 020	983 889	1 437 837	442 623	983 889	2 285 325
United States	2 783 235	3 422 293	13 619 023	2 694 014	4 809 587	9 813 545
Other developed economies	260 539	1 000 769	1 620 634	410 140	1 510 383	3 290 741
Australia	121 686	527 728	770 258	92 508	449 740	618 855
Bermuda	265[c]	2 837	2 678	108[c]	925	114
Israel	20 426	60 086	235 593	9 091	67 893	117 645
Japan	50 323	214 880	256 966[c]	278 445	831 076	1 983 858[c]
Korea, Republic of	43 738	135 500	263 253	21 497	144 032	551 549
New Zealand	24 101	59 738	91 887	8 491	16 717	18 720
Developing economies[a]	1 517 163	6 061 035	12 329 543	668 481	2 902 941	8 789 815
Africa	153 062	623 756	1 026 320	39 815	137 363	301 252
North Africa	45 590	201 109	326 091	3 199	25 770	40 050
Algeria	3 379[c]	19 545	33 977	205[c]	1 505	2 699
Egypt	19 955	73 095	137 543	655	5 448	8 848
Libya	471[c]	16 334	18 462[c]	1 903[c]	16 615	20 400[c]

/...

Annex table 2. FDI stock, by region and economy, 2000, 2010 and 2021 (continued)

Region/economy	FDI inward stock			FDI outward stock		
	2000	2010	2021	2000	2010	2021
Morocco	8 842[c]	45 082	72 941	402[c]	1 914	7 438
Sudan	1 398	15 690	29 728	-	-	54
Tunisia	11 545	31 364	33 440[c]	33	287	611[c]
Other Africa	107 472	422 646	700 229	36 616	111 594	261 202
West Africa	33 010	109 968	208 446	6 381	18 090	27 117
Benin	213	604	2 845	11	21	335
Burkina Faso	28	354	2 670	0.4	8	442
Cabo Verde	192[c]	4 745	2 453	-	2	94
Côte d'Ivoire	2 483	6 978	12 821	9	94	1 506
Gambia	216	323	915[c]	..	..	..
Ghana	1 554[c]	10 080	41 021	-	83	1 840
Guinea	263[c]	486	5 088[c]	12[c]	144	96[c]
Guinea-Bissau	38	63	316	-	5	11
Liberia	3 247[c]	10 206	8 929[c]	2 188	4 714	4 919[c]
Mali	132	1 964	6 407	1	18	275
Mauritania	146[c]	2 372[c]	9 995[c]	4[c]	28[c]	104[c]
Niger	45	2 251	8 275	1	9	423
Nigeria	23 786	66 797	91 857[c]	4 144	12 576	13 508[c]
Senegal	295	1 699	10 505	22	263	1 135
Sierra Leone	284[c]	482	2 438[c]	..	..	..
Togo	87	565	1 912	-10	126	2 430
Central Africa	5 053	39 227	118 702	1 651	2 217	4 661
Burundi	47[c]	13	242[c]	2[c]	2	6[c]
Cameroon	917[c]	3 099[c]	9 781[c]	1 252[c]	971[c]	1 128[c]
Central African Republic	104	511	749[c]	43	-	-
Chad	576[c]	3 594[c]	7 615[c]	-	-	-
Congo	1 893[c]	9 261[c]	36 653[c]	40[c]	34[c]	132[c]
Congo, Democratic Republic of the	617	9 368	29 149	34	229	3 241
Equatorial Guinea	1 060[c]	9 413[c]	15 585[c]	..	..	..
Gabon	-227[c]	3 287[c]	15 592[c]	280[c]	946[c]	79[c]
Rwanda	55	422	2 912	-	13	74
Sao Tome and Principe	11[c]	260[c]	426[c]	-	21[c]	2[c]
East Africa	7 202	38 085	96 547	387	1 474	2 255
Comoros	21[c]	60[c]	142[c]	..	..	..
Djibouti	40[b]	332	-2 073	..	..	..
Eritrea	337[c]	666[c]	1 267[c]	..	..	..
Ethiopia	941	4 206	31 596	..	..	..
Kenya	932[c]	4 967	10 458[c]	115[c]	62	50[c]
Madagascar	141	4 383	8 638[c]	9[c]	193	1 020[c]
Mauritius	683	4 658	5 355[c]	132	864	711[c]
Seychelles	515	2 960	3 335	130	290	300
Somalia	4[c]	566[c]	4 071[c]	..	..	..
Uganda	807	5 575	16 605	-	66	174
United Republic of Tanzania	2 781	9 712	17 153[c]	..	..	..
Southern Africa	62 208	235 365	276 534	28 198	89 813	227 169
Angola	7 977	32 458	13 166	-8	1 870	2 153
Botswana	1 827	3 351	5 100	517	1 007	970
Eswatini	536	927	1 103[b]	87	91	172[b]
Lesotho	330	929	1 114	..	..	..
Malawi	358	963	1 595[c]	-5	45	329[c]
Mozambique	1 249	4 331	50 068	1	3	7
Namibia	1 276	3 595	6 348	45	722	849
South Africa	43 451	179 565[b]	173 056[b]	27 328	83 249[b]	220 103[b]
Zambia	3 966[c]	7 433	18 912[c]	-	2 531	1 850[c]
Zimbabwe	1 238	1 814	6 073	234	297	737
Asia	1 023 690	3 872 409	9 130 113	575 247	2 348 151	7 745 454
East and South-East Asia	908 302	2 888 852	7 413 547	557 764	2 059 344	6 923 187
East Asia	650 700	1 738 193	4 275 933	473 708	1 455 117	5 089 251
China	193 348	586 882[c]	2 064 018[c]	27 768[c]	317 211	2 581 800

/...

Annex table 2. FDI stock, by region and economy, 2000, 2010 and 2021 (continued)

Region/economy	FDI inward stock			FDI outward stock		
	2000	2010	2021	2000	2010	2021
Hong Kong, China	435 417	1 067 520	2 022 195[d]	379 285	943 938	2 082 323[d]
Korea, Democratic People's Republic of	77[c]	236[c]	939[c]	..	..	..
Macao, China	2 801[c]	13 603	46 524[c]	-	550	13 670[c]
Mongolia	182	8 445	26 346[c]	-	2 616	810[c]
Taiwan Province of China	18 875	61 508[b]	115 911[c]	66 655	190 803[b]	410 648[c]
South-East Asia	257 603	1 150 659	3 137 614	84 056	604 228	1 833 936
Brunei Darussalam	3 868[c]	4 140	7 302	..	..	..
Cambodia	1 580	9 026	41 025	193	345	1 171
Indonesia	25 060	160 735	259 268	6 940	6 672	95 636
Lao People's Democratic Republic	588[c]	1 888[c]	12 208[c]	26[c]	68[c]	95[c]
Malaysia	52 747	101 620	187 375[c]	15 878	96 964	134 613[c]
Myanmar	3 752[c]	14 507	37 189	..	..	..
Philippines	13 762[c]	25 896	113 711[c]	1 032[c]	6 710	66 367[c]
Singapore	110 570	633 354[b]	2 007 270[b]	56 755	466 723[b]	1 346 395[b]
Thailand	30 944	142 334	279 140	3 232	24 418	177 044
Timor-Leste	-	155	554[c]	-	94	802[c]
Viet Nam	14 730[c]	57 004[c]	192 571[c]	-	2 234[c]	11 813[c]
South Asia	30 743	269 143	656 698	2 761	100 441	214 572
Afghanistan	17[c]	963	1 613[c]	-	16	165
Bangladesh	2 162	6 072	21 582	68	98	390
Bhutan	4[c]	204	409	..	..	..
India	16 339	205 580	514 292	1 733	96 901	206 378
Iran, Islamic Republic of	2 597[c]	28 953	60 136[c]	411[c]	1 713[c]	4 139[c]
Maldives	128[c]	1 114[c]	5 996[c]	..	..	..
Nepal	72[c]	239	1 850	..	..	..
Pakistan	6 919	19 828	32 931	489	1 362	1 979
Sri Lanka	2 505	6 190	17 891	60	351	1 522
West Asia	72 352	612 837	848 430	14 672	172 001	590 951
Armenia	513	4 405	5 631	-	150	519
Azerbaijan	1 791	7 648	31 607	1	5 790	26 692
Bahrain	5 906	15 154	33 471	1 752	7 883	19 007
Georgia	762	8 518	19 380	118	848	3 121
Iraq	-48	7 965	-	-	632	3 151
Jordan	3 135	21 899	37 305	44	473	697
Kuwait	608	11 884	14 799[c]	1 428	28 189	36 372[c]
Lebanon	14 233	44 285	68 905[c]	352	6 831	16 042[c]
Oman	2 577[c]	14 987	40 814[c]	-	2 796	12 769[c]
Qatar	1 912	30 549	27 534[c]	74	12 995	47 670[c]
Saudi Arabia	17 577	176 378	261 061	5 285[c]	26 528	151 499
State of Palestine	1 418[c]	2 176	2 976	-	241	332
Syrian Arab Republic	1 244	9 939	10 743[c]	-	5	5[c]
Turkey	18 812	188 324	120 700	3 668	22 509	57 356
United Arab Emirates	1 069[c]	63 869	171 563[c]	1 938[c]	55 560	215 047[c]
Yemen	843[c]	4 858[c]	1 942[c]	13[c]	571[c]	672[c]
Central Asia	12 293	101 577	211 438	49	16 365	16 745
Kazakhstan	10 078	82 648	151 953	16	16 212	15 666
Kyrgyzstan	432	1 698	4 233	33	2	610
Tajikistan	136	1 226	3 198[c]	-	-	271[c]
Turkmenistan	949[c]	13 442[c]	40 775[c]	..	..	..
Uzbekistan	698[c]	2 564[b]	11 278[b]	-	152[b]	198[b]
Latin America and the Caribbean[a]	338 557	1 550 176	2 142 727	53 170	416 598	741 119
South America	186 425	1 085 366	1 310 976	43 634	288 295	532 846
Argentina	67 601	85 591	98 928	21 141	30 328	42 452
Bolivia, Plurinational State of	5 188	6 890	10 734	29	8	893
Brazil	-	640 330	592 761	-	149 333	296 185
Chile	45 753	160 904	180 489	11 154	61 126	83 737
Colombia	11 157	82 991	218 928	2 989	23 717	68 804
Ecuador	6 337	11 858	21 388	..	..	..
Guyana	756	1 784	9 107[c]	1	2	57[c]
Paraguay	1 003	3 457	6 302	..	..	..
Peru	11 062	42 976	117 816	505	4 265	9 888

/...

Annex table 2. FDI stock, by region and economy, 2000, 2010 and 2021 (concluded)

Region/economy	FDI inward stock 2000	FDI inward stock 2010	FDI inward stock 2021	FDI outward stock 2000	FDI outward stock 2010	FDI outward stock 2021
Suriname	-	-	1 888	-	-	215
Uruguay	2 088	12 479	31 448	138	345	5 707
Venezuela, Bolivarian Republic of	35 480	36 107	21 187[c]	7 676	19 171	24 908[c]
Central America	139 768	417 113	755 450	8 534	126 008	204 732
Belize	294	1 454	2 535	42	49	75
Costa Rica	2 809	15 936	53 692	22	1 135	8 039
El Salvador	1 973	7 284	10 378	104	1	5
Guatemala	3 420	4 554	21 423	93	452	1 944
Honduras	1 392	6 951	17 598	-	850	2 830
Mexico	121 691	355 512	578 792	8 273	119 967	185 268
Nicaragua	1 414	4 681	11 206	-	181	811
Panama	6 775	20 742	59 825[c]	-	3 374	5 760[c]
Caribbean[a]	12 365	47 697	76 301	1 002	2 295	3 541
Anguilla	-	-	1 214[b]	-	-	124[b]
Antigua and Barbuda	-	-	1 516[b]	-	-	178[b]
Aruba	1 161	4 567	4 412[c]	675	682	658[c]
Bahamas	3 865[c]	13 160	26 352[c]	547[c]	2 538	59[c]
Barbados	308	4 970	8 344[c]	41	4 058	3 843[c]
British Virgin Islands	30 289[c]	265 783[c]	990 238[c]	69 041[c]	376 866[c]	85 497[c]
Cayman Islands	27 316[c]	161 916[c]	548 337[c]	21 643[c]	89 316[c]	344 445[c]
Curaçao	-	527	2 045[c]	-	32	721[c]
Dominica	-	-	526[b]	-	-	1[b]
Dominican Republic	1 673	18 793[b]	47 792[b]	-	743[b]	963[b]
Grenada	-	-	1 841[b]	-	-	109[b]
Haiti	95	625	2 001	-	-	-
Jamaica	3 317	10 855	17 814	709	176	1 076
Montserrat	-	-	38[b]	..	..	..
Saint Kitts and Nevis	-	-	1 636[b]	-	-	101[b]
Saint Lucia	-	-	1 685[b]	-	-	629[b]
Saint Vincent and the Grenadines	-	-	1 412[b]	-	-	99[b]
Sint Maarten	-	256	173[c]	-	10	106[c]
Trinidad and Tobago	7 280[c]	17 424[c]	8 694[c]	293[c]	2 119[c]	1 502[c]
Oceania	1 854	14 694	30 384	249	828	1 989
Cook Islands	-	-	131[c]	-	-	14[c]
Fiji	356	2 963	5 908	39	47	103
French Polynesia	146[c]	442[c]	1 120[c]	-	144[c]	348[c]
Kiribati	-	5	13[c]	-	2	1[c]
Marshall Islands	20	120	218[c]	..	..	..
Micronesia, Federated States of	-	7	235[c]	-	-	5[c]
New Caledonia	-41[c]	5 726[c]	16 211[c]	2[c]	304[c]	1 130[c]
Palau	173	232	511[c]	..	..	..
Papua New Guinea	935	3 748	3 887[c]	194[c]	209[c]	135[c]
Samoa	77	220	327	-	14	53
Solomon Islands	106[c]	552	651[c]	-	27	60[c]
Tonga	19[c]	220[c]	471[c]	14[c]	58[c]	111[c]
Tuvalu	-	5	9[c]	..	..	..
Vanuatu	61[c]	454	692[c]	-	23	30[c]
Memorandum						
Least developed countries (LDCs)[e]	35 974	161 938	414 411	2 604	11 528	22 434
Landlocked developing countries (LLDCs)[f]	33 630	177 269	431 130	1 025	29 288	51 892
Small island developing States (SIDS)[g]	17 133	65 139	97 115	1 906	10 332	9 873

Source: UNCTAD, FDI/MNE database (www.unctad.org/fdistatistics).

[a] Excluding the financial centers in the Caribbean (Anguilla, Antigua and Barbuda, Aruba, the Bahamas, Barbados, the British Virgin Islands, the Cayman Islands, Curaçao, Dominica, Grenada, Montserrat, Saint Kitts and Nevis, Saint Lucia, Saint Vincent and the Grenadines, Sint Maarten and the Turks and Caicos Islands).

[b] Asset/liability basis.

[c] Estimates.

[d] Directional basis calculated from asset/liability basis.

[e] Least developed countries include Afghanistan, Angola, Bangladesh, Benin, Bhutan, Burkina Faso, Burundi, Cambodia, the Central African Republic, Chad, the Comoros, the Democratic Republic of the Congo, Djibouti, Eritrea, Ethiopia, the Gambia, Guinea, Guinea-Bissau, Haiti, Kiribati, the Lao People's Democratic Republic, Lesotho, Liberia, Madagascar, Malawi, Mali, Mauritania, Mozambique, Myanmar, Nepal, the Niger, Rwanda, Sao Tome and Principe, Senegal, Sierra Leone, Solomon Islands, Somalia, South Sudan, the Sudan, Timor-Leste, Togo, Tuvalu, Uganda, the United Republic of Tanzania, Yemen and Zambia.

[f] Landlocked developing countries include Afghanistan, Armenia, Azerbaijan, Bhutan, the Plurinational State of Bolivia, Botswana, Burkina Faso, Burundi, the Central African Republic, Chad, Eswatini, Ethiopia, Kazakhstan, Kyrgyzstan, the Lao People's Democratic Republic, Lesotho, North Macedonia, Malawi, Mali, the Republic of Moldova, Mongolia, Nepal, the Niger, Paraguay, Rwanda, South Sudan, Tajikistan, Turkmenistan, Uganda, Uzbekistan, Zambia and Zimbabwe.

[g] Small island developing States include Antigua and Barbuda, the Bahamas, Barbados, Cabo Verde, the Comoros, Dominica, Fiji, Grenada, Jamaica, Kiribati, Maldives, the Marshall Islands, Mauritius, the Federated States of Micronesia, Nauru, Palau, Saint Kitts and Nevis, Saint Lucia, Saint Vincent and the Grenadines, Samoa, Sao Tome and Príncipe, Seychelles, Solomon Islands, Timor-Leste, Tonga, Trinidad and Tobago, Tuvalu and Vanuatu.

EXPLANATORY NOTES

The terms country and economy as used in this report also refer, as appropriate, to territories or areas; the designations employed and the presentation of the material do not imply the expression of any opinion whatsoever on the part of the Secretariat of the United Nations concerning the legal status of any country, territory, city or area or of its authorities, or concerning the delimitation of its frontiers or boundaries. In addition, the designations of country groups are intended solely for statistical or analytical convenience and do not necessarily express a judgment about the stage of development reached by a particular country or area in the development process. The major country groupings used in this report follow the classification of the United Nations Statistical Office:

- Developed economies: the member countries of the OECD (other than Chile, Colombia, Costa Rica, Mexico and Turkey), plus the new European Union member countries that are not OECD members (Bulgaria, Croatia, Cyprus, Malta and Romania), plus Albania, Andorra, Belarus, Bermuda, Bosnia and Herzegovina, Liechtenstein, the Republic of Moldova, Monaco, Montenegro, North Macedonia, the Russian Federation, San Marino, Serbia and Ukraine plus the territories of Faeroe Islands, Gibraltar, Greenland, Guernsey and Jersey.
- Developing economies: in general, all economies not specified above. For statistical purposes, the data for China do not include those for Hong Kong Special Administrative Region (Hong Kong SAR), Macao Special Administrative Region (Macao SAR) or Taiwan Province of China.

Methodological details on FDI and MNE statistics can be found on the report website (unctad/diae/wir).

Reference to companies and their activities should not be construed as an endorsement by UNCTAD of those companies or their activities.

The following symbols have been used in the tables:

- Two dots (..) indicate that data are not available or are not separately reported. Rows in tables have been omitted in those cases where no data are available for any of the elements in the row.
- A dash (–) indicates that the item is equal to zero or its value is negligible.
- A blank in a table indicates that the item is not applicable, unless otherwise indicated.
- A slash (/) between dates representing years, e.g., 2020/21, indicates a financial year.
- Use of a dash (–) between dates representing years, e.g., 2020–2021, signifies the full period involved, including the beginning and end years.
- Reference to "dollars" ($) means United States dollars, unless otherwise indicated.

Annual rates of growth or change, unless otherwise stated, refer to annual compound rates.

Details and percentages in tables do not necessarily add to totals because of rounding.

WORLD INVESTMENT REPORT PAST ISSUES

WIR 2021: Investing in Sustainable Recovery

WIR 2020: International Production Beyond the Pandemic

WIR 2019: Special Economic Zones

WIR 2018: Investment and New Industrial Policies

WIR 2017: Investment and the Digital Economy

WIR 2016: Investor Nationality: Policy Challenges

WIR 2015: Reforming International Investment Governance

WIR 2014: Investing in the SDGs: An Action Plan

WIR 2013: Global Value Chains: Investment and Trade for Development

WIR 2012: Towards a New Generation of Investment Policies

WIR 2011: Non-Equity Modes of International Production and Development

WIR 2010: Investing in a Low-carbon Economy

WIR 2009: Transnational Corporations, Agricultural Production and Development

WIR 2008: Transnational Corporations and the Infrastructure Challenge

WIR 2007: Transnational Corporations, Extractive Industries and Development

WIR 2006: FDI from Developing and Transition Economies: Implications for Development

WIR 2005: Transnational Corporations and the Internationalization of R&D

WIR 2004: The Shift Towards Services

WIR 2003: FDI Policies for Development: National and International Perspectives

WIR 2002: Transnational Corporations and Export Competitiveness

WIR 2001: Promoting Linkages

WIR 2000: Cross-border Mergers and Acquisitions and Development

WIR 1999: Foreign Direct Investment and the Challenge of Development

WIR 1998: Trends and Determinants

WIR 1997: Transnational Corporations, Market Structure and Competition Policy

WIR 1996: Investment, Trade and International Policy Arrangements

WIR 1995: Transnational Corporations and Competitiveness

WIR 1994: Transnational Corporations, Employment and the Workplace

WIR 1993: Transnational Corporations and Integrated International Production

WIR 1992: Transnational Corporations as Engines of Growth

WIR 1991: The Triad in Foreign Direct Investment

DIVISION ON INVESTMENT & ENTERPRISE

The UNCTAD Investment and Enterprise Division is a global center of excellence for all issues related to investment and enterprise development.

Two flagship products

World Investment Forum

World Investment Report

Seven core services

Global investment information & research

Core data products and services

Global Investment Trends Monitors

Transnational Corporations Journal

Investment policies & treaties

Investment Policy Reviews (IPRs)

International investment agreements (IIAs)

Investment Policy Hub

Investment promotion & facilitation

Investment facilitation and promotion

Business Facilitation Programme

Investment guides

Sustainable investment

Sustainable Stock Exchange Initiative

Family Business for Sustainable Development

Principles for responsible agricultural investment

Intellectual property for development

Sustainable Institutional Investment Partnerships

Enterprise development

Entrepreneurship Development

Empretec capacity-building programmes

Accounting and reporting

ISAR

World Investment Network

Five global policy frameworks

Investment Policy Framework for Sustainable Development

Reform Package for the International Investment Regime

Global Action Menu for Investment Facilitation

Entrepreneurship Policy Framework

Guidance on Core Indicator for entity reporting in the SDGs

worldinvestmentreport.org

HOW TO OBTAIN THE PUBLICATIONS

The sales publications may be purchased from distributors of United Nations publications throughout the world. They may also be obtained by contacting:

United Nations Publications Customer Service
c/o National Book Network
15200 NBN Way
PO Box 190
Blue Ridge Summit, PA 17214
email: unpublications@nbnbooks.com

unp.un.org

For further information on the work on foreign direct investment and multinational enterprises, please address inquiries to:

Division on Investment and Enterprise
United Nations Conference on Trade and Development
Palais des Nations, Room E-10052
CH-1211 Geneva 10 Switzerland

Telephone: +41 22 917 4533
Fax: +41 22 917 0498
unctad.org/diae

NOTES